The Atlantis Fragments

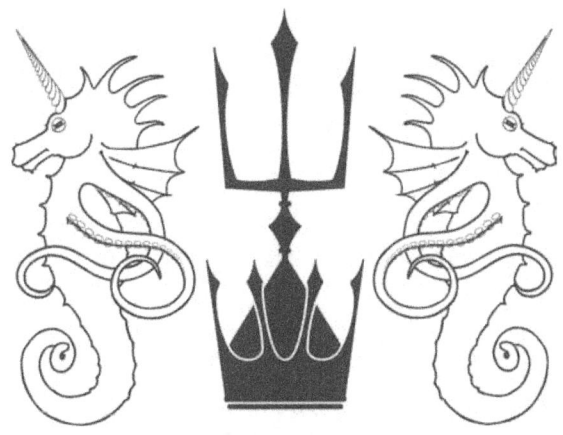

THE ATLANTIS FRAGMENTS

The Trilogy of *Songs and Sonnets Atlantean*

DONALD SIDNEY-FRYER

With illustrations by Lance Alexander

Hippocampus Press
New York

Copyright © 1971, 2003, 2005, and 2008 by Donald Sidney-Fryer
First paperback edition 2009

No part of this book may be reprinted without the permission of the publishers.
Printed in the United States of America.

ISBN-13: 978-0-9824296-5-5

Cover artwork by Gordon R. Barnett.
Cover design by Lance Alexander.
Interior illustrations by Lance Alexander.
Hippocampus Press logo designed by Anastasia Damianakos.

Published by Hippocampus Press
P.O. Box 641, New York, NY 10156

www.hippocampuspress.com

This omnibus edition of
The Atlantis Fragments
is dedicated by the poet-author
Donald Sidney-Fryer
to the two generous friends
whose hard work made it possible,
Alan Gullette and David E. Schultz.

Contents

The Atlantis Fragments: An Introduction, *by Brian Stableford* 13
Songs and Sonnets Atlantean: The First Series 19
    Introduction, *by Dr. Ibid M. Andor* 25
    Avalonessys 43
    The Crown and Trident Imperial 44
    Atlantis 45
    The Rose and the Thorn 46
    Rose Escarlate 47
    "O Ebon-Colored Rose" 48
    Your Mouth of Pomegranate 49
    As Buds and Blossoms in the Month of May the Rose 50
    To Clark Ashton Smith 51
    Pavane 52
    When We Were Prince and Princess 53
    The Crown and Trident 54
    Song 55
    "Thy Spirit Walks the Sea" 56
    Recompense 57
    To a Youth 58
    Spenserian Stanza-Sonnet Empourpré 59
    A Symbol for All Splendor Lost 60
    The Ashes in the Rose Garden 61
    To Edmund Spenser (1552?–1599) 62
    Rose Verdastre 63
    Ave Atque Vale 64
    Thaïs and Alexander in Persepolis 65
    A Fragment 66
    O Fair Dark Eyes, O Glances Turned Aside 67
    The Cydnus 68
    Golden Mycenae 69
    Lullaby 70
    Minor Chronicles of Atlantis 71
        Proem, *by Michel de Labretagne* 73
        The Hippokamp 74
        The Alpha Huge 80
        The River Called Amphus 81
        The Amphus Delta 84
        The Imperial Crown Jewels of Atlantis 85
        The Atlantean Obelisk 88
        The Garden of Jealous Roses 89

The Tale of an Olden Love	91
The Shepherd and the Shepherdess	94
Reciprocity	97
The Iffinnix	98
A Vision of Strange Splendor	99
Kilcolman Castle: 20 August 1965	101
Aubade	102
The Lilac Hedge at Cassell Prairie: 27 May 1967	103
Black Poppy and Black Lotus	104
The House of Roses	105
"The Musical Note of Swans . . . Before Their Death"	106
Green Sleeves	107
O Beautiful Dark-Amber Eyes of Old	108
The Forsaken Palace	109
For the *Shapes of Clay* of Ambrose Bierce	110
Connaissance Fatale	111
For the *Black Beetles in Amber* of Ambrose Bierce	112
Offrande Exotique	113
Sonnets on an Empire of Many Waters	115
Legend	117
I. Here, where the fountains of the deep-sea flow	119
II. Atlantis	120
III. Gades	121
IV. Atlantigades	122
V. Atkantharia	123
VI. Iffrikonn-Yssthia	124
VII. Atalantessys	125
VIII. Atlantillia	126
IX. Atatemthessys	127
X. At-Thulonn	128
XI. Avalonessys	129
XII. Poseidonis	130
XIII. The Merchant-Princes	131
XIV. An Argosy of Trade	132
XV. Memories of the Astazhan	133
XVI. A Letter from Valoth	134
XVII. No, not until the final age of Earth,	135
Commendatory and Dedicatory Poems	137
To an Atlantean Poet, *by Margo Skinner*	139
Inspiration, *by Ian M. M. Law*	140
Secretest, *by Fritz Leiber*	141
To Gloria Kathleen	142
For Master Edmund Spenser: His Great Song	143
Preliminary Note, *by Brian Stableford*	145
Notes, *by Dr. Ibid M. Andor*	147

Songs and Sonnets Atlantean: The Second Series 187

- Preface 191
- An Enchantress Out of Time 195
- A Summoning of Shadows 196
- Valediction 197
- In an Atlantean Bath 198
- Lo Primordial 199
- Strength of Dreams 200
- Copán 201
- Quo Vadis, California? 202
- Our Lady of the Unicorn 203
- Rêverie Gothique 209
- The *Monodon monoceros* 210
- Beyond Ultima Thule 211
- Midnight Visitant 212
- An Invocation 213
- A Miracle in Miniature 214
- Bialowieza 215
- Farewell to Zita 216
- *From the French of José-Maria de Heredia* 217
  - Oblivion 219
  - Pan 220
  - The Goatherd 221
  - The Shepherds 222
  - Hortorum Deus 223
  - On a Ruined Bust of Marble 228
- Return of the Conquistadors 229
- Enigma 230
- Pale Fragile Unicorns 231
- Fantaisie Médiévale 232
- Illumination 233
- Renewal 234
- Epiphany 235
- A Vision of a Castle Deep in Averonne 237
- *Some Further Fragments from Atlantis* 307
  - Pharanos Descending 309
  - My Mind to Me an Empire Is 312
  - Likewise My Mind to Me a Cosmos Is 313
  - Re-ascension 314
  - Pharanos at Sunset 315
  - Oneiromancy 316
  - At the Outhanox 317
- Beauty 318
- Notes 319

Songs and Sonnets Atlantean: The Third Series 347
  Foreword, *by Terence McVicker* 351
  To a Dead City 355
  Memorial 356
  The Herdsman 357
  Tropicality 358
  Totem 359
  Abandonment 361
  Amaranth 362
  Rapa-Nui 363
  Pendant 364
  A Game of Chess 365
  The Chest from Otherwhere 369
  Another Species of Epiphany 370
  A Ballade of Prospero 371
  The Reef of Coral 373
  Discovery 374
  The Bitch with Tits of Bronze 375
  Codicil of Contradiction 381
  As One Jaguär to Another 383
    Or So You Say 385
    The Warrior and the Jaguär 387
    Well Met by Midnight 389
    The Jaguär and the Astrologer 392
    The Apprentice and the Jaguär 396
    Quoctezu Bids Farewell 400
    The Passing of an Astrologer 404
    Epilogue 409
  Cephalopod in Residence 410
  Colossal Chambered Nautilus 411
  Hippokampoi 412
  As One Seahorse to Another 413
    The Little Horses of the Ocean Sea 415
    An Oldster Gives Advice 416
    A Mating Dance by Sunlight 417
    Labor and Deliverance 418
    A Proper Mode of Life 419
    A Ghostly Dance by Starlight 420
    Dominium atque Apotheosis 421
  Hadrian and Antinous 422
  Pan and Priapus 423
  A Ship Sails Out to Sea 424
  Barcarolle 425
  On Reading Edmund Spenser Once Again 426
  Nine Happy Goldfish 427
  An Archaeologist Uncovers the Past 428

Macabre Arabesque	439
The Scallop Shell	440
Triolets du Jour	441
A Villanelle Not à la Mode	442
Item: Ariel Sings	443
Ancestral Memory Revived	445
The Scroll	446
To a Conch	447
Of Some Eternal Realm	448
Past, Present, Future	450
Demeure Exotique	451
The Fugitives	453
The Music of the Spheres	489
To Rinaldo for Clark Ashton Smith	490
Forevermore the Rose	491
Tableau Sous-Marin	492
Predicament	493
Remonstration	494
Enlightenment	495
A Rendezvous with Pierrefonds	497
Rondeau of Winter	498
Rondeau of Summer	499
Pierrefonds, Poème en Pierre	500
A Ballade of Duality	504
Conundrum	506
Rondel of Time	507
Rondel of Space	508
The Ghost of a Dream	509
A Fanfare from Atlantis	510
Notes	511
Appendix	**539**
Index of Titles	**541**

THE ATLANTIS FRAGMENTS: AN INTRODUCTION

by Brian Stableford

Donald Sidney-Fryer is wont to describe himself as "the Last of the Courtly Poets, the One and Only Neo-Elizabethan Troubadour-Poet of Northern California." He accompanies himself during his performances on the chitarrone, a bass version of a Renaissance instrument ancestral to the guitar, just as the poems of Edmund Spenser—one of his principal idols—might have been accompanied in the court of Elizabeth I. In adopting this role, and the weight of its traditional associations, Sidney-Fryer views Spenser's poetry in an unusually wide context, whereby it becomes one of the most significant peaks of achievement in a vast spectrum, the past dimension of which extends through the Medieval troubadours of Brittany, whose own forebears might have played at the English court of King Arthur had there ever been such an institution, to further lost realms of the mythic past whose echoes resound in the lyrics and epics of ancient Greece. The forward dimension of the same spectrum extends, in Sidney-Fryer's perspective, to a group of Californian poets whose most important members—extensively represented in his performance repertoire—were George Sterling and Clark Ashton Smith.

Sidney-Fryer's own poetry, as befits art that is steeped in an awareness of finality, looks back across this entire spectrum to its mythic origins, thus completing a great circle by requiring the end to repossess the beginning, Ouroboros fashion—but with the precious awareness that the symbolic worm is not so much devouring itself as savouring itself, delighting in exotic gustation. Although there is a sense in which he might have selected anyone of a dozen mythical pasts in which to ground his work—most of his forebears selected breezy variants of the wooded hills of Arcadia—his own taste obviously tends to the briny, and his visual temperament to the contrasts between microcosms and macrocosms. When he occasionally leaves the shores of Atlantis to return to the present in the items collected in *Songs and Sonnets Atlantean* he is magnetically drawn to such ocean-isolated fragments as Rapa-Nui, only remaining on permanent land to visit the occasional Medieval castle—an environment as claustrophilic, in its own way, as the tiniest of islands. When he moves from actual to metaphorical oceans, as he often does, it is to cast himself adrift on a dark sea of cosmic space that makes reefs and islets of whole worlds.

The introduction to the first selection of *Songs and Sonnets Atlantean*, issued by Arkham House in 1971, went to some length to explain the ancestry of the featured works as indirect translations from the Atlantean—necessarily so, because that hypothetical language is not merely dead but utterly lost. Those individual works that are not actual translations, or reflections on lines penned by other poets within the tradition, pose as translations of translations, their Atlantean origins filtered through the work of Michel de Labretagne. Reading between the lines of his biography, the reader will realise that Labretagne must have been something of an anachronism himself: a last forlorn relic of Brittany's Age of Chivalry, which had faded into oblivion long before the final *coup de grâce* was administered to the last vestiges of Britanny's cultural and political independence by the Treaty of Sablé in 1488, five years before Labretagne's supposed birthdate.

Michel de Labretagne's primary legacy to the world was, according to the history enshrined in *Songs and Sonnets Atlantean*, an account of *La jouvence Bretagnesque*. That volume must, I presume (I have not had the privilege of reading it, alas, and can only presume), offer a far more wide-ranging and profound account of the scope and origins of ancient Breton lore than the Vicomte Hersart de la Villemarqué's woefully fragmentary and inexpertly-annotated *Barzaz-Breiz* (1839). Hersart never mentions Labretagne, and seems quite unaware of his work, but that is hardly surprising, given that he also pays scant attention to the *lais* of Marie de France, on the grounds that they are literary products produced for the amusement of Anglo-Normans and thus do not count as examples of "authentic" folklore.

Hersart was, of course, quite wrong to do that; although Percy Shelley was probably wrong to assert that poets are the true legislators of the world (the true legislators of the world are alas, the legislators) there is no doubt that poets are the true mythologists of the world, and no right-minded person would want it any other way. One only has to compare his version of the legend of Is with the one credited to Marie de France to realise that the lady was by far and away the better mythographer, even if she did not have access to the same sources of Michel de Labretagne, which evidently reveal that the drowned territory in question is more appropriately imagined as "Avalonessys." Sidney-Fryer is undoubtedly fortunate to have been able to draw inspiration from Labretagne rather than Hersart.

However crucial Michel de Labretagne was to the complex filtration process by which Sidney-Fryer's verse is connected to his remotest sources, he is only one link in a more extensive chain. The Atlantean lore preserved in Labretagne's posthumously-published 90-volume novel *Le roman de la princesse Aïs et du prince Atlantaryon* is supplemented in Sidney-Fryer's reflections by the scholarly analyses provided by the contemporary Atlantologist Dr Ibid M. Andor, who is credited with writing the introduction to the first collection of *Songs and Sonnets Atlanean*. Although the preface to the second series, first issued in 2003 by Wildside Press, reveals that Dr Andor had passed away in 1990, his authority clearly continued to exercise a significant influence over the poet's work, as evidenced by the note giving him due credit for his contribution to "Of Some Eternal Realm" and "Past, Present, Future" in the third series, first issued in 2005 by Phosphor Lantern Press.

Had the final phase in the filtration of Sidney-Fryer's Atlantean lore not been the cool archaeological perspective of a Dr Andor, the whole process of connection might have had a different result. The sceptical viewpoint that considers Atlantis to have been a fiction invented by Plato would doubtless have concluded that everything contained in Michel de Labretagne's legacy, including the man himself and the scholarship devoted to his work, would have to be interpreted metaphorically. In that case, Atlantis would become a proud symbolic representation of the mythic past, submerged and effaced in the mass by the relentless ocean of history, but stubbornly preserving a few mist-shrouded island peaks which can only contrive to *suggest* glories of expression now lost (lost not so much for lack of written versions as for lack of knowledgeable performers). Seen in the harsher light of that interpretation, *Songs and Sonnets Atlanean* would become, in effect, a long lament for absence and an exercise in inescapably-ironic substitution—but that would not be an inappropriate fate.

In fact, the sceptical view *is* a plausible account, made all the more plausible by the fact that one of the key features making Sidney-Fryer's work distinct and significant within his chosen tradition is the whimsical quality of his wit—which is expressed as frequently in his verses as in his commentaries thereon, though usually more delicately. Although the dominant concern of his kind of poetry has always been a calculated elegance of expression, its finest exponents have understood that the quest for such elegance cannot only accommodate an element of humour within its earnestness, but is bound to recognise an essential playfulness within its mission.

The three-volume sequence of *Songs and Sonnets Atlantean* is warmly bathed in wry humour by virtue of its expository materials—which adorn the greater number of its prose pieces as well as providing the metanarrative prefaces, commentaries, and notes—but the same wryness continually surfaces, ever more insistently as the sequence progresses, in deft intrusions of bathos into such verses as the ornately complex "A Vision of a Castle Deep in Averonne" and the coquettishly balanced "The Bitch with Tits of Bronze." The sequence makes much of the blithely paradoxical aspects of some of its key images—most notably the seahorse, whose manifestations from "The Hippokamp" to "Hippokampoi" and the subsequence "As One Seahorse to Another" provide fine exemplars of the poet's whimsical charm.

It is entirely appropriate that the voicing of this kind of playfulness should become more mordantly ironic as the tradition of Courtly Poetry attains its terminus, just as it is entirely appropriate that the voicing of the complementary earnestness should become politely and unashamedly insistent. Both sonorous expressions embody and maintain a plangent awareness of loss, as they must. When the poet opines in "Amaranth" that "That craving towards the transmundane can only turn— / Coiled—back upon itself, to mock that urge to yearn" he is perfectly correct, but the mockery in question is respectful; its effect is as much to ennoble as to ridicule the craving, as much to polish as to corrode its yearning.

Although the schools from which Donald Sidney-Fryer's poetry descends are broadly describable as Romantic, their extensions into the late 19th and 20th centuries had already become Decadent in the sense defined by Théophile's Gautier's introduction to the posthumous third edition of Charles Baudelaire's *Les Fleurs du mal*. Decadent style, according to Gautier, represents "Art arrived at that point of extreme maturity that determines civilizations which have grown old; ingenious, complicated, clever, full of delicate hints and refinements, gathering all the delicacies of speech, borrowing from technical vocabularies, taking colour from every palette, tones from all musical instruments, contours vague and fleeting, listening to translate subtle confidences, confessions of depraved passions and the odd hallucinations of a fixed idea turning to madness." Such a style is, according to Gautier, "summoned to express all and to venture to the very extremes" and Baudelaire's work thus partakes of "language already veined with the greenness of decomposition"—but that, Gautier argues, is inevitable in a civilization "where an artificial life has replaced a natural one and developed in a man who does not know his own needs."

That kind of decadence is very obvious in the work of Clark Ashton Smith, a great admirer of Baudelaire who consciously attempted to take the Baudelairean world-view to new extremes by transplanting it into new imaginative contexts—including a version of Atlantis. It equally obvious, albeit in a lighter shade, in the *Songs and Sonnets Atlantean*. It is no coincidence that the Brittany of Michel de Labretagne and the mighty Atlantis of Dr Andor's Atlantology are envisaged as quintessential embodiments of similar cultural phases, having not only reached and passed their climacterics but painfully aware of the inexorable processes of their own extinction.

Although Sidney-Fryer may indeed prove to be the last of the last of the Courtly Poets, he is certainly not the first to think of himself as the last and is well aware that his particular belatedness is best conceived as a further item in a pattern of echoes that had grown old even before it was first apprehended by the magical ear of inscription. In addition to their wit, the other markedly distinctive feature of the *Songs and Sonnets Atlantean* is their particular sense of remoteness: their acute consciousness of their own echoic fading.

Such representations of that diminuendo as a withdrawal into "the cosmic waste of Night" (as in "O Ebon-Colored Rose"), to become "Less than a speck of cosmic dust slow-dwindling on the Vast . . ." (as in the seventeenth and last of the "Sonnets on an Empire of Many Waters") are ostentatiously hyperbolic, because there is no other way to convey, whether by literal or metaphorical means, the sense of the furthest extreme. The indulgence of this kind of cosmic fatality is Sidney-Fryer's principal inheritance from the world-view of Clark Ashton Smith, but it is a torch he bears—or, as he prefers to express it in the concluding item of the series, a hymn that he extrapolates to its final fanfare—as if born to the role.

Like so many other Decadent writers, Sidney-Fryer is as fond of poetry in prose as he is of the stern formality of the Spenserian sonnet and the villanelle, and the scope of his work stretches to include fables, essays, short stories and narrative poems, as well as translations from 19th-century French. The elasticity of his method is another of his strengths, allowing the panorama of his work to take on a patchwork effect reminiscent of a crowded Medieval tapestry. However diverse it is though, his oeuvre retains the essential unities of outlook and ambition, ensuring that its sum is greater than its parts—a sum further enhanced by the performance aspect of his work, which is represented in such recordings as his CD-ROM of *The Hashish-Eater and Other Poems* [by Clark Ashton Smith] (2004). It is not always useful for a reader to know how a poet's actual voice sounds, but in this instance there is no risk and every chance of enrichment.

Jean des Esseintes, the protagonist of Joris-Karl Huysmans' À *rebours* (1887)—the Bible of Decadent prose—asserts that the prose poem is his favourite form of literature: the "osmazome of art." Although *osmazome* is nowadays translated as "essential oil," the term was coined to signify an imagined "savoury principle" of flesh that might be obtained in solution by steeping flesh in alcohol, and hence has aromatic associations that were particularly significant to Huysmans. Like Clark Ashton Smith, Donald Sidney-Fryer has an aromatic sensibility very different from Huysmans', but no less essential; from the conventional perfumes of roses and the sea it is distilled into something closely akin to the bouquet of what George Sterling called the "wine of wizardry": the nectar of pure exoticism.

That unifying sensibility extends like a subtle silken thread through the entire tapestry of Sidney-Fryer's works, binding them together into an intricate ensemble that is, at once, an "Offrande Exotique," a "Macabre Arabesque" and a "Rêverie Gothique." The heart of the enterprise, however—the core from which everything else ramifies, and whose beating supplies everything else with the oxygen of combustion—is the Atlantis series itself, whose fragmentary nature and double refraction through the contrasted but complementary perspectives of Michel de Labretagne and Dr Ibid M. Andor, condenses, crystallizes and clarifies the achievement of the work and the voice of the poet.

Reading, Berkshire,
England, United Kingdom,
2 February 2007

Songs and Sonnets Atlantean

The First Series

CREDITS

Some of the verses in this volume have appeared in the *Arkham Collector*, *Coven 13*, *Flame Annual*, *Galley Sail Review*, *Haunted*, *Macabre*, *San Francisco*, *Witchcraft and Sorcery*, and the *Young Physique*.

For permission to quote—in the Introduction or the Notes—passages from the following publications: *The Poetical Works of Edmund Spenser*, edited by J. C. Smith and Ernest de Selincourt, first published and copyright 1912 by Oxford University Press, London, etc.; *The Prince of Poets, Essays on Edmund Spenser*, edited by John R. Elliott, Jr., copyright 1968 by New York University; and *The Renaissance*, by Tucker Brooke and Matthias A. Shaaber, in A Literary History of England, second edition, Volume II, edited by Albert C. Baugh, copyright 1967 (original copyright 1948) by Appleton-Century-Crofts;—grateful acknowledgement is made to the following, respectively: Oxford University Press, Ely House, London; New York University Press, Washington Square, New York; and Appleton-Century-Crofts, Educational Division of the Meredith Corporation, New York.

ACKNOWLEDGEMENTS

For their warm interest and encouragement, and in some cases over the total period of approximately ten years, the author is indebted to many persons, especially Dr. Ibid M. Andor, August Derleth, Gloria Kathleen Fryer, George F. Haas, Helen French Hunt, Ian M. M. Law, Fritz and Jonquil Leiber, Kirby McCauley, Margo Skinner, and Genevieve K. Sully.

And for permission to quote—on the dedication-page—the line "Ah but in such an ugly time the true protest is beauty" from the record album *Pleasures of the Harbor*, words and music by Phil Ochs, issued by A&M Records, Hollywood, California, and copyright © 1968 by Barricade Music, Inc.;—grateful acknowledgement is made to Michael Ochs, president of Barricade Music, Inc., Topanga, California. The line in question occurs in the poem by Phil Ochs which appears on the back of the record-jacket and which begins "I've been away for a while but I hope to be back again soon."

Songs and Sonnets Atlantean

Fragments in Verse and Fragments in Prose

*Being translations from the Atlantean,
as well as from the French,
together with a selection of original poems
expressly created by the translator
for the present volume.*

Selected and translated
by DONALD SIDNEY-FRYER

With an Introduction and Notes
by DR. IBID M. ANDOR

Together with commendatory verses
by friends and well-wishers

And featuring numerous dedications
as well as quoted passages.

DEDICATED,
IN THIS THE REIGN OF ELIZABETH II,
TO THE MEMORY OF EDMUND SPENSER,
POET LAUREATE TO ELIZABETH I.

Ah but in such an ugly time the true protest is beauty.
—Phil Ochs, "Pleasures of the Harbor."

Ah! Colin, whether on the lowly plain,
Piping to shepherds thy sweet roundelays;
Or whether singing in some lofty vein,
Heroic deeds of past or present days;
Or whether in thy lovely mistress' praise,
Thou list to exercise thy learnèd quill;
Thy Muse hath got such grace, and power to please,
With rare invention, beautified by skill,
As who, I pray, therein can ever joy their fill?

O therefore let that happy Muse proceed
To climb the height of Virtue's sacred hill,
Where endless honor shall be made thy meed:

Because no malice of succeeding days
Can rase those records of thy lasting praise.

(The Amoretti and Epithalamion of Edmund Spenser, first published in 1595: the second of the two commendatory sonnets by "G. W. Senior, to the Author"—stanzaically emendated by Donald Sidney-Fryer.)

Introduction

In launching this little argosy of verse upon that vast, darkling, and potentially hostile Ocean Sea known as the general reading public; our poet, Donald Sidney-Fryer, offers for the first time in English an extensive selection of poems translated from the Atlantean, even if only through the French of Michel de Labretagne (1493–1550).

The poems have been selected largely from that unique collection by Labretagne, *La Jouvence Bretagnesque*, the original manuscript of which still exists in the Bibliothèque Nationale in Paris. These, the first serious poems by Labretagne after his ingenious but purely apprentice verses done under the tutelage of the Grands Rhétoriqueurs, never saw republication in French until their rediscovery in the nineteenth century by the great critic Sainte-Beuve, who devoted one of the best of his *Causeries du lundi* to Labretagne and his art. Clément Marot (1496–1544), a close personal friend to Labretagne during most of their comparatively short lifetimes, knew and praised the poems highly both before and after their publication. Marot and Labretagne first met in 1519 when Marguerite, later Queen of Navarre, then Duchess of Alençon and Berry, came to visit the Labretagnes at their principal estate located in Brittany, the Château Bretagnesque or Grand Château de Bretagne, bordering on the Gulf of Saint-Malo, not far from the Abbey of Mont Saint-Michel. Marot belonged at that time to the numerous retinue of Marguerite to whom François I had given him as a page in 1518.

Labretagne, a precocious poet, came of an ancient and noble family who had reigned as *grands seigneurs* in Normandy and Brittany for immemorial centuries and who claimed a direct descent from one of King Arthur's knights. By the time of Marguerite's visit in 1519, Labretagne had already gained an enviable reputation for himself as a distinguished and unique Atlantologist and a student of Atlantean literature, as well as a student of medieval poetry and of Arthurian history as manifested in the Keltic so-called romances of *le roi Artus et ses chevaliers de la Table ronde*. During the years 1517–19, he circulated his *Jouvence Bretagnesque* in manuscript, becoming widely known as a translator and a lyric poet of considerable distinction, even if of limited output. Marot and Labretagne became instant and life-long friends after a comparison of poetic notes, and Marot urged Labretagne to publish sans further delay his collection, which accordantly appeared in 1520. Labretagne in his turn encouraged Marot, and contributed financially to the publication, in 1532, of Marot's own first collection *L'Adolescence Clementine*, besides affording him a place of refuge on divers occasions when Marot was in disfavor with the King. But it was not until after his death that Labretagne achieved his greatest fame, and this as a novelist. His later poems, all original pieces, did not see publication until their inclusion, under the title *Dernier testament poétique*, in the *Oeuvres complètes* published in 1633.

Many of the early translations by Labretagne, sometimes considerably recast, reappeared in the author's famous romance, *Le roman de la princesse Aïs et du prince Atlantaryon*, published posthumously 1550–55 in Lyons, and issued in ninety volumes, the longest novel in any language, with the total pagination running over 30,000. All of these poems from the Atlantean (including those in this book) do not survive except in the French translations of Labretagne; unless the originals may be contained and yet identified on the recently-discovered volumes, or scrolls, from the submerged libraries of Atlantis and Poseidonis. In making his translations through the French, Sidney-Fryer has followed the text of the poems in their first appearance in *La Jouvence Bretagnesque*, preferring the simpler early versions to the elaborate, even if more polished, later ones.

Before we pass to a discussion of Atlantean poetry and its principal forms, as well as of how some of it happened to survive, we should consider, however briefly, the one and only collection of poetry published by Labretagne during his lifetime and the place it holds in the history of French literature. Although a former pupil of the Grands Rhétoriqueurs, little of the poetical tricks of the latter appear in this his first serious poetry. While some of his work in verse has a certain affinity with that of Marot (who had also been a pupil of the Grands Rhétoriqueurs), Labretagne anticipates the renaissance of French poetry brought about by the poets of the Pléiade, besides anticipating the work of Agrippa d'Aubigné. About one-third of the *Jouvence* are original poems influenced by medieval and Atlantean lyric poetry; the rest are translations of Atlantean odes, songs, "sonnets" (i.e, songs archroyal), etc., taken from the nigh-fabled *Codex Atlanteanus*. However, virtually all of the translations from the Atlantean are paraphrases in French prose, a sort of vers libre not unlike the verses in the King James Bible, nor unlike the *petits poemes en prose* of Aloÿsius Bertrand (1807–1841) in his *Gaspard de la Nuit* (1842). Labretagne and Marot, it will be noted, were among the first to cultivate the sonnet in French, and to do so with distinction. There can be little doubt but that *La Jouvence Bretagnesque* afforded a major impetus to the poets of the Pléiade, in showing them the possibilities of French in creating a poetry comparable to the best of the ancient Greeks and Latins, or of the ancient Atlanteans.

It is one of the greatest literary ironies of all time that the *Codex Atlanteanus*, that unique collection of Atlantean manuscripts, should have survived some 15,000 years, only to meet utter destruction during the French Revolution in the sacking and razing of the Château Bretagnesque. The history of the *Codex Atlanteanus* is so well known as scarcely to bear repetition; but perhaps the patient reader will bear with the present Atlantologist while he refreshes the reader's memory with a brief summary.

After the foundering of one-half or one-third of Atlantis the Archkingdom and virtually all of the Empire of Atlantis through the action of the Great Cataclysm about 13,000 B.C., the Atlantean garrisons were retained in the forts and watchtowers in what are now Cornwall, Wales, and southern Ireland. Aänsess, an Archknight, and the governor of the Atlantean holdings in these lands, was made a Grand Archknight by the King sometime shortly after the Great Cataclysm. After their thirtieth wedding anniversary, Atlantarion and Aïs, then King and Queen of the much-diminished Atlantean Empire, repeated the itinerary of their original wedding voyage (although taking much less time to do it the second time than the first), visiting the sites of the former island kingdoms—a rather gray and funereal trip save for their sojourn in Wales at Apenderragon the Great Watchtower in southern Valoth, or Wales, as guests of Aänsess. The King and Aänsess, both of them poets, had been close friends and correspondents, despite a considerable difference in age, ever since they had first met sometime before the Great Cataclysm. During this last visit with Aänsess in Valoth, the King made him a Grand Archknight Prince.

After the second wedding voyage of Aïs and Atlantarion, the governor and the King continued their correspondence, as well as their exchange of notes poetic and otherwise; and some thirteen years later, the garrisons were no longer considered necessary and were recalled by the King. The Grand Archknight Prince sealed his records, correspondence, and manuscripts with those of the preceding governors in the lowermost vaults of the central tower of Apenderragon (these were duplicates only—the originals had always been sent to Atlantis), and closed for the last time all the outer gates leading to the Great Watchtower. Thus, the Atlanteans abandoned their holdings in what are now the British Isles, leaving those lands forever. Escorted by a military flotilla, Aänsess returned in his own private trireme to Atlantis the Archkingdom. After a lengthy visit with the King at the Outhanox, the Great Citadel of Poseidonis (in Xonorr, the capital of that great mountain-heartland), he retired to his place of birth, his family's ancestral estate located in the great pastureland of the Astazhan, which occupied all of southeastern Atlantis. Upon his death, the King erected—within the castle-gardens of the old estate—an elaborate and beautiful monument to house his remains.

Centuries passed, and the duplicate scrolls of Aänsess, together with those of his predecessors, lay undisturbed in the lowermost vaults of the old central mass of the Great Watchtower whose upper and middle sections fell away into ruin, leaving only the massive foundations intact. Later, after many successive invasions by outlanders, a Cambrian, or Welsh, lord incorporated the ruined watchtower into the donjon of his castle. During the reign of Uther Pendragon, the resident family of nobles discovered the *Codex Atlanteanus*, as it became called. Later still, it was brought to King Arthur's court at Camelot (nowadays identified with the Dark Age reconstruction of the Iron Age fortress at Cadbury Castle in Somerset), and became part of the Royal Library there. Through the supreme intelligence as well as the arts magical of Merlin, both a great scholar and an archimage, the clerk-scholars at Arthur's court deciphered the *Codex* and translated it into Latin and Welsh. As pieced together by Merlin and as narrated by the troubadours and minstrels instructed by him, the story of the vanished world of Atlantis, and the last days of its Empire, created a great sensation at court, particularly the romance of the Princess Aïs and the Prince Atlantarion.

Long after Camelot had fallen into ruin, the *Codex Atlanteanus*, as well as the Latin and Welsh translations, somehow still extant in a now buried vault of the old Royal Library, were discovered in the thirteenth century and given as gifts by the then King of England to the Abbey of Mont-Saint-Michel, to form part of the library there. During the fourteenth century, the *Codex* and the translations of the same were acquired by the Labretagnes and became part of their library kept in an old tower called "la Tour d'yvoire"—there the young Michel de Labretagne discovered them in 1503, and with the aid of the earlier Arthurian translations, rendered the *Codex* into French. Much of the material he used in his famous *Roman*, incorporating some of it bodily into the novel. After an elaborate and painstaking preparation, Labretagne began the actual writing of his novel about 1529 and continued working on it until his death in 1550.

Although *Le roman de la princesse Aïs et du prince Atlantaryon* ranks as one of the first great novels of modern European literature, and although its publication in 1550–1555 marks one of the high watermarks of French Renaissance printing, strangely enough no one thought of issuing in published form the actual *Codex* itself, or any of the translations of the same. Thus, together with many beautiful and valuable medieval illuminated manuscripts, the *Codex Atlanteanus* as well as the Arthurian and French translations, survived until 1791 when the entire library containing these and other materials was utterly destroyed, or almost so, during the French Revolution in the general plundering and burning of the Château Bretagnesque.

Virtually all of our present information about Atlantis and Atlantean poetry derives either from the *Roman* of Labretagne, or from such of his notes as are preserved with *La Jouvence Bretagnesque* in the Bibliothèque Nationale in Paris. The principal forms of Atlantean poetry, according to Labretagne, are as follows: the song or little song, usually one to nine lines but never more than nine; the song or great song, or epic poem, generally employing all known forms, and of variable length; the sonnet or song archroyal, usually ten to twenty lines, rarely more; the ode or apostrophe, of any length but usually more than thirty lines; and finally a form very much like the French poem in prose as invented and elaborated by Aloÿsius Bertrand and Charles Pierre Baudelaire (poems of this nature were always written in a rich purple ink wherefrom derived the Atlantean names of the "purple patch" or "purple poem" or "purple prose"). The great song or epic poem was invariably used for detailed narratives whether long or short. The Atlanteans had a predilection for long, rather Whitmanesque, lines. True rime was not employed but something very much like assonance-rime was used, especially in poems of more than one stanza wherein the stanzas would be interlinked by rime. This use, in Atlantean poetry, of a system of interlinking rimes, whether assonance or otherwise, is somewhat analogous in English to the system of interlinking rimes employed by Edmund Spenser in the stanza that bears his name or by Spenser and Alexander Montgomery in their identically similar sonnet-form, evidently evolved independently of each other.

Unlike Labretagne who translated the Atlantean originals into French prose and who evidently despaired of achieving with true rime an effect in French similar to that achieved by assonance-rime in Atlantean; Sidney-Fryer—undeterred by the originals in Atlantean because of their express absence—has courageously elected to achieve, with true rime, translations into English verse that would approximate the original effect in Atlantean. It may be argued that the results are not real translations but recreations into another language, and through the possibly obfuscatory medium of yet another language at that. This may be true but we must grant Sidney-Fryer the right of his carefully considered choice, whether the poems assembled in the present volume fail or succeed simply as translations, or recreations, or original creations. As the most logical equivalent in English into which to translate the Atlantean "little song," he has chosen the Spenserian stanza. For the Atlantean "sonnet" or song archroyal, there is no true equivalent readily at hand. According to Labretagne, "this prince of fixed forms in Atlantean poetry" has three sections, with each one successively shorter than the preceding (although the lines of each succeeding section usually are progressively longer), and with each section linked to the preceding one by a system of assonance-rimes. To do justice to this unique tripartite form in Atlantean prosody as described by Labretagne and as manifested by him in his paraphrases in French prose, it has proven mandatory for Sidney-Fryer to innovate a special form of the Spenserian sonnet, consisting of a Spenserian stanza, a tercet, and a couplet. This innovation he terms, accordingly, the Spenserian stanza-sonnet.

The original Spenserian sonnet itself, unlike the Spenserian stanza, is a form that has found virtually no, or very little, employment in English since its use by Edmund Spenser, Alexander Montgomery, and a few other poets of their time. Devoting itself exclusively to the publication of sonnets, as its title indicates; the poetry magazine *The Sonnet, Dedicated to the Memory of Sir Thomas Wyatt and of Henry Howard Earl of Surrey*, and published in the first quarter of the present century, does not contain one single Spenserian sonnet in any issue of its complete run. The Spenserian stanza itself, in terms of its actual use by poets, has declined steadily since around 1900, and finds virtually no employment at all today, oddly enough, in this the Neo-Elizabethan Age.

The Spenserian stanza, it will be recalled, consists of two quatrains and a final alexandrine (or, very rarely, a fourteener), all of which are linked by rime: A B A B / B C B C / C. The Spenserian sonnet consists of three quatrains and a final couplet, with the quatrains linked by rime: A B A B / B C B C / C D C D / E E. The reader will note that the rime-scheme of the Spenserian stanza as well as that of the first nine lines of the Spenserian sonnet are thus exactly the same. The Spenserian stanza-sonnet wherein unite the stately Spenserian stanza and the even more stately Spenserian sonnet, consists of a Spenserian stanza, a tercet, and a couplet, with the Spenserian stanza and the tercet linked by rime, as follows: A B A B B C B C C / D C D / E E. Usually alexandrines or fourteeners, the tercet and the couplet are thus linked in terms of length of line. This further development will prove that the Spenserian sonnet—by showing forth the Spenserian stanza "hidden" within it, and by arranging the tercet and the couplet as lines longer than the usual pentameter—is as stately as, or is more stately than (due to its greater length), the Spenserian stanza, and is accordingly the stateliest of all sonnet forms in English or, possibly, in any language.

Another feature of the Spenserian stanza-sonnet which the reader will note in some of the poems assembled herein, is the rondeau-like device whereby line three more or less repeats as line thirteen (the first line of the final couplet), and line one more or less repeats as line fourteen (the second line of the final couplet); both lines usually lengthened, and hence both with appropriate additions or alterations. Through this device, amongst others, Sidney-Fryer hopes to restore to the sonnet or *sonetto*—that is, "little song" (in Italian)—some of its original, purely *singing*, qualities.

Needless to add, in view of the subject-matter and the consequent style of the poems originally in Atlantean or in French, as well as in view of the subject-matter of the original poems expressly created by the translator for the present volume, it has proven essential that Sidney-Fryer utilize (in his English) that which for lack of better terms we must call "the grand manner" and "the solemn tone"—in short, the incantatory mode—thereby restoring to poetic diction certain words or phrases ordinarily considered today as being outmoded, at least by the poetic fashions of the moment. These words and phrases our poet has found it highly necessary to use in view of certain subtle considerations of style, tone, meaning, and emphasis, as well as in view of certain similarly subtle effects which may be achieved thereby, effects impossible to achieve in any other way.

Thus, this volume has two principal purposes: to render into English the first considerable body of poems from the Atlantean, and to render direct homage to the *poet* (1552?–1599), and not the dramatist, whom the Elizabethans themselves held as supreme. That the poetry of Edmund Spenser should find comparatively little appreciation and admiration in our century, is of no great consequence; the reasons for this temporary neglect are perfectly apparent to the perceptive lover and student of literature; Spenser's time will come again as it did in Elizabethan times or in the time of the English Romantic poets, as well as in the time of their subsequent public vogue. But that the unique, merely historical, importance of Spenser's poetry should be obscured as a result of this curious neglect, is nothing less than a stain on the vast escutcheon of literature in English. If in 1912 Ernest de Selincourt could make the observation "that of late years the poetry of Spenser has occupied far less attention than is warranted either by its own intrinsic beauty or by its importance as a vital influence upon the development of our literature"—then we can make, alas! the same observation today with even greater truth.

Yet this is the man and poet of whom the same Ernest de Selincourt has written, and justly, in his magnificent Introduction to *The Oxford Spenser*: "The true memorial to Spenser is to be read in the work of his successors. He is among the very greatest of our poets, but the significance of his poetry in the history of our literature is even greater than its intrinsic value. He recreated English prosody, giving back to our verse the fluidity and the grace that it had lost since the days of Chaucer, and extending the range of its achievement; he created English poetic diction, lifting it from anarchy and stiffness, daring greatly, but triumphing whether in the simple or the ornate, widening its scope, but at the same time never failing to give it ease and flexibility, so that language became to him a willing servant, and could voice the subtlest shades of mood or fancy. By means of this rich and varied style, fully expressive of his high seriousness, his spirituality, his inexhaustible sense of beauty, he has exercised a spell that has been potent for three centuries, and none has called so many poets to their vocation."

True, there has appeared in the 1960s just past a goodly number of outstanding books on Spenser, each of them shedding a greater light on usually one or more facets of his extraordinary creative genius, and some of them emphasizing his unique formal as well as thematic originality. Some of these books must needs be mentioned here.

Short Time's Endless Monument, The symbolism of the numbers in Edmund Spenser's "Epithalamion," by A. Kent Hieatt (New York: Columbia University Press, 1960), brilliantly elucidates the ingenious numerological symbolism that forms the organic core of Spenser's own marriage ode.

A Preface to "The Faerie Queene," by Graham Hough (New York: W. W. Norton and Company, 1962), ably summarizes the sources and authors (the Carolingian and Arthurian mytho-poetic cycles, Boiardo, Ariosto, Tasso, etc.) directly or indirectly influencing Spenser, and makes a simple and brief but good beginning use of Freud's *Interpretation of Dreams* in an attempt at understanding the structure of *The Faerie Queene*, which thus becomes a dream-poem (with concomitant dream-symbolism) possessing (as John Symonds urges for Ariosto's epic *Orlando Furioso*) "the unity of a vast piece of tapestry rather than of architecture."

The Poetry of Edmund Spenser, A Study, by William Nelson (New York and London: Columbia University Press, 1963), contends that all of Spenser's poetry, but especially *The Faerie Queene*, is carefully structured around and out from an intellectual core or center; and that theme, rather than story, is the chief governing principle: over-all, this book is a carefully balanced and highly competent appraisal of the entire *corpus* of Spenser's poetry.

Spenser and the Numbers of Time, by Alastair Fowler (New York: Barnes and Noble, 1964), employing the *modus operandi* of *Short Time's Endless Monument*, ingeniously and brilliantly demonstrates how divers numerological systems (classical and medieval, popular and arcane) operate organically to create the unique structure of *The Faerie Queene*. In the words of the publisher: "Regarded in this way, the poem emerges as a cosmic model constructed in 'narrow verse' with masterful economy and subtlety."

The Kindly Flame, A Study of the Third and Fourth Books of "The Faerie Queene," by Thomas P. Roche, Jr. (Princeton, New Jersey: Princeton University Press, 1964), seeks to show, in an admirably clear and sensitive way, that Spenser was just as much in control of the structure of Books III and IV as he was in control of that of Books I and II; that the legends of chastity and friendship demand their complex and interwoven system of narratives to exemplify Spenser's or any other truly realistic conception of the virtues in question.

Spenser's Image of Nature, Wild Man and Shepherd in "The Faerie Queene," by Donald Cheney (New Haven and London: Yale University Press, 1966), in demonstrating that pastoral elements counterpoint the epic motifs throughout *The Faerie Queene*, attempts to follow the poem's overt sequence of presentation rather than forcing upon it a foreign conceptual framework, and argues for a parallelism of structure in Books V and VI similar to that in Books I and II: paramount in this study is the author's "close attention to continually shifting ironic perspectives."

Spenser's World of Glass, A Reading of "The Faerie Queene," by Kathleen Williams (Berkeley and Los Angeles: University of California Press, 1966), reveals with an admirable freshness, grace, and lucidity that *The Faerie Queene* depends for its unity upon a pattern of meaning established and expanded throughout the six books but coherent and self-consistent at the end of each; this particular study seems to sum up the new spirit in Spenserian criticism probably better than any other book mentioned here.

The Poetry of "The Faerie Queene," by Paul J. Alpers (Princeton, New Jersey: Princeton University Press, 1967), while indicating a variety of approaches to *The Faerie Queene*, urges readers and students alike to return to the surface metaphor (with emphasis on line and stanza rather than canto and book) for the poem's meaning rather than seeking that meaning in rigid and arid theories or conceptual frameworks; the author takes to task many of the other notable Spenserians of our time for approaching Spenser in a way either over-elaborate or inadequately simple.

Spenser's Images of Life, by C. S. Lewis, edited by Alastair Fowler (London and New York: Cambridge University Press, 1967), contends that much in Spenser must be seen as "pageant," that Spenser's pageantries must be experienced with some knowledge of Neo-Platonism and of Renaissance iconography (including pageant proper, tournament pageantry, masque, traditional images of gods, hieroglyphs and emblems, and philosophical iconography), and that *The Faerie Queene* is not an epic but rather is a grand pageant of the cosmos or of Nature and thus is Spenser's Hymn to Life: a worthy companion piece to Lewis's earlier and largely Spenserian study *The Allegory of Love* (Oxford: The Clarendon Press, 1936), even though Lewis himself did not live to write this book as extant in its published form.

Flower on a Lowly Stalk, The Sixth Book of the Faerie Queene, by Arnold Williams (East Lansing, MI: Michigan State University Press, 1967), gives a sensitive and perceptive reading of Book VI in the first book-length study devoted to the same, and presents a thorough, sound, lucid, and gracious analysis of Spenser's narrative, the meaning of that narrative, plus all the effects of "affect," with an especially welcome emphasis on Spenser's usually overlooked gift for comedy, as well as his gift for overt oral verse techniques.

Spenser's Allegory of Justice in the Fifth Book of the Faerie Queene, by T. K. Dunseath (Princeton, New Jersey: Princeton University Press, 1968), gives a thoughtful and long-overdue defense of the least liked, most neglected, and most misunderstood book of *The Faerie Queene* in the first book-length study devoted to the same, and shows that Spenser, in giving us a highly repressive picture of justice in a fallen world, was just as much in command of his fictional art in Book V as anywhere else in *The Faerie Queene*.

Reading Spenser, An Introduction to "The Faerie Queene," by Roger Sale (New York: Random House, 1968), emphasizes Spenser's sense of life rather than attempting to deal with his encyclopedic range of ideas and symbologies, and is remarkable for manifesting just how much even a person insensitive to his style can derive from *The Faerie Queene*, even if he deliberately underestimates or makes little of Books IV, V, and VI, as well as the Mutabilitie Cantos.

Some of the same writers whose books have been cited above contribute salient essays to the following three volumes which present much valuable supplementary material toward understanding Spenser's thought and style.

Elizabethan Poetry, Modern Essays in Criticism, edited by Paul J. Alpers (New York and London: Oxford University Press, 1967), containing much solid scholarship, devotes considerable attention to Spenser, with the last one-third of the book given over to *The Faerie Queene,* and helps provide a convenient index to the major re-evaluation of Spenser, and his oeuvre, that has come about in the 1960s.

Spenser, A Collection of Critical Essays, edited by Harry Berger, Jr. (Englewood Cliffs, New Jersey: Prentice-Hall, 1968), draws upon the ideas and literary techniques of all ages to provide a wide spectrum of thought and opinion on divers themes, metaphors, and problems inherent in Spenser's over-all oeuvre, from his earliest published work to his last.

The Prince of Poets, Essays on Edmund Spenser, edited by John R. Elliott, Jr. (New York: New York University Press, London: University of London Press, 1968), presents both a valuable documentary survey of Spenser's varying poetic reputation through more than three and a half centuries, as well as an introduction to the chief problems posed by his poetry to the modern reader, with especial emphasis on the poetic values of his own age.

It is highly significant that the editor of the last-cited volume not only employs the title that he does but moreover states in his Introduction: "Perhaps no major English poet has received a more appreciative rereading in recent times than Edmund Spenser. For years relegated to the dusty shelf reserved for authors politely honored but seldom read, Spenser has been one of the chief beneficiaries of our renewed interest in and understanding of Renaissance art. With the discovery by modern readers of the intellectual complexity and artistic coherence of literary forms that once seemed merely naive and disordered, Spenser has emerged from the shadow of Marlowe, Shakespeare, and Donne to lay claim once again to his title as 'the Prince of Poets in his tyme' [in the words of the inscription on the monument to Spenser in Westminster Abbey]."

Although Spenser—of all the great elder poets in English—has probably received the least circulation, the least understanding, and the least appreciation in the twentieth century until recently, yet it is heartening to observe how diverse have been the admirers of "the Prince of Poets" in our own time; these have included not only such recognized Spenserians like the great C. S. Lewis himself but—just as important—such unlikely figures (unlikely at least at first glance) as Virginia Wolff, T. S. Eliot, F. Scott Fitzgerald, Louis MacNeice, and Archibald MacLeish. But however heartening such an observation might prove, and however heartening the recent wealth of unusually intelligent and well-informed books on Spenser, yet we must repeat here the statement made in 1912 by Ernest de Selincourt, speaking apropos of Spenser, that "A full interpretation of his genius, worthy of its theme, is yet to be written." Such an interpretation would amalgamate the best and most generous approaches to Spenser whether made long ago or whether made in the present, especially those included in the outstanding studies on Spenser published in the 1960s. And such an interpretation would resolve as far as possible the problem of the over-all pattern structuring *The Faerie Queene*, and would syncretize the better solutions to this problem that recent scholars have proffered.

It may appear that we are laying an undue emphasis on the form, that is, the structure, and (evolving from the structure) the movement of *The Faerie Queene*. But it is only through an apprehension of its formal pattern (as the same circles or cycles through time and space) that we may gain any real understanding of this great poem's ultimate over-all meaning. Actually the truth of the structure of *The Faerie Queene*, as well as of its meaning, lies undoubtedly somewhere between Graham Hough's dream-poem with concomitant dream-symbolism, Alastair Fowler's numerological symbolism, and William Nelson's intellectual and thematic solution. Of course, in the most profound sense, this greatest poem by Spenser, with its ever-changing imagery, is a fantasy, a conscious dream, supremely a work of the imagination. This fact is in itself one of the first keys to understanding the poem and its peculiar construction.

Indeed, although the fact is often overlooked, *The Faerie Queene* is not only the first great fantasy in modern English, having crystallized many of what are now familiar conceptions of *faërie* and of the light fantastical, but it includes moreover—amidst its vast spectrum of tone and subject—the first delineation of the weird and the darkly fantastic as we understand them today. This is pointed out inferentially by the late great H. P. Lovecraft, that "literary Copernicus" (to use Fritz Leiber's memorable term), in his classic study "Supernatural Horror in Literature": ". . . by the time the old Northern myths take literary form, and in that later time when the weird appears as a steady element in the literature of the day, we find it mostly in metrical dress; as indeed we find the greater part of the strictly imaginative writing of the Middle Ages and Renaissance. The Scandinavian Eddas and Sagas thunder with cosmic horror, and shake with the stark fear of Ymir and his shapeless spawn; whilst our own Anglo-Saxon Beowulf and the later Continental Nibelung tales are full of eldritch weirdness. Dante is a pioneer in the classic capture of macabre atmosphere, and in Spenser's stately stanzas will be seen more than a few touches of fantastic terror in landscape, incident, and character." Indeed, properly defined, *The Faerie Queene* not only presents the first conscious "olden" style in modern English—or for that matter the first conscious style, or rather spectrum of styles, as we comprehend such today—but it also represents the first "Romanticism" (as understood in the sense of the Arthurian and Carolingian romances) as well as the first great "Gothic" fiction in modern English, in the most inclusive definition of those expressions.

To an earlier commentator, the French authority on English literature Émile Legouis (1861–1937), *The Faerie Queene* appears primarily as a dream-like pageant of constantly evolving and dissolving imagery the which, as presented through the recurring music of the Spenserian stanza, lulls the reader's intellectual faculties asleep. Legouis's book *Spenser* (New York: E. P. Dutton; London and Toronto: J. M. Dent, 1926) reduces itself in essence to a consideration of Spenser's poetry, and *The Faerie Queene* above all, as a tastefully assembled collection of imagery. Essentially it is a restatement of the stance of William Hazlitt and Leigh Hunt, or of the English Romantic poets, who certainly understood the poem in small parts and parcels but not in the mass, although undoubtedly they may have instinctively felt or sensed the over-all structure. (Coleridge comes the closest to a true comprehension and appreciation.) Legouis himself perceives nothing of the true structural principles animating *The Faerie Queene*, even though, unknown to him, he clearly held the first key to understanding the mystery. He does do justice to Spenser's overt, that is, surface, artistry. He does recognize "his inexhaustible sense of beauty" but of "his high seriousness," of "his spirituality," and of his over-all moral or ethical purpose (that is, in Spenser's case, his over-all *artistic* purpose), Legouis deliberately makes little. Typically, he is completely insensitive to the cosmic element in Spenser. To Legouis, Spenser is above all else a creator of imagery, and really little beyond this. But even this does not really minimize Spenser. To some critics and poetic mentors (e.g., Ambrose Bierce), imagery is the heart, the soul, the essense of poetry: it *is* the poetry. Even by such a restrictive definition as this one, Spenser still emerges as the most poetic of poets.

Whether one agrees or disagrees with their divers theses, such books as these are surely welcome, such books as these are surely needed. They widen our understanding of Spenser, or they stimulate us into providing our own solutions to certain mysteries inherent in his greatest work, and they enhance our appreciation of his unique genius. But they do so under a scholarly aegis rather than purely a poetical one. This is not a criticism, it is merely an observation. Today Spenser may be "the scholar's poet" but tomorrow he may yet again be "the poet's poet" as he was yesterday to the Elizabethans and to the English Romantic poets.

Whether Spenser could ever again become "the people's poet" remains to be seen. For, in spite of the fact that Spenser was the supreme literary celebrity of his own age; in spite of the fact that *The Faerie Queene* was to the Elizabethans themselves their supreme work of art; in spite of the fact that his poetry proved a great and beneficent influence—a source of delight, vision, wisdom, and technical instruction—to virtually all the other great English poets coming after him (beginning with Kit Marlowe and Will Shakespeare and continuing on through the English Romantic and Victorian poets); in spite of the fact that this same poetry, whether directly or indirectly, has continued to be a great and beneficent influence on virtually all of literature in modern English even into our own century; in spite of the fact that the recent wealth of unusually intelligent and well-informed studies on Spenser and *The Faerie Queene* has succeeded in rehabilitating his critical reputation; and in spite of the fact that Spenser is in essence the very father—the very fountainhead as it were—of literature, poetry, and fantasy in modern English;—it cannot be denied that for the average reader Spenser's great fairy tale has become the lost Atlantis of our older literature, the great "lost" classic of early modern English. For since around 1900, more or less coinciding with the death of Queen Victoria and with the inevitable decline of the British Empire, *The Faerie Queene* has fallen from the common currency that it once enjoyed in the homes of English-speaking families all over the world. For at one time Spenser's great myth—uniquely fusing as it does classical epic, medieval romance, and medieval allegory—was one of the great family classics, together with the King James Bible and the complete works of Shakespeare. If this great work—once universally accepted as the great *English* epic—does gain common currency again, it will not be primarily through the medium of the printed page but in some dramatic and novel fashion hitherto unsuspected. If this book of "songs and sonnets Atlantean" however modestly helps in any way to restore Shakespeare's own master to common currency—

whether amongst the poets or, more importantly, amongst the people—then its publication will be more than justified.

Thus, whether Neo-Elizabethan, Neo-Spenserian, Neo-Baroque, or Baroque Late Romantic—whatever designation seems most appropriate—the present volume is a deliberate postscript to that specific tradition of "pure poetry" begun in modern English by Edmund Spenser and more or less ended by such Californian lyric poets as George Sterling (1869–1926), Nora May French (1881–1907), and Clark Ashton Smith (1893–1961). If nothing else (and this alone might prove enough), this little volume bears witness to the fact that there are still more than a few brave souls who can see beyond the desolation of T. S. Eliot's *Waste Land* to the manifold and labyrinthine greenery of Spenser's Faeryland, to the allegorical dream-garden that flourishes in *Le Roman de la Rose*, to the primordial splendors of the archetypal Eden.

It is then altogether appropriate that this volume—dedicated as it is to the memory of the supreme poet of the Age of Elizabeth I (1558–1603)—should appear as of the nonce in this the Age of Elizabeth II (begun 1952). Thus, insofar as it brings together for the first time in English an extensive selection of poems translated from the Atlantean; and insofar as it brings to the attention of poets a new form well worthy of their use, to wit, the Spenserian stanza-sonnet; and insofar as it recalls attention, in however an humble manner, to one of the greatest of poets in English or any language, under a poetical rather than a scholarly aegis (and insofar as it attempts to recall attention, even if only incidentally, to one of the most magnificent forms in English prosody, to wit, the Spenserian stanza);—this major contribution to Plato's Atlantis Mythos (within the minor compass of "narrow verse") may be modestly recommended.

—Dr. Ibid M. Andor

Atlantis Hall, Terceira, the Azores.
30 September 1970.

If music and sweet poetry agree,
As they must needs, the sister and the brother,
Then must the love be great twixt thee and me,
Because thou lovest the one, and I the other.
Dowland to thee is dear, whose heavenly touch
Upon the lute doth ravish human sense;
Spenser to me, whose deep conceit is such
As passing all conceit, needs no defense.
Thou lovest to hear the sweet melodious sound
That Phoebus's lute, the queen of music, makes;
And I in deep delight am chiefly drowned
Whenas himself to singing he betakes.
One god is god of both, as poets feign;
One knight loves both, and both in thee remain.

—Shakespeare, *The Passionate Pilgrim.*

Songs and Sonnets Atlantean

The First Series

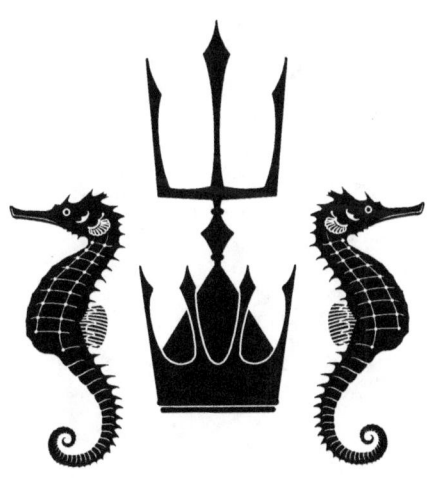

Avalonessys

Translated from the French of Michel de Labretagne.

When Avalon and Lyonnesse and Yss were one
Above the Ocean Sea's eternal hiss and spray;
Due northwest of Cornwall, Avalonessys lay—
That sea-green isle of apple orchards; where the sun
Would spin brave webs of time, in orbits never done;
Where lovers, in the midst of fountains and their play,
Upon the sea-green sod would seek some place away,
Whenas the world waxed old, with Time long since begun. . . .

It was then, it was there that I loved you, my love,
With paradisiac flames as ragingly afire
As any star within the empery of night;

Until that final day when ocean's wine, above,
Did loom afoam and, down, did fall—one wave entire—
To drown the fires of love, of life, and all of light.

The Crown and Trident Imperial

Translated from the Atlantean of an unknown poet.

1. Let us muse upon the more than splendor, upon the wonder and the marvel, that Atlantis was of old, and above all else, let us muse upon the crown and trident, and its ensamples manifold: Let us consider first the wide brow-encircling band from whose upper rim rise the nine tall, three-sided, and outward-pointing spikes . . . then, within and overtopping a little the encircling spikes, the conical cap . . . then, rising from the top of the cap, the smaller quasi-diamond-shape . . . then, rising from the diamond-shape, the short shaft that supports an imperial, rectilinear, and sharp-headed trident, of which the middle tooth overtops a little the two attendant teeth. Thus, the archetype, and innumerable the variants thereof devised by the artists and artisans of Atlantis, in substances multifarious, even in that rarest metal of all . . . the curious and costly alloy which immingles copper and gold with some silver . . . the pale flame-gold of orichalch. . . .

2. Of the crown and trident, once upon a time you could have found ensamples everywhere. . . . Useless abstraction to repeat them here, for the world in which they were once more than manifest has disappeared. Only in silhouette upon small coins preserved from the elder time can you still find this heraldry . . . or only fixed upon the top of single columns that still rise up in the wilderness, or by the lonely sea, or high in the desolate mountains. . . .

3. And shall anyone forge anew, and once more from orichalchum, the most sacred ensample of all? . . . the sceptre-staff now lost but once belonging to the Archking of the Empire of Atlantis . . . the thrice-tripled trident above the single crown. . . .

Atlantis

Translated from the Atlantean of Athallarion.

An alpha huge athwart the Ocean Sea,
The island continent Atlantis, old
In thrice-resplendent sovereign empery,
Uprose from deeps now deeper still. In gold
And orichalch it pleased her to enfold
The pomp, the pride, of her imperial court;
Where Beauty flamed her flambeaux manifold,
And blazing Wealth maintained its foremost port,
Enshrined—O Empire's heart—in Empire's uttermost fort:—

O fortress . . . pharos . . . archsublime acropolis of kings;
Where once the crown and trident swayed that pompous prideful court,
And Majesty in splendent state would muse on splendid things. . . .

O Splendor sunk, alas! beyond recall, that once of yore
Her crown and trident's empire stretched from east to western shore. . . .

Alas! And now no more . . . For ever more. . . . Alas!

The Rose and the Thorn

Translated from the French of Michel de Labretagne.

This red red rose, first rooted and tended tenderly
    in the red of my heart,
And then to the garden of our love transplanted
    with tender trembling art,
This red red rose, this life's love's heart's blood's
    bloom, this do you scorn,
Caressing instead, you sweet perversity shaped like a
    lass, its well-pricked guardians of thorn.

Rose Escarlate

Translated from the French of Michel de Labretagne.

In the garden of our love have we grown a scarlet rose
That flames it fiercely to the sun and gleams it to the moon;
But when our love falls to decay, and passion in silence goes,
Then the scarlet rose turns pale, lost in a deathly swoon.

"O Ebon-Colored Rose"

Translated from the Atlantean of Prince Atlantarion.

> Ces fleurs maladives.
> —Baudelaire, *Les Fleurs du mal*, dedication.

> . . . Ebon blooms that swell in ghastly woods . . .
> —Robert E. Howard, "Which Will Scarcely Be Understood."

> Not such as earth out of her fruitful womb
> Throws forth to men, sweet and well-savorèd,
> But direful deadly black, both leaf and bloom,
> Fit to adorn the dead, and deck the dreary tomb.
> —Edmund Spenser, *The Faerie Queene*, II: VII: LI.

The rose blooms ebon in these longsome latter years,

These long, too long, autumnal afternoons and nights.

Her darkling petals sparkle not with dew but tears. . . .

The dearling dew of lovers' dusk no more delights

Her languid leaves, nor traces errant loving flights

Upon her face, but in that same dew's sparkling stead

Burn bitter salty tears with pallid paling lights,

The paling mournful lamps of dying loves and dead,

Whose flames with oils of grief, and shame, and wan distress, are fed. . . .

Like night-black vipers that we overlate beware,

The darkling thorns lurk low, close to the rose's bed,

And sullenly distill the venom of Despair. . . .

And when the mournful lamps shall dim, shall fail, shall utterly leave
    no light,

Then shall the ebon rose be lost, lost in the cosmic waste of Night.

Your Mouth of Pomegranate

Translated from the Atlantean of Prince Atlantarion.

Your mouth of pomegranate mixed with musk is mine:
When I, and I alone, unseal your bright-red lips,
The bright-red pomegranate-blossom of your lips,
Your breath divine with musk breathes forth to me, and then
I breathe a fragrance as of pomegranate-wine,
A rich, rubescent wine long-stored in darkling vaults. . . .
And then, within the garnet cup that is your mouth,
I taste a savor subtly tart and subtly sweet,
The distillation of the pomegranate-fruit,
Such as might grow within a garden-close of gods. . . .

And thus, beneath the branches of these trees in bloom,
These Atlantean pomegranate-trees abloom
With the bright-red waxy stars of pomegranate-flowers,
When sinks and sets the pomegranate-colored sun
Beyond the wine of pomegranate-colored seas,
Then do I press my mouth on your mouth: O my love,
Your mouth of pomegranate mixed with musk is mine!

As Buds and Blossoms in the Month of May the Rose

Translated from the French of Pierre de Ronsard.

As buds and blossoms in the month of May the rose,
In all the youth and beauty of her firstling bloom;
With such a jealous flush the eastern skies illume
When tears of dew the dawn upon her face bestows;

Deep in her heart, empetalled Love and Grace repose,
Making the groves and gardens redolent with perfume;
But, when too harsh a rain or sun entrains her doom,
She languishes and dies, all petals in disclose;

Thus, in the very blossoming of thy youthfulness,
When heaven and earth paid homage to thy loveliness,
Fate struck thee down, as ash of petals to repose.

As fit funereal gifts, take thou these tears of mine,
And take these blossoms and this urn of milk as thine,
That thus, alive or dead, thine essence be but rose.

To Clark Ashton Smith

(13 January 1893–14 August 1961)

One with the stars and singing splendor of the night,
The alchemist of beauty and of bale is gone,
Leaving at last in long-delayed and stately flight
For worlds where never-ending suns of wonder dawn;
Where unicorned chimaeras all of crystal fawn
About the breast of sphinx and succubus asmile;
Where black, profulgent prodigies of horror spawn,
Alone or through the cunning necromantic guile
Of mighty and omniscient mages; where the vial
Of darkly glamourous night has poured its black above
Some Atlantean, enchanted, ocean-foundering isle
Where prince and princess prove the philtre-spell of love. . . .

One with all worlds and things of wonder lying lost of space and time,
He is at long last gone to claim, once more, his native sphere sublime.

August & December 1961.

Pavane

Upon hearing the Pavane *of Messire Gabriel Fauré.*

Where proud imperial peacocks pomp their many-pomped pavane,
Their stately dance of splendor pavonine,
And where courtier and courtezan
Mingle amid and mock those pomps of peacock eyne,
There the plenilune pours forth her flood of silence opaline
Within an inmost woodland glade,
While pipes of Pan combine
A poignant note of darkling light and lambent shade,
Of fingers yielding half-afraid,
As fingers touch and linger and then lightly pass
Within an inmost woodland glade
Of muted evergreen and muted gold-green grass,
Where courtier and courtezan,
And proud imperial peacocks pomp a many-pomped and many-hued pavane.

When We Were Prince and Princess

Translated from the Atlantean of King Atlantarion I.

When we were prince and princess deep in deepest love,
And roamed we at our will on Atlantean isles,
What deep delight to prove the philtre-spells of love!

The spells, the charms, the shy enchantments of our smiles,
And then the pulse of love within our hearts would rise,
Would put to lingering flight our shyness and our smiles. . . .

In secrecy we would dare love's great enterprise,
Its incandescent spells of passion, pain, and throe,
That proudly blazed the shield of love's great enterprise. . . .

But spell of spells of all those spells of long ago,
That last brief spell of splendor and of ecstasy,
When we were prince and princess oh so very long ago. . . .

And though our love, our names, in future cycles none
    May know and call to memory,
We shall not care, for once we were together one
    With splendor and eternity.

The Crown and Trident

Translated from the Atlantean of King Atlantarion I.

> ... And here, in the centermost heart of that immense, marvellous, and imperial city, Mount Atlantis, the Acropolis, like a first Olympus, soared eternally into the air. ...
> —Michel de Labretagne,
> from Le roman de la princesse Aïs et du prince Atlantaryon

High noon, and on this cloudless day how bright
The sun upon the arch Acropolis
From lowest slopes up to its utmost height;
From colonnades, towers, temples, palaces,
Fine-etched like sacrificial chalices,
To where a crown and trident huge aspires
To utmost—empyrean—synthesis;
To where the white-gold breath of sun conspires
With orichalch the most resplendent fires,
And where atop the mountain's mass of granite
Attains no sound of fanfares, flutes, and lyres,
Only the wandering notes of star and planet. . . .

Only this coin with crown and trident stamped in gold
Remains to speak the high-spired splendidness of old.

Song

Translated from the Atlantean of Athallarion.

O ebon-colored rose,
How much too darkly do you bloom!
Abyssal night bestows,
As from some vast, unlighted tomb,
Its utter black, its utter gloom,
Upon your stem, your foliage, and your face,
Your face wherefrom pours forth perfume,
A dark perfume . . . of pure and perfect grace. . . .
O aura fit for him that would have Death's embrace!

"Thy Spirit Walks the Sea"

Dedicated to Nora May French, in memoriam.

> What shifting films of distance fold you, blind you,
>   This windy eve of dreams, I cannot tell.
> I know they grope through some strange mist to find you,
>   My hands that give you Greeting and Farewell.
>   —Nora May French, "Ave Atque Vale."

Standing upon this lyric promontory

Which rises up beside the western sea,

We muse on Phyllis and her Sapphic glory:

Since that same time when you but seemed to flee

And in these waves they cast your ashes free,

Now more than half a hundred years have passed:

Beyond this world, its impure grief and glee,

You hold a greater world . . . the ocean's vast . . .

With whose untrammeled realms your spirit shall outlast:

Within what sunken colonnades and gardens do you roam,

Amid what palaces of some deep Atlantean past? . . .

Whose regal ways you have returned to claim once more as home:

And have you found—beyond this planet's barriers and bars—

Those greater spheres and realms . . . deep in the Ocean Sea of stars?

  Point Lobos: 31 December 1968.

RECOMPENSE

Translated from the Atlantean of an unknown poet.

All that the sea has taken, the sea restores.
—Clark Ashton Smith, "Sea Cycle."

The fabled wealth of the Atlantean kings,
Within the muck and slime of the ocean floor,
Lies far below with lost, forgotten things:
And can it be no splendor shall restore
The treasures of Atlantis that of yore
Her subject kings and queens in tribute gave?
The sunset and the sunrise evermore,
With gorgeousness extravagantly brave,
Invoke her stores of gold out from her vast sea-grave:

And in the twilight after sunset or before the morn—
Within the great, unending robe woven of many a wave—
The archimperial purple of Atlantis is reborn:

And in the night the white-gold stars that vibrate in the sea
Now hold her wealth of silver and of pale flame-gold in fee.

To a Youth

Whether in some palaestra of old Greece,
Your body nude, bronzed, glistening all with oil;
Or whether questing for some Golden Fleece,
A golden warrior in some Jason's toil;
Or whether through the Forum's noise and moil,
You passed, garbed in your noble *tunica;*
Or whether decked with ruff and pearls and foil,
You pomped within the court of Henri III,
The pampered and befeathered minion of a De Valois....

Or whether now, your golden body blazoned on the sun,
Surfing before the breaking wave with fierce, divine *éclat,*
Brave ocean cavalier, here, when you and the sea are one....

With mouth and eyes of mingled rapture and of mingled ruth,
Ever were you—and will you be—the same, O golden youth.

Spenserian Stanza-Sonnet Empourpré

> Strange pleasures are known to him who flaunts the immarcescible purple of poetry before the color-blind.
> —Clark Ashton Smith, *The Black Book*.

As if they waxed in Eden's garden-close;—
The iris, and the orchid, and the lyre;
The peacock, and the poppy, and the rose;
The phoenix, and his death and birth in fire;
The amaranth; the nenuphar; the choir,
Ere dawn, of little birds; the unicorn;
Amber, and ambergris; purple from Tyre;
The lover by the paramour forlorn;
Thus, all things "rich and strange" it seems are now forsworn:

But natheless I shall sing them in my minor mode,
The runes intoned by some faint otherworldly horn,
The melodies far-wafted from the antipode:

For such—the peacock, and the poppy, and the rose—
Still wax within some dim Aidennic garden-close.

A Symbol for All Splendor Lost

> Abides nor goal nor ultimate of peace,
>   Nor lifts a beacon on the cosmic deep
>   To guide our wandering world on seas sublime . . .
>   —George Sterling, "Sonnets by the Night Sea:" I.

No more, no less than Plato's quaint conceit,—
Atlantis,—more than myth, this memory
Of a paradise we may once more complete,
This image of an island empery
Supreme in wealth, extent, antiquity,—
Has now become my own arcanic lore,
But more, a torch deep in eternity,
A symbol for all splendor lost, and more,
A sign for all of loveliness evanished evermore. . . .

Forevermore? Perhaps there shall rise yet in far-off time,—
Beyond this bleak, blind interim of now and nevermore,—
Many a new Atlantis from "the cosmic sea sublime". . . .

And there, perhaps, in future gardens marvellous and vast,
Shall bloom again all splendor and all beauty lost and past.

The Ashes in the Rose Garden

*Dedicated to B. M. B., 1885–1965, in memoriam;
whose ashes lie buried in the Rose Garden of
Mountain View Cemetery, Oakland, California.*

The château by the châtelaine is now, alas! forlorn:
But for her, thus, a new domain,
A realm of rose, and through the rose her essence is reborn:
For her the air, the sun, the rain;
For her the rose that shall remain;
The bud, the rose, the bud again;
And for her, thus, a new domain,
Of dreams, and doubtful roses, in a fabled garden-close;
Of trouvère and fair châtelaine;
Of lovely antique tapestries, and gracious dim repose. . . .
Farewell, farewell, and thrice farewell, our lovely gracious lady all
    of rose.

To Edmund Spenser

(1552?-1599)

> ... The Prince of Poets in his tyme ...
> From the inscription on the monument to Spenser in *Westminster Abbey*.

Historiographers have said you died,
And were within Westminster Abbey laid
To rest—surely such worthies must have lied;
For at your seeming death you were conveyed,
While yet in courtly ruff and garb arrayed,
To Faeryland, and to Cleopolis,
That capital resplendently displayed,
And to the heart of that metropolis,
Panthèa,—the city's crown, and proud acropolis:

And there, within that crystal tower-palace's great hall,
The place of Gloriana's court, the one true Bowre of Bliss;
You have completed your great song, O gentlest bard of all:

Now rightly as *Sir* Edmund Spenser may you there be seen,
Both knight and poet laureate to Her Majesty, the Queene.

Rose Verdastre

Translated from the Atlantean of Athallarion.

. . . And so they laid the queen to rest in her own garden-close. . . .
By the Prince Atlantarion,
from the *Minor Chronicles of Atlantis*.

We wandered where the greenish roses grow
Close-gathered in the garden of a queen
Dead long ago from jealous love and woe:
Her jealous heart hath bred those roses green
And yellow-green whose phosphorescent sheen
Relumes the phosphors of her sepulchre:
Dire thorns, enormous and verdazurine,
Nourished from roots that subtly disinter,
Revive the piercing spites and jealousies that were:

The roses' fleshlike faces, velvet-soft, assume
Weird glamors gangrenous, whilst they administer
An overwhelming tide of strangely lush perfume:

We turned, our heart replete with jealous love and woe,
And wandered on from where those greenish roses grow.

AVE ATQUE VALE

Dedicated to R. G. P., in remembrance of March 1961.

Now, through the endless, void, and vasty halls of night,
The moon proceeds along her star-emblazoned way,
And pours deep in my heart her plenitude of light,
As in a Gothic hall, alone and old and gray:
Through shattered vaults, the reflex of a far-off day
Descends, and casts in ghostly wise a white-gold glow
On symbols of past loves, and comes at length to play
Upon a portrait I forevermore shall know,
The moon-bright likeness of the one so loved so long ago. . . .

Behold the gold flame of the mouth, the splendid body bare,
The face with beauty and with youth divinely all aglow,
The sea-green eyes, the gold-flushed skin, the darkling sea-gold hair:

Thus, hail and, thus, farewell to one who never shall return—
Although the flambeaux of the stars in unending vigils burn.

Thaïs and Alexander in Persepolis

Dedicated to José-Maria de Heredia, in memoriam.

Beneath the stars' impassive scrutiny they pause,
Outside the Apadana's western colonnade;
The villaged plain below—from garden, field, and glade—
Still wafts forth homage to the empery that was.

And everywhere but here—with laughter, song, applause—
The torch-lit, drunk, triumphant revellers parade;
But here, where destiny now is weighed and counterweighed,
Silence . . . while thought of retribution gnaws and gnaws.

Outlined against the splendent portico they stand,
Each richly robed, each with a gold wine-cup in hand:
She lifts her gaze towards him acclaimed by many fames. . . .

And the god-king observes with wonder and surmise
How, kindled by the Persian flambeau-fires, there flames
A splendor of destruction deep within her eyes.

A Fragment

Translated from the Atlantean of an unknown poet.

The flame-red sun was made a paling moon by mist
As by the Ocean Sea we stood and mused at dawn
And watched the ghostly waves uproll from out the east:
Fashioned of mist, fantastical creatures came to fawn
About our feet, there in that half-light of the dawn,
Bearing us gifts of shadowy crowns and shadowy gems:
Anon tall kings and queens with faces proud and wan,
With strange lights pouring from their crystal diadems,
Filed slowly past, garbed in great purple robes with white-gold hems:

Tridents upon their crowns and in their hands they bore—
Of orichalch the teeth, of orichalch the stems—
While winds blew fanfares for them as they paced the shore:

More and more thickly swarmed the mist billowing out of the east,
And more fantastical grew the shapes created by the mist....

O Fair Dark Eyes,
O Glances Turned Aside

Translated from the French of Louise Labé.

O fair dark eyes, O glances turned aside,
O ardent sighs, O tears poured forth in pain,
O endless nights whose vigils proved in vain,
O lustrous days whose charm did not abide;

O sad complaints, O obstinate desires,
O wasted time, O pains and pangs and cares,
O thousand deaths hid in a thousand snares,
O burning ills as of a thousand fires!

O mouth, O face, O hair, arms, hands, and fingers;
O plaintive lute, O voice that mournfully lingers;
So many flames to set a lass on fire!

Of thee I plain: for all the fires I bear,
For all that everywhere my heart I wear,
There has flown onto thee not one spark of desire.

The Cydnus

Translated from the French of José-Maria de Heredia.

Upon the darkling stream, within the sunset's blaze,
The purple and the white of the silver trireme loom;
Above her wake there trails a censer-borne perfume,
With flaffing of silken sails, with song of flute that strays.

Within the dazzling prow where Egypt's hawk displays,
Outside her royal dais, her glamour in utmost bloom,
Queen Cleopatra stands where sunset-lights illume,—
A great golden bird of prey with keen, attendant gaze.

Here rises Tarsus, where the disarmed warrior waits;
And in the enchanted air the enchantress elevates
Her amber arms that now the purple stains with rose;

She has not seen or sensed,—she has not felt Their breath,—
Beside her, scattering roses on the dark that flows,
The two Child-Gods: one is Desire, and one is Death.

Golden Mycenae

Citadel of gold and Cyclopean stone:
This proud lion couchant curled upon his dais,
With the mountains to the north as his great throne,
Southward sempiternally has fixed his face,
Gazing out across the sun-emblazoned space
Of the plains of Argos towards the sea's dark wine;
Patiently still searching for his golden race—
His first race of gods and godlike men—whose line
Blossomed, and then vanished . . . it would seem to no Design. . . .

It might be that no splendor passes evermore from Earth,
But that, through endless incantations—subtle, strange, divine—
It knows in far-off time and space a new resplendent birth:

In what age, in what world, shall this proud lion find again
Deep in the sea of stars—his race of gods and godlike men?

Lullaby

Translated from the Atlantean of Prince Atlantarion.

Here, where the earth and sea meet evermore,

And Mother Night takes all within her keep,

The waves wash quietly upon the shore:

The wild and white-maned horses of the deep

Have all been stabled, and are now asleep

Far down below where sunken triremes lie:

Above the shore, the sea-birds soar and sweep,

And through the trees that rise upon the sky,

A cool, soft sea-wind plays an old, old lullaby.

Minor Chronicles of Atlantis

Translated from the Atlantean of Prince Atlantarion.

Dedicated to Fritz and Jonquil Leiber.

Proem

Many and varied and curious were the stories, the histories, the miscellanea related by the poet Aon to the princess Aïs, during the time that they were sailing aboard the quinquireme of the Archking's eldest brother, the Grand Archknight Prince Anorthys, as the great ship was making her way across the eastern expanses of the Ocean Sea, and westward to Atlantis from the princess's native land located on, as well as to the south of, the shores of Ylliphya, in the very north of Iffrikonn.

Aon told the princess of quaint and fabulous monsters like the hippokampos; of the river Amphus that waters the Great Vale of Atlantis; of the delta of the Amphus and the seven principal streams thereof; of the gigantic nenuphars that blossom upon her waters; of the shape of the Archkingdom and the significance thereof; of the strange obelisks of Atlantis that line her metropolitan streets; of the loves and the sorrows and the deaths of olden lovers. Of these, and many other things, the poet descanted, to the delight or the wonder or the horror or the bafflement or the edification of the princess.

—Michel de Labretagne,
from *Le roman de la princesse Aïs et du prince Atlantaryon.*

The Hippokamp

High above the Ocean Sea weaving and reweaving her boundless tapestry of ever-cresting waves, within the prow of the great quinquireme ablaze with the late-afternoon sun, and just behind the huge heraldic sea-horse that crowns the stem, two figures are seated on a couch of ebony inlaid with silver and pale flame-gold. They look out over the westering sea.

One figure, attired in flowing scarves of violescent gauze, is the poet Aon, with his eyes green as the green of shoaling seas, and with his long and abundant mane of darkling sea-gold hair.

The other figure, to his right, is the princess Aïs, with her eyes blue like the azure of a tropical sky. Framed by her luxurious night-black hair that falls below her hams, and gowned in a simple flowing robe of green, she is leaning on a pile of iridescent cushions and fabrics.

Behind the couch rises up an enormous and purely ornamental zaör, the Atlantean harp and lyre, painted with a black, dimly refulgent lacquer, and strung with strings of a silver-seeming metal. The wind, sounding through the strings and within the hollowed body of the zaör, creates faint and bizarre sonorities.

Aon picks up from his left his great zaör of ebony strung with orichalch, and places it lovingly in his lap as though holding a child or a mistress. He shakes his great mane of hair, and strikes three ascending chords. He turns to Aïs, and gazes deep within her eyes. She looks back at her poet-mentor with serene attention and expectancy. They smile; and then Aon chants in his vibrant and sensitive tenor-voice.

"O Princess, although born an outlander, you have long known, from earliest childhood, I am sure, that all Atlantean ships—whether great or small, whether official or unofficial, whether for the transport of merchandise or of passengers—bear each upon their single or central rectangular sail an immense crown and trident woven in silhouette, just as this quinquireme bears one upon her own flame-colored central sail. . . . But enough of the crown and trident! I have sung that song enough. For the nonce I shall sing the song of the hippokamp."

He pauses and looks out over the westering sea, then points briefly to the huge sculpture at the summit of the prow, and then chants again but in an alien, deep, and hollow voice.

I

I am the hippokamp, or hippokampos, the sea-horse. Just as the crown and trident figures as the basic heraldic image, even so do I serve as the basic heraldic beast throughout the Empire of Atlantis, from the far north to the far south, from the far east to the far west.

Like most heraldic animals, I am—of course—a composite beast at best. The great Aÿsius created me three thousand years agone . . . Aÿsius, the chief court architect and sculptor during the reign of Poseidon III, called variously the Empire-Builder, the Earth-Shaker, and the First Lord of Sea and Land, amongst many another appellation.

Aÿsius had been seeking far and wide . . . to find a symbol for the dominion of many waters embodied in the Empire of Atlantis . . . and through that symbol an image for the very Ocean Sea herself.

Within these high seas, these great white-crested waves, or to use the traditional Atlantean figure of speech, these wild and white-maned horses of the deep, through which we are now sailing westward, he first discovered the idea of me.

Then he sought to find an avatar in which to render me concrete. From the land-horse he gave me my head, my neck, and my mane. From the little sea-horse that lives in tropical and semi-tropical seas, he gave me my body and my tail, magnifying both to monumental size.

Look how superbiously the long mane of the land-horse flows down over my neck and my back! Look how pertly the small fan-shaped fin of the little sea-horse is displayed at the bottom of my back and at the beginning of my tail!

But my tail—how pleased I am by that! My tail is longer and thicker and wider than that of the little sea-horse. It divides at the end into two proud fins which thrust out at right angles to the tail, and which are fashioned like those of leviathan, or of the veridical or actual sea-horse. Gradually tapering towards the outer end, my tail curls back down towards my body, and thus into itself, shell-wise.

Whether hewn from granite or malachite or marble, or whether carven from rosewood or ebony or cypress, or whether cast entirely in bronze, in silver or in gold, or in the pale flame-gold of orichalch, I flaunt my imperious and imperial beauty everywhere.

Rampantly perched upon high rectangular pedestals, often with jewelled eyes whose dark profounds hide an unknown and unknowable fire, I proclaim the image of myself in vasty numbers throughout the Empire of Atlantis. Uncounted and uncountable is the population of my kind.

Eternal souvenir of the Ocean Sea, I rear up in gardens or in desert-wastes, I keep guard on either side of the thrones of kings, I stand in avenues within temples and palaces as well as without, I pleasantly disturb the monotony of long colonnades, or I piquantly cap the corners where two or more streets merge or pass through each other.

Or often I appear featured as the very figurehead itself on the summit of some ship's prow, just as I sit here crowning the stem of this quinquireme. Rather like large quizzical eyebrows forever arched in metaphysical doubt, inquiry, or speculation, my fanciful shape in bas-relief is emblazoned on either side of the stem on virtually all Atlantean ships, just above the huge eyes which, carven and painted, peer out over the unceasing waves.

Oftentimes I may seem wild and fierce, with my neck triumphantly arched, with my mouth agape, with my nostrils flared, and with my proud, regal, and abundant mane tossed madly about. But at other times I assume a mien calm and majestical, as befits a beast so frequently found at the ancient courts of kings.

I have lived in every time and clime of the Great Imperial Age that began three thousand years agone. For three thousand years my nostrils have respired exotic and opulent perfumes, the sweet or lethal breath of autumnal or vernal flowers, and the winds and vapors of manifold oceans.

For three thousand years my ears have resounded to the sophisticated jargon of courtiers, the aggressive and competitive sibilance of merchants and merchant-princes, the cryptic utterances of sages and prophets, the mystic poetry of philosophers and metaphysicians, the clouded lore of mysteriarchs, the music sublime of poets, the whispers and raptures of lovers, and the imperious discourse of kings and prelates.

For three thousand years my stoned and implacable gaze has testified: to the pageant of an empire transpiring through the sovereign alkahest of time. I know the history of imperial Atlantis at first sight and sound and smell—whether originating in the marketplace or the temple or the court—and just as well I know much never chronicled by the royal or archroyal historiographers. And I shall outlast until the dissolution of that pageant, so long as one piece of Atlantean earth looms yet above the waves.

Oddly but characteristically, poets and visionaries claim to have seen me—in all veridicality—as early as the great Aÿsius had unveiled the first carven example of myself. And since I am the quintessence of these great white-crested waves, I would say that they have seen me for a fact, and moreover on innumerable occasions.

Although I am a composite beast at best, I have had many another heraldic animal patterned after me, the taurokamp, the leokamp, the sea-satyr, the unicorned sea-horse, as well as the giant sea-scorpion. I am the hippokamp, or hippokampos, the sea-horse.

II

I, too, am the hippokamp, or hippokampos, the sea-horse. But whereas my brother hippokamp, the heraldic beast fashioned in substances multifarious, exists only through the medium of the mind of man and only through the means afforded by his hand; I am the veridical and actual hippokamp, even though the numbers of my kind have dwindled almost to the point of extinction.

Alas! as the Empire of Atlantis and her commerce have increased, so has my species decreased in the over-all total of our far-flung population. And great is the pity and the pain of this fact, for we are a choice and strangely beautiful animal.

Prone to wandering like the whale, we range all the way from the equatorial seas to the seas of the far north or of the far south. Peaceable and shy, we live in those places usually inaccessible to men and to the ships of men.

By preference as well as by olden tradition, we inhabit those areas where the sea and the land meet in an ever-changing welter of tides and currents and winds . . . raving and roaring around sea-caves and shelving sea-cliffs . . . and in and around the weirdly sculptured rocks of great sea-labyrinths.

Like the leviathan, we are a mammal and have evolved from the land-horse over a period of manifold aeons, and thus we still bear many points of resemblance to our brother species.

Our eyes, protected and encircled by thick protuberant muscles, project out from our head. Some small distance back from our eyes, our ears rise up, now hardly more than low vestigial cones.

Our mouth, too, has changed, for in adjusting to our new diet of seaweed and sea-flower, mollusk and crustacean and fish, our upper and lower sets of teeth have metamorphosed into continuous ridges of an extra-sharp and extra-hard enamel-covered bone.

Our neck has become even thicker than that of the land-horse. Between the eyes and the ears, and a little bit back from the eyes, there lifts up a low serrulate crest which runs down the back of our neck and then disappears into the skin of our upper back.

The girth of our chest is considerable and exceeds even that of the great bull; like the leviathan, we can submerge for extended periods of time deep within the exquisite oblivion of Mother Ocean.

Our front legs, thick and short, have developed semi-prehensile appendages; our hind legs now form part of our long and sinuous tail which, muscular and supple, has thickened to such a degree that at the widest it easily equals our neck in girth.

Our tail rapidly tapers towards the outer end, and the tail's end itself, consisting of two fins issuing at right angles to the tail, we employ in the same way that the helmsman employs the rudder on one of your great Atlantean ships, to guide and govern the course.

And we have no pelt—only a thick, smooth, rubbery skin like that of the whale, and gray-green in hue, rather like the dull-toned, gray-green patina that forms on bronze and on brass, as well as on the darker, more copper-laden orichalchums.

Rarely will you witness us now, rarely do we let a man or a woman or a child behold us; just often enough so that mankind shall know for a verity that we still exist, even though we are, alas! gradually becoming a legendary and a mythical creature.

And though we make love with a passion, a fury, and an ingenuity that have no parallel or equal, our sea-dams hardly ever conceive anymore. And on those rare occasions when one of our females does give birth to a sea-foal who is perfect and who does not perish from the manifold hazards of our existence, supreme is our joyance and our delight.

And then supreme is the joyance and the delight, the fervor and the freshness with which we, the sea-studs, can once more mount our sea-dams, hoping that the fruit from our labor of love shall also prove more than a momentary exaltation of the senses.

In the late afternoon the sea-studs and the sea-dams will court each other and then pair off. Then as the sun's fierce disk of rubescent gold sinks and sets in the far west, we will join and, thus united, we will dive into the upper levels of the sea stained with the flames of sunset.

Then as the dusk of evening changes the upper sea into one enormous dark-gray pearl, we glide into those lower levels of twilight. Then as twilight passes into night, we descend still further, and roam those yet nether regions of eternal night. Thus deep within that womb of waters, and secure from all pursuit, we make love while Mother Ocean caresses us with her pervasive and inexorable affection.

Then after seemingly unending hours of making love—when we have lost all sense of time and space and self, when we can no longer distinguish the night of waters from the night of stars, and when the dusk before dawn has once more changed the upper sea into one enormous dark-gray pearl—we reach our final and supreme climax.

Still united, after that little death which is love's ecstatic finish, we once more swim gradually towards the upper sea, and away from those regions of death and love and eternal night. At last, in the midst of waves aflame with the incandescent gold of sunrise, we once more break through the surface of the upper sea. Then, with a strange awe and rapture commingled of lingering ecstasy and prescient sorrow, we part and then swim on upon our individual ways.

But sooner or later, after the due passage of time, when no little seahorse finally succeeds our amatory labor, then we make love once more with our tragic and wonted irony. And surely, because of this, we have become a sad and sorrowful species, and the warm salty tears that we weep are now more of grief than of joy, and immingle easily with the greater salt and the greater grief of Mother Ocean.

My brother hippokamp, no disrespect nor less love to him for this, is an illusion, a pretty piece of heraldic imagery, but he cannot ever become extinct. Having never truly lived, never can he truly die. Do not forget me, however, for I am alive. Do not consign my species to the realms of myth and legend yet. Remember me. I, too, am the hippokamp, or hippokampos, the sea-horse.

The Alpha Huge

> . . . Shaped like as an alpha huge . . .
> Old Atlantean figure of speech

A sacred mark of the most profound significance, featured extensively in the older imperial heraldry, the alpha huge has discovered its most monumental expression in the shape of the Archkingdom: A shape which may find abstraction in the figure of a tall isosceles triangle of which the two long sides project a little bit below the base, this design usually in an equal mix of or and vert and on a field azure: Thus, the Archkingdom with the massive prongs of her three great land's-ends—southeast, southwest, and north—lying athwart the great blue shield of the Ocean Sea. For principles arcane as well as practical, the alpha huge is the first glyph in the official alphabet of imperial Atlantis as created by—as well as at the behest of—the First Lord of Sea and Land, Poseidon III.

From furthest eld, speaking as the result of a wisdom both sublime and occult, seers and mysteriarchs have averred that the alpha huge is a sign descended from Earth's prime as well as a sign to represent or envision somehow the same, A symbol for the vernal paradise, the world in the first flowering of existence, as well as a symbol for the autumnal paradise, the world that has grown old and that waxes towards the inevitable decline, a world such as Atlantis, alas!—this image adumbrates also the beginning of creation as well as the mysteries of the further prime.

A sacred mark of the most profound significance, the alpha huge—according to the revelations of yore—shall emerge again but only in the latter cycles just before the end, to remind and reassure the soul prophetic of the inevitable birth or rebirth which always lies beyond that final death of all things.

The River Called Amphus

The great river-system . . . the Amphus . . . watering the very heart itself of the island continent which is the Archkingdom . . . begins in the springs and streams and rills fed by the eternal snows crowning the altitudinous mountains that surround the Vale of Mythnom . . . north of the great mountain-heartland Poseidonis . . . cradled by the clouds and by the sky . . . where the snow-like clouds and the snow-clad mountains are one to the distant eye of vision. . . .

Descending the sharply decadent slopes of the mountains . . . the brooks and streams . . . soon on the floor of Mythnom-Vale . . . intone their way into the little rivers, into the pools and lakes and ponds, into the interconnecting canals . . . all these in turn ultimately playing forth into the valley-centered and southward-streaming Monamphus . . . past the myriad farms and estates, past the innumerable houseboats and floating palaces, past the woods and orchards and parks. . . . The high garden-valley canal-world of Mythnom-Vale . . . the Great Garden in the Sky. . . .

Now the southern end of Mythnom-Vale . . . the Monamphus divides her solemn hymn at the great city At-Tho-Then . . . descending down into the great mountain-heartland Poseidonis . . . as the eastern and western branches of the Poämphus . . . flowing south through the Great Vale to-East and the Great Vale to-West that lie between the three great ranges of the sky-cleaving Eiphlox Mountains . . . . And in the Great Vale to-East, on both sides of the eastern Poämphus midmost, the great city Zaära . . . and in the Great Vale to-West, on both sides of the western Poämphus midmost, the great city Zhaärth. . . .

In turn the western and the eastern branches of the Poämphus gather into the great lake . . . the Gates of Day . . . to the east of the Outhanox, the Great Citadel of Poseidonis, and to the east of the attendant great city Xonorr just north of the ancient fortress . . . and the lake, the fortress, and the city . . . all this lies at the foot of the southernmost mountains of the great central Eiphlox range. . . .

Now the waters of the great lake descend southward in spectacular fountains and waterfalls . . . down over a gradual series of ever-widening terraces . . . the Steps of Day . . . with peculiar out-jutting rocks eroded by the ever-falling waters into bizarre and often colossal shapes ... with towered isles crowned by lush and turreted greenery, and fraught with strange vivid blooms.... Now the upper and northernmost floor of the Great Vale of Atlantis.... The great flood of waters ... as the eastern branch of the Amphus proper ... pursues an eastward-projecting concave-course ... rushing past the paralleling eastern mountain-girdle of the Great Vale of Atlantis....

Meanwhile, to the west, and separated by a wide ridge of ruinous rock interspersed with copses of dark tall trees ... the great Lake Yllthyrrya ... fed by natural subterranean tunnels that accumulate the considerable seepage from the western Poämphus high above the tunnels, and just to the north of the great lake ... from Yllthyrrya flows the western branch of the Amphus proper ... pursuing an inversely similar course to that of the eastern Amphus....

Between these two major branches of the Amphus ... the vast sea of verdure called the Great Vale of Atlantis ... the great grainery that feeds an Empire ... crisscrossed with canals for irrigation and navigation ... cinctured by mountains and by hills on all sides ... from the rich alluvial soil the farmers mine the opulent and multi-varied gold of cereal-grains both summer and winter.... On the eastern bank of the western Amphus midmost, the great city Izzarth ... on the western bank of the eastern Amphus midmost, the great city Sfarnyx.... At last, at the southern and lowermost part of this greatest of valleys, the eastern Amphus and the western Amphus gather into the vast Lake of Lotus choked with water-lilies ... upon the southern marge of the lake, the Ampheum, the great fane to and of the Amphus, adumbrates her massy outlines from amidst her environing verdure....

At last the southern midmost marge of the island continent which is the Archkingdom ... the great river called Amphus pushes down from the Lake of Lotus and through the low mountains and high hills of the coast ... facing the Ocean Sea to the south ... lavishly spreading out her delta shaped like a vast full-blown lotus ... a lotus like one of the manifold gigantic nenuphars that haunt the turgid waters of her mouth of seven mouths....

Between the two midmost streams of the Amphus delta and close to the Ocean Sea ... the great imperial seat Atlantis the City ... the capital of Atlantis the Archkingdom as well as of the Empire of Atlantis ... and thus chief of the seven great cities located within the island continent.... At last, like a huge and multi-coiled serpent with one enormous head of manifold mouths, the Amphus disgorges her abundance of dust and dirt and detritus into the ever-attendant waters of Mother Ocean . . . thus immingling her streams with that greater flux which has no end and no beginning. . . .

But in time some of these identical particles of water, some soon, some later, rise up from that great flux yclept Mother Ocean but in the form of manifold vapors that pass up into the clouds far overhead. . . . And in time some of these clouds moving northward over the Great Vale of Atlantis change into rains that fall lightly or precipitously down upon and into the land. . . . Other clouds moving further northward change into blizzards or caresses of snow, to coronate with dazzling splendors the mountain peaks of that great mountain-heartland Poseidonis or, yet further north, the peaks of the altitudinous mountains that surround the Vale of Mythnom . . . cradled by the clouds and by the sky . . . where the snow-like clouds and the snow-clad mountains are one to the distant eye of vision. . . . And thus those particles of water turn and return in that cycle of cycles which never can have an end and which never can have a beginning. . . .

The Amphus Delta

> Alpha, Delta Plane and in the Round, and Three.
> —Old nonsense jingle of Atlantis.

Shaped like a vast full-blown lotus as observed in silhouette, the delta of the great river called Amphus hath seven principal streams. From west to east these are by name: the Alphis, the Aälphis, the Amnaältis, the Amphorial, the Amphamar, and flowing southeast from the Amphamar half-way down her course, the Ataämphus, and finally the Alphessys. Between the two midmost streams, the Amnaältis and the Amphorial, the great imperial capital Atlantis resplendently displays the vast circle of her megalopolis.

The old nonsense jingle which virtually all Atlanteans will utter ever and anon, often irrelevantly, it would seem, is facile enough to explicate. The alpha—of course—refers to the Archkingdom, the delta plane to the delta of the Amphus, the delta in the round to the towered cone of Mount Atlantis, the Acropolis, arising from the centermost heart of the great capital city, and the three refers to the trident on the huge crown and trident atop the apex of the Acropolis. Thus, the main or concrete level of meaning, but there are others . . . of course . . . as always. . . .

Upon the delta's bayous, upon her marshes and pools and ponds, wherever and whenever the river waters run quietly, the broad flat leaves and the deep, broad, and multi-petalled cups of the manifold gigantic nenuphars blossom forth, revealing their simple but still cryptic signs to any and all who may care to look . . . sometimes in the sunlight, sometimes in the shade, crimson or white or yellow or blue or purple . . . or, rarest and most beautiful of all, the giant black lotus. . . .

The Imperial Crown Jewels of Atlantis

Mount Atlantis, the Acropolis of Atlantis the City, and the arch Acropolis in all the Empire of Atlantis! Close to the Ocean Sea, and between the two midmost streams of the Amphus delta, the Amnaältis and the Amphorial, the great imperial capital Atlantis resplendently displays the vast circle of her megalopolis. From within the third and innermost ring of the three great harbors, or rings of water, that lie concentered thus at the very heart of the city . . . there lifts up the towered cone of the arch Acropolis . . . completely surrounded by the great Sacred Grove planted by Poseidon III three thousand years agone. . . .

Mount Atlantis! O Empire's heart piling relentlessly up towards the heavens . . . O high-spiring crown soaring over three thousand imperial feet into the air . . . O great aspiring mass of stone as much of marble now as originally of granite . . . O tremendous and constantly evolving conspiracy between man and nature . . . O huge treasury compact of Atlantean life and art and culture. . . .

Mount Atlantis! How much without! The great imperial terraces aflame with the royal blooms of rose and lily and poppy . . . the colonnades . . . the towers and turrets . . . the garden-bowers . . . the temples . . . the trees that rise in tall and royal assemblies on the middle and upper slopes . . . the palaces . . . the great portals with double doors . . . the great flying buttresses topped by sculptures of every description and of every enduring material . . . the great imperial staircases ascending from level to level . . . even to the very summit surmounted by the archroyal observatory. . . .

Mount Atlantis! Whether within the Acropolis . . . within the unending spaces hewn out of the living stone . . . or whether without . . . out upon the multi-leveled slopes of the mountain . . . are the great halls of state . . . the throne-halls . . . the banquet-halls . . . the treasuries . . . the gatherings and avenues of statues and other sculptures . . . the great jetting fountains . . . the pools and basins and waterfalls . . . the shrines of divinities manifold. . . .

Mount Atlantis! How much within! Housed within this huge treasury are treasures beyond count . . . treasures that come from all over the Empire and the world . . . treasures given as tribute for over three millennia by a grateful and worshipping people to their living deity, the Archking, and through the sacred prism of his being, proffered thus to Atlantis herself . . . but chief of these treasures are the imperial crown jewels. . . .

But first and foremost of the ordinary treasures . . . the strange scrolls inscribed with curious lore and perilous mysteries, and illuminated with metallic inks and with precious feathers and metals and stones. . . . The costly and exotic fabrics of subtle weave . . . cloth of silver . . . cloth of gold . . . cloth of electrum . . . cloth of orichalch . . . cloth of copper for lovely copper skins. . . . Tapestries and carpets created from furs or woven from choice fabric-threads in accordance to fantastical designs. . . . Dyes rich and rare . . . the black ink manufactured by the giant squids of Atatemthessys . . . the opulent red-purples of Murexidia . . . that easternmost realm bordering on the easternmost of the Seas Within . . . the Seas Within the Gates of Gades. . . . The strange and endless minerals teased into extraordinary shapes. . . . Giant urns and vases carven from gigantic masses of cinnabar imported from the remnants of the vast island kingdom of Lemuria lying athwart the great tropical ocean south of Yndessys and east of southeastern Iffrikonn. . . .

But the treasure of treasures are the imperial crown jewels of Atlantis. . . . Pearls that still retain the cool and opalescent gloom of Yndessessian seas. . . . Pomegranates with rind of beaten flame-gold and with seeds of garnet. . . . Giant snowflakes chiseled from purest crystal. . . . Madrepore from the far-western tropical seas that wash above the sunken fields and plains of the monstrous and now lost continent of Mu. . . . Coral red as the red wine of autumnal sunsets in Avalonessys. . . . Coral white and candid as the candid white of the single wondrous horn sported by the unicorn. . . . Amber . . . black amber . . . white amber . . . as white as the opaque ice of old icicles frosted over. . . . Heraldic beasts hewn from uncommon minerals or cast entirely out of precious metals . . . silver unicorns . . . emblematical squids of lapis lazuli . . . golden leokamps . . . giant sea-scorpions in tattooed and armored mail of electrum-plates . . . amber taurokamps . . . Atlantillian jaguärs of malachite with bright polished eyes of yellow jasper . . . hippokamps of orichalchum . . . swans of roseate ivory with bills of black onyx. . . . Scepters and maces and sceptre-shafts . . . almost all surmounted with crown and tridents. . . . And here and there and everywhere blaze out the manifold and variegated splendors of tridented crowns in substances multifarious . . . tridented crowns that have often sat heavy but always proud upon the heads and brows of many royal generations. . . .

But the most perfect and beautiful treasure of the imperial crown jewels ... the crown and trident whose nine spikes form three individual tridents of which the bottom-pieces adhere to the wide brow-encircling band of the crown proper, thus making over-all a total of twelve teeth, the refulgent thorns of royalty and of divinity.... This type of crown and trident is usually made entirely of rare gem-stones fitted together with the finest pale flame-gold ... a dazzle of light and weight.... This is the same as that huge crown and trident-fashioned of purest orichalchum—which crowns the great lanthorn or beacon which in turn roofs the central and highest edifice of the archroyal observatory which in turn arises from the highest heights of Mount Atlantis.... Here, at high noon, on a clear day, the sun and the pale flame-gold conspire to adumbrate certain ultimate splendors, and here still reach, however faintly, vagrant and random echoes of those greater harmonies created by the stars and planets and galaxies ... in that orbiting and balancing which has no end and no beginning ... the music of the perfect spheres moving through the pregnant emptiness of perfect space....

THE ATLANTEAN OBELISK

Like the heraldic sea-horse, the peculiarly Atlantean, nine-sided, and always ithyphallic obelisk, a characteristic feature of Atlantean architecture, usually slightly tapered towards the upper end, and almost always topped with a crown and trident, will rear up virtually anywhere and everywhere . . . whether within sleeping chambers . . . on either side of the bed or couch . . . or whether within parks and gardens . . . rising up from the midst of the perennial roses or within the midst of the towering yews and cypresses with their proud aspiring shafts . . . or whether within temples and palaces or whether without . . . on either side of the thrones of kings or of gods . . . or whether within city-streets . . . along the wide thoroughfares of the great cities . . . especially within the great imperial capital Atlantis. . . .

The Atlantean obelisk, although thus used in a variety of ways, is above all featured in order to outline the great colonnaded city-streets . . . particularly during the long and star-bright or fog-tapestried vigils of the night . . . many obelisks are first surmounted with a tall effulgent lamp, or lanthorn, and are then surmounted with a crown and trident, and hence are yet one more type of common street-illumination. . . . Like the heraldic sea-horse, the peculiarly Atlantean, nine-sided, and always ithyphallic obelisk will rear up virtually anywhere and everywhere . . . both expectedly and unexpectedly. . . .

The Garden of Jealous Roses

This history happened shortly after the 1,001st-Year Jubilee of the Empire of Atlantis, during the reign of Atlas LII, called Ataquor, whose Queen Consort Archroyal was the Sovereign Lady Lillittis, belovèd over all. Anon, by some foul necromancy beyond precedent, a weird change came over the queen; from being a warm, compassionate, and loving person Lillittis became at irregular intervals imperious and haughty and hateful, to such an extent that the Archking and his people could only conclude that an ancient succubus, a monstrous persona from the black abyss of elder time, had somehow invaded the body of their queen and was desperately striving to win control. For all did mark the great jealousy that the new personality bore to the old one, and she to her, above all in regard to their individual amour for the Archking. In one thing alone did the two personalities accord: in their love and cultivation of the queen's rose-garden located in a garden-bower on the lower western slopes of Mount Atlantis and thus in the primordial twilight afforded by the great Sacred Grove.

In vain did the Archking summon the most celebrated necromancers and the most learnèd of doctors; in vain did the men of medicine administer to the queen their most renowned and reputedly efficacious potions and nostrums; and in vain did the mages perform their most potent spells and rituals of exorcism above and around the person of the Sovereign Lady. Gradually the struggle for domination between the two personalities enfeebled and then killed the queen, dead thus from jealous love and woe. But upon her death-bed, when she had once more become the warm, compassionate, and loving person whom everyone did love with such dearling regard, Queen Lillittis made her last and very last request, that her body be buried in her own garden-close, instead of being lapidified and then enthroned—according to the olden custom—within the funereal halls of the Outhanox, the Great Citadel of Poseidonis.

The Archking, acquiescent to his queen's dying request but bewildered and saddened beyond measure by these monstrous and sorrowful happenings, broke thus with the immemorial tradition, charging the grave and holy men of death to bury the body of Lillittis within a sepulchre just below those roses that she had nurtured with such care and with such rare accord, and so they laid the queen to rest in her own garden-close with the utmost of due funereal pomp.

But the roses growing above her body changed their wonted and variegated hues of red and white and orange and yellow to green and yellow-green, assuming a weird phosphorescence, and soon sporting enormous blue-green thorns. And their new fragrance was not as the fragrance of other roses—delicate and subtle—but was overwhelmingly luscious like the breath of the night-blossoming jasmine. And the people of the court and the city could only reach the lamentable conclusion that the same foul necromancy that had come upon the queen during life had now pursued her into death. And an even greater sorrow, mingled with terror and horror, fell upon the already grief-pierced hearts of the Archking and of his people ... and the garden-close became shunned by all, except by poets and by other solitary lovers, often also jealous, who well understood the meaning and the bitter appeal of that thrice-accursèd place. . . .

The Tale of an Olden Love

In the little village of Noöm, just south of the metropolis At-Tho-Then, in the southernmost part of Mythnom-Vale, where the Monamphus divides her solemn hymn into the western and the eastern branches of the Poämphus, there lived with their families the maiden Lailis and the youth Ampara. Now this happened in the reign of Atlas LXXVII, called Naörthris, during the fifth century of the second millennium of the Atlantean Empire.

Playmates and friends from earliest childhood, Lailis and Ampara, upon attaining to middle adolescence, became something more than brother and sister to each other. They were standing by the eastern shore of the western Poämphus, in the pearl-gray dusk just before the morn, when they kissed for the first time as man and woman. With a trembling thrill, and with the dawning of fierce and incredible suns within their hearts, they realized that they loved each other but no longer as brother and sister. And a great fear and a great joy caught at their hearts. And they sank in each other's arms down upon a blossom-embroidered hillock; and so they made love there by the river, on the green turf, in the midst of the flowering trees, where the glories of the early morning sun found them thus at length.

Shortly thereafter, and alas for the lovers, they became separated: Lailis, by virtue of her great beauty, had been invited to the court of the Archking, to fulfill her novel duties as one of the archroyal concubines.

Ampara, overwhelmed with grief and carrying his bardic lute, wandered forth from Noöm, never to return; and simply wandering wherever life happened to lead him, he sang of his lost love with a poignant beauty, gratefully recreating his private pain into a royal pleasure for others. And people hearkened to his lyrics, and great became the rumor of Ampara's invocations, eternally calling back a goddess who has eternally departed. Anon, in the course of his wanderings, the lyric poet came to the imperial seat, Atlantis the City, the greatest of the seven great cities located within the island continent. Introducing himself into the artistic life of the City, Ampara gradually gained unique fame for the songs he sang, and the manner in which he sang them; and the arbiters of creative elegance gave him their official acceptance, pronouncing him a wandering poet of recognized genius.

Soon did Atlas Naörthris invite Ampara to sing for him and the imperial court. Lailis had by now become the favorite concubine of the Archroyal Majesty, and she alone of all those assembled in that great court knew of whom Ampara sang. Royally did the Archking and his court acclaim the poet, but the lovers, dissimulating their true feelings of mutual passion, smiled at each other with a strange and secret look understandable to none but themselves. And once again, as in some olden play of paradise and hell, there flamed within their hearts the dawning of fierce and incredible suns, and Lailis and Ampara knew then that their love had never died but had only smoldered until they could meet yet once again.

Their olden love thus revived, the lovers found ways and means to meet in privacy, and to plan a flight incognito from Atlantis the City. Disguised as wandering minstrels, they met one night at midnight in the plaza due south of Mount Atlantis, and crossed over the divers plaza-bridges and rings of land into the Outer City, going from there into the low mountains and high hills of the coast west of the City and the Amphus delta. And thus they fled the Atlantean court and capital. . . .

For three days and three nights of mad happiness, the lovers journeyed west, safe for awhile from any pursuit, receiving food and hospitality at isolated farms and villages, or eating from the abundance provided by a wild and fruitful nature. They travelled along the southern marge of the island continent, on roads rarely used but which led eventually to the little seaport of Aliddium that lay where the great prong of southwestern Atlantis joins the larger mass of land. From Aliddium the lovers were planning to win passage—by assuming the position of ship's minstrels—aboard some argosy of trade going to Atlantillia and thence to the Antillias. But they somehow became lost in a series of valleys running ever west.

On the fourth day Lailis and Ampara wandered into an ineffably lush-green valley fraught with such grand and umbrageous trees as they had never known or seen before; trees with enormous orchid-like flowers wherefrom poured forth strange and subtle aromas. . . . Anon, late in the day, just before the twilight yielded to the night, they discovered within a lowland a natural pool with a great jet in the middle thereof eternally rising and falling. Now the lovers, upon seeing these pure and crystal waters, felt a great thirst, and rapidly and unreflectingly they bent down and drank deep, noticing a curious metallic aftertaste which soon passed, however. Suddenly Ampara remembered old stories about a natural spring with attendant pool located somewhere in this general area . . . a spring whose waters did not give life but only took it away . . . the dread Fountain of Ddath. . . . But Ampara said nothing and only smiled.

Now the lovers felt an unwonted lassitude and then a black tide of mortal fatigue . . . swiftly and with great passion, Lailis and Ampara, somehow both suddenly understanding all, kissed and embraced each other . . . smiling tranquilly amid their soft and sudden tears, they perceived far within each other's eyes the ghostly renascence of fierce and incredible suns . . . and now giving up to the torpor induced by the waters of the lethal fountain, they sank in each other's arms down upon a blossom-embroidered hillock. Here the following day the glories of the early morning sun found the lovers thus at length, dead amidst the great flowering trees.

And here an archroyal searching-party finally discovered their bodies, already beautiful with dissolution, some thirty days later. Noting their nearness to the dread Fountain of Ddath, the officials comprehended at once the sad issue within that place. And thus did the end come upon the lovers Lailis and Ampara, and poets everywhere sang of their love and of their sad conclusion, and the Archking himself, among many, mourned their passing.

The Shepherd and the Shepherdess

Now here we have a pretty tale of a shepherd and a shepherdess, Lailliquis and Xilvaä ... this happened in the sixth century of the third millennium of the Atlantean Empire. And it came to pass that of the seven sons fathered by Atlas CXXIX, or Atlas Lissarion, the youngest one, to wit, the Prince Atlantaon, once again wearied of the perennial splendor, the everlasting pomp and pageantry, of the imperial court and capital. Aon, as his close friends and relatives would sometimes call him, decided to leave Atlantis the City for awhile, and to become a shepherd once again but this time somewhere in the eastern range of the Eiphlox Mountains which dominate and cradle the great mountain-heartland Poseidonis. In addition, and of far greater import, the time had come for Aon to find himself a wife, according to that immemorial custom which dictates that the males of the upper classes must—almost always—choose their spouses from the lower classes.

With his dark-blond hair and his sea-green eyes, and with his unpretentious and practical garments of simple design and weave, Aon made a very pretty shepherd indeed. Leaving the imperial seat, he journeyed afoot north through the Great Vale of Atlantis, and then northeast into the eastern Eiphlox Mountains. On a warm and vernal day he wandered into the high mountain village of Quolyx, a sheepherding community, close to two large sylvan lakes that lay just to the north like two huge light blue eyes eternally gazing at the sky. Now the villagers did mark the great comeliness of the stranger who, holding converse with some elders in the village square, let it be known that he, Lailliquis, an itinerant shepherd, was looking for work. And the elders, pointing to a large cot standing on the northern side of the square, advised the stranger to ask of old Septemmis, the wealthiest shepherd in the village.

Now Septemmis had just lost the shepherd of his flocks pastured at the western end of the western lake. After questioning the applicant closely, the squire pronounced himself satisfied, and instructed Lailliquis to claim charge of the flocks that very day. The newly-hired shepherd assented but as he was leaving the house of Septemmis he noticed a girl with dark-blue eyes and raven-black hair ... a girl of wondrous beauty and gracious bearing and enigmatical presence whom the squire introduced as his daughter Xilvaä.

And the maiden and the youth ... each intrigued and enchanted the other. ...

Every day Xilvaä came to visit the handsome stranger who told her of the great world that lay beyond the little village; and he charmed her with stories of the great imperial court and capital that flourish in everlasting splendor close to the Ocean Sea. Deeply but gradually the youth and the maiden fell in love with each other. After careful deliberation, the lovers decided to ask permission for their union from Xilvaä's father.

Septemmis not only refused, explaining that he had hopes of a high-placed husband for his daughter, but reprimanded Lailliquis and instructed him to return to his flocks. Also, wishing to keep the lovers apart, the old shepherd banished his daughter to the eastern end of the eastern lake, to tend his flocks thereat.

Greatly did the lovers grieve at being parted, and every morning and every evening they both wept into the opposite ends of their respective lakes. Anon a strange phenomenon occurred: the western lake slowly changed its wonted light-blue color to a lovely sea-green, like that in the eyes of the shepherd Lailliquis; and the eastern lake slowly changed its wonted light-blue color to a rich azurine, like that in the eyes of the shepherdess Xilvaä; and the waters in the passage connecting the two lakes turned to an aquamarine.

Now all the villagers did mark this weird occurrence, and many of them spoke sternly with Septemmis, advising him that surely he did an evil thing, thus to part two lovers whose love had proven so great that their tears of grief at being parted could alter the color of two large bodies of water. But Septemmis would not be moved, maintaining that the weird change of color was purely coincidental, and had resulted without a doubt from some natural cause.

Lailliquis got word of his plight to his father, and anon the Archking with great pomp and with a great entourage sought the solace of the high mountain country in and around Quolyx, ostensibly to hunt. Great was the joy of them that dwelt in the village at having their living deity in their midst, and great was their delight to see the grand pavilions of the archroyal encampment, gay with rich and brilliant colors, rising up like bright enormous flowers in the glades and on the hillocks environing the village. Privately Atlas Lissarion spoke with Aon, advising him not to grieve: he, the Archking, would intercede with Septemmis.

Summoning the old shepherd, the Archking told him that he had heard that Septemmis dreamt of a high-placed husband for his daughter. The old man, amazed at the Archking's private knowledge, became confused and uncertain, but assented to the fact. Then Lissarion inquired closely of the old man whether he would oppose a match between Xilvaä and the Archking's own youngest son, to wit, the Prince Atlantaon. In even greater amazement the old man stated not only an emphatic nay but also that he could only regard such a match as the greatest he could possibly *imagine* for Xilvaä.

Then the Archking inquired more closely, "But why do you then oppose this match in fact, even though you say that you would not? For is not Atlantaon, sometimes called Aon, sometimes called *Lailliquis,* my very own son, who presently grieves, as does indeed your very own daughter, that you should separate them? And has not their weeping, as a very proof of their great love, changed the color of the twin lakes hereby? Do you still refuse to be moved now?"

And now the amazement and the wonder of Septemmis grew to their greatest; and covered with confusion immingled with some shame, the old man sheepishly but gladly gave his official approval to the union of the shepherd called Lailliquis and of the shepherdess called Xilvaä.

Reciprocity

This is a tale that Pharanos, the present astrologer to the Archking, loves to tell about his former astrological magister, to wit, Ullfanon. Ullfanon, it will be recalled, served as Astrologer Archroyal—and hence as Prince of Astrologers in All the Empire of Atlantis—first of all to Atlas CLII, or Atlas Quomequa, and then to his widow, the former Queen Consort Archroyal, and the first and only queen regnant in all the history of Atlantis, the Great Queen Archroyal, to wit, Atlaïs Atalantossa. Once a year, usually after the autumnal aequinox, and always at night, during a time whenas neither clouds nor mist nor fog would obscure the heavens, Ullfanon was wont to sit in full astrological robes and regalia upon the great astrological throne that centrally stands within the central and highest edifice of the archroyal observatory rising from the highest heights of Mount Atlantis.

Thus would Ullfanon hold solitary court from the dusk of evening until the dusk of morning, virtually unmoving, wrapped in meditation, and listening to the music of the spheres. Above him would loom his largest heaven-sweeping telescope, but with the thick cylinder of the telescope completely reversed, and thus with the eyepiece proffered as it were for the possible use of anyone or anything out in sidereal space, anyone or anything that might care to look down and inspect the old astrologer. Then, on that one unique night, he would ceremoniously invite the stars, the very stars and suns themselves, to study him, Ullfanon, as he had studied them, the stars, on all the other nights whenas the local meteorological conditions permitted such scrutiny and contemplation. Thus did Ullfanon allow the stars, if so they deigned, to give him something equivalent to that scrutiny and love that he proffered them in his eye and in his heart eternally.

This tale I have on the best confidence from the present astrologer to the Archking, to wit, Pharanos, who (it will be recalled) studied with Ullfanon as his last pupil and apprentice.

The Iffinnix

The poets and the prophets, those masters of strange lore and knowledge, assert that somewhere high in the highest mountains of the great central range of the Eiphlox Mountains, and thus north of the Outhanox, the Great Citadel of Poseidonis, there abides—according to the most reliable traditions—the now near-legendary bird called the iffinnix, who can fly to greater heights than any other wingèd creature, although the peaks of the greatest Eiphlox Mountains rise up even beyond the reach of the iffinnix.

They say that now but one last iffinnix lives on, a miracle of avian loveliness, with pinions of murex and gold and flame, and that all the others of his kind have long since departed for other worlds, but that he, the very last one, cannot leave our sphere until the eventual foundering of Atlantis, that will come about sometime during these latter cycles.

And both the poets and the prophets predict that when the very last iffinnix leaves Atlantis, when Atlantis has thus verily come to know an empire of many waters, then and then only shall he sing at last his only song, ineffable and canorous and poignant like the musical note of swans before their death.

A Vision of Strange Splendor

1. I dreamed a dream: a million-colored rose unfolded to my view. Standing on an empty plain beneath an empty sky, I watched both the plain and the sky gradually disappear, and I myself became concentered only to one enormous eye that could see in any direction, an eye that also had the power somehow to apprehend sound, an essence of audient vision somehow suspended in pure space. But somehow I knew that I lay at the bottom of some innominate abyss.

2. Of a sudden a great mass of ever-seething flame and smoke uprose, seemingly from nowhere. With sonorities as of a million thunders, the great mass of smoke and flame, firmly fixed upon the nothingness of the nadir, uncoiled swiftly to the zenith, with lights upon lights upon lights of a strange, septuple splendor.

3. Anon a weird, half-veiled illuminescence hovered over and out from this outré phenomenon, and suddenly at the top of the great mass of smoke and flame, a rosebud appeared, a rosebud curiously black and white and gray, a rosebud which waxed fuller and fuller, suddenly to burst forth in riotous bloom incredible, with a million petals and with a million colors, filling space as far as the eye could see.

4. Now this million-colored rose began to expand further and further, again filling space as far as the eye could see. And anon, deep within the profounds of the million-colored petals, I perceived tiny particles of incandescent matter which I suddenly recognized as innumerable stars around which there circled in unending cycles other stars as well as moons and planets.

5. Now all these atoms or stars began to circle around the great central eye which, I belatedly noticed, could perceive in all directions at once, not just all around but likewise above and below. Over and over, the atoms or stars wheeled around the great central eye in a deliberate and pre-measured music that seemed to have no end and no beginning. And now the splendors of that far-flung rose waxed ever brighter, with colors and lights never imagined and never to be imagined.

6. And once again the million-colored rose began to expand further and further, again filling space as far as the eye could see. And somehow I knew that the million-colored rose had reached her uttermost growth, her utter-

most bloom. What an infinity of atoms and stars nestled in her petals! In that one great expansive jet of light . . . a resplendent fountainhead or matrix of innumerable and innominate shapes and forms and fantasies . . . I perceived and understood the essential unity of everyone and everything.

7. Anon the stars or atoms grew faint and began to fail, and the million-colored rose began to withdraw back upon and into herself. Then with a suddenness unexpected as it was frightening, the rose burst into great and all-consuming flame. But through the flames I was able still to perceive a rosebud of pristine beauty, a rosebud curiously black and white and gray. The rosebud vanished and in her place a fiery alpha appeared, endued with incredible splendors. Anon the multi-colored splendors of the alpha changed to a single phosphorescent and compassionate blue, and then the alpha disappeared. And then I and the eye and the vision became one. And then I woke.

*And here concludes
the little book yclept the*
Minor Chronicles of Atlantis.

KILCOLMAN CASTLE: 20 AUGUST 1965

(In the fellowship of Kirby McCauley.)

> Yet all these were, when no man did them know,
> Yet have from wisest ages hidden been;
> And later times things more unknown shall show.
> Why then should witless man so much misween,
> That nothing is, but that which he hath seen?
> What if within the Moon's fair shining sphere,
> What if in every other star unseen,
> Of other worlds he happily should hear?
> He wonder would much more: yet such to some appear.
>   Edmund Spenser, *The Faerie Queene*, II: Proem: III.

Here, where the wind, the rain, the muted sun combine
To form the glistening dream of this cool summer's day,
To this place have we come as pilgrims to your shrine:
Here, where these hills, these fields, this little lake still stay;
Where, arrased on this tower, the ivy's rich display
Of deep green still keeps green the bay-leaves in your crown:
The one white swan upon the lake in some strange way,
However brief, renews far better your renown
Than monuments which man puts up . . . which time and man bring
    down. . . .

Now soon, as you yourself presage, the knights of Earth shall wend
Upon their quest, their destined quest, with all the stars for crown,
Into the hypercosmic Vast sublime and without end. . . .

Then, to the sound of otherworldly harp and flute and horn,
The phoenix heart and soul of man shall once more be reborn.

AUBADE

Translated from the Atlantean of Prince Atlantarion.

. . . The choir, / Ere dawn, of little birds. . . .

The early morning dew lies over all—
The garden-close, the field, the woods, the glade—
Now, ere the dusk yields up her pearl-gray pall:
Restless, alert, the little birds invade
This tapestry of pallid light and shade,
And fill the air with many a radiant cry:
While yet the birds attend with serenade,
Out of the east where never sunsets die,
The sun's fierce disk of pale flame-gold climbs up the sky.

The Lilac Hedge at Cassell Prairie: 27 May 1967

Dedicated to August Derleth, in gratitude.

Within this round of farms and far-off hills,
Within the greater round of space and sky,
Amid the calls of owls and whippoorwills;—
This third successive twilight bids goodbye
To us alone below this one great eye
Whose deeper light of stars will soon descend:—
Here, by these lilacs breathing to the sky,
Three stand enchanted at the twilight's end,
Linked in this mystic round of friend to friend to friend:

But this remains of Cassell Prairie now: this lilac hedge
Extending more than half a mile, this line without a bend,
Beside this old road paved with earth, touching the future's edge:

In future worlds of further stars, what friends will stand at dusk
By Earth-born lilacs all abloom with lavender and musk?

Black Poppy and Black Lotus

Translated from the Atlantean of Athallarion.

Black poppy and black lotus in the dusk:
Behold! hard by a still and night-black pool,
And fraught with faint airs as of ghostly musk,
The night-black poppy-petals, twilight-cool,
Pour out their dew, their opium-laden drool,
Deep in the heart of night-black nenuphars
That lie upon that still and night-black pool:
Wafted by Beauty's darkling avatars,
The wan luxurious airs lift up . . . up towards the stars. . . .

The House of Roses

Dedicated to George Sterling, in memoriam.

> Oh! mystically strange
> That speechless things should so have power to hint,
> With subtle form and tint
> That seize the heart's high memories unaware,
> The sorrow and the mystery of Change,
> And elements in Fate's controlling plan
> Not altogether ministrant to man
> Nor mindful of his care.
> —George Sterling, *The House of Orchids*.

In midnight dream we wandered far afield,
And came to where outspread a garden-close
Both shaped and quartered quaintly like a shield:
There, in the middle of the shield, uprose
A Gothic chapel fashioned like a rose,
With living walls of rose and leaf and stem:
There, past the reach or ken of any foes,
The great rose towered up like a diadem,
Secure within its crystal moat, beyond the garden's inmost hem:

Within the chancel latticed off with rose-rubescent bars;
Half-seen, there pulsed eternally, like some huge vital gem,
A rose-white immanence of fire drawn from the hearts of stars:

Ciphered upon the marble floor, for hour on hour on hour,
There flamed: "To him that joined the star, the wine stone, and
    the flower."

"The Musical Note of Swans ... Before Their Death"

Translated from the Atlantean of Athallarion.

And first from great Antiquity,
and before the Melody of *Syrens*,
the musical note of Swans hath been commended,
and that they sing most sweetly before their death.
—Sir Thomas Browne, *Pseudodoxia Epidemica*,
The Third Book, Chapter XXVII, part "1," the first period.

The musical note of swans before their death
Sounds only where the lonely waters run
In dark and far-off tarns: With dying breath,
Upon the splendors of the dying sun,
He singeth out against oblivion,
Like some blind woman singing in a crowd,
The weird, slow, plaintive melody of One. . . .
And thus he dies in splendor lone and proud,
With all of night's black pall for his imperial shroud.

Green Sleeves

(1967)

Upon hearing the Fantasia on "Greensleeves"
by Ralph Vaughan Williams.

Forth from the heart of hill and field and hearth;
Of castle, palace, manor house and cot;
Of lush-green park and woods and garden-garth;—
This tune, quick with the beat of life and fraught
With long-dead voices otherwise forgot,
Still sings today with slow, deliberate breath;—
This melody that centuries have wrought;
Born long before the first Elizabeth
Out of Old England's earth, but past all earthly death:

Elizabeth the Second reigns throughout these years—
Today—so that this twice-old air gains now new breath,
To mingle with the music of the far-off spheres. . . .

This tune, the breath of lush-green park and woods and garden-garth,
Forever sings forth from the heart of hill and field and hearth.

O Beautiful Dark-Amber Eyes of Old

Translated from the French of Michel de Labretagne.

O beautiful dark-amber eyes of old:
Did I not know them in the long ago?
Within a boscage deep and manifold,
Again I am the unicorn . . . and, lo!
You are the maid, the cause of all my woe,
Dressed in a gown of sendaline and gold,
To whom in gentle trust and love I go,
To lay my horn upon your lap. . . . Behold!
These beautiful dark-amber eyes I know from old.

The Forsaken Palace

Dedicated to Algernon Charles Swinburne, in memoriam.

> In the world of dreams I have chosen my part,
>   To sleep for a season and hear no word
> Of true love's truth or of light love's art,
>   Only the song of a secret bird.
>   —Swinburne, *A Ballad of Dreamland*, Envoy.

An endless maze of colonnades, it lies
In a vast woods to-north, yet always green,
Beneath eternally mist-haunted skies:
Amid the countless courts that lie between
The colonnades, full in the pallid sheen
Of sun or moon, great fountains roar and gush:
Telling of legends tragic or serene,
Vague-figured tapestries of purple plush
Hang in the gloom of halls and chambers all ahush....

Where dawn-red roses bloom deep in the innermost court,
A golden bird, within whose plumes wild splendors flush,
Sings yet a sea-like song, and holds his lonely court:

With notes and chords and overtones that endlessly prolong,
Not far away to-west, the sea forever sings her song.

For the *Shapes of Clay* of Ambrose Bierce

Lo! vague, inchoate shapes of clay that stand
Alone upon a bleak and moonlit sweep
Of desert barren save of night-black sand:
Lo! in their midst, huge marble gods that keep
Close watch upon those shapes of clay, and weep
Forth tears of ebon amber all around:
Lo! far above, deep in the cosmic deep,
A vast and kaolin moon whose rays astound
That land of spellbound sight forever to no sound.

Connaissance Fatale

Where gnarled gnomes and where haggard hags convene
In some huge sepulchre deep in the earth;
There, where the lovely lamia reigns as queen
Amid Walpurgis revelry and mirth;
There, where the basilisk gives loathsome birth
To monstrous brood; there, there I met my love,
That Atlantean solace for all dearth,
That primal goddess from domains above,
Fair Lilith,—she wherein unite the serpent and the dove:

We kissed but once—but once!—eternity of heaven and hell—
And then she vanished instantly: And now what other love
Could give me her warm lips of mandragore and asphodel?

For me, no place to rest, no time for love, no end of pain,
Until sometime, somehow, somewhere, I claim her lips again.

For the *Black Beetles in Amber* of Ambrose Bierce

Night-black heraldic scarabaeuses
Painstakingly carven by a master hand
Out of the blackest of black onyxes:
Then through the black arts of an elder land
Set in a cartouche of golden amber and,
At last, ensepulchred within the earth:
Then aeons later from the amber sand
Reborn, in blackly splendor-fraught rebirth,
Thus to attest the Night, and Her eternal worth.

Offrande Exotique

Dedicated to Eulalie, in memoriam.

> 'Tis a sweet theme,
> Which many a muse before has tried;—
> Let none now deem
> The hands profane which touch the lyre;
> They but essay (it were no crime t' aspire)
> To sing again that oft-sung tale:
> The May-Rose and the Nightingale!
> —Eulalie, "Approach of May."

These little buds, these blossoms, and these leaves,
I proffer but in vain: For who shall take
These now? or sun-proud fruit? or gold-green sheaves
Of grain? or sunlight on a sylvan lake?
Or foam that flowers forth within the wake
Of some great quinquireme ablaze with light?
Or all such things that make the spirit ache
And thrill with yet an ever-new delight?—
But manifold are those who take these blooms that grow by night:

Mandragoras in pale or purple avatars,
Huge calla lilies of a pure but deathly white,
Black roses, and black poppies, and black nenuphars:

Take then these coronals of blossoms dark or wan,
And seek no more those blooms that have forever gone.

Sonnets on an Empire of Many Waters

Dedicated to Kirby McCauley.

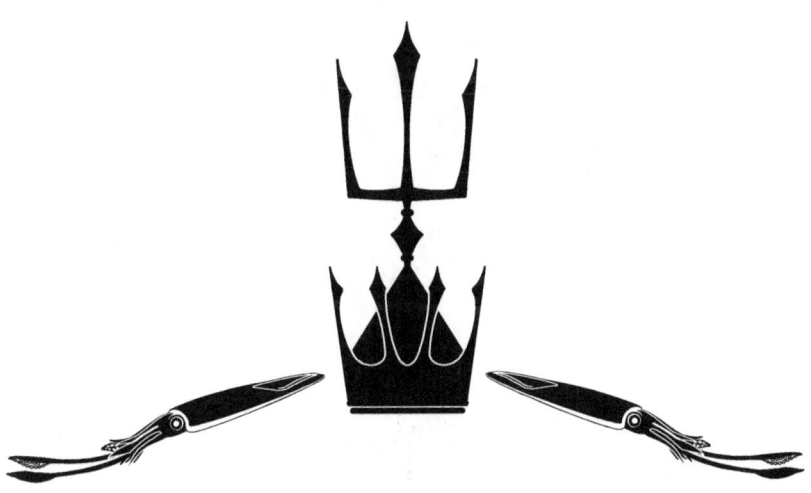

Legend

The Empire of Atlantis

1. Atlantis (at-LAN-tiss), the Archkingdom:
    the Mid-Atlantic Ridge and the Azores.
2. Gades (guh-DEEZ):
    a projection of land off southwest Iberia.
3. Atlantigades (AT-Ian-TIG-uh-deez):
    the Madeira Islands.
4. Atkantharia (AT-kan-THARR-ee-uh):
    the Canary Islands.
5. Iffrikonn-Yssthia (IFF-rih-konn, ISS-thee-uh):
    the Cape Verde Islands.
6. Atalantessys (AT-uh-lan-TESS-iss):
    the St. Peter and St. Paul Rocks.
7. Atlantillia (AT-Ian-TILL-ee-uh):
    island between Greater Antilles and Lesser Antilles.
8. Atatemthessys (AT-uh-TEM-theh-siss):
    the Bermuda Islands.
9. At-Thulonn (AT-thu-LONN):
    island off southeast Greenland.
10. Avalonessys (AV-uh-law-NESS-iss):
    island in the Irish Sea.

11. Poseidonis (PO-see-DONN-iss),
    the Archprincedom:
    the mountain-heartland
        of the Archkingdom:
        the Azores.

1

Here, where the fountains of the deep-sea flow
In fair resemblance of eternity,
And where the lights of deep-sea creatures glow
But faintly in the black infinity;
There stand vague shapes of huge antiquity—
Colossal fanes, and vasty palaces,
And markets once alive with merchantry,
And obelisks, like monstrous phalluses,
Outline the streets of this deep-sea metropolis:

And where proud kings and princes pomped in splendor near-divine,
Within the Great Thronehall Archroyal, within the Acropolis;
The tentacles of giant squids in darkness now entwine. . . .

Yea, even as foretold by mystic prophets long ago,
A boundless ocean-empire hath Atlantis come to know.

11. Atlantis

Translated from the Atlantean of Athallarion.

With land's ends three, southeast, southwest, and north—
An alpha huge athwart a great blue shield—
This mighty island kingdom stretches forth:
From inland mountain and from inland weald
To where the ocean's many waters yield
To coastal mountain, tableland, and vale:
From upland forest and from upland field
To where the sea-grove stretches from the gale;
To fiords, to bays, to gulfs where sports the migrant whale:

And in the southern midst, circled by mountains and by hills,—
The Great Vale of Atlantis,—where the harvests never fail,
But always yield rich gold of grains for Atlantean mills. . . .

Behold how this almighty island kingdom stretches forth:
One, to the southeast; two, to the southwest; three, to the north!

III. Gades

Translated from the Atlantean of Athallarion.

Land of the taurus and the taurokamp,
Keeper of the Gates to the Seas Within,
And of the eastern realms the guardian-lamp:
In puissance and in wealth the closest kin
Unto Atlantis—Lo! her royal twin—
This is the port for ships from every part
Of the lands that front on the Seas Within . . .
Vessels that bring their goods, their works of art,
From many a mart nearby, from many a far-off mart. . . .

Here, at the brave sunsetting, with strange reverence and rite,
Out of his steaming chest, nude youths wrench forth the great
    bull's heart,
To read therein deep omens, ere the imminence of night:

Yes, of the Empire's eastern realms the guardian and the lamp,
This is the strong domain of the taurus and the taurokamp.

IV. ATLANTIGADES

Translated from the Atlantean of Athallarion.

This kingdom of the Yndessessian vine,
The green, the purple, and the yellow grape,
The opulent and multi-varied wine;
Regally spreads out upon her three-pronged shape,
West, east, and south—from mountaintop to cape—
Her lush-green vineyard-forest without end;
None of whose ripe grape-clusters can escape
The keen, sure eye of harvesters who wend
Throughout those wilding labyrinths wherein the berries pend:

Give me to drink of your good wine, your vintage made for kings—
Quintessence wherewithin the earth, the rain, the sunlight
    blend—
Till I, like Majesty, shall muse on thrice-resplendent things:

Between Atlantis and Gades, replete with grapes and wine,
There stands up out of the ocean's deeps this grand realm of the
    vine.

V. Atkantharia

Translated from the Atlantean of Athallarion.

Upon the huge crescent of this arid isle,
These irrigated pomegranate-trees
Thrive in unending orchards, mile on mile:
Like images depicted in a frieze,
They scarcely move within the ghostly breeze
Breathing from off the sea-foam all in bloom:
Thrust up above the rows on rows of trees,
The stark and snow-topped mountains loom and loom,
Yet fires from eld still flow throughout their deep-set womb:

And fires from eld still burn deep in the garnets of these pomes,
Still flame deep in these flowers, these bright-red stars without
    perfume,
Still illuminate these leaves where yet some primordial splendor
    homes:

These irrigated pomegranate-trees, for mile on mile,
Flower, leaf, and fruit . . . upon the huge crescent of this arid isle.

VI. Iffrikonn-Yssthia

Translated from the Atlantean of Athallarion.

Above the tropic seas' dark azurine
Which mirrors back the sky's unbroken dome,
There rises up this labyrinth of green:
Below these proud and snow-crowned peaks there roam
Those cats that have within these woods their home,
Tiger and panther, lion and spotted pard:
Fantastic orchids white as arctic foam,
Against the deep and mothering jungle starred,
Blossom above the night-black shores which granite headlands
    guard:

In answer to the roaring breakers out beyond the lee,—
From deep within those glooms with twisting vines and branches
    barred,—
The great bull elephant roars out his challenge at the sea:

With tall proud peaks, this jungle-isle, a labyrinth of green,
Looms up above the tropic seas and their dark azurine.

VII. Atalantessys

Translated from the Atlantean of Athallarion.

Far southern kingdom of gigantic flowers,
And marble palaces upon the shore,
Or in the midst of gardens, groves, and bowers:
Great golden poppies in the sunlight pour
Forth auras like a dust of golden ore—
Huge orchids in the shade bloom ebon-hued:
While grossly grow the flowers called mandragore,
Deep nenuphars, with tropical suns endued,
Spread out on pool and stream their own tremendous magnitude:

Borne on cold ocean-streams from ultimate antarctic bournes,
Masses of ice, like ships arch-fantasy-wise carved and hued,
Sail up offshore to melt away . . . whose passing no one mourns:

White palaces upon the shore, in gardens, groves, and bowers. . . .
Out of far southern seas there lifts the realm of gigantic flowers.

VIII. Atlantillia

Translated from the Atlantean of Athallarion.

This island kingdom of the jaguär,
The orange, and the lemon, and the lime,
Is but the gate to realms more strange and far:
Like some fair visne surviving from Earth's prime,
With green growth never breathed upon by rime,
Between the twin Antillias lies this land:
But far more fair than any worldly clime
Is what the sunset and the clouds command,
Now, to the west, eternally beyond that further strand. . . .

And yet this island realm were paradise enough . . . for *here*
Can I not grasp these green, gamboge, and golden fruits in hand,
Can I not breathe the citrus flowers perfuming *everywhere?* . . .

This paradise enough, the gate to realms more strange and far,
Remains the green and regal isle where homes the jaguär.

IX. Atatemthessys

Translated from the Atlantean of Athallarion.

Within this round the giant squid resides—
A circle vast, volcanic, submarine—
And in the midst thereof this isle abides:
Superbious, majestical, serene,
The archimperial peacocks pomp and preen
Amid this paradise of flowering trees:
Both flowers and fruits peculiar to this visne,
Together with attendant courts of bees,
Hang out over the flood and ebb of semi-tropic seas:

Enthroned amid the water's many mansions and domains,
A great pulsating brain . . . encircled with arch-mysteries,
Far down below the giant squid in strange effulgence reigns:

Beyond the rise and fall of elder worlds, this isle abides
Within this mantic round wherein the giant squid resides.

X. At-Thulonn

Translated from the Atlantean of Athallarion.

Far northern kingdom of the northern lights,
Of ice and snow and evergreen and frost,
Of endless twilights and of sunlit nights:—
Where winter winds work miracles embossed
With evanescent lights the skies have lost,
Preparing countless fantasies for view:—
Where lovely lad and maiden may accost
The unicorn, entrapping him; but few
Hunt other than the seal, the musk ox, or the caribou:

In autumn and in spring the northern lights unfurl,
With ever-changing veils of purple, green, and blue;
Orange, and red, and gold; and silver shot with pearl:

Endowed with ice and snow, with unending dusk and sunlit nights,
Southeast off Mhu Thulan there lies the land of strange north
    lights.

XI. Avalonessys

Translated from the Atlantean of Athallarion.

Island of apples and of apple-wine,
Where rich and year-round crops of apples grow,
And apple-blossoms bloom above the brine!
You grant fair haven to the ships that go
Upon the Shoaling Seas' green crystalline flow—
Fair haven, with great harbors, and green coves:
Refuge and rest you grant; soft sea-winds blow
Adown your arbors where the sea-bird roves;
And lovers love to loiter deep within your groves. . . .

Pausing upon their northern or their southern flight,
To take a brief refreshment of your water-troves,
Amid your fragrant isle the great wild swans alight:

Island where apple-blossoms bloom above the brine. . . .
O realm divine with apples and with apple-wine!

XII. Poseidonis

Translated from the Atlantean of Athallarion.

Cradle of empire and of mighty kings—
Great mountain-heartland whose great mountains rise
Up far beyond the reach of any wings!
Tremendous bulks ascending to the skies
Beyond the heights whereto the phoenix flies,
Hereat they stand like puissant kings of old:
Upon their robes of evergreen there lies,
In lavish wise, the sunlight's breath of gold,
And fires their silver crowns with splendors white and cold:

Poseidonis, within the matrix of your Citadel,
The endless halls and corridors in funeral pomp enfold
Over three thousand kings and queens who thus for aye shall
      dwell:

Lo! these great peaks which rise beyond the reach of any wings,
Cradle this cradle-realm of empire and of mighty kings.

XIII. THE MERCHANT-PRINCES

Translated from the Atlantean of Athallarion.

Outside the Great Gate Acropolitan,
Due south of Mount Atlantis, they await
In splendor more than necropolitan:
Their crowns and great rich robes all aureate,
The morning's white-gold rays irradiate
With lusters and with lights ineffable:
And shall he still come forth? The hour is late.
The tremors of suspense they cannot quell,
Nor yet the love and awe that in their hearts foretell. . . .

Now fanfares and alarums. . . . Soon shall he, the King, come
    forth,—
Empanoplied with archimperial splendors nonpareil. . . .
The merchant-princes have all faced the Gate upon the north:

In splendor more than that of those in some necropolis,
They wait within the Plaza south of the arch Acropolis.

XIV. An Argosy of Trade

Translated from the Atlantean of Athallarion.

Like some strange beast called forth from deep-sea caves,
With triple banks of oars on either side,
Westward the barque pavanes across the waves:
The sign and sigil of an imperial pride,
A crown and trident spreads against the wide
And bleached-white sail its woven silhouette:
No land nor other ship may be descried
Here where dark seas and empty skies are met . . .
Where soon in fierce flame-gold the sun shall sink, and set:

A vast rich hoard the trireme holds within her cargo-glooms . . .
Furs from the north, wines from the south, lanterns and lamps of jet;
Argent, and or, and rare gem-stones, and opulent perfumes:

Westward an argosy of trade pavanes across the waves,
Like some strange beast with many legs called forth from deep-sea caves.

XV. Memories of the Astazhan

Translated from the Atlantean of Aänsess.

Beyond this tapestry of mist and rain
Which winter weaves about these northern hills,
Fair southern realms in memory still remain:
The Astazhan with all her splendor fills
This heart of me—her springs, and streams, and rills;
Her pools, her lakes; her pastures—lush and green—
On plains, in valleys, and on rolling hills;
Her parks, her woods; the warm but gentle sheen
Of the sun touched with mist above her large demesne. . . .

Between the cots and castles graze the cows and goats and sheep,
While herdsmen, decked against a grass well-near aquamarine,
Still play upon rude pipes their song of peace and rest and sleep:

Here, in the north, fair southern realms in memory still remain
Beyond this tapestry which winter weaves of mist and rain.

XVI. A Letter from Valoth

Translated from the Atlantean of Aänsess.

From Aänsess, Archknight, Archroyal Governor of the Atlantean Forts and Watchtowers in Valoth, Karanak, and southern Ivvrinaä; to His Majesty, King Atlantarion I, Overlord of the Empire of Atlantis; Dictated from Apenderragon the Great Watchtower in southern Valoth but Three Days after the Great Cataclysm.

My prince, our Avalonessys is now no more:
Upon that single day and night of rain,
Beneath the threshold of the deepest shore,
With all earth shuddering as in fear and pain,
Slowly the island sank below the main,
Leaving behind a foam-filled wrath unknown,
More bleak and barren than an arctic plain,
A desolation utterless and lone,
Where winds and waves now mourn, and make imperial moan:

The blossoms of the foam, a white and fatal green,
Now bloom above those miles of apple-blossoms flown
Beneath a deeper sea no longer fair and green:

Submerged beneath the threshold of the deepest shore,
Alas, my prince, our Avalonessys is now no more!

XVII

No, not until the final age of Earth,
When man has gone, and nothing claims the land,
Shall this proud city know a new rebirth:
The sea shall dwindle to its utmost strand;
The deep-sea silt shall change to fine gray sand,
Then like a vasty pall shall fall away:
And then Atlantis once again shall stand
Resplendent in the splendidness of day;
Until—at last—her last, and very last, decay. . . .

When all her fair proud ruin shall dissolve to dust,
And thus, to dust dissolved, forevermore shall stay;
For *in* the end, unjust or just, the end *is* just:

For in the end the Earth itself shall surely not outlast,
Less than a speck of cosmic dust slow-dwindling on the Vast. . . .

FINIS

Commendatory and Dedicatory Poems

To an Atlantean Poet

For D. S. F.

Dear friend, you walk alone in Atlantean fields,
So long enshrouded by the water's swell,
Where coral-encrusted palaces beneath the waves
Dream in sea change the dreams no man can tell
Save you who sing of lovers long rememberèd,
Of older glories in a shining world,
Of banners, pageants, distant sea-drenched drums
Vibrating in the waters:
Then once more there comes
The lord of sea and land,
And by his side,
Iridescent his bride,
And the older loves that are rememberèd.

Glory fades, dreams die.
We live in the gray land.
Touch for a moment my hand.
We remember the king and his immemorial queen.

Margo Skinner.

San Francisco, California.
11 August 1967.
(By permission of Margo Skinner.)

INSPIRATION

Dedicated in sincere friendship to D. S. F.

Bared branches wave leafless fronds
    Aloft, and my eyes ascend
Yet farther and above
    To limpid folds of blue and flakèd white
Wherein the portraits of the Gods
    Find place in fitful majesty
Commanding the minds of men
    To behold Omnipotence. . . .
In spheres of sapphirine splendour.

From beyond, in rich Atlantean climes
    Across those lulling waters,
I hear swelling chorus mass
    Upon swelling chorus
Billowing forth into One
    Eternal Note
Sustaining Universes
    In its wake
And of its substance I partake
    As with each and all.

                      IAN M. M. LAW.

Beckenham, Kent, England.
9 December 1967.
(By permission of Ian M. M. Law.)

SECRETEST

To Donald Sidney-Fryer,
upon his nearing completion of Songs and Sonnets Atlantean.

Andromeda and Messier Twenty-Five;
Black shadows of the planets and the moons;
Unseen electric rays, vocal and terse;
Caverns within Altair and Deneb Two;
From mists 'round Procyon, a priceless dew;
The deepest secrets of the universe!
And beauty's sweep in Mars's red sand dunes—
Dry, baked by gamma rays, and still alive!

The bathysphere falls down the ebon height,
Bearing adventurers extramarine;
Ooze, and the pillowed stop; the searchlight's beam
Shows great Atlantis standing still supreme—
Might of the depths!—and so much to be seen.
Just so, through modern glooms, Fryer shines bright.

FRITZ LEIBER.

Composed on PSA flight 722,
San Francisco to Los Angeles,
22 June 1969.
(By permission of Fritz Leiber.)

TO GLORIA KATHLEEN

For my very own Queen Gloriana.

Life is a pure flame, and we live by an invisible Sun within us.
—Sir Thomas Browne, *Urne-Buriall.*

My lover-lass, my lady fair, my friend,
You are the sole illusion worth my while
This moment just before the cycles end:
Our love creates an Atlantean isle
Where hell with paradise must reconcile,
And heaven and hell subsume the masque of pain:
For still, within our kiss, within our smile,
Inheres the still small point beyond all bane,
Inheres the loss of self and, thus, the loss of all things vain. . . .

The vanities that fret shall fall from us, and all things chime
In chords tremendous, deep, sublime . . . that endlessly wax and wane
To pulsings of that one pure fire beyond all space or time:

The sole illusion worth my while before the cycles end,
You throne supreme . . . my lover-lass, my lady fair, my friend.

DONALD SIDNEY-FRYER.

San Francisco, California.
Christmas 1969.

For Master Edmund Spenser: His Great Song

Two stanzas for The Faerie Queene.

VII: Proem: I.

You ask, Who *is* this famous Faerie Queene,
Whom we so much do praise, yet nowhere show,
But always vouch, although but seldom seen?
Mistress of shapes and changes whom we know,
Transcendent, immanent, both weal and woe,
The source of all things noble, just, serene;
This sovereign lady fair from long ago,
This presence often felt, yet seldom seen,
Lo! Sapience or Mother Nature *is* our Faerie Queene.

VII: VIII: III.

But since that Sabaoths sight may never be
Whilst here on Earth we needs must wend our way
And suffer changeful state, then list grant me,
O that great Sabbaoth God, the strength to play
My bardic lute, and sing my wonted lay,
My song of wars and loves which will not cease
Until the reckoning of that seventh day
Whenas all things from change will find release,
To rest back in their source, that still small point called peace.

MASTER DONALD SIDNEY-FRYER.

San Francisco, California.
30 September 1970.

Preliminary Note

N.B. Mr. Stableford preceded his present introduction to the over-all cycle of *Songs and Sonnets Atlantean* with an appraisal written in late October 2003, thus three years and three months [*sic*] beforehand. The full text of the earlier appraisal follows.

In Re: Songs and Sonnets Atlantean, by Brian Stableford

The second and third series of *Songs and Sonnets Atlantean* augment the enterprise begun in the Arkham House volume of 1971, further elaborating its multidimensionality and continuing the evolution of its witty and whimsical elements—which belong as much to the commentary as to the poems themselves, but are intrinsic to the enterprise.

The longest single item in the second series, "A Vision of a Castle Deep in Averonne," is a wonderful extravagance—a fast-flowing narrative neatly balancing past and future in a relationship that is poignant, complex, and altogether apt. The translations from Heredia are cleverly wrought, and their Parnassian theme is carried forward ingeniously into such sonnets as "Rêverie Gothique" and "Epiphany," whose inventive use of an unusual stanza-scheme is admirably suited to the wry note with which their subject-matter is interwoven. The new "Atlantis Fragments" look forward as well as back, such meditative items as "My Mind to Me an Empire Is" and "Likewise My Mind to Me a Cosmos Is" providing a bridge to the contemporary cosmological poems of the third series: the "Rondel of Time" and its companion "Rondel of Space," and the Hawking-inspired "The Music of the Spheres." This group provides a neat counterpoint to, as well as extension of, the visionary elements of much earlier poems, which is carefully preserved and maintained in other items, especially in the most extravagant of the many heartfelt tributes included in the third series: "Memorial" and "Enlightenment."

The metafictional stratification of the whole body of work is fascinating in its depth and complexity, moving from the bedrock of a beautifully ornate version of the legendary Atlantis (complete with such marvels as iffinixes!) through the Elizabethan fabulations of Edmund Spenser, the neo-paganism of the French Parnassians, and the unrepentant fantasizing of the American

Bohemians of the West Coast, to a fresh and deftly-stylized present day. Such scope is rare; coherence of vision and supple exploitation of exotic method within such scope is even rarer. The accomplished dexterity with which so many innovative links are forged and sewn is remarkable, and the whole tapestry is a brilliant achievement.

Reading, Berkshire,
England, United Kingdom,
27 October 2003

NOTES

BY DR. IBID M. ANDOR

To an Atlantean Poet, by Margo Skinner; *Inspiration,* by Ian M. M. Law; *Secretest,* by Fritz Leiber; *To Gloria Kathleen,* by Donald Sidney-Fryer; and *For Master Edmund Spenser His Great Song,* by Master Donald Sidney-Fryer.

These six poems are included here in the same way as commendatory verses by friends and well-wishers, as well as dedicatory verses by the poet himself, were included in collections of Elizabethan poetry, thus to invoke a favorable ambiance for the author and his book. The title "The Lord of Sea and Land" (see line 10 of Margo Skinner's poem "To an Atlantean Poet") was one of the official designations of each of the ten Atlantean kings.

Dedicated, in this the reign of Elizabeth II, to the memory of Edmund Spenser, poet laureate to Elizabeth I.

Since most of the poems in verse included in this book are cast in some form of the Spenserian sonnet, the Spenserian stanza, or both, the entire volume constitutes in effect an extended act of homage to "England's Archpoët"—to wit, Edmund Spenser—hence, the dedication.

The Spenserian stanza-sonnet by "G. W. Senior, to the Author" forms (that is, in terms of what has reached us from the Age of Elizabeth I) the most pointed anticipation of the form devised or innovated by Sidney-Fryer from Spenser's own sonnet-form as well as from his own stanza. Line 1: "Colin" or "Colin Clout" is of course Spenser himself. Lines 1–2: A reference to Spenser beginning his career "in lowly vein" with the twelve "aeglogues" that make up *The Shepheardes Calender,* first published in 1579. Lines 3–4: A reference to *The Faerie Queene.* Lines 5–6: A reference to the *Amoretti and Epithalamion.* Lines 13–14: The recent restoration of Spenser to his place of pre-eminence in English letters, by the outstanding Spenserian scholars of the 1960s, thoroughly vindicates the sentiment voiced with such confidence by "G. W. Senior" in these lines. Spenser proved indeed the "perfect guide" to the Elizabethan poets.

Introduction, by Dr. Ibid M. Andor.

Unless otherwise indicated, all quotations—used to identify the particular topic or point under discussion—derive from the *Introduction,*

Pronunciations for Atlantean proper names, etc. Atlantean: AT-lan-TEE-un. Atlantis: at-LAN-tiss. Poseidonis: PO-see-DONN-iss. Codex Atlanteanus: CO-dex AT-lahn-tay-AH-noose. Aänsess: AY-ahn-sess. Atlantarion: AT-lan-TARR-ee-un. Aïs: eye-EESS. Apenderragon: AH-pen-DARE-uh-gonn. Valoth: vuh-LOTH. Outhanox: OO-thuh-nox. Xonorr: k'zo-NORR. Astazhan: AH-stuh-ZHAHN.

For those readers who are interested in learning more about the history of the *Codex Atlanteanus*, as well as about its actual form and substance (as derived from the *Roman* by Labretagne, as well as from such of his comparatively few notes as are preserved in the Bibliothèque Nationale in Paris), the monograph by the present annotator entitled *The Codex Atlanteanus Reconstructed* (first published in 1936, and now in its 31st edition) will provide the most extensive and authoritative detail (The New England Institute of Oceanography Press, Provincetown, Cape Cod, Massachusetts).

Virtually all the Atlantean poetry surviving either through *La Jouvence Bretagnesque* or through the *Roman* by Labretagne, dates from the last hundred years or so *before* the Great Cataclysm or from the seven-and-thirty years *after* the Great Cataclysm, more or less.

"The Spenserian stanza itself, in terms of its actual use by poets, has declined steadily since around 1900, and finds virtually no employment at all today, oddly enough, in this the Neo-Elizabethan Age."

The use of an isolated Spenserian stanza as a vehicle for lyric expression, it may be mentioned here, is rare. The form has usually been used of course in long poems, as part of an over-all series of Spenserian stanzas. The great Irish fantaisiste, Lord Dunsany, was one of the few poets of the 20th century who would on occasion favor the Spenserian stanza as the basis for a single short lyric.

"The reader will note that the rime scheme of the Spenserian stanza as well as that of the first nine lines of the Spenserian sonnet are thus exactly the same."

Neither Spenser nor his contemporaries were unaware of the over-all similarity between the Spenserian stanza and the Spenserian sonnet, or of a natural formal break that could occur between lines 9 and 10, and between lines 12 and 13, in the Spenserian sonnet. Spenser evidently evolved his particular sonnet-form just sometime previous to the publication of the first three books of *The Faerie Queene* in 1590: the Spenserian sonnet-form made its official literary début in the 17 dedicatory sonnets included at the end of this first quarter of his magnum opus. It is most likely that the system of interlinking rimes in the stanza that he created for *The Faerie Queene* suggested to him a sonnet-form with a similar system of interlinking rimes: from the A B A B B C B C C of the Spenserian stanza it is an easy and logical step to the A B A B B C B C C D C D E E of the Spenserian sonnet.

Spenser's contemporaries would have remarked the similarity between the stanza and the sonnet not only by the interlinking rime-scheme: just as the Spenserian stanza concludes regularly with an alexandrine, six of the

17 dedicatory Spenserian sonnets conclude regularly with an alexandrine; these are numbers 7, 9, 10, 14, 15, and 17.

In 1595 appeared the 89 sonnets included in Spenser's *Amoretti and Epithalamion*, and addressed for the most part to his second wife Elizabeth Boyle. All of the sonnets in this remarkable and beautiful sequence are Spenserian, with the exception of VIII which is Elizabethan, or Shakespearian, in form. Only two sonnets conclude with an alexandrine; these are numbers X and XLV.

But the second of the two commendatory sonnets (prefacing the *Amoretti*) by "G. W. Senior, to the Author"—the which appears on the dedication page of the present volume—remains the most pointed anticipation of the Spenserian stanza-sonnet, and proves as much as any by Spenser himself to what extent both Spenser and his contemporaries were aware of the over-all similarity between the Spenserian stanza and the Spenserian sonnet.

"The Spenserian stanza . . . consists of two quatrains and a final alexandrine (or, very rarely, a fourteener), all of which are linked by rime. . . ."

Few scholars appear to have commented on the fact that, whether line 9 of the Spenserian stanza is an alexandrine or a fourteener, or a sixteener for that matter, the effect is the same just so long as this last line succeeding eight decasyllabics is a line longer than the usual pentameter. There is only one official fourteener (by Spenser himself) ending a Spenserian stanza, out of the thousands of such stanzas that make up *The Faerie Queene*. This is at the end of stanza 42 in Canto XI of Book III, and runs as follows: "On whom he got faire Pegasus, that flitteth in the ayre." (This line refers to Neptune begetting the wingèd horse on "snaky-locke Medusa.") It may be mentioned here that both Shelley and Dr. Johnson have also written Spenserian stanzas ending with fourteeners.

Also, even if a Spenserian stanza is arranged in alexandrines (lines 1–8) and a fourteener or a sixteener (line 9) instead of being arranged in the usual decasyllabics and alexandrine; the effect again remains the same, just so long as the poet retains the over-all proportions; the principal difference being an increase in stateliness gained by the Spenserian stanza created in longer lines.

Likewise, few scholars appear to have commented on the formal advantage of the riming arguments that precede all the cantoes in *The Faerie Queene*. Each argument is cast in the old ballad metre (8: 6: 8: 6) or in the form of two fourteeners arranged in ballad metre (the effect of course remains the same), with the break or caesura usually falling nicely at the end of lines one and three; that is, at the end of the eighth syllable. These riming arguments not only inform the reader apropos of the substance of each canto; but metrically, in terms of a line longer than the wonted decasyllabic, they anticipate the stately beauty of the alexandrine that almost always closes each stanza, and oftentimes they possess the same alexandrine-like pendulum-effect.

"Another feature of the Spenserian stanza-sonnet which the reader will note in some of the poems assembled herein, is the rondeau-like device whereby line three more or less repeats as line thirteen (the first line of the final couplet), and line one more or less repeats as line fourteen (the second line of the final couplet); both lines usually lengthened, and hence both with appropriate additions and/or alterations."

The rondeau-like device could perhaps be called with greater propriety the rondel device, and here we are thinking in particular—anent the effect of repetition—of the Swinburnian variation of the roundel, the English adaptation of the French rondel. This last form, the rondel, usually contains fourteen lines, of which the first two repeat as a refrain at lines 7 and 8, and again at lines 13 and 14. Compare this to the rondeau-like device whereby lines 1 and 3 more or less repeat as lines 14 and 13, respectively.

"Thus this volume has two principal purposes: to render into English the first considerable body of poems from the Atlantean, and to render direct homage to the *poet* (1552?–1599), and not the dramatist, whom the Elizabethans themselves held as supreme."

That the Elizabethans regarded Edmund Spenser as their supreme poet is demonstrated manifold, both during his lifetime and posthumously. This fact has been well summed up by Tucker Brooke writing on the English Renaissance in *A Literary History of England* (edited by Albert C. Baugh and published by Appleton-Century-Crofts, Inc., New York and London, 1948): "Nothing in Elizabethan literature, perhaps nothing until Byron's time, equaled the over-night fame of *The Faerie Queene*. Spenser became at once 'the only living Homer' and the supreme literary celebrity of the age." Many other experts on Elizabethan literature will attest to the poetic supremacy of Spenser. The first collected edition of Spenser's works appeared in 1609; this was the first folio. The second folio appeared in 1611–1612–1613. The title page of this last edition refers to him as "England's Arch-poet" as follows: "The Faerie Queen: The Shepheardes Calender, together with the other works of England's Arch-poet, Edm. Spenser. Collected into one volume, and carefully corrected. H. L. for Mathew Lowens, London, 1611–1612–1613."

"Actually the truth of the structure of *The Faerie Queene*, as well as of its meaning, lies undoubtedly somewhere between Graham Hough's dream-poem with concomitant dream-symbolism, Alastair Fowler's numerological symbolism, and William Nelson's intellectual and thematic solution."

Spenser's great fantasy is an Arthurian romance cast in Virgilian epic form. Like *The Aeneid*, it contains 12 books, or would have contained 12 books, if Spenser had lived to finish it; moreover, each book, like a smaller epic, is divided into 12 cantos. Outwardly, it appears a discursive romance with acute allegorical features, or a unique type of allegory told in the form of a discursive romance.

The Faerie Queene is a dream-poem in the manner of the French medieval allegory *The Romaunt of the Rose,* by Guillaume de Lorris and Jean de Meung, which last inspired many similar works, and which was one of the first major works in literature deliberately to create an imaginary place as a background for a narrative. But whereas the *Romaunt* merely creates an imaginary garden, *The Faerie Queene* creates an entire land, an entire world, an entire cosmos, of the imagination, and one which somehow reflects the world we know. This is in itself a great feat of creative originality with Spenser. Also, whereas the *Romaunt* concerns itself mainly with love courtly and otherwise, the scope of Spenser's epic-poem is enormous: it attempts to reflect all of life, and not just human life.

The main or central structural principle of this enormous quasi-medieval dream-poem is most likely, as William Nelson contends, intellectual and thematic; that is, the central structural element is theme expressed through fable, allegory, and symbol. The center or the central core is the principal theme of glory, or spiritual splendor, and gravitating around this arch-center are the subsidiary centers or themes; but with everything guided or directed, in terms of over-all architectonics, by formal symbolic or numerological principles, as elucidated by Alastair Fowler: hence, a cosmic model, or a microcosmos reflecting the macrocosmos: if nothing else, the over-all cyclic movement of *The Faerie Queene* would indicate that the poem is a cosmic model. The result is Graham Hough's "Freudian" dream-poem: a high-fantastical Renaissance tapestry, replete with dream-symbolism as more or less understood in terms of *The Interpretation of Dreams* by Sigmund Freud (1900). And this brings us back, strangely enough, to the medieval dream-poem based ultimately on the fantastic allegory *The Romaunt of the Rose.*

Spenser undoubtedly derived the idea of the cyclic structure—as well as of the cyclic movement—of his epic poem from the Arthurian and Carolingian mytho-poetic cycles. Further, the effect obtained by the typical Spenserian stanza is all part of the cyclic/circular ambiance created by Spenser for *The Faerie Queene*: a deliberate, usually slow-paced music as of a planet moving in its processional-like orbit around the sun; a music that purposes to reflect the order and harmony of the cosmos, or (more aptly) the music of the spheres; in the same way that the great circular maze, which is the overall structure of *The Faerie Queene*, purposes to reflect the great circular maze of the macrocosmos, of the stars and planets moving in their predestined orbits through the heavens.

It should be clear from the above that the present attempt at defining the over-all structure, movement, and meaning of *The Faerie Queene* in no way excludes Émile Legouis's conception of Spenser's epic as a dream-like pageant of constantly evolving and dissolving imagery, and in no way excludes C. S. Lewis's conception of the poem as a grand pageant of the cosmos or of Nature and, hence, as Spencer's Hymn to Life. "A full interpretation of his [Spenser's] genius, worthy of its theme," would cogently and harmoniously syncretize all these divers attitudes and approaches towards, as well as conceptions of, *The Faerie Queene*.

"Indeed, properly defined, *The Faerie Queene* not only presents the first conscious 'olden' style in modern English,—or for that matter the first conscious style, or spectrum of styles, as we comprehend such today—but it also represents the first 'Romanticism' (as understood in the sense of the Arthurian or Carolingian romances), as well as the first great 'Gothic' fiction in modern English, in the most inclusive definitions of those expressions."

It may be argued that *The Shepheardes Calender* (1579) presents not only the first conscious "olden" or rustic style in modern English but simply the first conscious style, or spectrum of styles; except that we intend the statement above to be relevant to a conscious work of fiction, *qua* fiction, and not to a poeticized form of overt autobiography, which is what *The Shepheardes Calender* is in all verity. To the Elizabethans *The Shepheardes Calender* would have appeared more a *Portrait of the Artist as a Pastoral Poet* than anything else. This is not to deny the pivotal artistic and historical significance of this earlier major poem by Spenser.

"For since around 1900, more or less coinciding with the death of Queen Victoria and with the inevitable decline of the British Empire, *The Faerie Queene* has fallen from the common currency that it once enjoyed in the homes of English-speaking families all over the world."

This statement, however extreme it might appear at first, is perfectly true in regard to the homes of the more self-consciously *cultured* English-speaking families, whether they formed part of the British Empire or of the United States of America.

"If music and sweet poetry agree"

This sonnet is also attributed to Richard Barnfield, but the present annotator agrees with Ernest de Selincourt that it seems much too good to have as its author anyone other than Shakespeare.

Avalonessys.

This is one of the comparatively few original poems in verse included by Michel de Labretagne in *La Jouvence Bretagnesque,* and typically shows the influence of the medieval and Atlantean lyric poetry that Labretagne studied with such care in his youth.

The Crown and Trident Imperial.
Through the French of Michel de Labretagne.

By an Atlantean poet of the Post-Cataclysmic Age. The three principal types of tridented crowns in ordinary use throughout the Empire of Atlantis, whether as heraldic silhouette or as heraldry in the round, are as follows: First, the archetypal crown and trident, used simply to indicate Atlantis in general, or by any royalty or any kingdom in the Empire. Second, the archroyal crown and trident (simply a tripled trident above a single crown), used exclusively by the Archroyal Family or the Archkingdom. Third, the thrice-tripled trident above the single crown, the exclusive property of the Archking, and handled only by himself or any of his personal trident-bearers.

Atlantis.
Through the French of Michel de Labretagne.

The original sonnet, or song archroyal, Athallarion (ATH-uh-LARR-ee-un) created about 13,000 B.C., shortly after the Great Cataclysm, the which in a single day and night had caused the submergence of virtually all the Empire of Atlantis, including between one-third and one-half of Atlantis the Archkingdom, and including Atlantis the great capital city of both the Empire and the Archkingdom. Athallarion was 97 at the time and died soon after creating this his final poem.

In recognition of his services to the crown and state of Atlantis, and above all for his great epic *The Song of the Archking* (created for the 3,003rd-Year Jubilee of the Empire of Atlantis), the last Archking, Atlas CLIII, called Sfamoönophamos (SFAH-mo-on-NOF-uh-moss; "born during the epiphany of Sfamoön"), made him a Grand Archknight Prince, and gave him a series of vast estates in the Great Vale to-West located in Poscidonis. In addition to his original title of "Poet Laureate of Poets Laureate at the Court of the Archking," Athallarion assumed, at the behest of the Archking, the new title of "Prince of Poets and of Poets Laureate in All the Empire of Atlantis" especially created for him.

After the Great Cataclysm, this last great Atlantean poet journeyed from his estates in the Great Vale to-West in Poseidonis to the Outhanox (OO-thuh-nox), the Great Citadel of Poseidonis, to the south of which he now saw, instead of "The Sea of Verdure" that had been the Great Vale of Atlantis, the dark and turbulent waters of the Ocean Sea. It was this view, as well as the attendant extraordinary sense of loss common to all surviving Atlanteans, which inspired Athallarion's famous threnody.

Rose Escarlate.

Escarlate, thus in the original French title: the old French form for "scarlet"—from which derive both the English word and the modern French "écarlate."

"O Ebon-Colored Rose"
Through the French of Michel de Labretagne.

Created sometime before the 3,003rd-Year Jubilee of the Empire of Atlantis. A rare expression of melancholy from Prince Atlantarion.

Your Mouth of Pomegranate.
Through the French of Michel de Labretagne.

Created by Prince Atlantarion during the wedding voyage of the Princess Aïs and himself amid the divers island kingdoms of the Empire of Atlantis; and in particular while visiting the island kingdom of Atkantharia (the Canary Islands), far-famed for her endless pomegranate-forests and for her ineffable wine of pomegranates. The pronunciation of the word "pomegranate" used in this poem (as well as in number V of *Sonnets on an Empire of Many Waters*) is "POMM-uh-GRANN-it."

When We Were Prince and Princess.
Through the French of Michel de Labretagne.

Created by King Atlantarion and presented to the Queen Aïs on the occasion of their 30th wedding anniversary, and in memory of their wedding voyage amid the divers island kingdoms of the Empire of Atlantis, in the years just before the Great Cataclysm, when they were prince and princess. . . .

The Crown and Trident.
Through the French of Michel de Labretagne.

Created by King Atlantarion in the latter decades of his life, evidently sometime after the death of his beloved wife, the Queen Aïs, but sometime just before the withdrawal of the Atlantean garrisons in what are now Ireland, Wales, and Cornwall.

The "crown and trident" was also both the principal coin of the realm and the basic medium of monetary exchange throughout the Empire of Atlantis.

Song.
Through the French of Michel de Labretagne.

From Athallarion's first collection *The Book of Athallarion,* the product of his first poetic youth.

"Thy Spirit Walks the Sea"
Dedicated to Nora May French, in memoriam.

Although born in Aurora, New York, 1881, Nora May French lived most of her 26 years in California, first in the Los Angeles area and then in San Francisco and Carmel just before she died. "Phyllis," a name she adopted while residing in the Los Angeles area, she preferred to "Nora May." She committed suicide—for her own good reasons, we may be sure—in November 1907 while a guest at the home of George and Carrie Sterling in Carmel. Her sister Helen (later Mrs. Helen French Hunt) and a group of friends (the early group of Carmel writers and artists headed by George Sterling) with appropriate ceremony scattered her ashes into the Pacific Ocean from Point Lobos.

Henry Anderson Lafler, with the assistance of Sterling and the critic Porter Garnett, gathered and edited her verses which appeared posthumously in 1910, published simply as *Poems* by The Strange Company, San Francisco. The lines quoted to head the present tribute form the third and last stanza of the last poem included in her volume. Both Sterling and his protégé Clark Ashton Smith considered her one of the most naturally gifted poets of her sex ever to have appeared in America. She ranks as the West Coast equivalent of Edna St. Vincent Millay.

"... This lyric promontory" in line 1 is a deliberate reminiscence of stanza II of Swinburne's great elegy to Baudelaire, "Ave Atque Vale":

> For always thee the fervid languid glories
> Allured of heavier suns in mightier skies;
> Thine ears knew all the wandering watery sighs

> Where the sea sobs round Lesbian promontories,
> The barren kiss of piteous wave to wave
> That knows not where is that Leucadian grave
> Which hides too deep the supreme head of song.
> Ah, salt and sterile as her kisses were,
> The wild sea winds her and the green gulfs bear
> Hither and thither, and vex and work her wrong,
> Blind gods that cannot spare.

Sterling created two beautiful tributes to her, the sonnet "Nora May French" which begins "I saw the shaken stars of midnight stir" (collected in the volume *A Wine of Wizardry* etc., 1909), and the longer poem "The Ashes in the Sea" / N. M. F. (collected in the volume *The House of Orchids* etc., 1911). Clark Ashton Smith created a magnificent elegy in blank verse entitled "To Nora May French." The title of the present tribute is a quotation taken from lines 76–77 of Smith's elegy: "But I will dream thy spirit walks the sea, / Unpacified with Lethe." This elegy first appeared in Smith's collection *Ebony and Crystal, Poems in Verse and Prose,* published by the author himself in December 1922 at Auburn, California.

Recompense.
Through the French of Michel de Labretagne.

By an Atlantean poet of the Post-Cataclysmic Age. The terror and horror of the Great Cataclysm had already faded considerably before the unknown poet who wrote this could have created it.

To Edmund Spenser.

When Spenser's grave in Westminster Abbey was opened in the present century—not to recover the elegies to his memory which noblemen and poets had written and thrown into his grave at the time of interment; but to discover proof that Sir Francis Bacon had written the plays of William Shakespeare—neither poems, pens, nor remains were found; nor the proof the zealous pedants were hoping to discover. Since no remains were found, the truth can only be that Spenser was "translated" to the Court of Faeryland, indubitably at the express behest of his beloved Faerie Queene.

Line 12: "You have completed your great song. . . ." Although *The Faerie Queene* as presently extant may be experienced as a complete work by the reader, formally it is unfinished. However, Spenser had every intention of completing it and, if his lifetime had proven equal to the task, had also every intention of creating a sequel of similar length to it, an epic revolving around

King Arthur and his Knights of the Round Table, and most likely under such a title as *The Briton King*.

Line 14: "Both knight and poet laureate. . . ." Although Elizabeth I never knighted him—as odd as it might seem—Spenser did fill the position of poet laureate for the years 1590–1599.

Rose Verdastre.
Through the French of Michel de Labretagne.

Verdastre, thus in the original French title: the old French form for "greenish"—from which derives the modern "verdâtre."

Like the "little song" which begins "O ebon-colored rose," the product of Athallarion's first poetic youth, and included in his first collection *The Book of Athallarion*.

A Fragment
Through the French of Michel de Labretagne.

By an Atlantean poet of the Post-Cataclysmic Age, not the same as the author of *Recompense*.

Lullaby.
Through the French of Michel de Labretagne.

Created for their children by Prince Atlantarion during the wedding voyage of the Princess Aïs and himself amid the divers island kingdoms of the Empire of Atlantis; and in particular while visiting the island kingdom of Atatemthessys (the Bermuda Islands), during their sojourn on the western end of the island.

Minor Chronicles of Atlantis.
Through the French of Michel de Labretagne.

General note: According to Labretagne, all of Prince Atlantarion's original "minor chronicles" were not poems in verse but were "purple patches" instead—that is, poems in prose.

Proem.

Pronunciations, etc. Aon: AY-on. Aïs: eye-EESS. Anorthys: uh-NORR-thiss. Ylliphya: ILL-lih-FEE-yuh or ill-LIF-fee-yuh (the northern shores of Africa, from Egypt to the western end of the Atlas Mountains abutting upon the Atlantic Ocean). Iffrikonn: IFF-ri-konn (Africa). Amphus: AM-fuss.

The Hippokamp.

Pronunciations. zaör: ZAY-ore. hippokamp: HIH-po-kamp. hippokampos: HIH-po-KAM-poss. Aÿsius: eye-EE-see-uss. Poseidon: PO-see-DONN. taurokamp: TORR-o-kamp. leokamp: LEE-o-kamp. taurokampos and leokampos: in the same way as hippokampos.

The real sea-horse that still existed in the last days of the Empire of Atlantis, the French sculptor Marcel Loyau has magnificently reconstructed for the Clarence Buckingham Memorial Fountain located in Grant Park, Chicago, Illinois, immediately west of Lake Michigan. For this fountain (dedicated 26 August 1927) Monsieur Loyau conceived and executed four pairs of hippokampoi, situating each pair in each of the four corners of the fountain's great basin.

The Atlanteans also featured other creatures or devices, heraldic and otherwise, as figureheads on their ships and barges. The great central island, the Archkingdom, usually featured on her ships the mythical sea-horse; on the ships of her nobility and royalty a unicorned sea-horse who sported a crown or coronet around his neck and who brandished a trident at the end of his unicorn. Gades would feature on her ships a taurokampos or taurokamp. Atlantigades would feature a sea-satyr wreathed and crowned with grapes and grape-leaves. Atkantharia, a giant sea-scorpion. Iffrikonn-Yssthia, a leokampos or leokamp. Atalantessys, anyone of several, characteristically gigantic flowers grown uniquely on that island. Atlantillia, a jaguär. Atatemthessys, a giant squid. At-Thulonn, a unicorned sea-horse, usually erminewhite. Avalonessys, a swan. Poseidonis, the mountain-heartland of the Archkingdom, featured on her great barges (which floated adown the Amphus to the great imperial seat Atlantis) the giant sea-ram, half sea-monster, half wild-mountain-sheep. But almost always, above each of the huge eyes carven and painted on the prow (of every ship) high above the water-line, there would appear in bas-relief an archetypal heraldic sea-horse.

The River Called Amphus.

Pronunciations. Mythnom: MITH-nomm. Poseidonis: PO-see-DONN-iss. Monamphus: mo-NAM-fuss. At-Tho-Then: with an equal accent on each particle of speech. Poämphus: po-AM-fuss. Zaära: zay-ARR-uh. Zhaärth: zhay-ARTH. Outhanox: OO-thuh-nox. Xonorr: k'zo-NORR. Eiphlox: EYE-flox. Yllthyrrya: ill-THEER-ee-uh. Izzarth: iz-ZARTH. Sfarnyx: SFAR-nix. Ampheum: am-FEE-um.

The Amphus Delta.

Pronunciations: Alphis: AL-fiss. Aalphis: ay-AL-fiss. Amnaältis: AM-nay-AL-tiss. Amphorial: am-FORR-ee-uhl. Amphamar: AM-fuh-MARR. Ataämphus: AT-uh-AM-fuss. Alphessys: al-FESS-iss.

The Imperial Crown Jewels of Atlantis.

Pronunciations. Murexidia: MYU-rek-ZIDD-ee-uh. Lemuria: lee-MYURR-ee-uh. Yndessys: in-DESS-iss. Yndessessian: IN-deh-SESS-ee-un. Mu: MOO.

"O high-spiring crown soaring over fifteen-hundred imperial feet into the air. . . ." An "imperial foot" was the basic metric unit in the Empire of Atlantis, and was established by Poseidon III from his own right foot as the ultimate authority over competing pedal measurements. Others have estimated the height of Mount Atlantis at over 3,000 feet.

The Garden of Jealous Roses.

Pronunciations. Ataquor: AT-uh-kworr. Lillittiss: LIH-lih-tiss.

The Tale of an Olden Love.

Pronunciations. Noöm: NO-omm. Naorthris: NAY-or-THRISS. Lailis: LEYE-liss. Ampara: am-PARR-uh. Aliddium: uh-LIDD-ee-um. Antillia: an-TILL-ee-uh. Ddath: DAHTH.

"Ampara, overwhelmed with grief and carrying his bardic lute, wandered forth from Noöm, never to return. . . ."

Virtually all Atlanteans, especially the young people, were singers and either musicians or poets, or both. Just as the purely musicianly lute (usually strung with eleven strings or more, and designed to be fretted by the fingers of the left-hand, and played largely by the fingertips of the right hand) was a far more complex instrument than the purely bardic lute (usually strung with six strings, and designed—in the manner of the purely musicianly lute—to be fretted by the fingers of the left-hand, but played by the fingernails of the right-hand), similarly the bardic lute was far more complex than the bardic lyre but with one major difference from the purely musicianly lute: the bardic lute was employed less to create music per se than it was to create an appropriate ambiance for and around the poetry, and to space out the words, phrases, and lines with a para-musical punctuation, but of such a simplicity that the poet could chord and pluck without distracting either himself or his audience from the poetry. Nevertheless, this ancient Atlantean, bardic-type accompaniment had predictably evolved into a highly complex art before the Great Cataclysm, and both the Prince Atlantarion and the last great Atlantean poet, to wit, Athallarion, were among the outstanding bardic-musical performers of their time. The zaör, or Atlantean harp and lyre combined, possessed certain distinct differences from the lute, being indeed closer to the basic seven-string lyre than to any other stringed instrument.

The Shepherd and the Shepherdess.

Pronunciations. Lailliquis: LEYE-lih-kwiss. Xilvaä: k'zil-VAY-uh. Lissarion: lih-SARR-ee-un. Atlantaon: AT-lan-TAY-on. Quolyx: KWO-lix. Septemmis: SEP-teh-miss.

Reciprocity.

Pronunciations. Pharanos: FARR-uh-noss. Ullfanon: ULL-fuh-nonn. Quomequa: kwo-ME-kwuh. Atlaïs Atalantossa: AT-leye-EESS AT-uh-lan-TOSS-uh.

Atalantossa, a name assumed by Atlaïs at her coronation, is that of the great Atlantean earth-mother-goddess within whom was essenced the Atlantean continent and about whom there centerd elaborate cults throughout the Empire of Atlantis, especially in the kingdom of Gades.

The Iffinnix.

The Atlantean IFF-in-nix: phoenix or iffinnix.

Kilcolman Castle: 20 August 1965.
In the fellowship of Kirby McCauley.

Here, from about 1587 until October 1598, resided Edmund Spenser, the first great Elizabethan poet,—and by that token the first great English poet after Geoffrey Chaucer, as well as the first great poet in modern English,—and one of the greatest poets in English or any language. Here at Kilcolman Castle in County Cork, Ireland, Spenser created most of his mature poetry, including most of *The Faerie Queene.*

To this place, Sidney-Fryer's great and good friend Kirby McCauley, then of Minneapolis, Minnesota, travelling in Ireland on vacation, made a pilgrimage on 20 August 1965, to pay homage to the elder bard, on behalf of the author at that time unable to make the pilgrimage himself. Subsequently, in his cards and letters to the poet for August, September, and October 1965, Kirby detailed his adventure at Kilcolman Castle, an adventure summarized in lines 1–9; hence, the Spenserian stanza was made possible only through the unique fellowship afforded by this friend. The castle, today scarcely more than an ivy-covered tower, is presently located on a private farm. No monument of any type whatsoever indicates that one of the greatest poets in English lived here for a considerable part of his life and created some of his greatest poetry here.

Aubade.
Through the French of Michel de Labretagne.

An early morning serenade created for their children by Prince Atlantarion during the wedding voyage of the Princess Aïs and himself amid the divers island kingdoms of the Empire of Atlantis; and in particular while visiting the island kingdom of Avalonessys (in the Irish Sea), during their sojourn at Apenderragon the Great Watchtower in southern Valoth, or Wales.

The Lilac Hedge at Cassell Prairie.
Dedicated to August Derleth, in gratitude.

Cassell Prairie, Wisconsin, was founded by an English colony in the 1850s. "Cassell" is very probably an English place-name carried over to America, and is most likely not the name of one of the early settlers. The lilac hedge, more than half a mile in length, was planted by Deacon Thomas probably sometime in the 1880s, and is laid out in a straight line beside the road, with only three or four small breaks in it now. Not far from Cassell Prairie stands Place of Hawks, alias Arkham House, the home of August Derleth, which is located on the outskirts of Sauk City, some thirty miles northwest of Madison, the state capital. (Historical data courtesy of August Derleth.)

To Arkham House the author came on 25 May 1967 and stayed through the 29th. This was the author's first personal visit with Derleth at the latter's home even though their friendship had begun through correspondence in 1954. On three successive evenings (the 25th through the 27th) Derleth, Dennis Mack (one of Derleth's helpers), and the author visited Cassell Prairie while out on a drive in Derleth's car. The poem commemorates the third and final visit, and is dedicated to Derleth in gratitude for his friendship, encouragement, and hospitality.

Black Poppy and Black Lotus.
Through the French of Michel de Labretagne.

The product of Athallarion's first poetic youth, and included in his first collection *The Book of Athallarion*.

The House of Roses.
Dedicated to George Sterling, in memoriam.

From 1903 until his death late in 1926, George Sterling (born 1869) reigned as a prince of poets on the West Coast (of the U.S.). One of California's greatest lyric poets, he is second only to his own protégé Clark Ashton Smith. His line of general poetic descent is from the English Romantic and Victorian poets, especially Tennyson and Swinburne; his line of immediate poetic descent is from Ambrose Bierce. It may be mentioned here that, in the tradition of Edgar Allan Poe, the American and now largely underground school of "pure poetry" has been peculiarly associated with Bierce, directly or indirectly.

Line 14: "To him that joined the star, the wine stone, and the flower." In the over-all *corpus* of Sterling's poetry collections, this is a reference to his first three: "the star" refers to *The Testimony of the Suns* (1903); "the wine stone" to *A Wine of Wizardry* (1909); and "the flower" to *The House of Orchids* (1911). All three books were published by A. M. Robertson of San Francisco.

"The Musical Note of Swans . . . before their Death."
Through the French of Michel de Labretagne.

In the original French paraphrase in prose, the equivalent of the first line reads "La mélodie des cygnes avant de mourir"—whose interesting similarity to the phrase by Sir Thomas Browne prompted the quotation therefrom.

Green Sleeves.

Although registered in 1575 at Stationer's Hall, London, as the Ballad of my Lady Greensleeves, the tune itself was already old by Elizabethan times.

O Beautiful Dark-Amber Eyes of Old.

In the original French, a deliberate fragment in rhythmical prose, doubtless inspired (in regard to form) by Labretagne's translations of Atlantean "little songs" into French paraphrases in prose.

For the Shapes of Clay *of Ambrose Bierce.*

Shapes of Clay, Bierce's second published volume of verse, first appeared in 1903, published by W. E. Wood, Publisher, San Francisco; and dedicated by Bierce to his two favorite and greatest poet-pupils, George Sterling and Hermann Scheffauer. The collection reappeared in 1910, as volume IV of Bierce's 12-volume *Collected Works* (1909–1912), published by the Neale Publishing Company, New York.

For the Black Beetles in Amber *of Ambrose Bierce.*

Black Beetles in Amber, Bierce's first published volume of verse, first appeared in 1892, published by the Western Authors Publishing Company, San Francisco. The collection reappeared in 1911, as volume V of Bierce's *Collected Works.*

Offrande Exotique.
Dedicated to Eulalie, in memoriam.

The particular choice of the words *buds, blossoms,* and *leaves,* in the first line, is by way of tribute to Eulalie (1824–1854) and her one and only collection of poems *Buds, Blossoms and Leaves,* published by Moore, Wilstach and Keyes; Cincinnati, November 1854. Eulalie (pronounced YOU-luh-LEE) was the *nom de plume* of Mary Eulalie Fee, of New Richmond, Ohio (not far from Cincinnati); who, shortly after her marriage to John Shannon in late January 1854, accompanied her husband when he returned to Auburn, California, in late March or early April; making her home in Auburn until her death in childbirth in late December 1854.

Although she lived in Auburn thus but a poignantly brief period of time, the Auburn Poetess (as she was called) had become, by the time of her death, fairly widely known in her adopted state, at least in the vicinage of Auburn, Sacramento, and the general gold-mining area thereabouts. According to an old resident of the area, "The retiring and idealistic poet . . . was the object of pride, love and interest to hundreds of young mining adventurers . . . and her fame became wide in the mines." Eulalie ranks as California's first woman poet in English; in her own modest way—her best poems reveal her as a careful craftswoman—Eulalie anticipates the work of such East Coast poetesses as Emily Dickinson and Edna St. Vincent Millay, beside beginning a West Coast tradition continued by Ina Coolbrith, Nora May French, and Susan Myra Gregory (of both Monterey and Auburn, and the sister of the popular novelist Jackson Gregory), a tradition somewhat analogous to that of Dickinson and Millay on the opposite side of the continent.

The verses quoted to head *Offrande Exotique* are the last seven lines of a poem by Eulalie never collected but first published in an early Auburn weekly newspaper (printed and published by her husband John Shannon), *The Placer Democrat* for Wednesday morning, April 19, 1854 (this was the first issue).

Line 10: "Mandragoras in pale or purple avatars . . ." The mandrake, mandragore or mandragora may refer to two entirely different plants. The first and usual reference is to the *Mandragora officinarum,* an herb of the nightshade family growing in southern Europe and northern Africa, an herb which possesses ovate leaves, small white or purple flowers, and a large homuncular-shaped root. The second reference is to the Mayapple or mayapple, the *Podophyllum peltatum*, an herb that grows in North America and that bears a small egg-shaped yellow "apple" (edible but nauseous in flavor) as well as a large solitary flower, highly distinctive in appearance; this herb is known in the United States as either the mandrake or the mayapple. The mandrake or mandragora is a typical item in the paraphernalia of the English Decadent poets, artists, and writers. For example, Oscar Wilde makes use of it in his poem "The Sphinx," that masterpiece of fantastic imagery; and the great artist Aubrey Beardsley employs, in place of the usual mandragora, the American mandrake or mayapple in the lower right-hand quarter of his well-known drawing wherein Siegfried has just slain the dragon. In the line cited above, our poet Sidney-Fryer is referring to the American mandrake-blossom as though it possessed both the white and purple hues of the flower of the *Mandragora officinarum*; the modern Anglo-Saxon plural above (in line 10) is not to be confused with the Greek and Latin singular *mandragoras*.

Sonnets on an Empire of Many Waters.
Through the French of Michel de Labretagne.
Dedicated to Kirby McCauley.

General note: Sonnets II–XIV, all created by Athallarion. Sonnets II–XII, part of a series describing the divers island kingdoms, island princedoms, etc., of the Empire of Atlantis. Sonnet XIII, one of a series describing the different classes of Atlantean society. Sonnet XIV, one of a series describing the different classes of Atlantean ships. All these sequences of songs archroyal were created by Athallarion when he was middle-aged.

Most of the material in the following notes apropos of each of the ten island kingdoms of the Empire of Atlantis, etc., has been abstracted from the single outstanding book on Atlantean geography, *Atlantis: A Travelogue,* which was originally given by the present annotator as a series of lectures at The New England Institute of Oceanography, Provincetown, Cape Cod, Massachusetts, during the autumn and spring semesters of 1929–1930, respectively. Subsequently the material was expanded and arranged as the book above, and was first published in 1931 by The New England Institute of Oceanography Press at Provincetown. The most recent edition, the ninth, was published in 1967.

Sonnet II. Atlantis.

Capital and principal port: Atlantis the City.
Principal heraldic beast: the hippokamp, or hippokampos. See both the prose-poem *The Hippokamp* and the note to this.
Atlantis the Archkingdom, as distinguished from Atlantis the Empire,

and as distinguished from Atlantis the great capital city of both the Archkingdom and the Empire, was a small continent located in the North Atlantic Ocean and closer to Europe than to North America. In size it was about halfway between the continent of Greenland (the ancient Mhu Thulan) and the over-all terrain of the British Isles (considered as one island). Its southernmost latitude was about the same as that of Madeira; its northernmost latitude was about the same as that of central Ireland.

This the Archkingdom, shaped like a huge alpha or a capital A, possessed seven great cities, and five principal divisions. The title "The King of the Seven Cities"—one of the official designations of the Archking—had long passed into legend before the Great Cataclysm. The five principal divisions of the Archkingdom included the great prong of southwest Atlantis; the great prong of southeast Atlantis, the Astazhan (AH-stuh-ZHAHN); and between these two great prongs, the great southern inland valley, the Great Vale of Atlantis; then the great mountain-heartland Poseidonis, whose southern boundaries marked the northernmost reaches of the three previous divisions; and last, the great northern prong of Atlantis, including the large and landlocked Vale of Mythnom lying immediately north of the central mountain range of Poseidonis.

Accordingly the climate of the island continent varied considerably: for example, the great northern prong of Atlantis, as well as the high mountains, received a goodly amount of snow in the winter, but the Great Vale of Atlantis, in the south, enjoyed a mild rainy winter and a dry summer.

The western mountains, running along and inland of the western coast of the Archkingdom, were the second highest in the Empire (together with the mountains of Atkantharia), and of an Andean height and character, a true cordillera. The great central mountains of Poseidonis, together with certain peaks in the western and eastern ranges, were the highest in the Empire, some estimates making them as high as the Himalayas. The eastern mountains were the lowest of the three ranges, and leveled out in southeast Atlantis into the vast pastoral plateau of the Astazhan. A considerable population inhabited the mountain valleys as well as the wealds or upland plains. These were in the main a semi-agricultural, semi-pastoral people.

Atlantis the Archkingdom was the first and foremost of the ten island kingdoms, and the first of the first pair of the same. The name of the Archkingdom, styled thus after Atlas I, called Pharanomion (FARR-uh-NO-mee-un), or the Founder, simply means "land, or island, of Atlas." The heart of the Archkingdom was the Great Vale of Atlantis, called "The Sea of Verdure," which produced most of the Empire's grain, watered in winter by the rains and in the summer by the elaborate system of irrigation-canals.

The great imperial seat Atlantis the City was not only the greatest port in the Empire but also the greatest port in the entire Pre-Cataclysmic world, possessing three great harbors, or rings of water, concentered thus at the very heart of the megalopolis.

Sonnet III. Gades.

Capital and principal port: Tartessoös (tar-TESS-so-oss).

Principal heraldic beast: the taurokamp, or taurokampos (the bottom half like that of the mythical sea-horse, the upper half the same as the head, horns, neck, and upper torso, but sans the legs, of the great bull).

The Gates of Gades: the then landlocked Straits of Gibraltar.

With special cults centering on the great Atlantean earth-mother-goddess Atalantossa, as well as around the idealized bull or taurus; this second of the ten island kingdoms, and the second of the first pair of the same, raised large herds of beef cattle for export. The guardian as well as the cultural and spiritual leader or "lamp" for the eastern realms of the Empire, "gades" or, in old Atlantean, "gaädesh" (GAY-uh-DESH) means "fort, fortress, castle."

The kingdom of the taurus and the taurokamp (and an island kingdom in name only) was a roughly triangular-shaped projection of land (pointing south-southwest) off southwest Essperya (ess-PAIR-ee-uh; Iberia), with its longest side contiguous to what is now the Iberian shore from the Straits of Gibraltar to the tip of southwest Portugal. The climate featured cool rainy winters as well as semi-tropical summers.

The so-called river—actually an interconnected system of lakes, streams, marshes, and canals—the Esquillantrion (ESS-kwih-LAN-tree-un) separated Gades from Essperya, and ran in a roughly northward-projecting arc beginning north of the northern side of the Gates of Gades and flowing out into the Ocean Sea just below the southwest "chin" of Iberia.

Beyond the Esquillantrion, to the east and to the north, there lay the Essperyan Marches, a semi-desolate tract of land, featuring on the Gadean side a great system of castellated forts which protected this kingdom from invasion by outlanders.

The great bay called the Horn of Plenty (and shaped roughly like one) separated Gades from Iffrikonn, and provided along the first 30 miles of its northern shore a magnificent natural harbor for Tartessoös. This second greatest port in the Empire handled the bulk of the commerce coming from the Seas Within the Gates of Gades (the twin basins of the Mediterranean), and possessed some thirty miles of colonnaded docks, behind which lay the city, a thin ribbon of settlement extending along the same roughly southwest-northeast axis as the harbor. Immediately above the city there uprose those lofty palisades upon which stood the immensely elongated royal palace or system of palaces.

Two archipelagoes lay stretched between Gades and the eastern shores of the Astazhan, the southeast prong of the Archkingdom. Iöcia (ee-O-sha; now Joséphine Seamount) dominated the northern island-chain, the Iöphemnonian (EE-o-fem-NO-nee-un) Isles, and Amphrysthion (am-FRISS-thee-onn; now Ampere Seamount) dominated the southern island-chain, the Yphisthirides (IFF-iss-THEER-ih-deez). Over both of these archipelagoes Gades ruled as the suzerain, as did she over the Gates of Gades unto their eastern marge upon the western basin of the present Mediterranean.

Apart from the Gates of Gades and a few odds and ends of land that were once parcel of the Essperyan Marches, nothing survives of this kingdom that was once "the royal twin" of Atlantis.

Sonnet IV. Atlantigades.

Capital and principal port: Ymstryllys (IM-stril-iss).

Principal heraldic figure: the sea-satyr (wreathed and crowned with grapes and grape-leaves, and holding a great goblet against his chest and stomach, with both hands around the stem, the left hand above the right).

Shaped like a cluster of three large pointed oval grapes, or prongs (west, east, and south), grouped with their stem-ends together; the third of the ten island kingdoms, and the first of the second pair of the same, possessed a lush spring-like climate almost all year long apart from the cool winter rains and fogs. Almost completely covered by the great vineyard-orchard-forest of so-called grape-trees, this kingdom of the wine grape produced not only all manner of both wine grapes and eating grapes but also, and particularly, all manner of grape wines, which Atlantigades exported throughout the Empire. The cuttings for the wine grapes had originally come from Yndessys (in-DESS-iss; India).

Each of the island's three prongs had a high mountain range running lengthwise. Ymstryllys lay at the head of the bay bound by the western and southern prongs. Behind Ymstryllys, between the western and southern mountain ranges, in their foothills in fact, there stood the first palace of the kings of Atlantigades, the so-called Palace in the Vale. Where the mountain ranges of the island's three prongs almost met, their height dropped off and leveled into a weald which the kings of Atlantigades had caused to be terraced and gardened; upon this vast parterre stood the second palace of the kings, the so-called Palace in the Mountains.

Atlantigades was the suzerain over the pastoral island and princedom of Lesser Atlantigades that lay north-northeast of the eastern prong that pointed in the same direction. The island's highest mountaintops have survived as the Madeira Islands, and were, together with those of Iffrikonn-Yssthia, the third highest in the Empire.

Sonnet V. Atkantharia.

Capital and principal port: Phaär (fay-ARR).

Principal heraldic beast: the giant sea-scorpion (the bottom half like that of the mythical sea-horse, the upper half—thus emerging from the lower part of the sea-horse's neck—a giant scorpion with his body curving upward and outward frontally, and with all his legs outspread).

Note: The pronunciation of the word "pomegranate" used in this poem (as in the earlier piece of hexameter blank verse *Your Mouth of Pomegranate*) is "POMM-uh-GRANN-it."

Shaped like a large and bumpy crescent with one end pointing north and with the other end pointing west, and with the crescent's concavity thus facing largely northwest; the fourth of the ten island kingdoms, and the second of the second pair of the same, lay (with but a narrow channel between) just west of that part of Iffrikonn south of the Atlas Mountains, or the Mountains of the Moraänon (mor-RAY-un-NONN), where they abut on the north-northwestern coast. Between the two ends of the island's crescent, north of the outer Bay of Atkantharia, lay the desert isle of Lesser Zaäzran.

A very mountainous kingdom with both interior and coastal ranges, Atkantharia possessed not only an extremely rocky coast (with fantastic spires, bays, coves, arches, and islets) but also the second highest mountains in the Empire (together with the mountains running along and inland of the Archkingdom's western coast)—the highest being, of course, the Eiphlox Mountains in the Archkingdom's mountain-heartland Poseidonis.

Dry and hot apart from the rains and only moderate warmth of the brief winter, the desert kingdom (so called on occasion) endured her hottest weather when the scorching desert winds, or siroccos, would blow west off the Zaäran (ZAH-uh-RRAHN), that greatest of deserts we now call the Sahara.

At one time the only naturally fertile country, the northernmost fourth of the island—with lush pastorage and with the original pomegranate-forests growing there wild—gradually changed into a desolation, almost lunar in its austerity, the Atkaharan (AT-kuh-huh-RRAHN), due to the sudden shifting of the winds that supplied the rains to this part of the kingdom. The original capital Alpaär (AL-pay-ARR) was located here inland but with the shifting of the rain-winds the capital was relocated onto a small bay opening out of the northern shore of the western part of the island's crescent.

As Atlantigades was almost completely covered with "Her lush-green vineyard-forest without end," so was Atkantharia—or kingdom of the Atlantean pomegranate, or *atkanthar* (AT-kan-THARR)—almost completely covered with her cultivated and largely irrigated pomegranate-forests, located for the most part on the coast, in the valleys, and on the lower slopes of the mountains. The orchards were watered either directly by the winter rains or through the elaborate irrigation-system whose waters were supplied from the winter snows melting down from the high peaks.

Far-famed for her endless pomegranate-forests but most of all for her ineffable pomegranate-wines of all varieties, the desert kingdom exported both her pomegranates and her pomegranate-wines throughout the Empire, out through some ten major ports, of which the capital Phaär was the principal. She also exported certain highly desired inks, dyes, and cosmetics—of all shades of red—which she produced from the pomegranate-rinds left over after the crushing of the pomegranates for wine.

The Atlantean pomegranate, or *atkanthar*, it must be noted, was much larger than its modern counterpart, indeed being as large as a large man's head, with the seed-pulps as large as cherries. The bright-red waxy flower-stars were also much larger than the modern blooms, although like the latter they possessed no perfume.

This island kingdom's loftiest peaks have survived as the Canary Islands.

Sonnet VI. Iffrikonn-Yssthia.

Capital and principal port: Yssthia (ISS-thee-uh) .

Principal heraldic beast: the leokamp, or leokampos (the bottom half like that of the heraldic sea-horse, the upper half the same as the head, neck; mane, and upper torso, but sans the legs, of the male lion).

Shaped like a pair of lion's jaws opening out onto the west—popularly called the Jaws of Iffrikonn—the fifth of the ten island kingdoms, and the first of the third pair of the same, was almost completely covered with lush tropical vegetation—apart from certain rocky portions of the coast, and apart from the higher slopes and the snow-topped peaks of the highest mountains. The jungle kingdom possessed a typical rain-forest climate, very hot and very humid. It rained all year round but the heaviest rains fell during the rainy season.

The island kingdom of the leokamp was almost as mountainous as Atkantharia: one long range stood in the upper jaw, two ranges in the lower jaw (these three ranges all on a basic east-west axis), and one range between (on a north-south axis), which formed the eastern part of the kingdom, and which connected to the upper jaw by a low, marshy isthmus. Most of the island's population centered in the capital—the fifth greatest port in the Empire—and received about half its basic diet from small farms and fruit-orchards located in the jungle; the other half of its food Iffrikonn-Yssthia imported from Iffrikonn and from the rest of the Empire.

Almost completely filling the Vale of Yssthiomm (ISS-thee-omm)— which was located between the lower jaw's two mountain ranges, and which thus opened out onto the northern shore of the lower jaw—Yssthia handled virtually all of the trade and commerce coming from all along the entire western coast of Iffrikonn, as well as from the subcontinent of Yndessys; indeed, the name "Iffrikonn-Yssthia" means "port, or harbor, for Iffrikonn." The remaining few ports on the island were hardly more than fishing villages. The Vale of Yssthiomm sloped gradually upwards to the break between the two mountain ranges of the lower jaw, and thus opened out onto the southern coast of the same. Displayed upon the bottom of the break between the two mountain ranges, the palace of the kings of Iffrikonn-Yssthia—surrounded by elaborate gardens—dominated the upper or southern end of the valley, and thus looked south out over the Ocean Sea, as well as looked north out over the city, the harbor, and the Bay of Iffrikonnis (IFF-rih-kuh-NISS), which lay thus between the Jaws of Iffrikonn.

In addition to receiving all manner of precious and exotic materials—ivory, furs, pelts, etc.—coming from Iffrikonn, the jungle kingdom was famous for her own mines of precious and semi-precious metals and stones. The Atlanteans also maintained a few mining communities deep in the interior of Iffrikonn, such as the famous city of Opar. Thanks to the considerable intermarrying that had been going on for about 3,000 years between the Atlanteans and the Iffrikonnian (IFF-rih-kuh-NEE-un) peoples, most of the island's inhabitants possessed a dark gold complexion, although typically Atlantean in structure. During the local annual Council of the King, leading Iffrikonnian chieftains, brought over from the continent by Atlantean ships, would gather into Yssthia, to exchange gifts and to feast with their Atlantean brothers.

The kings of Iffrikonn-Yssthia kept their jungle kingdom well stocked with elephants and other typical wild animals imported from both Iffrikonn and Yndessys (in addition to the fauna native to the island).

This kingdom's highest mountaintops have survived as the Cape Verde Islands, and were, together with those of Atlantigades, the third highest in the Empire.

Sonnet VII. *Atalantessys.*

Capital: the entire island of Atalantessys.
Principal port: the entire island of Xalporal.
Principal heraldic device: anyone of several, characteristically gigantic flowers grown uniquely on Atalantessys (gigantic poppies, orchids, roses, mandragoras, nenuphars, etc.—all truly of monstrous dimensions—usually grouped in threes, with the central bloom higher than the two attendant ones).

The sixth of the ten island kingdoms, and the second of the third pair of the same, was different from the rest of the Empire in a number of unique ways. The chief island Atalantessys, just north of the equator, survives (in reduced form) as the St. Peter and St. Paul Rocks; about 400 miles to the southwest lay the two lesser islands Manthos (MAN-thoss) and Xalporal (zal-PORR-'l), which have survived (similarly in reduced form) as Rocas and as Fernando de Noronha Island, respectively. Manthos, which produced most of this realm's basic diet, lay about 200 miles northeast of the present-day Cabo de São Roque (that northeastern corner of the "nipple" on the great eastern-projecting "breast" formed by the subcontinent of Brazil); about 100 miles to the east (of Manthos) there lay Xalporal—the sixth greatest port in the Empire—whose entire coast, with multiple harbors large and small, served as the port of Atalantessys, and handled virtually all the trade and commerce coming from all along the entire eastern coast of what is today South America, from southernmost Lesser Antillia to the southernmost tip of the continent. Today the St. Peter and St. Paul Rocks, Fernando de Noronha, and Rocas are all Brazilian possessions.

About as large as Manthos and Xalporal combined, Atalantessys—an oval island wider east and west than north and south—served as the administrative and esthetic center of the realm. The entire island, with her gently rolling terrain (low hills near the coast, and slightly higher hills toward the center), and with her eternal warm summer, resembled a great lush-green garden-park studded everywhere with palaces great and small. The principal residences of the kings of Atalantessys were two: the half-ruined Old Palace that spread all along the northern coast; and just inland of it, to the south, the New Palace, environed with elaborate formal gardens.

Although typically Manthos and Xalporal were tropically hot and wet, Atalantessys had an unexpectedly cooler climate than the jungle kingdom (that lay north-northeast of this southernmost realm of the Empire), due principally to the cold currents that came flowing out of the great southern ocean, bypassing Manthos and Xalporal to the west, and washing around this northernmost part of the equator kingdom, or the garden kingdom (as it was also called on occasion). Accordingly the island lay at the center of a vast and near-eternal cloud of fog or mist that dissipated only on a few rare days during the entire year; at such times the heat and the light would prove almost unbearable; much of the vegetation that flourished in the cooler climate would wilt, some of it would die, and almost the entire population, human and otherwise, would seek the cooling waters along the coast or in the island's innumerable pools, lakes, and streams. It rained on Atalantessys virtually every day, once in the morning, once in the afternoon, and sometimes during the night; the rain fell heavier of course during the rainy season per se.

Due to the peculiar climate possessed by the chief island of the realm and certain recondite features of the soil, the Atlanteans cultivated uniquely on Atalantessys divers gigantic flowers (many of them hybrids), much desired throughout the Empire, and exported everywhere as potted plants. These floral prodigies, although most of them could not reproduce, enjoyed nonetheless a long life.

Carried on the cold currents coming ultimately from the great frozen continent that lay far to the south, great icebergs, in the ultimate season of their dissolution, would sail up offshore from out of the southern ocean. The inhabitants of Atalantessys would approach these ice-islands in their unireme barges, and then land thereupon, to picnic or to explore the fantastic grottoes and other extraordinary features of the icebergs' mutable architecture. Few or none were those who mourned the passing or melting of these icebergs as they constituted an eternal menace to the shipping both of the equator kingdom and of the Empire.

Atalantessys was about the same size as Avalonessys—both were among the smallest royal islands in the Empire—and with his characteristic irony Poseidon III endowed this isle with the name "Atalantessys" or "island kingdom of great Atlantis" when he subsumed the realm into the Empire.

Sonnet VIII. Atlantillia.

Capital and principal port: Atzatlan (AT-zuh-TLAHN).
Principal heraldic beast: the jaguär.
The so-called Pearl of the Antillias, the rounded isle of Atlantillia lay between Greater Antillia and Lesser Antillia. But the island herself constituted only a fraction of the total Atlantean holdings in the twin Antillias; the seventh of the ten island kingdoms, and the first of the fourth pair of the same, included the actual isle of Atlantillia herself, the easternmost end of Greater Antillia, and the northernmost end of Lesser Antillia.

The landmass of Greater Antillia (on an axis running east and west, or east and west-northwest) included the present-day Cuba, Hispaniola, Jamaica, Puerto Rico, and the Virgin Islands; the eastern end of this near-continent would be marked today at the southeast corner by St. Croix and at the northeast corner by Anegada (more or less due north of St. Croix). Lesser Antillia (on a largely north-south axis) included both the present-day Leeward Islands and the Windward Islands; the northern or northwestern end of this landmass would be marked today at the southwest corner by Saba and at the northwest corner by Anguilla (more or less due north of Saba). Between what is now St. Croix and Saba there stretched a low, narrow isthmus—the Isthmus of Atzatlan or Quoätzl (kwo-AT-z'I)—through which the Atlanteans had excavated nine canals (which thus ran north and south).

The last 100 miles or so of the eastern end of Greater Antillia constituted Outer Atlantillia West, known as the Itzl (IT-z'l), and the last 100 miles or so of the northern or northwestern end of Lesser Antillia constituted Outer Atlantillia East, known as the Oöxochl (O-okk-ZO-k'l). Greater Antillia and Lesser Antillia, centuries before the arrival of the Atlanteans, had formed a great unified empire, both politically and economically; the Antillian suzerain maintained his imperial seat in Quoätzl, a great city that once covered almost all of the island later named Atlantillia. When the Atlanteans settled here during the reign of Poseidon III, the great Antillian empire had long since disintegrated into divers rival territories, the island abounded with jaguärs, and the semi-tropical jungle had grown up over the ruins of the old abandoned Antillian capital Quoätzl.

The Atlanteans decided to maintain the island's plateau for the most part as a wild area, as a natural garden-park, and to build their city Atzatlan along the western, southern, and eastern shores of the island (this constituted Inner Atzatlan), as well as (just across the channel of Atzatlan Harbor) on the Isthmus of Quoätzl, along the easternmost shore of Greater Antillia, and along the northwesternmost shore of Lesser Antillia (all of these last three areas constituted Outer Atzatlan). Great gardened bridges joined the inner city to the outer. The Atlantillian kings built their palace in the northern part of the island's plateau and thus facing north out over the ocean.

Most of Atlantillia proper was covered by a plateau of moderate height with gently rolling terrain, but the entire realm enjoyed a semi-tropical climate, and thus was neither as hot nor as wet as the jungle kingdom. The island kingdom of the jaguär was famous for extensive citrus forests (producing fruits which were similar to the present-day citron, lemon, orange, lime, grapefruit, etc.) located for the most part on the Itzl and the Oöxochl. The Atlanteans also cultivated in these areas one of the sacred fruits from the ancient continent of Mu, a fruit much like the present-day pineapple. Although she exported most of her fruit, Atlantillia imported most of her own food from the twin Antillias.

Atzatlan, the third greatest port in the Empire, handled most of the trade and commerce coming from Greater Antillia, Lesser Antillia, and the lands of Oöxathan (O-okk-zuh-THAHN; Central America), and all the other lands bordering on the Seas of Antillia (the western sea is the present-day Gulf of Mexico, the eastern sea is the present-day Caribbean).

North of the palace of the Atlantillian kings and upon a great bluff that looked out over the sea, there stood a curious outdoor thronehall yclept the Great Jaguär Throne, which faced east-northeast toward Atlantis the City.

Here the Atlantillian king held regular audience unless wind or rain or both together prevented such.

The mere presence of the Atlanteans for some 3,000 years had created a comparative peace and sense of order (or harmony) amongst the warring Antillian chieftains and petty kings. Out of gratitude and courtesy the native Antillian peoples acknowledged the Atlantillian king as their nominal suzerain. Thus Atzatlan served as a focus for the political, economic, and esthetic life of the twin Antillias.

Line 9: "that further strand" or shore, in this case, could be either Outer Atlantillia West (that is, the Itzl) or the entire landmass of Greater Antillia.

What was once the island proper of Atlantillia now lies at the bottom of Anegada Passage, the channel which separates the Virgin Islands from the Leeward Islands.

Sonnet IX. Atatemthessys.

Capital and principal port: Meirion (MEER-ee-un).
Principal heraldic beast: the giant squid.

A large rounded island, the eighth of the ten island kingdoms, and the second of the fourth pair of the same, lay about 1,000 miles almost directly north (just a little to the west) of Atlantillia proper. Atatemthessys was originally, sometime during the dim geological past, an active volcano surrounded by a circle of other active volcanoes. The central volcano became extinct but the "wide round [about 300 miles across] of volcanoes submarine" remained. Within this orbit of volcanic activity and consequently warmer waters there lived not only the giant squid, the *Architeuthis princeps*, but many species of sea-life, reportedly including a species of the archaic armored squid, that were extinct anywhere else in the oceans of the Pre-Cataclysmic world.

The Issvess Mountains dominated the interior of the island; this was a low, verdure-clad range, shaped like a great fish-hook, on an axis running northeast to southwest, with the "hook" at the southwestern end curling northward. The island was famous for her forests of fruit-trees, the principal ones under cultivation being similar to the modern peach, plum, cherry, apricot, etc. The peaches and apricots were about as large as modern grapefruits; the plums and cherries were about as large as apples. From these the Atlanteans made preserves, glacéd fruits, wines, liqueurs, etc. The island was also famous for her honey and honey-bees, which she exported together with her fruits and fruit-products. Atatemthessys produced most of her own food.

Apart from a comparatively brief winter (rainy, windy, cool at night but warm during the day), the island kingdom of the giant squid enjoyed an exquisite spring climate the rest of the year, with a consequently lush semi-tropical vegetation.

The capital and principal port, to wit, Meirion, spread along the middle southern coast, facing south toward the southern and principal break in the wide round of undersea volcanoes, the Gates of Atatemthessys (marked by a pair of colossal pharoses carved from towering chaotic masses of rose-flushed lava-stone tapering upwards).

The state palace of the kings of Atatemthessys rose up at the center of Meirion but the ordinary residential palace, the Temthorial (tem-THORR-ee-ul) with its incredibly elaborate roof, stood in the middle of a vast garden-park located between the eastern shore of the island and the eastern end of the Issvess Mountains. The Temthorial and its principal throne-hall alike faced east toward Atlantis the City.

Atatemthessys—or island kingdom of the giant squid, or *atatemth* (the common Atlantean word for squid *is* "temth")—also exported jet-black inks, dyes, and cosmetics produced from the black "ink" of squids. The Atlanteans regarded cephalopods, especially giant squids, as essences or symbols of omnipotence, omniscience, and good fortune.

Line 9: "the flood and ebb of semitropic seas" does not refer to the *lunar* tides but to the comparatively low swell of the *solar* tides. The moon during Atlantean times was a small planet called Sfamoön (sfah-MO-on), with a weak orbit of its own, vacillating between the greater gravitational pull of Earth and Mars; it approached the Earth every five and six years in regular alternance; until finally, yielding to the greater gravity of Earth (at a time when Mars was at its farthest point away from both Earth and Sfamoön, and when the small planet itself was at its closest point to our own world), it was "captured"—thereby triggering the Great Cataclysm that spelt the end not only of the Atlantean Empire but, in addition, of virtually the entire Atlantean world as well.

As a result of the Great Cataclysm the "wide round of volcanoes submarine" became dormant and lapsed back into the ocean floor, thus more or less completely disappearing. The Issvess Mountains of Atatemthessys have survived as the Bermuda Islands.

Sonnet X. At-Thulonn

Capital and principal port: Ymnoth (IM-noth).
Principal heraldic beast: the unicorned sea-horse, usually ermine-white, and usually with a coronet around his neck.
Shaped roughly like a large diamond whose two lower sides are longer

than the two upper sides; this ninth of the ten island kingdoms, and the first of the fifth and last pair of the same, lay (somewhat south of the present Cape Farewell) just off southeastern Greenland, the ancient Mhu Thulan (MOO, thoo-LAN), then as now covered with an ever-enduring mass of ice, and fabled to have formed the ultimate peninsula of the legendary continent called Hyperborea. Heavily forested with evergreens and with such deciduous trees as were sturdy enough to flourish in this far northern latitude, the winter kingdom possessed a rolling terrain with low hills, very rocky in places, especially along the island's coast.

A great bridge (protected at either end with great castellated fortresses) of stone and crystal of divers textures and colors (fitted cunningly together without cement, and allowing for the contraction and expansion caused by the extreme changes in temperature from summer to winter) connected the island's northern point to the forested southern marge of Mhu Thulan which stretched from somewhere east of Cape Farewell to somewhere west of the present-day seaport Julianehaab.

This southern margin, called the Lonnthulan (LON-thu-LAN), and protected at her northern boundaries from the worst of the winter weather by great natural barriers of stone (which now form part of the high cliffs of Cape Farewell presently fronting the ocean at this southeastern tip of Greenland), served as a buffer for At-Thulonn against the terrible hyperboreal cold breathing off the great sheet of ice during the winter.

The winters here were very long; those in the kingdom of the unicorned sea-horse were not as long or severe as those in Mhu Thulan, due to the warm currents (coming ultimately from tropical and semi-tropical seas) washing around the island. With but a brief spring, summer, and autumn, the winter kingdom was usually self-sufficient in producing her own food during the warm weather (there were many small farms located all over the island) but she had to import most of her food for the long hyperboreal winter.

Located just south of the island's eastern point and with a magnificent harbor (but completely ice-free only during the warm weather which lasted some 90 days), the capital Ymnoth was the fourth greatest port in the Empire, and handled virtually all the trade and commerce coming from the eastern Seas of Naörth (NAY-ORTH; these stretched between Greenland and Norway, and included all the islands located within those waters as well as in the waters north of that stretch of ocean, as well as all the lands contiguous thereunto). To Ymnoth the Northkings would bring within their vessels—their dragon-headed uniremes—all manner of merchandise (smoked meats, smoked fish, lumber from northern trees, pelts and furs, etc.) in exchange for Atlantean products.

The state palace of the kings of At-Thulonn was located in the capital but the ordinary residential palace stood in the midst of the great royal estate that completely filled the island's southern point.

The northern lights actually unfurled their multi-colored veils all year round but the most spectacular displays occurred in autumn and in spring.

The unicorn that lived in the forests of southern and western Mhu Thulan, was ermine-white in winter and a delicate shade of light gray during the warmer weather (as contrasted to the perennially fawn-colored unicorn that lived in parts of Scotland, England, Ireland, and Wales). The female unicorn looked rather like a doe but with a long, pointed, convoluting horn issuing from her forehead. The male unicorn looked identical, but with that additional and nether horn unique to the male (this nether horn was *just* half as long but thrice as thick).

Super-gentle and super-timid animals, the unicorns were protected by royal and archroyal law—it was forbidden to kill them—and were therefore rarely hunted by most of the adventurous young people. The unicorn could be captured only through blandishments, through overt demonstrations of affection, in short, through love and kindness; but then the youth and the maiden capturing it had to let it go; however, only after they had convinced the male or female unicorn of their enduring love for it.

Both the upper and lower classes hunted both on the ice-cap and in the Lonnthulan, as well as on the western coast of Greenland, from somewhere south of present-day Godthaab to somewhere north of present-day Godhavn on Disko Island. A variety of animals were hunted—deer, bear, fox, etc.—but in his sonnet on this island kingdom Athallarion has naturally selected for mention a more typically exotic assemblage such as the seal, the musk ox, and the caribou.

Nothing survives of this island kingdom save for a few rock formations projecting up out of the sea south of Cape Farewell but once contiguous to the northern end of the great bridge of stone and crystal that connected At-Thulonn to Mhu Thulan.

Sonnet XI. *Avalonessys*.

Capital and principal port: Ysstralot (ISS-truh-lot).
Principal heraldic bird: the swan.
The tenth and last of the ten island kingdoms, and the second of the fifth and last pair of the same, lay more or less in the middle of the Shoaling Sea West (Irish Sea), almost equally distant from the middle southern shore of Ivvrinaä (IVV-rih-NAY-uh; Ireland), and from the westernmost points of Valoth (vuh-LOTH; Wales) and Karanak (KAR-ruh-nahk; Cornwall). Iv-

vrinaä connected at the northeast with Ultimate Allbeyonn (Scotland), and Allbeyonn (ALL-be-yonn; England) connected at the southeast with Nys (NISS; Europe) by the land-bridge Ym-Rith (IM-RITH), which sealed off at her eastern end the Shoaling Sea East (English Channel). Avalonessys herself, with rolling hills and with apple-orchards of great extent, enjoyed a near semi-tropical climate like that of the Scilly Isles, with such mild winters that apple-blossoms bloomed, and crops of apples ripened, all year round.

Celebrated for her forests of apple trees and of rose-trees, this kingdom of the swan, the rose, and the apple, exported apples, all manner of apple wines and apple-cordials, preserved apples, etc., as well as all manner of rose-clippings and roses, which the Atlanteans particularly cultivated on this island. What with the perennially light-green leaves of the apple-forests, this almost perfectly round island was about the same size as Atalantessys, and verily did resemble "A sea-green pearl in a shoaling sea" (in the traditional phrase)—the shoaling sea in question being the Shoaling Sea West.

The capital Ysstralot was displayed, together with her palatial suburbs, along the southern shore of the island, southwest to east-southeast. The state palace of the kings of Avalonessys rose up at the center of the capital but, as in other island kingdoms, the regular residence was located outside the principal port and capital; in this case, on a low but vast and multi-terraced hill north of a large lake north of Ysstralot, all in the midst of great formal gardens.

We must make mention here of the extraordinary color, together with certain other peculiar and striking characteristics, of the two Shoaling Seas, the surface of which was rarely ruffled by other than the most moderate of storms, usually during the wintry season. As their name implies, these were comparatively shallow bodies of water with numerous bars of sand, and with a consequent color and over-all appearance rather like those of the seas around the Bahamas. The principal colors were yellow-green, green, dark-green, and aquamarine. Since much of the ocean floor around Avalonessys was largely composed of a white sand comparatively free of marine growths, the over-all effect was, to say the least, unusual. When Athallarion descants of ". . . The Shoaling Seas' green crystalline flow—" (line 5), he is not indulging in any poetic exaggeration.

The name of Avalonessys, possessing as it does a double suffix, means "the island kingdom, or royal isle, or island realm, of apples." The single for "apple" is "aval" (uh-VAHL); the plural *is* "avalon" (av-uh-LONN). ("Avalonessys" was pronounced either "av-uh-law-NESS-iss" or, more rarely, "av-uh-LONN-ess-iss,") The "ys" or "is" designates of course "island," and the "ess" preceding it designates "kingdom" or "royal," "Nys"—the name for Europe—is a contraction for "nay is," which simply means "no island" or a continent.

There was a great cult in Avalonessys centering on the swan. The many lakes, ponds, and streams within the island served as resting places for all manner of migrant birds, but especially for the swans. The more extravagant of their admirers would cast small necklaces of Yndessessian pearls around the necks of the swans as they would float hither and thither and yon upon the surface of the island's "water-troves."

The only other places in the world at that time besides Mhu Thulan where the unicorn lived (to the best of the information available to the present annotator for the nonce), were parts of Ultimate Allbeyonn, Allbeyonn, Valoth, and Ivvrinaä. This unicorn (as contrasted to the ermine-white or pearl-gray unicorn that inhabited the southern and western coasts of Mhu Thulan) was a rich golden-fawn in color, but was as timid and gentle a beast as his brother species living north of At-Thulonn.

Many of the Atlantean forts and watchtowers in Ivvrinaä, Valoth, and Karanak have survived in varying ruinous conditions. However, nothing survives from the isle of Avalonessys herself save the memory and the name.

Sonnet XII. *Poseidonis.*

Capital and principal inland port: Xonorr (k'zo-NORR).

Principal heraldic beast: the giant sea-ram (the bottom half like that of the heraldic sea-horse, the top half the same as the head, horns, neck, and upper torso, but sans the legs, of the giant wild mountain ram).

See both the prose-poem "The River Called Amphus" and the note thereto.

An elongated oval running west-northwest and east-southeast, Poseidonis the Archprincedom possessed the highest mountains in the Archkingdom and hence in the Empire: three tremendous ranges, western, central, and eastern, called the Eiphlox Mountains. Their topmost peaks now survive, respectively, as the three main groups of the Azores. Leading Atlantologists, including the author of these notes, estimate that they rose at least as high as the Himalayas. There were two principal valleys in Poseidonis: the Great Vale to-West and the Great Vale to-East; although comparatively narrow east and west, they were as extensive north and south as the Great Vale of Atlantis.

Line 5: The Atlantean phoenix, or iffinnix, a semi-mythical bird reputed to live high in the central Eiphlox Mountains. Hence, any eminence ascending "Beyond the heights whereto the phoenix flies," is indeed of an extraordinary height.

At the northern end of the Great Vale of Atlantis, where the western and the eastern branches of the Poämphus met in the great lake yclept the Gates of Day (wherefrom flowed the eastern branch of the Amphus River); and on the verge of the plateau lying thus at the southern base of the central Eiphlox Mountains; there stretched the Outhanox, the Great Citadel of Poseidonis, along an east-west axis. The Citadel served as a fortress to the city just north of it, to wit, Xonorr (this metropolis was one of "the Seven Cities" figuring in one of the Archking's official titles, to wit, "King of the Seven Cities"). Lying thus long and low (there was only one principal storey but arranged on two or three main levels), the Outhanox possessed a great battlemented southern terrace which ran along the southern verge of the plateau, crowning thus a series of great stone palisades, and looking out into the upper or northern reaches of the Great Vale of Atlantis, or "The Sea of Verdure" as it was called.

To the Outhanox there were brought, from all the ten kingdoms, the dead kings and queens who, after suitable mummification and enrobement, sat enthroned along both walls of the seemingly endless halls and corridors. At the time of the Great Cataclysm, the Outhanox ensepulchred more than 150 generations of kings and queens from all over the Empire; thus, there were over 3,000 crowned heads.

When after the fall of Atlantis the City to the Northkings the child-king Poseidon II (PO-see-DONN), called the Son, fled north with his court and with such of the Atlanteans as had not been enslaved by the Northking invaders; it was here in Poseidonis that they set up their temporary government in exile as it were, a kingdom that was to endure through the three hundred years of the great feudal age that preceded the Empire of Atlantis. After winning back the Atlanteans' first realms in the south of Atlantis, after conquering the entire island, and then after establishing the Empire on an official basis; Poseidon III, called the Earth-Shaker, the Empire-Builder, the First Lord of Sea and Land, etc., made Atlantis the City—now recovered from the Northkings—the capital of his empery. But the old city in the north, the old Citadel, and the entire upland country, remained the spiritual home of the Atlanteans. They thus always cherished an especial affection for Poseidonis, a cradle-realm of empire and of mighty kings, and a place of refuge when the Atlanteans' very life and culture were threatened with extinction.

Officially the Archprincedom was virtually the equivalent of one of the ten island kingdoms. The Heir Apparent, usually the Archking's eldest son, the Archprince, maintained his court in the old Citadel. In his governing of the Archprincedom he would pass his apprentice-kingship. Thus, when upon the incapacity or retirement or death of the old Archking, the Archprince came to the supreme throne of the Empire, he had usually proven himself a thoroughly experienced ruler.

One of the five principal divisions of the Archkingdom, Poseidonis grew a variety of crops in abundant harvest, and together with the Vale of Mythnom, as well as the island kingdom of At-Thulonn—and together with the great northern prong of Atlantis, as well as all the high mountain-lands of the Archkingdom—the Archprincedom enjoyed a true cycle of the four seasons. The name of the Archprincedom, styled thus after Poseidon II (as well as in memory of Poseidon I, called the Father), simply means "island of Poseidon" the island in question referring to the great "island of mountains" that was Poseidonis rising up from within the midst of the Archkingdom.

Sonnet XIII. *The Merchant-Princes.*

Line 14: "the arch Acropolis" (as in line 2 of "The Crown and Trident"): that is, the leading acropolis in all the Empire of Atlantis.

Once every ninety days the Archking would summon all the great merchants and merchant-princes resident in and around Atlantis the City, to meet him at dawn within the Place (or Plaza) Acropolitan, just outside the Great Gate Acropolitan which afforded unique access to the Acropolis from the Plaza and from the City. But, although he would summon them to meet him there at dawn, the Archking would sometimes make them wait upon his late arrival, and sometimes he would not appear at all; however, only after making them wait upon him a due period of time, thus merely to show them that there was indeed some power or authority higher than their own merchantry.

Sonnet XIV. *An Argosy of Trade.*

A word of explanation is needed here to detail certain distinct peculiarities about not only the Atlantean trireme but also about the Atlantean galleys in general: unireme, bireme, quinquireme, etc. Unlike the galleys used in the Middle Ages or in classical antiquity—which were large, low, usually one-decked, usually flat-bottomed, and propelled by both sails and oars—the Atlantean oar-banked vessels were ocean-going ships which—while certainly large, and propelled by both sails and oars—sat high in the water, were usually multi-decked (rather like a galleon, all proportions guarded), and always equipped with a deep, large, and permanent keel designed not only as part of the over-all engineering of a given vessel but principally for sailing over the deep waters of the Ocean Sea.

Sonnet XV. *Memories of the Astazhan.*

Created by Aänsess (AY-ahn-sess) in Valoth (vuh-LOTH) but a year or so before the Great Cataclysm, and in memory of his birthplace, the Astazhan (AH-stuh-ZHAHN).

The great prong of southeastern Atlantis, and one of the five principal divisions of the Archkingdom, the Astazhan occupied a vast pastoral plateau surrounded by low coastal mountains on the west, south, east, and northeast, and by inland mountains of a largely medium height on the north and northwest (these last were the southernmost ranges of the eastern Eiphlox Mountains). This area enjoyed outstanding fame not only for its dairy products, especially for magnificent and variegated cheeses, but also for dairy cattle, which the local dairy merchants exported throughout the Empire, out through Atlantis the City and her merchant fleets, of course.

Many distinguished persons had been born in the Astazhan, including the last Queen Consort Archroyal, to wit, Atlaïs Quolaïtho (AT-lie-EESS KWO-lie-EE-tho). A woman of great beauty, charm, distinction, and intelligence, as well as a poetess of considerable originality and accomplishment, Quolaitho bore Atlas CLIII, called Sfamoönophamos (SFAH-mo-on-NOF-uh-moss), seven daughters and nine sons. The last-born son was the youngest child of the Archking, to wit, the famous poet Prince Atlantarion whose marriage to the Princess Aïs of Ylliphya became one of the marvels of late Atlantean and Post-Cataclysmic poetry and romance.

Aänsess was one of the last great masters of the song archroyal.

Sonnet XVI. A Letter from Valoth.

Created by Aänsess at Apenderragon (AH-pen-DARE-uh-gonn) the Great Watchtower in southern Valoth during the first three days following the Great Cataclysm, and dictated by him to his scribe on the third day.

In a single day and night, as veraciously described by Plato himself (in his principal accounts of the Atlantis Mythos, to wit, the dialogues *Timaeus* and *Critias*), the Great Cataclysm—preceded and accompanied by a succession of terrific earthquakes and tsunamis had lowered extensive areas of the ocean floor, and had caused the submergence of virtually all the Empire of Atlantis: all of the nine lesser island kingdoms, and between one-third and one-half of the Archkingdom. Of the nine lesser island kingdoms, nothing survived above the waves but a comparatively few mountain peaks. Of the Archkingdom herself, there survived only the great mountain ranges, including the central mountain-heartland Poseidonis. The great prong of southeastern Atlantis, the Astazhan, also survived.

Only the fact that they were visiting Poseidonis on official business just prior to the Great Cataclysm, and prior to their scheduled return to the capital of Atlantis, preserved the King Atlantarion and his own immediate family from the general destruction. They had gone to Xonorr, the capital of Poseidonis, in order to ensepulchre within the Outhanox the Pan-Atlantean royalty, most of whom had perished in the catastrophic Battle Before Athens but a short period of time before.

In his accompanying commentary in prose, Aänsess informs Atlantarion that the highest tsunamis had washed the foot of the huge battlemented walls environing the Great Watchtower. Apenderragon, it must be noted, crowned an only slightly lower spur of one of the highest mountains in southern Wales, or Valoth, and commanded from this eminence a sweeping panoramic view of the Shoaling Sea West and of Avalonessys herself lying in the midst thereof.

The waves caused by the submergence of Avalonessys, and by the lowering of the ocean floor of the Shoaling Seas both East and West—terrible as these waves may have proven—were nothing compared to those caused by the accompanying submergence of one-third or one-half of the Archkingdom. These last waves came rolling out of the west, the southwest, and the south, only a little later than the waves created by the sinking of Avalonessys.

While the geological causes and forces that created the Great Cataclysm had been building up for an extremely long time, it has now been established beyond any doubt that it was the "capture"—by and into Earth's orbit—of our later moon, the small planet Sfamoön (sfah-MO-on), which triggered the grand catastrophe—with its attendant outrageous earthquakes and tsunamis—which not only submerged most of the Empire of Atlantis but swept away most of the Atlantean world as well.

Sfamoön, with a weak orbit of its own, had been vacillating for aeons between the greater gravitational pull of Earth and Mars. It would approach the Earth every five and six years in regular alternance. It was at the end of these five- and six-year periods that the Pan-Atlantean royalty, together with many other Atlanteans of all classes, would gather to Atlantis the City from all over the Empire: in order to reconsider the old laws, to codify new commandments (which would sometimes change or modify the old ones), to discuss common interests, to resolve any problems affecting any and all parts of the Empire, to plan the common future, and to hold high festival for thrice-thirty days, etc. This was the Grand Council of the Kings—the Atlantean festival of festivals—a kind of combination Easter-Thanksgiving-Christmas-and-New-Year.

By a supreme irony, the closer epiphany or manifestation of Sfamoön almost invariably happened at the time of the vernal aequinox—which marked not only the Atlantean New Year but also the official commencement for the Grand Council of the Kings. Sfamoön was thus the particular star of good fortune to the Atlanteans, associated by them with their festival of festivals, and thus with all things joyously beginning anew. However, at the time of the last regular manifestation of Sfamoön, Mars was at its farthest point away from both Earth and Sfamoön, and the small planet itself was at the closest point it had ever been to our own world. Yielding finally to the superior gravity of Earth, Sfamoön was "captured"—yet its greater proximity was now to bring only death and destruction to the Atlantean world.

The actual Cataclysm occurred about a year after the "capture" of Sfamoön (some experts dispute the approximate length of time). During that one year our new satellite changed visually from a large star of dazzling brilliance into the familiar silver disk the size of a small coin that we now know. Also during that one year, the oceans of the world came increasingly to feel, in addition to the old and gentle *solar* tides, the new and increasingly greater *lunar* tides. Thus, following the Great Cataclysm, a succession of tremendous waves—unutterable in the havoc and the destruction they created—battered the shores of the entire basin of the North Atlantic Ocean, but the effects of these waves were manifest in all the oceans of the world, especially the Seas Within the Gates of Gades (the twin basins of the Mediterranean). The waters of the Ocean Sea burst through the great land-bridge at the Gates of Gades (which connected Gades to Iffrikonn), creating the present Straits of Gibraltar therethrough, and then burst through the great land-bridge between the present Sicily and Tunisia, creating a permanent passage therethrough, also. Thus, the two great basins of the Mediterranean were joined, and the over-all sea level was raised to its present measure. The tremendous waves caused by the Great Cataclysm gradually lessened everywhere over a period of many days. In consequence of the lowering of their ocean floor, both Shoaling Seas had assumed the darker hues of other seas—now being indistinguishable therefrom—and had thus lost forever their former characteristic hue of green and aquamarine.

> *O Splendor sunk, alas! beyond recall, that once of yore*
> *Her crown and trident's empire stretched from east to western shore....*
>
> *Alas! And now no more ... For evermore.... Alas!*
>
> * * *
>
> *Forevermore? Perhaps there shall rise yet in far-off time,—*
> *Beyond this bleak, blind interim of now and nevermore,—*
> *Many a new Atlantis from "the cosmic sea sublime"....*
>
> *And there, perhaps, in future gardens marvellous and vast,*
> *Shall bloom again all splendor and all beauty lost and past.*

Songs and Sonnets Atlantean

The Second Series

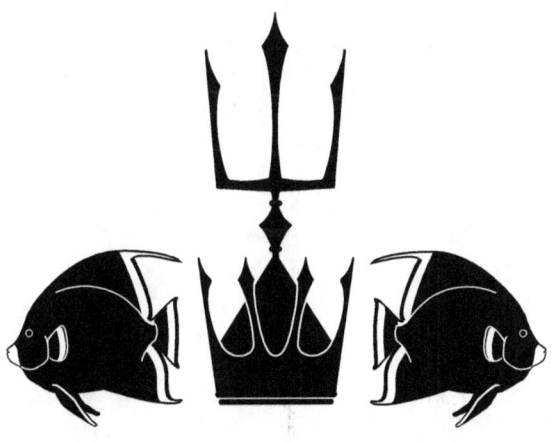

CREDITS

Some of the poems in this collection have appeared in *The Cthulhu Codex, The Galley Sail Review, Nocturne, The Romantist, Worlds of Fantasy and Horror,* and *Weird Tales.*

ACKNOWLEDGMENTS

For their warm interest and encouragement during the creation of these poems, the author wishes to thank G. Sutton Breiding, Kenneth and Lois Davis, Michael and Renée Halverson, Gerda Hoefert-Kennedy, Don Herron, Ronald and Michelle Hilger, Kathryn Hohlwein, Louis A. Irmo, Jesse F. Knight, Philip Lamantia, Stanley D. McNail, David A. McClintock, John C. Moran, Jr., Brent Morgan, Nancy J. Peters, Paul Toffaletti, Henry and Kim Vester, and Celeste Turner Wright.

DEDICATED

with affection

to Henry and Kim Vester

in gratitude and appreciation

for their kindness, generosity,

and special friendship.

PREFACE

Twenty-seven years have elapsed since Arkham House published on 16 June 1971 the First Series of *Songs and Sonnets Atlantean* as the author's first book. Between that event and the completion of the Second Series, Dr. Ibid M. Andor has passed away. Among many other distinctions that worthy scholar and general man of letters was the second principal contributor to the First Series; that is, after the author himself. Given the obvious inability of Dr. Andor to furnish an introduction and notes to the Second Series, the author has perforce himself taken on the task.

The introduction and notes provided to the First Series by Dr. Andor, as the premier Atlantologist of the twentieth century, not only added materially to the actual substance of the first book but also assisted in its public success thanks to the weight of his fame and prestige. The author owes a tremendous debt to Dr. Andor, and he regrets only that he must acknowledge it in memoriam. Born in 1895, Dr. Andor died in 1990 at the advanced age of ninety-four, fortunately in good health and happily occupied until almost the very last. His two principal monographs are still in print, and moreover in a variety of languages: the first, *Atlantis: A Travelogue*, remains the single best work on the geography of the Empire of Atlantis (first published in 1931); the second, *The Codex Atlanteanus Reconstructed*, constitutes his magnum opus (first published in 1936). Aside from his unique professional attributes and abilities, Dr. Andor possessed many endearing and unforgettable personal qualities, to which all who knew him will readily attest.

In addition to the special debt of gratitude that he owes Dr. Andor, the author owes an equal one to Harry O. Morris, Jr., of Albuquerque, New Mexico, editor of that adventurous and innovative journal of curious lore and artwork *Nyctalops*, which published its final issue (no. 19), that for April, during 1991. For the latter half of the special double issue of April 1976 (no. 11–12), he generously departed from his usual fare of horror supernatural and otherwise to devote it instead to what was essentially a festschrift honoring the First Series of *Songs and Sonnets Atlantean* and its poet-author-translator. The author owes a particular and paramount indebtedness to the editor of *Nyctalops* for honoring thus a contemporary book and writer in such an abundant and unique manner. That author is more than happy and willing to acknowledge such a debt, and he closes on a note of gratitude.

Sacramento, California, 27 June 1998   Donald Sidney-Fryer

Songs and Sonnets Atlantean

The Second Series

An Enchantress Out of Time

Dedicated to Indus Arthur, the harpist-singer.

A strange magnificence past all forgetting,
Above a sea too sullen for her song,
The wine-dark sun had tarried long in setting:

She looked back towards her castle, its huge throng
Of towers, outlined against the night full strong—
The high slit windows flaring still with day:

The sun flamed out, the twilight lingered long,
And where she sat safe from the sea's blind spray,
Her hands awhile made loud her great gold harp at play:

She gave her sorrow to the winds and to the waves below,
A rhapsody of harp and voice thrilling out over the bay,
Singing again that old, old song of extasie and woe:

And yet her dress, her hair, her lips,
    and—yes! above all else—her eyes,
Ineffably agleam, held hints
    of other times . . . and other skies. . . .

A Summoning of Shadows

Dedicated to Fritz Leiber.

Black suns, black wine, and blue-eyed vampires!
—G. Sutton Breiding.

Upon his uttermost peak, beyond the void Abyss,
In light septuple and supernal fitly robed,
With powers of Paradise, of Limbo, and of Dis;
The Mage convokes once more the darkness all-englobed,
By thunders fanfared and by lightnings tensely probed:
A wild weird globe, a world where antic daemons teem,
And strange-loined mermaids mate with monsters heavy-lobed;
Where dolent griffins weep for some forgotten dream,
And crowns and thrones and tridents lost from old Atlantis gleam:

Attended then by a vast rush of wings unseen but without number,
He summons yet those further shadows—from beyond the cosmic
    stream—
More dark than dark, more deep than deep, ineffable as dreams in slumber:

Endued with all the appanage of dreams, and loves, and fears;
The Mage stands firm upon that peak, the dominus of strange spheres.

Valediction

To H. Warner Munn: 1903–1981.

Like some eternal sunset brave with gold.
—Clark Ashton Smith, "Fetlain's Elegy to Vixeela."

Dear friend, romantist, and romanticist,
Within whatever sphere you find yourself,
May you fare well: in extasie outblissed!

Though less than angel, but far more than elf,
With heart intent on more than trade or pelf,
Your mind has lit a last but lasting fire:

Now you have found, once more, that greater Self
That looms beyond this world of fear and mire,
And thrones in majesty there where the stars respire:

Yea, now for you, dear friend, the sunset holds, without surcease,
A glow, a flame, like as the phoenix towering from his pyre,
A glamour deeper than the paradise of love and peace:

Yea, now you know that million-colored splendor manifold,
Forevermore, "like some eternal sunset brave with gold."

In an Atlantean Bath

Translated from the Atlantean of Prince Atlantarion.

As the night around us grew dark and cool
While the warm spring-fed waters laved our limbs
In the white basin of the marble pool,—
We laughed at odd conceits and curious whims,
Splashing small waves out towards the outer rims
Where trees and bushes closed us all around:
The sky's last waves of red like giant scrims
Faded to grey, far off we heard a hound,
Nearby a bird, then we fell silent, and there came no other sound:

Anon a soft refrain arose from harp or lute or lyre
Whose maze of counterpoint a poignant voice of crystal crowned
With words, half spoken and half sung, of liquid light and fire:

Anon the voice and music ceased, whose provenance we did not know,
But left within our hearts a joy as keen as any plangent woe.

Lo Primordial

Dedicated to Jesse Allen.

We have seen where the suns, like a host of great shields,
Swarm and swim all displayed in a sky without end,
Speeding through Time and Space as light to more light yields:

We have flown with great birds where the winds and waves blend
In a wild surge of spume, to descend and ascend
Where leviathan lifts, and spouts up from the main:

We have stood where huge trees tower and interdepend
At the base of volcanoes whose breath is of bane,
But on the rim of their mouths, flame the pure blooms of fire as if out of
    another domain:

From far up in the sky, with a scream and a joy fierce and bare,
The eagle strikes, the hare screams out his agonized fear, but in vain;
For the scream of the eagle must meet thus with the scream of the hare:

Parrot screech, snarl of cat, barking of baboon . . . what infinite passion
    yearns!
The silence profound and primeval that held sway beforetime now returns.

STRENGTH OF DREAMS

*Per Filippo della mantia
ed il su' occhio di fantasia.*

(For Philip Lamantia, ecc.,
by way of tribute to him both as poet and as person.)

Thou art one with those hawks, fierce on the wing,
That hover on the updraft with their young
Where the winds on their wingtips whistle and sing:

Thou art one with those greater vultures, flung
Before the storm, huge birds that long have hung
Unmoving till blown far by wind and rain:

Thou art one with those mightiest eagles, sung
And still extolled, that still soar without strain,
That still throne then on high, yes, as sovereigns dare to reign:

Nor cunning Zeus himself, for all his fecund brow,
Nor bearded Proteus, uprising from the main,
Were yet more fierce, more deep, more manifold than thou!

The lightning bolts of thy mind's eye to furthest ends, like laser beams,
Leap out at once, with all the depth and weight and height and strength
    of dreams!

Copán

Wednesday afternoon, 14 September 1988.

Still standing near the ancient riverbed,
Amid the park where dark green depths advance,
The ceremonial center looms ahead:

To-north, the central plaza's broad expanse,
Where stelae rise in hieratic trance;
To-south, the acropolis's carved stone height:

Where ceiba-trees, to-west, twist in their stance,
And shadows form the green and filtered light,
The ambient gloom seems richer still, by far, than purest night:

When was it that the quetzal-bird last chanced to grace these stones?
Withdrew, when last, its miracle of plumage emerald-bright?
So must we sigh, and ask, where silence only stalks and thrones:

The shadows on the grass describe an infinitely slow pavane
Until the twilight with far greater shadows overtakes, and overwhelms,
    Copán.

Quo Vadis, California?

New Year's Day, 1991.

Garcí Ordóñez de Montalvo told
Of militant Queen Calafía who
Once ruled a farther western realm of gold:

Called California, this changed in plain view
From an exotic island kingdom to
A great long valley and an almost isle:

But she had long since left with all her crew
Of Amazons, yea, for a termless while,
Her once domain of gold transformed, profaned, and vile:

So, whither goest, O thou California, next?—
Now that our teeming millions throng her erstwhile isle,
By people and by problems plagued, perplexed, and vexed:

Why—from her new and now yet farther western realm
Should she return?—To claim once more this kingdom's helm?

Our Lady of the Unicorn

Litanie en l'honneur d'Elle.

"A mon seul désir." [To my one desire.]
　　—Motto from a late mediaeval tapestry.

*Dedicated to Thomas and Linnea Hall
in remembrance of Eric.*

I

She holds forevermore in fee
All tides, all treasures, of the sea,
But never would she flout or scorn
The empire of the rose and thorn,
Or yet the kingdoms of the dew
Nor those of cypress and the yew.

She of the pure and only horn,
Our Lady of the Unicorn.

II

Where coldest ocean currents run
In seas below the midnight sun,
Cloud-borne, she hovers in the air
To watch the sport and frolic there
Of one-horned narwhals through the waves
Like jousting knights with ivory staves.

She of the pure and only horn,
Our Lady of the Unicorn.

III

Where gardens gleam with rose and leaf,
With promise of delight or grief,
She stands amid the shadowed brake
By fountains gushing near a lake,
To wait for that One sure to come,
Driven there by his heart's own drum.

She of the pure and only horn,
Our Lady of the Unicorn.

IV

Where morning dew and evening dew
With gems and filigree bestrew
Their traceries, their treasure-troves,
Upon the fields, upon the groves,
She skims above the level grass
Like phantom gliding over glass.

She of the pure and only horn,
Our Lady of the Unicorn.

V

Where graveyard cypress, graveyard yew,
And grimmest ilex-oak endue
The silent space between the tombs
With but the purest gloom of glooms,
She watches through the midnight hours
To heed the bloom of ebon flowers.

She of the pure and only horn,
Our Lady of the Unicorn.

VI

Attended in her tented bourn
By maiden, lion, unicorn,
She looms inside the tapestry
Amid its figured imagery
Where, summing all of love and fear,
The motto reads: A *mon seul désir.*

She of the pure and only horn,
Our Lady of the Unicorn.

VII

So thus and yea—yes, in this way—
To trumpets or to lutes at play,
Whether by night or yet by day,
She holds forevermore in fee
All tides, all treasures, of the sea,
But never would she flout or scorn
The empire of the rose and thorn,
Or yet the kingdoms of the dew,
Nor those of cypress and the yew.

She of the pure and only horn,
Our Lady of the Unicorn.

Elle de l'unique et pure corne,
Voilà Notre-Dame à la Licorne.

Rêverie Gothique

The first faint flush of light had scarcely crept
Into the woods when, all at once, that glimmer
Dimmed to the gloom innate within the crypt:

The skies themselves grew dim, and then still dimmer,
Their vault a weight grave, grim, and even grimmer;
The sun rose up at last, a dark small coin:

Nearby a figure sat in a pale glimmer
While holding up his massive clublike loin—
It seemed some daemon satyr-faun with both hands near his groin:

This imp just sat there on a knoll, grinning from ear to ear,
A radiant, joyful demigod safe in his pagan quoin,
Laughing at all that darkness with a fine show of good cheer:

One moment, blackest gloom—the next, a blaze of light—but gone,
Alas! quite gone, out from those woods, that daemon satyr-faun.

The *Monodon monoceros*

> The little whale with rare and giant horn,
> The narwhal is one type of unicorn.
> —Anonymous Rime.

As grand as any fierce rhinoceros,
Archaic and majestic and uncouth,
Behold the *Monodon monoceros!*
His own straight horn is nothing more, in truth,
And nothing less, than one long, huge, front tooth,
Evolved through time from need per nature's law:
Once prized for oil and ivory horn, forsooth,
As well as for those ivories in his jaw,
The narwhal yet lives on!—a thing of miracle and awe:

Into what further stars, beyond all earthly care,
Might he, like other species past, himself withdraw,
With all his kind, to seek the seas of Otherwhere?

No fancy lingo can disguise that everything is linked:
His gain to Otherwhere means . . . here he would become extinct!

Beyond Ultima Thule

Translated from the Atlantean of Prince Atlantarion.

Way past the northern end of Mhu Thulan,
Out on the plains of frozen-solid floes,
Let me go where there lives nor beast nor man:
Full many a fathom deep, the frozen snows
Descend in seas where never human goes
Except with arms and armors resolute:
For league on league the frozen plains expose
What never any human could refute,
A wind-swept waste of ice, bare, lethal, absolute:

At the top of the world where the elements brawl,
Lie those vast frozen seas, ineffable and mute,
Save the sounds of the wind and the ice over-all:

Out on those frozen plains where the winds howl and moan,
 Let me go forth by myself . . . at last quite alone. . . .

Midnight Visitant

Dedicated to Stanley D. McNail.

The old grandfather clock out in the hall
Strikes twelve, then stops, its monstrous tick-tock stilled,
As if in answer to some daemon's call:

Silence profound . . . might it be daemon-willed?
He sits unmoving, but much more than chilled;
He feels such fright, he scarcely dares to breathe:

Will his own pulse be likewise daemon-stilled?
Why do such fears at midnight need to seethe,
Or as . . . in *whose* firm flesh some baleful daemon's teeth may teethe?

A prodigy comes forth, a presence out of time antique—
Whose tall and all-aspiring horns vertumnal flowers enwreathe—
A snub-nosed, goat-legged lad, moustached, with beard and bristled cheek:

The man leaps up, renewed; his heart from fear shall not convulse;
The shape moves out of view, beyond; the clock resumes its pulse.

An Invocation

The vast, ebullient maelstrom of the sun,
The pale, blank desolation of the moon,
The nothingness where one and none are one:—
The sunset of an autumn afternoon,
The poignant call of owl or gull or loon,
The keen enchantment of outmoded rime:—
The canticle of some forgotten rune,
The tintinnabulation of a chime,
The dissonance of chaos which moves not in time to time:

The breath of roses in a garden's hidden glade,
The kiss of lovers at some cloister's hour of prime,
A love-knot sewn upon a piece of old brocade:

Let us invoke all these, and more:—
    From macrocosm to microcosm,
    From commonplace to totally awesome,
Let the untrammelled phoenix soar!

A Miracle in Miniature

*(Concerning the miniature portrait by Nicholas Hilliard
of Elizabeth I playing the lute, c. 1580.)*

Dedicated to Donna Curry, lutenist-singer nonpareil.

Our dear Elizabeth still plays the lute
Enshrined in Hilliard's painted medium
Where otherwise all else might well be mute:
What other means were there at maximum
To shadow forth the once rich minimum
Of sound where now she sits with calm regard?
Is it perchance Kemp's jig she chose to strum,
Or some grave tune by Dowland to have starred,
Or is it her own counterpoint her fingertips retard?

From her enchanted bourn, by time immured and fossed,
She is *not* gone while we still hold this perfect shard,
This lone memorial, of a nobler music lost:

To Her, the Faerie Queene, belongs the song,
    and only Beauty is of consequence:
      Where only Beauty is the only sense,
to Her the stars' own melodies belong.

Bialowieza

(The primaeval forest at Poland's eastern edge.)

Dedicated to George F. Haas, in memoriam.

Encompassed by the greater vast of trees,
The still vast inner core of woods endures
To lift this massive and majestic frieze:—
In these dim purlieus come no ax-armed hewers;
The shade from towering oaks and elms obscures
The muffled ground with lichen, moss, and fern:—
Here, where this ancient woodland still matures,
Some forest bison at their grazing turn
As if restored to life all at once out of Death's old urn:

No kings, grand dukes, or tsars shall hunt here evermore;
The village's old hunting lodge shall not return
To life; the huntsman's horn shall sound here nevermore:

However vast these woods may stretch in space,
    their trees abide so vaster still in time:
        What greater miracle—out of earth's prime!—
is there than such survival as this place?

Farewell to Zita

Zita von Hapsburg: 1892–1989.
Empress of Austria, and Queen of Hungary: 1916–1918.
Funeral in Stephansdom: Saturday, 1 April 1989.

When Marc Aurelius built his palace here
In ancient Vindobona, here in Wien,
He came to push the tribes off the frontier:

The centuries pass. By sybil unforeseen,
New emperors command a new demesne
From here ere forced to leave their vast estate:

In Stephansdom, in Innere Stadt Wien,
Beneath the Gothic ceiling's vaulted weight,
The last—unabdicated—Austrian ruler lies in state:

Zita von Hapsburg, Empress, has at last come home;
The last imperial echoes fade, but not abate,
While ringing ever back through time to ancient Rome:

Celestial echoes from terrestrial thrones,
    Orbiting ever outward through the Void,
      Past satellite and star and asteroid,
Forever—and forever—ring those tones. . . .

From the French of José-Maria de Heredia

Unriming translations from *Les Trophées*:
Sonnets on Oblivion, Pan, and Priapus.

*Dedicated to Stanley D. McNail
in gratitude and in memoriam.*

Oblivion

The temple stands in ruins atop the promontory.
Here Death has all mixed up, in this fawn-colored ground,
The marble Goddesses and Heroes cast in bronze,
Whose high renown the solitary grass enshrouds.

Alone, sometimes, a drover leading his oxen to water—
With his conch from which yearns an ages-old complaint
Filling the tranquil skies and the marine horizon—
Lifts his dark form against that infinite clear-blue.

The Earth, maternal, and kind to the ancient Gods,
Every spring still makes green—how eloquent in vain!—
One more acanthus for the broken capital;

But Man, unmindful of his forebears' dream itself,
Without a tremor hears—from the depth of calm nights—
The Sea who grieves for her lost Sirens by herself.

PAN

On through the thickest growth, by way of secret paths
That are lost in the depth of the green avenues,
The Cloven Foot, divine huntsman of naked nymphs,
Glides past, his eyes aflame, underneath the high forest.

How sweet it is to hear the sighs and fresh cool sounds
That lift up at high noon from springs and streams unseen
When the bright, burning sun, conquistador of clouds,
In the night of the shade darts the gold of his rays.

Some lone nymph wanders by, and then stops. She gives ear
Where the tears of the morning rain down, drop by drop,
Upon the moss. Rapture overwhelms her young heart.

But, with one single bound, the God from the dark thicket
Is launched, seizes her, strikes the air with his mocking laugh,
Disappears . . . And the woods once more fall back to silence.

The Goatherd

Herdsman, do not pursue within this harsh ravine
The willful bounds and leaps of that indocile buck;
On Menalus's slopes, where summer exiles us,
The night comes up too fast, and your hope is in vain.

Remain here, do you wish? I have some wine, some figs.
We shall await the dawn here in this wild retreat.
But speak low, Mnasylas! The Gods are everywhere.
Hecate looks at us with her one eye divine.

That shadowed hole down there is the cave in which lairs
The Satyr, our familiar daemon of the heights;
If we don't alarm him, perhaps he will come forth.

Do you hear the reed pipes that sing out on his lips?
There he is! His two horns beckon down the moon's rays;
And look, my goats, there in the light, he makes them dance!

FROM THE FRENCH OF JOSÉ-MARIA DE HEREDIA

The Shepherds

Come. The path sinks down in Cyllenius's ravines.
Here's the cave and the spring. There it is that he likes
To sleep on his own bed, made of grass and wild thyme,
In the shade of that big pine-tree where his breath sings.

Tie here to this old moss-grown trunk our pregnant ewe.
Do you know, before a month goes by, nursing her lamb,
She will furnish him our offerings of cheeses and milk?
The Nymphs will weave for him a mantle from her wool.

Bless us, Pan! oh thou Cloven Foot, thou guardian self
Of the herds nourished by the mountain Arcadian,
Thee I call . . . He hears! I just saw his pine-tree shudder.

Come, let's go. The sun dives, all ablaze, to its setting.
A poor man's gift, my friend, is worth a marble altar
If offered to the Gods with a heart pure and simple.

Hortorum Deus

[God of Gardens]

I

Don't come near! Get away! Pass at a distance, Stranger!
Deceitful pillager, you would like, I suppose
To pick, and walk off with, my grapes, and olives, and
Eggplant as well, sun-ripened in this orchard's shade?

This place I guard. With billhook blows a shepherd, once
In Aegina, hewed me from some hard fig-tree's trunk;
Mock the sculptor, Passerby, but think on the source
Of Priapus, that he can take unkind revenge.

Long ago, loved by sailors, on a galley's beak
I stood erect, bright-red, overjoyed by the sea's wrath
All afoam, or by the smile, bedazzling, of the waves;

Now, lowly guardian of these fruits and salad greens,
Against marauders I defend this garden-close . . .
And no more shall I brave the laughing Cyclades.

From the French of José-Maria de Heredia

II

Respect, oh Traveller, if you do fear my wrath,
This humble roof woven out of sword grass and rushes.
There, amid his offspring, lives a robust old man;
He is the master of this close and that pure spring.

And he it is who planted straight up in the air
My emblem quarried out of a linden-tree's heart;
He has no other Gods—I alone also guard
This orchard that he tills, and with flowers, to please me.

Here live but humble folk, direct, simple, devout;
Picked by them, these dark poppies and these violets
Adorn my sheath, alongside these green barley-grains;

And always, twice a year, the rustic altar drinks—
Under the farmer's sacred knife slashing the throat—
The blood of some young buck in heat and with a beard.

III

Stop, you damn kids! Beware the noose, the trap, the dog!
No longer do I want, I who defend this place,
People to come, feigning to fetch one garlic clove,
But instead, stealing my fruits, and gleaning my grapes.

Besides, down there, from the stubble where he cuts the thatch,
The farmer spies you, and if he comes, by my club!
Your back will soon find out just how much weighs a God
Of hard wood hefted by a strong man's arm that strikes.

Quick, take the path on the left, follow to the end
Of the hedge where that beech-tree grows tall, and right there
Profit by this advice that slips inside your ear:

A negligent Priapus lives in that next close;
From my place you can see his trellis's supports
Where the grapes have turned red in his vine-branch's shade.

FROM THE FRENCH OF JOSÉ-MARIA DE HEREDIA

IV

Enter then. My supports have been recently plastered,
And under my new trellis, where the sunlight steals,
Sweeter still is the shade. Honey perfumes the air.
April spreads her fresh carpet on this flowering earth.

The seasons, one by one, adorn me: yellow grains,
Ripe grapes, green olives, or springtime's first blossom-cup;
Still curdling on the cheese-wattle is the morning's milk,
Which the she-goat gives me from udder and from teat.

This garden's owner honors me. I deserve it,
For never thrush or thief has pilfered from his vine,
No one is better guarded in all the countryside.

The sons are handsome, the wife is virtuous, the man,
After market at night, clinks the coins in his hand,
Pure silver denarii that he brings back from Rome.

V

What cold! the frost is bright on the last green vine-branches;
I track the sun, because I know that exact hour
When the dawn makes the snows of Soracte turn red.
The plight of a rural God is harsh. Man is perverse.

Within this ruined close, alone, for twenty winters
I have grown chill. My beard is hirsute and compact,
My bright-red paint chips off, and my wood shrivels up
And then splits, and I fear being eaten by worms.

Would that I were a household god, just a mere Lar
New-painted, offered food, and always overjoyed,
Gorged on honey and fruit, or girded with April's flowers!

Near the forebears of wax, deep in the vestibule,
I would grow old, and the sons, on their virile day,
Would come hang at my neck their childhood's amulet.

From the French of José-Maria de Heredia

ON A RUINED BUST OF MARBLE

The moss was pious when it closed his mournful eyes;
For, in this untilled wood, he shall await in vain
The Virgin who poured out the pure milk and the wine
On the earth in whose name he once marked off the bounds.

Today the hops, the ivy, and the honeysuckle,
Which loop themselves all over these godlike remains,
Not knowing them for Pan, Faunus, Hermes, or Sylvanus,
Twist up their fresh green horns onto his damaged brow.

Look there. The slanting sunlight, still caressing him,
Within his snub-nosed face has placed twin orbs of gold;
Look how the wild grapevine laughs there like some red lip;

And—glamour unforeseen!—a murmur of the wind,
The leaves, the roving shade, and the sunlight that stirs,
Out of this ruined bust have brought a God to life.

Return of the Conquistadors

Unriming translation from the French of Paul Valéry.
Dedicated to José-Maria de Heredia, 7 January 1891.

Victorious evening catches fire in the waves.
And, on the virgin water, like exalted laughter,
The bugles announcing sumptuous destinies
Astonish the wyvern bewildered in the gloom.

For, with her giant sail broaching the sea that steams,
The vessel plunges forth, overburdened with spoils,
On the orb of the sun—chimaera faraway—
And shoulders up, aghast, the fire-bedazzling foam.

Look! on the prow in flame, a grand Conquistador
Towards Palas in triumph lifts up a bar of gold
Whose blaze recalls the shore that lured those heroes on!

And, glory for our eyes, there then burst out in rays
The metal pure, matured inside the caves of Dream,
The fabled gold that you grasp forth, Heredia! . . .

Enigma

[Wyvern, as exhibited in heraldry or by Paul Valéry (proclaiming the "return of the conquistadors") on a ship's flag (standard, ensign, or banner), is a purely fabulous, two-leggèd, and wingèd creature, somewhat like a cockatrice or basilisk, but with a dragon's head, whose breath, or even glance (like those of cockatrice or basilisk or even Medusa), could bring death to the active spectator or merely passive onlooker.]

To turn to stone a wyvern
On some ship's flag at sunset's close
Would make just any eye turn!

To change an orchid to a rose,
Its face at once in full disclose,
Would not form startling miracle the less!

Is it but metaphor we pose,
Some conjurer's cheap trick, with words to bless,
Or some sublime enigma, more, beyond all power to guess?

Pale Fragile Unicorns

Dedicated to Jacques and Adelle Foley, con recuerdos.

> In some green island of the sea,
>   Where now the shadowy coral grows,
> In pride and pomp and empery
>   The courts of old Atlantis rose.
>   John Masefield, "Fragments."

Pale fragile unicorns of mist and light
That flash from shore to sea, from sea to shore,
And seldom loiter in their restless flight!
They manifest or vanish, evermore,
Upon the strand between the sea and shore
In some antique, phantasmagoric dance!
Evanescent, are they not less or more
Than any world of humans or of ants—
Where, in this twilit space, the creatures preen and prance?

Dear little beasts, they serve—as heraldry supreme—
The cause, the quest, the enterprise of High Romance,
The aspiration, and the glamour, and the gleam:

Back to the black profounds of Mother Ocean Sea,
    There where her mothering darkness lives and rules and grows,
Shall they not find again that vanished empery,
    Where once the old resplendence of Atlantis rose?

Fantaisie Médiévale

Dedicated to Valerie K. Beatts, with all my thanks.

There is a concourse of heraldic beasts
That some attend at midnight in their sleep,
And there they celebrate with lavish feasts:
In that enormous castle's donjon-keep,
Proud peacock pies in dishes wide and deep
They serve with plumes, along with roasted swan:
Fabled liqueurs upon those tables heap,
And fabled wines, that none but they might con,
Or drink, those beasts, their guests, from midnight into dawn:

The unicorn, the gorgon, and the manticore?
Such never lived, they say, save in the long agone—
If then—and other beasts emblazed in fabled lore:

No shape that heraldry, howevermuch involved,
    Has made—beyond all reason and all rime—
As yet exceeds those entities that have evolved,
    Those captured on the palimpsest of Time.

Illumination

Abraxas, Abrasax, and Abracadabra.
Verbal charms from Antiquity,
to procure protective magick.

For Andrew Joron, in appreciation.

Both candle and chandelle, and more—abracadabra!—
Shall they preserve the light lost from the lamps that wane,
From chandelier and chandelabre and candelabra?

How shall a charm protect us from all bale and bane,
Ensure a lasting light that shall not prove in vain,
But wax invincible just like the sun's own sphere?

What art or science could produce and then sustain
A fire *like that*, assisted by what sage or seer?
No, none!—so light the candle-flame, and hold it close in fear.

RENEWAL

(20–21 October 1992)

The first rain of the season came and went
Within a space of hours, leaving behind
The mid-October leaves that came and went:
A light and gentle rain that fell by night,
It brought to life the clang of tiny chimes,
The breath of sweet and all-engendering earth:
After the long, long drouth of summertime,
The rain but served to wake a deeper thirst,
A greater appetence, an overwhelming sense of dearth:

Albeit the cool, wet, verdant season has commenced,
What might assuage that appetence, existing first
Before the world began, which nothing can quite quench?

The very same as that near void named the universe,
      Our own dearth is no less enormous and unhoused;
         We search the labyrinths of mirrors and Minotaurs,
Always we seek past our own selves that Some Thing Else.

Epiphany

*Dedicated to John Law
by way of tribute to him for the Burning Man.*

The statue of the bearded Christ stood where
The park had made a shaded niche of trees;
The old priest came and sat on a bench there.

He listened. What a tuneful hum of bees!
Or were the sounds archaic melodies
Played on reed pipes? Was it a Christian hymn?

He dozed, then woke up, somewhat ill at ease,
Expecting neither miracle nor whim,
When—mute with shock—he saw the statue wink at him!

Emerging from behind the plinth, quite in command,
A youthful Faunus, fair of face and fair of limb,
Walked smiling past, a luscious nymph at either hand.

The old priest then looked back, by solemn wonder drawn;
With more than shock he stared: the statue, it had gone!

A Vision of a Castle
Deep in Averonne

Dedicated to Ronald and Michelle Hilger.

This narrative is founded
on a legend of the Auvergne
concerning the Citadelle de Merle.

A vision of a castle deep in Averonne.

Stark-alert, she woke up all at once, her heart thudding:
Once again, that same dream haunting her since her youth!
How many times had she seen the same battlements
Looming up like big teeth out of the darkest night?!
The scene was more or less almost always the same:
The structure stood in ruins, or else it rose intact,
Sometimes by day, or by moonlight, or just by night—
Mostly by night, with cressets flaring, or torches flaming,
Vast walls, turrets, towers, all with massive stonework poised
Solidly far above the river's deepest gorge.

That vision of a castle deep in Averonne.

She sat up in her bed, and then lit the large candle
On the stand at her bedside as she paused to think,
"Ancestral memory?"—and smiled. Her heart had calmed.
Within the candle's pallid sphere of light and shade,
Clad in her blue nightgown, her beauty bloomed anew,
A beacon to the pier glass on the wall across,
Whose depths had once thrown back the image of her lovers
Ferociously twining in her secure embrace.
How long ago that was!—even though she remained
As lovely as ever, her blonde hair now pure white;
She did not look that old—well, at least from a distance.

That vision of that castle deep in Averonne.

Why had her father and mother altered her name?—
Now Christabel Hawthorne. True, they had changed their own

At the same time, but how could hers compare at all?
Christabelle Delaubépine. That was not the same.
Indeed, why had her parents altered all their names?
Just to become like the other Americans?
De l'Aubépine? Close, but not quite: *De l'Aube-épine*—
Not just *Of the hawthorn*, but more, *Of the dawn-thorn*—
A curious name from somewhere in the south of France.
Provençe, Languedoc, Guyenne, Aquitaine, Averonne?
Averonne! That was it. Her father had made sure,
Once hiring an expensive genealogist,
But where had she put all those papers and reports?

That vision of that castle deep in Averonne.

Le Châteaufort des hirondelles! There, that was it!
(Or Englished as *The castled fortress of the swallows*,
From all the swallows that still flocked around its towers.)
A mediaeval citadel, a feudal town,
A great *cité* like Carcassonne, but not restored.
Had she perhaps not seen a print of it somewhere?
Marriage, children, family had taken all her time,
And now?—she was alone. How much had she forgot!
Yes, the *De l'Aube-épine;* they had been grands seigneurs,
Princes ruling from their stronghold on the Faronne,
The stream that flowed into the deeper Haute-Isoile,
The greater stream that watered most of Averonne.
Why not go there from America with some friend?!
She had the friend, she had the time as well as money.
If he were free, then they would go to that old realm—
She would arrange it all with her own travel agent.

That vision of that castle deep in Averonne.

Leaving her fancy farmhouse in New England, she
Met her friend in New York, a lover once, and still
A friend, still young in looks, dapper, slim, and moustached.
Such was Perceval Jones, aged sixty-two like herself,
Artist, sculptor, writer, poet, and journalist,
Handsome, a *bel-esprit*, her favored kind of man.
They embraced with real warmth, holding each other close,
Each one with a big smile. They eyed each other long.
"You look well, and handsome," each said at the same time,
Doing a double take, then bursting out in laughter.
"I'm so glad that you are free, and could come along,"
She said. He rejoined, "It is your treat after all,
And, yes, I did accept. Many thanks, my dear friend!"

That vision of that castle deep in Averonne.

The cruise across the Atlantic took about a week,
Then a few days to pass through the Straits of Gibraltar
And on across the western Mediterranean,
Disembarking at Marseille. There they took the train
That went up by the Rhône on into its great canyon,
Getting off—north of Viviers and south of Tournon—
At Pont-Vieux, where it sits on the stream's western bank,
And the cliffs on the north have at last levelled out.
Here the old picturesque Roman bridge makes the link
South to north, where the Basse-Isoile meets with the Rhône
Here Christabel and Perceval leased them a car,

At long last heading towards the realm of their desire,
To-west across the northern reaches of Languedoc.

That vision of that castle deep in Averonne.

Talking, singing, laughing, they took turns at the wheel
Of their big touring car, piled high with all their bags.
English they spoke sometimes, but mostly they spoke French,
They needed the practise, now that they were in France,
That ancient country of the Gauls and then the Franks:
La belle France, mère des arts et des sciences
(Beautiful France, mother of arts and sciences).
Acting almost like some young couple newly wed,
They made a dapper pair, she in blue, he in green.
She favored blue since it flattered her style and color;
Now she looked like some châtelaine of olden times.
Just in the selfsame way green suited Perceval;
In truth he might have been her master of the hunt.
He said, "Let's make up a song," and then began to sing,
Christabel joining Perceval in this refrain:

    Allons-nous-en envers le pays de Cocaigne,

    Le pays de gâteau, de vin, et de châtaignes.

    (Let's go away on towards the country of Cockaigne,

    The land of cake and wine, the land of chestnuts, too.)

That vision of that castle deep in Averonne,

They saw but few châteaux, and chiefly dairy farms,
Small, like most farms in France. The land was rich and green,
Lush meadows marked here and there with stands of trees.

By slow degrees the terrain rose as they drove west;
This was the valley of the Basse-Isoile whose hills
To north and south were lined with terraced vineyards on
Their upward slopes, the famous *Côtes de Basse-Isoile*,
Justly famous for choice grapes and for choicer wines.
Delighting in the green of late spring, they had come—
The river on the north, parallel to the road—
To the place where the Basse, or Lower, Isoile begins,
The rapids that divide Languedoc from Averonne.
Here they found a small inn, the Auberge de la Frontière,
Where they would stay the night, to resume the next day.
They wondered at the name, just as if Averonne
Might be some foreign land, rather than part of France.

That vision of that castle deep in Averonne.

They agreed, in advance, to pass as man and wife,
Both of them slipping on some former wedding rings;
This had its advantages, and both loved such ruses.
They signed the register, as Monsieur et Madame
Delaubépine, des Etats-Unis d'Amérique.
The landlord and his wife then introduced themselves
At once as Monsieur et Madame Daubervilliers.
"America?" repeated Madame l'Aubergiste,
The landlord's wife, in French, her face lit with a smile.
"We're doing research on our family's history,"
Volunteered Christabelle. "Is that here in Languedoc?"
"No, it's in Averonne, where they had an estate."
With a curious expression their hostess looked at them,
Repeating, "Averonne?" Her smile had gone, she paused,

She smiled again. She said, "Well, good luck with your search."
They went up to their room with only a few bags.

A vision of a castle deep in Averonne.

In the inn's dining room they ate a gourmet meal,
Accompanied by one of the fine local wines,
And ordered a bottle to be sent to their room
While they went on an evening walk around the inn.
It was dark with no moon but the stars had emerged
All the more brilliantly for the moon's utter absence.
In the near distance the mountains of Averonne,
And their hills, lifted up like a wall on the west.
They returned to their room; the wine had not arrived.
A knock resounded on the door; they opened it.
There stood Madame l'Aubergiste, supporting a tray
With two wineglasses, a corkscrew, and a large bottle.
"Mon Dieu, what a big bottle!" exclaimed Perceval.
They asked her in. She entered, smiled, put down her tray;
With her smile still in place, she looked at them again:
"Finding the wine took me longer than I had thought.
You would like to sample one of the good red wines
Of Averonne? They are potent wines, but delicious."
"Fortified like Madeira?" asked Perceval. "No,
Just very strong," said their hostess. Then Christabelle
Exclaimed, "Good, let's drink it! Uncork it, if you will."
Madame obliged, they thanked her with much warmth, she left.
At long last the two were quite alone for the night.

A vision of a castle deep in Averonne

They drew the drapes, and changed into their night attire,
Getting ready for bed. Christabelle had put on
A rich wine-dark nightgown, and he had clothed himself
In a grey dressing gown. They sat down at the table,
Lit the two candles, poured the wine into the glasses.
This ritual done, they looked into each other's eyes,
Smiled, and then sighed, quite comfortable, but alert.
He put his hand on hers. "I've never seen you look
More beautiful than you look tonight." He spoke softly,
But with an extra warmth. "Thank you for your gallantry,
And, yes, I feel younger than I have in years.
We should travel together more often. It's fun!"
The fire upon the hearth had burned low. Perceval
Got up, added a log, sat down again, and said,
"This wine has such a deep red hue. Let's have our toast!"
She proffered, "To romance!" He agreed, and they drank.
The bouquet, taste, and aftertaste, all were unique,
"Like liquid rubies" with a heart of chastened fire,
More sweet than sharp, leaving a sweet warm afterglow.
She said, "Let's have some more." He was glad to oblige.
"Now, that's a magic wine," he said. "I feel no pain!"
She agreed, "Yes, it is! A royal anodyne."
They leaned across the little table towards each other,
Their lips meeting, and holding, so it seemed, forever.

A vision of a castle deep in Averonne.

They stood up, and embraced, again it seemed forever:
How light they felt, and yet charged with such strange fierce powers,
Like tides flooding and ebbing in rapid succession

Around, between, deep in their bodies and their cores,
Dazing, dazzling, dizzying them, uniting them once more.
They clung to each other, catching their breath and balance:
Inside its golden sphere love buoyed them up as one.
She undid her gown, and next he undid his robe,
Both letting their clothes fall unheeded to the floor,
Turning then towards the canopied and curtained bed.
Perceval: "The candles?" Christabelle: "Let them burn."

A vision of a castle deep in Averonne.

How long had they made love? For an hour? Or for hours?
She remembered, they took a break, drinking some wine,
Then returning to the deep maelstrom of their passion.
They had drunk all the wine, the candles had burned out,
Burning down and flowing into small mounds of wax.
It must have been sometime following midnight when
Christabelle ceased to sleep while her lover slept on.
Their chamber had turned cool, some light came from the hearth,
The fire was almost out, some small embers remained.
All her tensions gone, she felt content and at peace,
Falling asleep again—my, how they had made love!—
A deep sleep with no dreams until they woke at dawn
When both she and he seemed to have had the same dream,
And such a curious dream it was, the one they shared.

A vision of a castle deep in Averonne.

In this eccentric dream they were standing near the edge,
The grass-grown verge, above some river's deepest gorge.

Across the gorge there loomed a long and massive ridge
Like some enormous backbone running east and west,
Lifting up from great depths upon its landward side,
Its northern side, its other side, away from them.
Those great depths formed a dry moat where no river flowed,
A rock-bound trench not as deep as the stream itself
Upon whose edge they stood. The edge beyond the ridge,
Their edge, the ridge itself, lay within a vast bowl
Made by still higher hills or mountains verdure-clad.
The approach to the ridge must have perched on the land,
Quite out of sight, beyond the ridge's northern side.
But everything else took a second position,
A place subservient, to the site's commanding feature:
Yes, all else paled beside the vasty citadel
That raised its bulk up from the ridge's great long rock.
Tremendous bastions, donjons, turrets, towers, and walls,
The structure was immense; the site, impregnable:
Such an edifice was in fact, beyond all doubt,
A feudal city, or a *cité féodale*.
No need to perceive it, the dreamers now knew that
One bridge alone gave access to the single entrance
Into the citadel upon its landward side,
And this bridge, too, was castled at its outer end,
A massive gatehouse-tower with its own smaller moat.
Not only no scaffold but almost not any missile
Could span that wide gorge, or the ridge's landward gulf;
And on that landward gulf's own landward side or edge
There was not enough space to set up and manoeuvre
The catapults and other engineries of war

Needed to bombard and subdue such a great castle.
Châteaufort, Châteaufort, et encore, Châteaufort!
Châteaufort, Châteaufort, yet again, Châteaufort!
Early on such became the slogan or devise
Of the serfs, or the peasantry, of *L'Hirondelle*,
Or of *Les Hirondelles*, that southwesternmost part
Of Averonne. There Châteaufort had long ago
Provided not merely defense but also refuge
Against all outlanders, against invading armies.
That the structure was old, and had already passed
A long sequence of growth, was manifest at once:
From west to east, three donjons rose, with each one grander
Than the last. East of the easternmost, the great hall stood,
A marvel of Gothic Flamboyant, lifting up
With soaring stained-glass windows, buttresses, and spires:
A grandiose construction more of glass than wall,
It took away the breath to contemplate its wonder.
But in their dream the dreamers paid it little heed,
Knowing it almost better than each other's face.
She, the châtelaine; he, her master of the hunt;
Both were absorbed in some lover's feud or fight.
It was probably spring or, more probably, summer—
To judge from all the green leaves, from the lack of flowers;
And the time of day must have been around midmorning.
That was all. They woke up (it was dawn), then slept on
After falling asleep once more for a few hours;
But the dream had not continued in their new sleep,
Though the sense of that dream, and the feeling, lived on
In their new dreams. They woke from them just at midmorning.

That vision of that castle deep in Averonne

Such was their curious dream; they marvelled at it greatly,
Discussing it, comparing notes, while still in bed.
They rose, they washed, they dressed. Then a knock on the door;
They opened it once more to Madame l'Aubergiste;
She was holding a tray with coffee and croissants,
This food to break their fast following their long night.
They smiled, and asked her in. She smiled, and made her entrance;
Then she put down her tray. "Did you have a good night?
Did you enjoy the wine?" she asked them. They said yes,
In fact much more than what they had thought in advance;
Never had they drunk such a wine before, they stated.
They thanked her, smiled at her, and then smiled at each other
But they did not tell her about their curious dream.
She smiled, then bowed, and left. They packed up their few bags
While drinking their coffee, and eating their croissants.
With their bags packed, they went downstairs, and said au revoir,
Handing over a generous gratuity,
That is, to Madame et Monsieur Daubervilliers.
They thanked her, and her husband, for food, room, and service,
Declaring that they hoped to stay another time,
Most probably on their return from Averonne.

That vision of that castle deep in Averonne.

"But where had she put all those papers and reports?"—
Christabelle had not found them before leaving home.
Before they drove on, she conferred with Perceval,
But mulling over a few plans, their ways and means,

Rather than seeking out Châteaufort first of all,
She decided to go to the town of Vyônes.
There they could search and read the parish registers
That had been gathered there by the Archbishopric
From every part of Averonne sometime ago.
All of these were still maintained in the cellar-vaults
Belonging to the great cathedral of Vyônes,
That splendid pile, half Gothic, and half Romanesque,
Completed in Eleven Hundred Thirty-Eight.
After adding their bags to those in the back seat,
At long last they drove off in their big touring car.

That vision of that castle deep in Averonne.

Going south of the rapids, they continued west—
Those rapids that divide Languedoc from Averonne,
And flow down to become the Basse, or Lower, Isoile—
The road zigzagging up a rather steep ascent,
And coming out at last upon the tableland
That constitutes the greater part of Averonne.
Our couple drove on west for a number of leagues
Through wooded areas of beeches and of oaks
Before the road curved north. The highway had been skirting
Les Grands marais, or *Le Pays marécageux*,
The inland delta of the Haute, or Upper, Isoile,
A great stretch of marshland, not easily traversed,
That drains into the Basse-Isoile down through the rapids.
The channel of the upper river does not cross
On over into the channel of the lower one;
There is no direct link from the one to the other,

Not even by canal, albeit often projected.
The contours of the land do not permit such linkage,
Nor the barrier of big rocks, just before the rapids,
That thrust up from the delta's lower or southeast end.
Christabelle and Perceval decided to stop;
They pulled off the road, and got out to take a look.
What was it that they saw? A vasty wilderness
Of willows, alders, osiers, rushes, and sword grasses;
Of stagnant pools, of sluggish channels, of wide waters,
Of shuddering quagmires, of perilous quicksands;
Islands of dry terrain with beeches and with oaks,
And sometimes with stands of evergreen trees and shrubs.
And all this was vibrant with almost every kind
Of bird, insect, reptile, rodent, and other mammal,
Or thus it would appear: storks, herons, ibises;
Blackbirds and thrushes with sparrows, and swallows, too;
Sparrow hawks, falcons, other hawks, along with owls;
Terns, geese, ducks, and swans; with buzzards, vultures, and eagles;
Butterflies, dragonflies, mosquitoes, gnats, and moths;
Dayflies, harvest flies, cockroaches, beetles, and spiders;
Grasshoppers and cicadas with locusts and crickets;
Snakes, tadpoles, frogs, toads, lizards, tortoises, and turtles;
Salamanders, chameleons, fresh-water fishes;
Mice and rats, moles and water rats, beavers and squirrels;
Little herds here and there of miniature red deer;
Wolves, foxes, catamounts, and lynxes. And all this
Bewildering kaleidoscope of form and motion
Is fed, watered, and maintained by the Haute-Isoile,
As it slackens, then meanders, and overflows,

After it leaves the great Forest of Averonne
By some distance on the north, where those woods take up
Much of the province's level and central space
Between Ximes on the east and Vyônes on the north.
Both Christabelle and Perceval absorbed the scene,
Its beauty and its life. "Look at those water lilies,"
She cried out in a voice of awe. "How beautiful!"
But Perceval advised, "We had better leave soon,
If we are to make it to Vyônes in good time."
Reluctantly they turned away, and then drove on,
Heading north, and passing through a lush pastureland,
Just as lush as the valley of the Basse-Isoile,
Again with terraced vineyards on the nearby hills—
These were the no less famous *Côtes de Haute-Isoile*—
Again with few châteaux, but many dairy farms.
In their midst there stood the village of Les Hiboux,
Where Christabelle and Perceval stopped to have lunch,
Then driving on from there, and heading north again.
At last they got on the main road of Averonne
That comes in from Ximes and Malnéant on the east;
And from that junction they drove straight north to Vyônes,
Arriving and settling there in the late afternoon.

That vision of that castle deep in Averonne

They had no great luck with their search in Vyônes,
But they did enjoy themselves while sojourning there.
The great cathedral was imposing and immense,
The cafés and restaurants were in fact quite good,
The local people were helpful, warm, and friendly.

After our couple got the requisite permission,
They thoroughly perused the parish registers,
Scrutinizing those records for her family's name;
And while it was not common, it was not unknown,
But one Delaubépine was not in truth another.
So, every now and then they would take the day off,
Sometimes driving around the local countryside,
Or passing the day or more in one special place.
They spent about a week just on the great cathedral,
A hybrid marvel of Gothic and Romanesque,
Full of decorative freaks and anomalies;
But all such whimsies paled next to the first-rate gargoyles,
Often fantastical or grotesque beyond measure;
And in particular those carved by Blaise Reynard,
Who had died untimely, inspecting his own work,
Extensively repaired after the sculptor's death.
Then or later his two remained pre-eminent:
A daemon-horned satyr with wings of giant bat,
And a griffin-cat malignant and murderous.
In this way the two expatriates passed their days,
In research and outings, while they stayed in Vyônes;
But because they had no great luck in their enquiry,
The priest who had charge of the parish registers,
At last counselled them to pursue their quest in Ximes.

That vision of that castle deep in Averonne

While driving through the great Forest of Averonne,
Somewhere not quite halfway between Vyônes and Ximes,
Around noon the next day, our couple stopped, and parked

Off the road in some thicket-hidden cul-de-sac.
They got out to have their lunch in the open air,
Carrying a basket of food and a blanket while walking,
And seeking some proper spot not too far away,
Going a little farther than what they had planned.
Such a spot they soon found near a half-ruined tower,
The remnant of some castle to the west of the road.
They spread their blanket on the sunlit grass-grown mound;
Then they placed thereupon the wine, bread, cheese, and fruit
Out of the basket, finally sitting down with a sigh.
"My, how hungry I am," she said. "Me, too," he smiled.
"Let's eat then," Christabelle urged. They began at once.
 Afterwards he asked her, "Well, you aren't discouraged'?"
"In my search?" she asked back. "Yes, in your search," he said.
"No, not really. I have the feeling that once in Ximes
 We will have better luck." Cuddling, they fell asleep.
The wine and the food and the sun had made them drowsy.
When they woke, it was midafternoon. What was *that?!*
Was it a masquerade? Or were they half-asleep?
They seemed to see some woman with an entourage.
Were those reed pipes they heard, that thrilled upon the air
With tambourines and tabors beating out the rhythm?
The woman wore an antique gown. Her entourage?
Were men? Or were beasts? With horns, hooves, and shaggy legs?
In unmatched beauty, this woman came forward smiling,
Her creatures capering around her, and then the mound
On which lay our lovers, unmoving, scarcely breathing,
A mood of awe and marvel holding them in thrall.
The woman came right up to them, and then she vanished

Along with her entourage, as they seemed to merge
Into the lovers where they lay. Joy sharp as pain
Thrilled them through and through, while a wave of dark and light,
And then of heaviness, engulfed them, and they fell unconscious.
When they woke, it was late afternoon. They embraced,
Needing that comfort of each other's arms and body.
Both felt elated and exhausted all at once,
But energy soon poured back into them. They roused,
Then stood up, as they swayed, holding on to each other
For support, still overwhelmed. What could *that* have been?!
They looked into each other's eyes, where water flowed.
Christabelle smiled. Perceval sighed, "Well, I suppose
We should be leaving soon, before it gets any darker."
She repacked the basket while he folded the blanket,
And in the late sunlight they returned to the car.
Nothing had disturbed it, it started with no trouble,
Soon they were speeding south and then east on towards Ximes,
Arriving and settling there after night had fallen.

That vision of that castle deep in Averonne.

At first having no luck in Ximes, as in Vyônes,
They visited the local sights:—the great cathedral,
Which replaced the very first church that had burned down;
While not as grandiose as the one in Vyônes,
It remained a prime example of Gothic Flamboyant,
With flamelike traceries on ceilings and in windows,
On pillars and on walls;—the monumental Tomb
Of Saint-Azédarac, said to have been assumed
Bodily into heaven itself;—the Bishop's Palace,

Largely constructed by Azédarac himself;—
The Town Hall, or Hôtel de Ville, also conceived
In the selfsame extravagant style as the church.
And once they had exhausted all the local sights,
Our couple even went beyond the eastern border,
Just outside Averonne, over in Lyonnais,
To see the strange cathedral town of Malnéant,
Encircled on all sides by great walls and high towers,
A darker Carcassonne, completely dominated
By the church at the center; otherwise it was
A labyrinth of streets and gabled inns and houses.
Meanwhile Perceval and Christabelle persevered
In their search for vestiges of her family's past.
Then after Malnéant the major breakthrough came
When Christabelle insisted on *De l'Aube-épine*,
And not *De l'Aubépine*—that is, *Of the dawn-thorn*,
And not *Of the hawthorn*. That made the difference,
And that alone. Why had she not done so before?!
Our couple was talking with the priest who had charge
Of the Church Library next to the Bishop's Palace.
He bowed his head, and smiled, but his manner was grave,
"Yes, I can tell you something of your family's past;
But please come into my office, where we can talk."
They did just as he asked, and sat down, facing him
Where he sat at his desk, his hands clasped before him.

That vision of that castle deep in Averonne.

Then the priest addressed these alleged French descendants:
"Very well, M'sieu' et Madame de l'Aube-épine,

Or to use your last name in its earliest-known form
(Here he stressed the final e's almost like final a's),
Mon Sire et ma Dame de l'Alba Espina
(His listeners enjoyed this fine display of wit),
Or to use more modern French, *De la Blanche épine*
(So the name meant more *the white thorn* than *the dawn-thorn*),
Yes, I shall tell you something of your family's past
As you request, but in generic terms, and succinct.
But first, have you gone yet to your family's estate?—
Châteaufort, or *Le Châteaufort des hirondelles*—
No, not yet? You will? Good, but in your own good time!
The family first achieved some widespread prominence
In the reign of Charlemagne but after he was crowned
At Rome as Emperor of the West in Eight Hundred.
By then they had settled in southwestern Averonne;
It was Charlemagne who raised them to the rank of princes.
But from the first they made a point to hold themselves
As aloof as they could from the center of things,
A wise procedure over time, as it turned out.
From the Tenth and on through the Fifteenth Century
The family flourished at its greatest. In the Tenth
They built the first, the western, part of what was later
To become their citadel, founded on a ridge.
This first castle they built inside a Roman fortress;
From the start they maintained what was a brilliant court,
To which there came troubadours and philosophers,
With clerics and poets, with wandering knights and monks,
With jongleurs. Nor did their court ever lack for women
Who were at once adroit, brilliant, and beautiful,

Including the mistresses of the citadel;
And some of those fair châtelaines ruled, and held power.
Such was the court of the Princes de l'Aube-épine,
And then arrived the terrible Thirteenth Century.
Averonne over-all survived almost by chance
The severe crusade led by Simon de Montfort
Against the provinces of southern France; a war
That destroyed a people, their art, their way of life;
A war from whose effects they never could recover.
How did it come about that Averonne survived?
Prizes much more accessible, and not to mention
Richer treasures, existed in surrounding realms.
That was the chief reason, with a lot of good luck;
But the De l'Aube-épine and their vassals endured
Only because of the stout walls of Châteaufort,
And the impregnability of its location.
De Montfort pushed that far, took good note of the place,
And then pushed on elsewhere with his armies and allies.
All through those centuries, on into the Renaissance,
The De l'Aube-épine continued to build their fortress;
The family thus continued to survive with grace,
Withstanding wars and plagues, with losses and reverses.
Especially humane, they always paid attention
To the needs and concerns of their own farming class.
Keeping close to their citadel, they took no part
In La Fronde, the cabal against young Louis Quartorze,
And rarely were summoned to Versailles later on.
In this way they survived until the Revolution
During the last decade of the Seventeen Hundreds.

Only then it was that some disgruntled servitor
Betrayed the family, and betrayed the citadel,
By letting in a mob that destroyed, in large part
Through fire and other means, much of the ancient castle.
Those of the family who were not murdered outright
Escaped only with their lives, and thus became dispersed,
Fleeing to other lands, even to America."
Heaving a big sigh, here the priest briefly stopped talking,
His voice choked with sadness; he cleared his throat, and added:
"I, Father Jean-Paul Pierre, am a De l'Aube-épine,
A direct descendant myself." He had stopped talking.
And looked at his listeners with a furtive smile.

That vision of that castle deep in Averonne.

A long silence ensued; nobody said a word;
More than surprised, his listeners just sat there stunned,
Quite unable to move. Then everyone got up,
The two approached the priest, and everyone embraced,
Crying, laughing, still dazed. Our couple thanked the priest,
Then everyone sat down again, bemused, and smiling.
Next Christabelle and Perceval glanced at each other,
He nodded at her, and she nodded back at him,
Exchanging a few words in English and in French.
Looking at Father Jean-Paul, Christabelle announced,
"Well, we have a little confession to make you
Ourselves. Perceval, here, and I are just old friends—
For convenience we are just posing as man and wife—
It is I alone who am the De l'Aube-épine.
We intend no harm." Father Jean-Paul merely smiled,

And said, "I forbear to sit in judgment on you,"
Adding mock-solemnly, "The moral choice is yours."
Jean-Paul himself was a young, handsome, well-knit man,
As handsome in his way as Christabelle in hers.
Suddenly, as they continued their conversation,
Perceval noticed the resemblance between them,
Between Jean-Paul and Christabelle, making the comment,
"At least to me you two do look somewhat alike,"
Adding, as he glanced at Christabelle with a smile,
Dressed as she was again in the blue that she favored,
"And you today look all the more the châtelaine."
Side by side, the two looked at themselves in a mirror;
Yes, there was a certain resemblance between them.
"I have yet another confession to make you,
Dear Jean-Paul," she announced. "I have dreamed the same dream,
Off and on, since my youth. It still haunts me today,
And it is more or less almost always the same:
A vision of a castle deep in Averonne.
The place? It is none other than our own Châteaufort.
Even Perceval has dreamed the same dream while in France."
"Now, that is strange!" said Jean-Paul. He seemed rather puzzled,
"But Châteaufort has haunted more than a few people.
In case you have not learned of this, I should tell you,
The Ministry of Historical Monuments,
At Paris, has made it an historical landmark;
They have begun to do repairs and restorations.
It is, of course—today—just a colossal ruin,
Its days of magnificence are now gone forever.
Meanwhile do not hold off visiting Châteaufort.

There's a village nearby with a small but choice inn
Where you would be welcome, as well as comfortable."
They said au revoir, and embraced. Our couple took
Their departure back out into the world outside.

A vision of a castle deep in Averonne.

Early in the morning of the very next day,
They drove from Ximes, crossed the Isoile and the Faronne,
And took the road that paralleled the lesser stream,
Going on deep into southwestern Averonne.
A heavy mist hung on the heights and on the lowlands,
Obscuring at times the roadbed and its environs.
Perceval was at the wheel. He drove with great care,
And slowly. They advanced into a world of white
And silver, damp and cold, a ghostly universe
That was muffled, silent, endlessly dripping, dripping.
At length they came to the village of Châteaufort,
And parked next to the Auberge de la Bergerie,
The small and ancient inn, so called, of the sheep-fold.
The mist was lifting. They went inside, and secured some rooms.
They had their bags brought in, and then tipped the innkeeper.
This landlord and his wife had introduced themselves
At once as Monsieur et Madame Montalambert,
And seemed rather impressed by our couple's last name,
But they disclaimed a close link with the De l'Aube-épine.
They would now have to walk the pathway to the castle,
But first they wanted to see it viewed from the south,
South of the river's gorge, the same side as the village.
A sign gave advice; "Historical monument.

This way to southern view of Cité féodale."
Our couple found the path, and took it through some trees
Until the path came out into a wide open space
Where the mist lingered still, above the river's gorge.
Here the sunlight filtered down through the rising mist
In which vague shapes loomed up—archaic, dim, inchoate.
So, Christabelle and Perceval had come at last
To the place that gave birth to the dream haunting her,
Haunting them, there by the edge of the river's gorge.
No one else was in sight. They found themselves alone.
Like a diaphanous curtain before a stage,
The last of the mist was lifting before the castle,
A thin sheet spread out wide. Our couple gasped as one.
There, limned upon the mist, lay a broad panorama:
The castle in the dream that they had dreamed together,
Châteaufort at the height of its magnificence,
The soaring marvel that was the vasty citadel—
Its donjons, turrets, towers, its buttresses and spires—
Its bastions, massive walls, its deep-set battlements:
That vision of *that* castle deep in Averonne!
The splendor of that sight blinded them, and bewildered;
Then the last of the mist lifted up, and was gone.
Stunned, Christabelle and Perceval stared at each other,
And looked again across the gorge at Châteaufort.
Involuntarily, they both cried out, "Oh, no!"
There stood the great long ridge; there sat a colossal ruin,
Battered, blighted, riven from above and below.
The bastions and the walls remained; many towers and turrets;
Much of the inner fabric, and most of the foundation;

But the three donjons, all were gone; the chapel, gone;
The towering mass of the great hall, all of it gone:
The stained-glass windows, buttresses, arches, and spires
Were less than the mist that had vanished in the sunlight.
Christabelle was weeping; Perceval wept with her,
And there above the gorge he held her in his arms,
As they gave each other such comfort as they could.
When they had recovered, they went back to the inn,
Where they could rest, could sleep, could then recover further.
They would go to the castle, but not until tomorrow;
Exhausted, they had seen quite enough for one day.

A vision of a castle deep in Averonne.

In the candle-lit privacy of their own chambers
Christabelle that evening conferred with Perceval.
"At this point both of us, I am sure—you agree?—
Are just a little tired, or more than just a little,
Of ruins and old buildings. Yet we both desire
To observe at close hand Châteaufort as it is,
Such as it is today. You agree? Very well.
I suggest therefore that, after tomorrow's visit,
We take a rest, a good long rest, from all of it.
Let's get to know the local people and this place,
This village, as well as the local countryside.
We could pass a week or a few weeks doing this,
And then I would suggest that we go more or less
For a month on a wine-tasting tour of the province."
She looked at Perceval. "Please tell me what you think."
Pondering, abstracted, he thought hard for some while,

And then he declared, with a twinkle in his eye,
"I can't imagine anything more perfect than
What you have suggested. May I come along, indeed?!"—
He asked her teasingly, and somewhat roguishly.
For answer she kissed him on the nose. They embraced.

That vision of that castle deep in Averonne

Early and fresh the next morning our couple rose,
And prepared themselves for their visit to the castle.
They took the old road, now a pathway, to the bridge,
To the old Roman bridge, that spans the river's gorge,
From one bluff to another, with one, high, far-flung arch.
The bridge, like the village, lies eastward of the castle,
Its masonry well surviving its weight of years.
Our couple crossed the bridge, glancing into the gorge;
The old Roman road went westward, and so they followed,
Arriving at the bridge that led into the castle,
The bridge whose middle span was the drawbridge itself,
With towers and portcullis, guarding the single entrance:
This was the landward side of the great citadel,
Whose only bridge was castled at its outer end,
A massive gatehouse-tower with its own smaller moat,
A dry moat, moreover, like the deep trench before them,
Dividing the citadel from the outer world.
As Christabelle and Perceval approached the castle,
The crowds of birds that soared and wheeled caught their attention,
The swallows that gave both land and fortress their name,
The clouds of swallows that still flocked around the towers.
Arriving at the gatehouse-tower, they paid the fee,

That is, for two adults, and from this vantage point,
Before they crossed the bridge, they took the time to note
The multitude of towers, the massiveness of walls,
With such multiple fortifications in places,
Double, triple, even quadruple, that it seemed
That this Châteaufort out-Carcassonned Carcassonne.
Across the bridge from them, the single gateway stood,
A barbican almost beyond belief in size,
With towers on either side, each higher than the other.
The portcullis was up, and the gate behind it:
Our couple crossed the bridge, and entered through the portal;
They found themselves at last in a great outer courtyard,
Facing south. On their right, to the west, what was left
Of the first castle stood, enclosed in what survived
Of the old Roman fort, the original structure.
They began at random to wander here and there,
From one spot to the next, as in a labyrinth,
Often meeting the laborers, and those in charge.
Christabelle did not reveal her true name or self,
Perceval and she posed just as Delaubépine.
Enthralled in spite of themselves and their weariness,
Forgetting drink and food, at least for the time being,
For hour after hour they wandered around the ruins,
From courtyard to courtyard, from one place to another.
Whether as it had stood in the past centuries,
Whether now as an archaeological site,
What a tremendous enterprise this Châteaufort!
The architects and archaeologists had come,
To take their measurements, to draw their plans and views;

Already they had made repairs and restorations.
Christabelle and Perceval spent quite a long time
At the site of *la salle*, what had been the great hall.
Such was in fact all gone except for the foundation,
The vast wide floor, the lower courses of the walls,
The bases of the columns that were fixed in rows,
That stood on either side of the great central aisle.
Still they had only seen a small part of the castle
When late in the afternoon they felt exhausted,
As well as hungry and thirsty. So, with mixed feelings
They returned to the world outside, then to the inn.
Once again, they had seen quite enough for one day.

A vision of a castle deep in Averonne.

As they had both presaged, they had become burned out
Once they had gone for the first time to the citadel.
Christabelle had been right: it was time for a rest,
A complete rest, from all ruins and from all old buildings,
Insofar as that was possible in Averonne.
They put into action Christabelle's first suggestion:
They got to know the local people and that place,
That village, as well as the local countryside;
They spent a week or more doing nothing but that.
Already on good terms with their hosts at the inn,
So now they through Monsieur et Madame l'Aubergiste,
That is, through Monsieur et Madame Montalambert,
Came to know the villagers, first the shopkeepers,
Then the farmers who worked the local countryside,
Christabelle helping out with a loan here and there,

More a gift than a loan, or with an outright gift,
As the case appeared apt. As we know, Christabelle
Aside from her great beauty had a lot of charm,
And soon she had won everyone over as friends,
Perceval helping out with his own brand of charm.
They explained how he had assumed her own last name
As part and parcel of their own marriage agreement
By reason of her wealth and of her family's name,
Delaubépine, no mention of *De l'Aube-épine*,
At least not yet, it seems, but that would come in time.
Nobody minded that she seemed to take control;
As Francophone descendants they became accepted,
And universally liked, admired, and respected.
Her then behavior caused Perceval to remark,
"Even if I did not know the details of your birth,
And much more than that, your over-all ancestry,
You seem in fact to have been to the manor born."
Just as Jean-Paul, when informed of Christabelle's dream—
In their interview with him—had seemed rather puzzled,
So now her old friend appeared utterly nonplussed,
Yes, at a loss for words, if not a twinge afraid.
She held his hand, and said, "Please trust me. All is well."
He relaxed, smiled, then took her other hand in his.
They had arrived in France during the latter spring;
Early summer now saw them leave Les Hirondelles,
Which was their new home base, for their wine-tasting tour
Of the province over-all and perhaps beyond.

That vision of that castle deep in Averonne.

Hardly had they left, hardly had our couple left,
When an army of carpenters, with some engineers,
Descended in full strength upon the citadel;
Horse-drawn wagons followed at once with tons of lumber,
Of all types, including the entire trunks of trees;
All of this must have cost a veritable fortune.
A year ago, it seems, some crazy millionaire—
American, of course—had made a large donation
To the Ministry of Historical Monuments,
But on the condition that it was for the castle,
For Châteaufort alone—less for its restoration,
And more for some proposed historical display,
A pageant that would show the life at Châteaufort
During the Middle Ages or the Renaissance—
The late Fourteen Hundreds, or early Fifteen Hundreds—
Which, properly announced, would then attract attention,
The right kind of attention, to the citadel.
The carpenters would build some solid full-sized mock-ups
That would replace the structures that had disappeared.
The pageant would employ the local folk as actors;
The attention, thus focussed, would then in turn attract
The larger donations needed to reconstruct,
In stone, the missing portions of the citadel.
The mock-ups would remain in place until they were,
One after another, replaced by reconstructions.
Directed by the foremen equipped with their blueprints,
The carpenters put up with astonishing speed
The solid mock-ups that were temporary structures.
The citadel once more, as though by necromancy,

Took shape and form right there before everyone's eyes.
The donjons, one by one, went up, and then the chapel;
The missing walls and towers; the great hall, most of all.
This happy change of fortune for the villagers,
They dated from the arrival of our own couple,
Perceiving it as the bright shape of things to come;
They felt for Christabelle more gratitude than ever.
Almost at summer's end the mock-ups neared completion,
The painters painting the wood to look just like stone,
Just like the greyish stone that came from local quarries;
The workers applying all the finishing touches;
They had even brought in a little furniture.
The glaziers had arrived from Paris and from Brussels,
About a month beforehand, to install the stained glass
In the windows of the great hall and the large chapel,
As well as elsewhere, though somewhat less, here and there.
Right at the autumnal aequinox all was ready,
At long last the entire citadel stood complete:
What a tremendous task that everyone had finished!
So much work to make a mere image, an illusion,
A vision of a castle deep in Averonne!
Everyone was amazed, even the local people,
Solid and steady types not easily impressed.
The autumn had arrived with its threat of cold weather,
And stormy, that could mar the opening events
From late September and on through to mid-October,
The first pageant of all; but then, to gild the lily,
The summer promised to lengthen into the autumn
With an exquisite *Eté de la Saint-Martin*:

All was ready when our couple made their return,
Not knowing what had happened, hearing only rumors.

A vision of a castle deep in Averonne

Meanwhile our couple had prolonged their wine safari
From one month to two months, and finally to three,
Visiting most of the old province in that time.
At the start, while in Ximes, they had paid a brief call
On Jean-Paul, but he was far too preoccupied
With some new acquisitions, some splendid old tomes,
To spend much time, right then and there, with his new friends.
These old books of great value had just come to light
In an old monastery somewhat east of Ximes:
They seemed to be unique texts from the ancient world—
Yes, from the ancient Mediterranean world—
Texts otherwise uncatalogued, unknown, or lost.
Our couple congratulated him on his find;
He was brief, but cordial, in his manner towards them.
"So, you went to Châteaufort. It's quite a place, yes?!
But, I do understand how you feel as of now,
Rather burned out. Well, your wine-tasting tour should help:
You have a beautiful summer for such a trip.
Do either or both of you read Latin or Greek?
Who knows what treasures are here that we have unearthed?!
Some lost works by Sappho, by Plato, by Plotinus?
We should know by whenever it is that you return.
Well, have a good time. This province is something else,
As you should know by now. Agreed? It really is!"
Our couple bade him farewell; he bade them farewell,

Adding, "Please don't forget the wines of La Frênaie!"
They promised to try them, and at last they drove off.
First, they toured the countryside all around Vyônes,
Visiting Périgon, Faussesflammes, Sainte-Zénobie.
The sweet white wines of northwest Averonne were grand,
As fine as any *Liebfraumilch* from the Moselle,
Or almost as that vintage named Château Yquem.
From there they drove across to northeast Averonne
To the vineyards of the Cistercian Monastery,
The Abbaye d'Ylourgne, famous for its *vin rosé*.
From Ylourgne they drove south at last to La Frênaie;
This estate made not just Averonne's best red wines,
And the most potent ones, but the best dessert wines
In all the province. The restored château received—
With meals, lodging, and service—a few guests for money.
The meals were divine, the service excellent,
The mediaeval chambers were luxurious:
Both Christabelle and Perceval felt quite at home.
They stayed there about one month, which did not come cheaply;
But Christabelle reckoned, the money was well spent.
From there they drove south to the Château de Sylaire—
Sometimes also known as the Château de Cromlech—
Which also received guests, and at transcendent prices.
Here our couple remained for only a few nights
Despite the room and board. Both the red and white wines
Produced here, they perceived to be out of this world!
They decided, this place was well worth its own trip,
And a much longer stay, but at some future date.
From Sylaire they drove south once again, but this time

To the village of Les Hiboux, bypassing Ximes.
Here they stayed at a small but comfortable inn,
Securing two connected chambers for the nonce.
From this inn as their base they went forth to explore,
Each day, the celebrated *Côtes de Haute-Isoile*,
To walk those terraced vineyards on the nearby hills,
To visit the wineries, whether large-scale or small,
That were rife throughout that over-all countryside.
The vintages here were no less diversified
Than in the other regions where they had gone tasting.
It was now but two or three weeks from summer's end:
Our couple wished, for sure, to spend a week or more,
And roam around, among the *Côtes de Basse-Isoile*,
Between the rapids at the border and the Rhône,
The realm through which at first they drove to Averonne.
In a few days they departed from Les Hiboux,
Driving south once again, before the road curved east,
While skirting all the while the vast reaches of marshland
That form the inland delta of the mid-Isoile.
They stopped only briefly where they had stopped before,
A place that they hated to leave, it was that peaceful;
But there they would spend much more time on their return.
Going south of the rapids, they continued east—
Those rapids that divide Averonne from Languedoc—
The road zigzagging down the rather steep descent,
And coming out at last upon the level ground,
To-east across the northern reaches of Languedoc.
Thus bypassing this time the Auberge de la Frontière—
There they would spend a night or two when they returned—

Our couple drove straight through to the Rhône's western bank,
Arriving and securing some rooms at Pont-Vieux.

That vision of that castle deep in Averonne.

Now, before they continued their wine-tasting tour,
Our couple wanted to explore this ancient village,
This miniature town, established by the Romans
At the top of the bank, and safe from any flooding,
Just north of where the Basse-Isoile meets with the Rhône.
Here Christabelle and Perceval passed a few days,
Wandering in and out of the town's little shops,
Some filled with antiques, others with more modern art.
In a store that sold art of all kinds, old and new,
Perceval insisted that he pay, this one time,
When Christabelle found a statuette to her liking,
A dazzling creation with a gold and green finish,
A nineteenth century duplicate, done in bronze,
Of an ancient, and in fact archaic, Greek sculpture:
A satyr with horns, but more like a horse than a goat,
With large, liquid, staring eyes like those of a deer,
But otherwise a satyr impressively rampant.
At this Perceval raised his eyes in mock-wonder
When he viewed it, and quipped, "Undoubtedly a male,
And it might be that this was modelled from the life,"
Adding, "That is, by the sculptor in antiquity.
Who knows?!" She merely smiled, holding her statuette,
And said, "I love his eyes." Our couple wandered off
In the large store, each in a different direction.
All at once he cried out, and called Christabelle over:

Her good friend had just found an incredible painting,
A magnificently fantastical tableau.
Perceval stood looking near an old, mullioned window
Where the late afternoon sun came streaming in.
The first thing that he noticed was the frame itself,
The fancy but now somewhat tarnished golden frame,
Heavy, massive, carved of teak, gold-leafed long ago;
But it took much more time to focus on the painting,
With its brilliant center, with its much darker background.
Both Perceval and Christabelle stood there, transfixed;
He exclaimed, "We must absolutely buy this painting!"
On a small metal strip at the base of the frame,
It read: "Titania atque Auberonnius."
Underneath that title, another legend read:
"Leur Rencontre dedans la Forêt d'Averonne."
("Their Encounter in the Forest of Averonne,"
 Or which could also be translated in this way,
"Their Meeting *inside* the Forest of Averonne,"
 As if inside the woods were like inside a building.)
 Both of them noticed that use of *dedans* for *dans*,
 Of the adverb as an intensive preposition,
 Unless it were a purposely archaic usage.
"What a curious usage," he remarked to her,
 But she said back to him, "No, not if you remember."
(Yes, she said back to him, "No, not if you remember.")
 He said nothing. What was he supposed to remember?
 He thought, then asked himself, "*A Midsummer Night's Dream?*"
 He cried out, "*A Midsummer Night's Dream!*" She just smiled,
 And asked, "Is it not more a late summer night's dream?"

He shrugged his shoulders, and merely smiled back at her.
Of course, they knew Titania, and from Shakespeare's play,
As the queen of the fays, or of the *faieries*,
Of Faërie, the form of the word in Old French.
Auberonnius was the same as Oberon,
Which was just the same as Auberon in Old French,
Thus the king of the fays, or of the *faieries*,
A role that he fulfilled in mediaeval folklore.
But on one point did Christabelle and Perceval accord:
Our couple had each come to the selfsame conclusion,
That Fairyland could be just anywhere at all,
And what is more, could happen just at any time.
On the back of the large-scale canvas the date read,
And in Arabic numbers, Eighteen Ought Seven;
Right next to this, someone had written. "Fragonard?"
Fragonard? Was this Jean-Honoré Fragonard?
But Fragonard, he had died in Eighteen Ought Six.
Was this the work of someone who had been his pupil?
Someone else had penned, but much below that notation:
"Théophile Aristophane de Saint-Rayonnant,
Elève de Fragonard, mais juste avant sa mort."
("Pupil of Fragonard, but just before his death.")
This was an artist who was otherwise unknown;
But our two continued to look at that large picture,
With its brilliant center, with its much darker background.
Inside the oval at the center of the painting
Stood the two figures, thus: Titania to the left,
Oberon to the right. Both wore gowns, both wore capes
With voluminous trains, both wore wide and high collars

Of shimmering lace, translucent, and edged with pearls.
Scintillating coronets crowned the head of each;
Little crystals twinkled on their persons and their clothes
As they faced each other, each with a mocking smile.
His gown was amethyst; his cape, a rich blue-green;
Her gown, a rich blue-green; but her cape, amethyst.
They stood in a bright glade inside the darkling forest,
Each with an entourage gathered in the penumbra,
And with much stranger creatures in the zones of darkness.
Faierie courtiers comprised each entourage;
On both sides of the oval in the painting's middle,
Inside the zones of darkness, lurked the woodland folk,
Fauns, wood nymphs, water nymphs, mountain nymphs, elves, and satyrs;
In the darkest corners lurked giant vampire bats.
The woodland, clearly the Forest of Averonne
With the massive trunks of its ancient oaks and beeches,
Inhered on all sides, and at the top and the bottom,
A swirling mass of greys and browns, dark greens and golds:
The light came from either the full moon or the dawn.
Transfixed, our couple suddenly looked at each other:
"We must buy this painting, and let's divide the cost
Between us," Perceval said; Christabelle agreed.
They found the storekeeper, who was cordial and friendly;
He sold them the painting for a mere hundred dollars,
Such a painting with all its jewelled surfaces.
Our couple was amazed, and they thanked him profusely.
They had already renewed the lease on their car,
And stored the painting with great care in the back seat;
Once again it was time to head west for the nonce.

A vision of a castle deep in Averonne

As before, they continued their wine-tasting tour,
But now through the long valley of the Basse-Isoile.
By slow degrees the terrain rose as they drove west,
Stopping often to taste, and staying overnight.
Their days had now become a pure and perfect idyll
As they meandered their way west by slow degrees.
In the far distance the mountains of Averonne,
And their hills, lifted up like a wall on the west.
How impressed they had been by the fine local wines
When first encountered on their way to Averonne,
But now, following their province's own vintages,
The local wines, however fine, seemed somewhat lacking,
Missing a certain ineffable character.
Nevertheless, they still gave their own unique pleasure,
Above all a supersweet wine liqueur made from raisins.
Thus in a few weeks Perceval and Christabelle
Completed the distance from the Rhône to the border,
To the rapids that mark the climb to Averonne.
There once more they lodged at the Auberge de la Frontière,
Where Monsieur et Madame l'Aubergiste were quite pleased
To have them as guests yet again, and so this time
For a number of nights, rather than for just one.
Monsieur et Madame Daubervilliers then asked them,
What had brought them back to this corner of Languedoc?
Our couple then explained, how they had occupied
Their last two or three months on a wine-tasting tour
Of Averonne over-all and somewhat beyond,

Including last of all the *Côtes de Basse-Isoile*,
  Thus clear across the northern reaches of Languedoc.
  Monsieur l'Aubergiste allowed himself a rare comment:
"You have found a perfect way to get to know France,
  Not only through her art, but through her drink and food.
  In drink and food and art is found the soul of France,
  Above all in her wine, the product of her earth;
  That is as true of Averonne as any other province."
  Here Madame l'Aubergiste politely posed the question,
"You have done well in your search for your family's past?"
  Christabelle replied, "Yes, thank you for your interest.
  This Averonne is distinct from the rest of France,
  Is it not?" Madame l'Aubergiste nodded her head,
"I almost told you so, but thought that it was something
  That you should get to know, but strictly on your own."
  Here Christabelle nodded her head back at her hostess;
  With such these two had reached their first real understanding.
  Perceval that first night conferred with Christabelle.
"Well, here our wine-tasting tour has come to an end,
  The one most fantastic vacation of my life!
  For making it possible, thank you, Christabelle,
  And thank you very much. What do you have planned next?"
"To return to Châteaufort, and by way of Ximes,
  So we can visit with Jean-Paul on our way back.
  I'd like to know more about those books he found
  In that old monastery somewhat east of Ximes.
  He had hopes of finding some otherwise lost works
  From the ancient world. What might he have not discovered?!
  Moreover, I'd like to be back in Châteaufort

Right at the autumnal aequinox if we can.
I've reserved our same rooms beginning from that day."
Perceval did not see why they could not be back
By then. So he agreed, such would make up their plan.
After their second night our lovers left the inn,
Feeling well content once more with food, room, and service,
Voicing that contentment in no uncertain terms,
Declaring that they hoped to stay some other time,
And handing their hosts once more quite an ample tip,
That is, to Monsieur et Madame Daubervilliers.
Like so their hosts felt contentment towards them as guests.
At their request the innkeeper's wife had made them
A lunch to have somewhere picnic-style on the road.
Both guests and hosts then said au revoir to each other
While Christabelle and Perceval drove off at last.

That vision of that castle deep in Averonne.

Once again they had stopped where they had stopped before
While skirting the great marshland of the mid-Isoile.
Not far from where they parked, they consumed picnic-style
The lunch that Madame l'Aubergiste had fixed for them.
It was just past high noon when they sat down to eat
On the blanketted mound from which they viewed the swamp
With all its rich mix of animal and plant life.
There was no need of undue haste to get to Ximes,
Where they would spend the night; so they had lots of time
To dawdle over lunch, and then to laze about.
They even ventured into the marshland a little
Before the deepening water blocked their advance:

Without waders one could not go very far in.
How peaceful and how beautiful all of it seemed!
A flock of cranes, colored pearl-grey, flew overhead
Just then, and landed in a shallow pool nearby.
With long legs, with long necks, with long bills, with large wings,
These birds whose legs came up high out of the dark water
Seemed not just impressive but also somewhat comic.
At this point Perceval asked Christabelle a question:
"Here we are like gypsies, moving from place to place,
 Without a fixed abode. Does it unsettle you?"
"No, not at all. And you?" "I feel the same as you.
 How many people could afford to live this way?"
"Well, since we can, let's be as unchained as those birds
 Over there. What is more, since my last husband's death,
 When I took back my maiden name, my dear children
 Have become quite preoccupied with their own lives.
 They don't miss, it would seem, their own mother that much;
 If they do, then absence only makes the heart grow fonder.
 Besides, I'm content to claim my life back from them,
 And their constant jockeying for my special favor.
 I send them and their children gifts and little notes
 From time to time. I have my own life to live now!
 Enough! That's my declaration of independence.
 I feel no guilt at all. They'll see me soon enough."
"Well, I have neither wife nor children, Christabelle,
 But I think I understand how it is you feel.
 Besides, it is your choice, and not anyone else's."
Again reluctantly, as on their first stop there,
 They packed up their basket and blanket, then drove on.

Our couple reached Ximes without incident or mishap,
Securing, and settling in, some rooms with no problem;
There they passed a pleasant evening and a good night.
In the morning, before leaving for Châteaufort,
They managed to have a real visit with Jean-Paul,
Who now had the time that he did not have before.
After the usual greetings and courtesies,
Jean-Paul remarked how rested and how fit they seemed;
Then he said, "So, your wine-tasting trip went quite well?
Three months! You had a good long trip. And La Frênaie?
Indeed, a special place with special wines. Well done!"
Christabelle asked about the books that he had found.
With a rather wry smile, Jean-Paul gave this response:
"Well, so much for works by Sappho, Plato, or Plotinus!
So much for highfaluting hopes and expectations!
Those ancient books apparently originated
In the scriptorium of an early monastery
Built on a castled rock in the Aegean Islands.
I do not know how they came here to Averonne,
But they were obviously brought here in some way.
And the volumes appear to be some kind of codex
That systematize information on Atlantis—
Yes, the Atlantis that Plato himself describes
In his dialogues *Timaeus* and *Critias*—
The codex is in Greek, and has to be translated.
Will marvels never cease?! I would only hope: Never!
The volumes are unique, and therefore have great value."
Both Perceval and Christabelle expressed surprise
At this news of Plato's old Empire of Atlantis;

And just before they left, Jean-Paul posed them this question:
"Do you know what's been happening at Châteaufort
  While you've been gone? Have you heard anything at all?"
  Perceval answered, "Yes, they've been making repairs,
  We've heard, and other restorations. That *is* true?"
"Yes, in general that *is* true," Jean-Paul made answer.
"But, you'll see for yourselves, and in your own good time.
  I don't want to spoil the surprise that's in store for you.
  On your way back you'll have a nice puzzle to ponder!"
  Here Perceval and Christabelle looked at each other
  With wonder and surmise writ large upon their faces.
  Our couple bade him farewell; he bade them farewell,
  Adding, "You'll see me there soon while I'm on vacation.
  Oh, make sure to see the place first from south of the gorge!"
  They promised that they would: it was a favored view.
  Our couple took their leave, and after lunch drove off.

A vision of a castle deep in Averonne.

  Meanwhile, back at the citadel of Châteaufort,
  Right at the autumnal aequinox all was ready,
  On the very same day that our couple returned,
  Not knowing what had happened, hearing only rumors,
  Arriving in the middle of the afternoon,
  Securing, and settling in, their rooms at the inn.
  The inn was full, and the village itself was packed,
  Families having taken in out-of-town guests
  From near and from far, from Paris and overseas.
  When our couple asked why, Monsieur l'Aubergiste answered,
  Some special events were taking place at the castle

Starting that very night. Everyone seemed to be waiting
On something that was just on the verge of happening.
Our couple was amazed, if not in fact astonished,
But they wasted no time, and went at once to the place
Where they had gone before when they had first arrived.
Unlike that first time, some few folk stood here and there;
And it was then that our couple first took good note
That the leaves on the trees were starting to turn color.
So, once more they had come full circle to this place
Just south of the edge by the river's deepest gorge.
Across that space they looked again at Châteaufort;
Stunned, Christabelle and Perceval stared at each other.
What was this?! The entire citadel stood complete!
Neither uttered a word; they were truly dumbfounded.
Meanwhile behind them the wide open space had filled
With people from the village and the countryside.
At the head of a hand-picked group of citizens,
Madame l'Aubergiste arrived where our couple stood;
This was none other than Madame Montalambert.
The group all wore smiles as she bowed her head, and spoke:
"Madame Delaubépine—" "Christabelle, s'il vous plaît!"
"Bien, Madame Christabelle! We would like you to take
Part in our pageant starting tonight in the castle.
And because of your name, and because you might be
More or less related, we would like you to play
The role of Lady Christabelle de l'Aube-épine,
The châtelaine ruling in Fifteen Hundred Thirty,
Whose husband had passed on in the preceding year,
She who disappeared with her master of the hunt

At the stroke of midnight in full view of the people
Gathered in the great hall on Thirty-One October,
And who then reappeared right at the stroke of midnight,
Still with her master of the hunt, on One November,
In full view of those regathered in the great hall,
As recorded in the chronicles of that epoch.
A thing of wonder, it has never been explained.
The two themselves had no concept of what had happened,
But they were otherwise all right, and in good health.
Will you agree to our request? And your own husband
Could then play the role of her master of the hunt."
With a charmed and charming smile, Christabelle said, "Yes!
Thank you! I would be delighted to play the role
That you request of me!" She bowed her head to them,
And all of them in turn inclined their heads to her.
She looked at Perceval with an enquiring smile,
"And you?" Her good friend smiled, bowing his head in turn.
Standing at her full height, Christabelle took control:
"You need not be concerned about what we should wear.
We have clothes that will suit, or that we can adapt."
She nodded at the crowd; and they bowed back to her.
It was late afternoon, and everyone dispersed,
To regather that night inside the citadel.

That vision of that castle deep in Averonne.

In the candle-lit privacy of their own chambers,
As the two of them dressed, and adapted their clothing,
Perceval that evening remarked to Christabelle:
"I suppose we'll meet tonight this Alphonse Dello Beppin;

Most everyone should be on hand in the great hall.
Who would have thought of it, of solid full-sized mock-ups?—
But our own millionaire of Dello Beppin Tires,
Of yet another branch of the De l'Aube-épine,
The man who has financed these temporary structures,
Who is behind everything that is taking place.
He isn't crazy, so much as he is inspired.
He may not speak much French, I hear; but he speaks English,
No problem there for us." Perceval smiled at her;
Christabelle smiled all the time that she went on sewing.
She had a long dress of dark-blue wool—with full skirt
And long sleeves—that she was adapting as she needed,
Dropping the bottom hem so that it hid her ankles,
Opening the sleeves from the elbow to the wrist,
And filling in with some extra cloth that she had,
So that the sleeves hung down, and more than just a little,
And making new tight-fitting sleeves to fit inside.
Yes, Christabelle was quite a quick, proficient sempstress.
She showed no décolletage, and kept the high-necked collar;
It was autumn after all, she needed no chill.
Perceval, already dressed in his dark-green clothing
Adapted with great skill, looked just like a forester,
Or like some châtelaine's own master of the hunt,
Which was in fact what he was pretending to be.
Christabelle laid her sewing down, and shook out her dress,
Removing the one she wore, and putting on the other.
Then she let down her thick long hair, letting it fall
In a great cloud of shimmering white and of silver,
Lustrous, coiled, and curling. Next she twisted a loop,

A long loop, of pearls twice around her high-necked collar,
While holding her long hair. Now she put on pearl earrings,
Followed by matching pearl bracelets. One more loop
Of pearls twisted twice around the top of her head,
She added, like a low coronet. She had finished,
And stood still, a vision of loveliness unrivalled.
Startled beyond measure, Perceval then cried out—
His eyes and voice trembling with tears of adoration—
"Oh Christabelle, you look divinely beautiful!"
She smiled, and then put on an all-enclosing cape;
They blew the candles out, and went outside their chambers,
To join all the others on their way to the castle.
She had placed her hand on the arm that he had proffered
When she whispered, "Thank you for your enthusiasm!"

Lanterns lit the way from the village to the castle,
Then torches lined the route inside the citadel,
First from the gatehouse-tower, and then across the bridge,
Right through the barbican, on into the great hall,
Rebuilt in wood and glass in all its magnificence,
Where quite an assemblage had already convened.
The great hall was ablaze with torches and with candles,
But carefully placed to avoid the threat of fire,
In sconces, in candelabras, in chandeliers.
How distinct the effect was from electric light!
The radiance came down in waves of red and gold,
And fired the soaring stained-glass windows from inside,
Displaying as they did the same obsessive pattern
Of red roses, of green branches, of big white thorns,

All convoluted, over and over again,
As though the great hall screened an idyllic dream-garden.
Topped by pinnacles, finials, and other spires,
A forest of flying buttresses pressed outside
The north and south walls along the length of the structure
In support of the fabric more of glass than wall,
So that they seemed almost completely built of glass:
It took away the breath to contemplate their wonder,
Illuminated as those walls were from inside;
But only a few flying buttresses upheld
The west and east ends or walls of the massive structure,
Walls that were more solid than those made out of glass.
The great hall was like the Sainte-Chapelle, but much larger,
Like the Sainte-Chapelle inside the Palace of Justice,
At Paris, located on the Ile de la Cité,
That was the ancient Lutetia Parisiorum,
The capital of northern Gaul under the Romans.
The two chief entrances, each one placed in the middle
Of the north and south walls, stood thus facing each other,
Each approached by an avenue flanked on both sides
By carved beasts of heraldry set on pedestals.
Our couple entered through the portal on the north,
Through what had always been, as now, the favored entrance.
Christabelle had thrown back her cape, tied at the neck,
To reveal the beauty of her dress and her pearls.
They made a dapper pair, she in blue, he in green,
But she purveyed a magnificence nonpareil,
Most likely not viewed there since Fifteen Hundred Thirty.
Thus the crowd fell away on both sides as they entered,

Leaving the passage clear and straight through to the throne
Where it stood on the dais against the western wall
Under a canopy that was a perfect marvel
Of Gothic Flamboyant fantasy and invention.
Directly from *la galerie des ménestrels*,
That is, the minstrels' gallery, from where it opened
Far up within the eastern wall, a choir of boys
With high, pure voices burst all at once into sound,
Startling the assemblage with unexpected song,
With opulent and polyphonic melody,
As our couple had entered through the northern portal,
And then turned, going along the wide central aisle,
That which ran east and west between the rows of columns.
They marched with dignity and with grace to the dais,
Which they mounted, and where they sat down on their chairs,
He on a simple armchair, but she on the throne,
Against the back of which she had done off her cape:
Their sitting down signalled the program to begin.
The Ministry of Historical Monuments
Had sent some officials and others to attend
The opening night of the pageant. The chief one,
Who introduced himself as Apollon Dubois,
Started the program with a brief but pointed speech
From a rostrum fixed at the center of the hall.
"Mesdames et messieurs, welcome to Châteaufort,
Whether you are local people, or from elsewhere,
Whether friends or members of the De l'Aube-épine.
We start here tonight what is an experiment,
A notable first for our ministry in Paris,

Made possible by the kind openhandedness
Of Monsieur Alphonse Dello Beppin and his family,
An American but of ancient French descent,
And that descent from the De l'Aube-épine themselves."
Here Monsieur Dubois nodded at him and his group
Where they sat in a space cordoned off from the rest;
They all smiled and nodded back at Monsieur Dubois.
"For this evening we have arranged a special program
Of music, vocal or instrumental or both,
Selected exclusively from the Renaissance,
And in several cases from the Middle Ages.
We wish to thank the musicians who have come here
To restore this music among us all tonight,
The singers, the players of lute and flute and viol.
We wish to thank, as well, all of you who prepared
Painstakingly and patiently for this commencement,
Especially the local people who appear
Here tonight, garbed in the costume of their ancestors.
Thank you! Let's allow the musicians to take over."
Loud applause for Monsieur Dubois as he sat down.
Then a consort of lutanists began to play,
As rearranged for those four instrumentalists,
A series of fantasies by Albert de Rippe,
Or Alberto da Ripa, who came from Mantua
During the spring of Fifteen Hundred Twenty-Nine
To become court lutanist to François Premier.
All during Monsieur Dubois's speech, and afterwards,
Our couple was looking discreetly around them,
Bemused by the interior of the great hall.

Like the great cathedral at Ximes, though but a mock-up,
This formed a supreme example of Gothic Flamboyant,
With flamelike traceries on ceilings and in windows,
On pillars and on walls, a kind of Gothic Baroque.
Inside or outside, it seemed a forest of columns,
But those inside were colossal, each one being made
Out of the single trunk of one gigantic tree.
Swords, shields, lances, and heraldic banners were hung
Between the windows. At the eastern and western ends
Vivid-hued hangings, no less than tapestry mock-ups,
Concealed the unfigured surfaces of the walls.
Tiered above and below, five massive chandeliers
Of iron hung from the length of the vaulted ceilings.
Such was the solid full-sized mock-up of the great hall;
It amazed our couple no less than anyone else.
During the long interlude between the two halves
Of the program with all of its delicious music,
When people talked and relaxed, refreshments were served—
Simple sandwiches, elegant cakes, glasses of wine—
By village lads and maidens dressed like servitors.
Why, here was their Jean-Paul, already on vacation,
Bringing Alphonse and his own group to meet our couple.
When Jean-Paul had said that they would see him there soon,
That was precisely what he had meant, namely, soon!
Both Christabelle and Perceval arose at once,
And embraced Alphonse, his wife, and all their grown children;
After all they were all related more or less.
Christabelle's warmth and charm were a joy to observe;
Her graciousness alone could have served as a model.

Alphonse complimented Christabelle on her warmth,
On her charm, on her beauty, on her graciousness.
She complimented him, and moreover thanked him,
For the miracle that he had wrought at the castle
Through his discerning and inspired philanthropy.
They all talked for awhile, getting to know each other,
And finding much with which to build a true rapport;
During the time of the pageant and afterwards,
They would all of them be seeing much of each other.
Christabelle and Jean-Paul managed to talk alone:
He asked her, "Well, what do you think of our rich kindred?"
She answered, "They are not only rich, but quite pleasant,
And as we know, the two don't always go together.
So, I'm happy to claim them as our kin. And you?"
He answered, "I agree, and they will make good allies."
The last half of the program was about to start,
And so people returned to their accustomed places.
The concert now continued with some plaintive tunes,
Troubadour airs that sang of love, despair, and longing,
As arranged for, and performed by, the viol-players
With violin bows on their viols, or *violes*.
Next the singers took over, soloists and groups,
To furnish the program almost until the finish.
Then the consort of lutes performed some lively dances
From the book of them that one Pierre Attaignant published
At Paris in the year of Fifteen Hundred Thirty—
These brought the concert to a suitable conclusion.
The audience with cheers applauded the musicians,
Dressed up as all of them were in period costume;

They smiled, and bowed modestly to their audience.
Christabelle with Perceval rose, and approached them,
Dispensing words of praise and even of affection,
A gesture observed as appropriate for princes.
Nodding in salutation, our couple returned
To their seats so that Christabelle could then receive
Fit homage in her assumed rank as châtelaine.
It was close to midnight, near the time to disperse.

The architects and archaeologists had come
To the fore, in one group, to give Christabelle something.
All of them wore broad smiles, and the chief architect
Was carrying a cushion covered with a cloth
Under which something sat, waiting to be revealed.
How fantastically their modern dress contrasted
With the surroundings that they had helped to create
In reconstructed form, in solid full-sized mock-ups!
The chief architect, Michel Saint-Ange, then spoke up,
After bowing his head, quite aptly in character.
"Princess and châtelaine, we have discovered something—
In the walls of the castle—that belongs to you,
Or that seems to have belonged to you formerly,
Before someone secreted and walled it away;
And we would like to give it to you at this moment."
Christabelle smiled, inclining her head in acceptance.
With a bow he kneeled on one knee in front of her,
With the other knee then extended before him.
Like an adroit magician performing a trick,
He lifted up the dark-red velvet cloth with one hand

Off the dark-red velvet cushion resting on the other.
Simple and elegant, there both glittered and glimmered
A coronet of silver with teeth or tines of gold,
Thus brought forth after a sleep of four hundred years.
Deeply moved, Christabelle first flushed, and then turned pale;
But she soon regained control, smiled, and said, "Thank you."
She leaned forward, and closely viewed the little crown;
Then she picked it up, and placed it upon her head,
Above the double loop of pearls around the top.
Briefly a cloud of light seemed to play about her
Before she spoke. She said, "For seeming to dissemble,
Even when asked explicitly, pray forgive me.
Until this moment I could not reveal the truth,
But at long last, right now, my lips have been unsealed.
Je suis descendue des châtelaines de Châteaufort,
Ou si vous voulez, des castellanes de Castelfort."
Then for those who spoke and understood little French,
She repeated in English what she had just said:
"I am descended from the châtelaines of Châteaufort,"
But in her French she had repeated the main phrase
In the more ancient words proper to southern France,
Including the original name of Castelfort.
A long silence ensued; nobody said a word;
More than surprised, her listeners just stood there stunned.
Then everybody burst into applause, with cries
In fact of sympathy, such as "Well done, Madame!"
Christabelle just sat there, head unbowed, but eyes lowered;
She made no sound, but lines of tears ran down her cheeks.
Perceval had reached on over, and held her hand,

Speaking in a low voice words of comfort and support.
Here Madame l'Aubergiste, that is, Montalambert,
Had come forward herself, nodding her head, to say,
"Was I then the only one to suspect the truth?!"
No one answered. "Bien, if I was, then so be it.
Madame, I do not blame you for having dissembled;
You must have had your own good reasons, I am sure.
But to pass to another, more pertinent subject:—
We all know the grave wrong that was done to your family.
Do *you* know just how that great injustice came about?
They had survived quite well until the Revolution
During the last decade of the Seventeen Hundreds.
A disgruntled servitor it was who betrayed
Your own family by betraying the citadel,
By letting in a mob that destroyed, in large part
Through fire and other means, much of the ancient castle.
Those of your family who were not murdered outright
Escaped only with their lives, and so became dispersed,
Fleeing to other lands, even to America.
Your family had done nothing to earn such a fate.
We still remember how good they had been to us,
And what is more, over quite a long space of time,
From Eight Hundred to Eighteen Hundred, more or less,
An over-all term of about one thousand years.
Especially humane, they always paid attention
To the needs and concerns of their very own vassals,
Of their serfs above all, of their own peasantry,
Often putting those needs above their very own.
They never insisted on their own ancient rights

At the expense of those of their very own people,
An almost unique phenomenon at that time,
And not at all typical of their especial class.
What of that servant, that disgruntled servitor,
Who let in the mob that destroyed the ancient castle?!
It was André, called the Malcontent, who did it.
An ingrate, he had been magnificently treated
By the De l'Aube-épine, but he came to be peevish
Over a mere trifle, and plotted his revenge:
Your family's murder, and the citadel's destruction.
What of that mob, that infamous and angry mob?!
All of them were conspirators and criminals,
The dregs of society hired for the occasion,
Who only posed as honest revolutionaries,
Using the occasion to rob, to kill, to ruin,
And the De l'Aube-épine became their ideal target.
In this way did that great injustice come about."
Madame Montalambert had ceased; she bowed her head:
All of the De l'Aube-épine family who were present
Had become rather grave in their mood and demeanor.
Christabelle had become the same, but now she smiled,
And said with her accustomed grace, "Thank you for speaking,
Madame Montalambert. Your words instruct and heal.
It is now past midnight, more than time to retire."
Perceval helping Christabelle on with her cape,
Our couple then arose, and walked out of the great hall,
Followed by most of the people who had attended;
The rest of them put out the torches and the candles.
The first night of the pageant had come to its finish.

A vision of a castle deep in Averonne

From the autumnal aequinox to mid-October
The pageant ran its course, becoming more authentic
And historical as the days and weeks went by.
The tourists or guests could wear modern dress, of course;
But the rest of them had to sport period costume,
Whether servitors, musicians, or what have you.
All those who thus took part had become quite adept
At olden modes and manners by the pageant's end—
Christabelle's example served everybody else—
And the pageant itself in almost every way
Proved successful, attracting those larger donations
Needed at least to start reconstructing in stone
Those portions of the citadel ruined or lost.
The architects' first choice? To rebuild the great hall;
But they would not begin the work until next spring.
A special hour occurred near the end of the pageant:
Father Jean-Paul had presided at the first mass
To be intoned inside the reconstructed chapel,
The first mass there since the destruction of the castle.
The last night had finished with a tide of applause,
Loud and long, on behalf of Alphonse Dello Beppin,
In gratitude for what he had made possible;
He took a bow then in gracious acknowledgment.
Including Alphonse with his group, and our Jean-Paul,
Most of the guests and the De l'Aube-épine dispersed
Until another year's historical display:
The first enactment thus had come to its conclusion;

The old clan at long last had united once more.
Our couple would remain until sometime November,
When they would go back to America by ship,
Possibly to return to France another year.
Now Christabelle proposed a choice event for those
Left behind, including the villagers themselves.
She proposed to them a British-style Halloween,
Such as they staged throughout the English-speaking world,
Including the United States of America,
To take place, of course, on *La Veille de la Toussaint*,
Or Allhallows' Even, the day before All Saints' Day.
This was not so startling as it appeared at first;
All that she proposed was a simple masquerade
Such as people put on during the Renaissance—
As, among other times, the early Fifteen Hundreds—
With costumes and disguises, and often with masks.
At such times people impersonated those gods
And goddesses of old, the Twelve Olympians,
Or more local and elemental deities,
Or such as our own Titania and Oberon,
And their strange court of daemons, elves, and *faieries*.
The masquerade was to take place during the evening,
All inside the magnificence of the great hall.
Christabelle's proposal rapidly found approval,
As much for its oddity as for its novelty:
A British-style Halloween might be a lot of fun—
It would be curious and quite original—
The French had forgotten much of their Keltic roots.
For a week more or less our couple stayed in Ximes,

Where Christabelle had found a marvellous dressmaker,
To help her make the costumes for her and Perceval.
Also, she had a coronet fashioned for him,
But with one curious distinction from her own,
Which was at least on loan, but not an outright gift,
From the Ministry of Historical Monuments.
Only one detail formed this curious distinction:
At the top and center of his own coronet,
From within the circle there of the teeth or tines,
A pair of goat-horns, just like those of Pan, came forth.
Of course, our couple had brought with them the large painting
That they had purchased at Pont-Vieux, so that the garments
Displayed by Titania and Oberon could serve
As models for the costumes that our couple planned
To wear during the masquerade at Châteaufort.
At last Christabelle with the help of the dressmaker
Had finished the outfits for her and Perceval:
They fit perfectly, and what is more, they looked stunning;
They would cause a sensation at the masquerade.
After Christabelle paid the dressmaker her fee,
Plus an ample bonus, our couple then returned
At once to Châteaufort, to the inn at the village.
To make a proper entrance at the masquerade,
Our couple then engaged some village lads and maidens
To pose as *faierie* courtiers, as well as pages,
To hold up the long trains of their enormous capes.
The young people were free to vamp up their own costumes,
As they saw fit, but still within certain broad guidelines,
Or they could use the garments worn during the pageant.

Finally the evening of the masquerade arrived;
Everyone convened in costume inside the great hall,
Which once more was ablaze with torches and with candles.
Our couple made their entrance last, just for effect;
The other masqueraders looked on in mute wonder,
As though Titania and Oberon for a fact
Had made their arrival into the world of mortals
As goddess and as god. Both wore gowns, both wore capes
With voluminous trains, both wore wide and high collars
Of shimmering lace, translucent, and edged with pearls.
Scintillating coronets crowned the head of each;
Little crystals twinkled on their persons and their clothes
As they walked side by side, each with a mocking smile.
His gown was amethyst; his cape, a rich blue-green;
Her gown, a rich blue-green; but her cape, amethyst.
Faierie courtiers comprised each entourage,
And pages were bearing the long trains of their capes.
They mounted the dais where two thrones had been prepared;
Next the pages removed the long trains from their capes.
So that our couple could then sit down with some ease.
At a signal from Christabelle the fun began
With dances and with games, with mummers and with mimes.
Buffoons and other jesters trod a merry measure,
With antic steps and gestures that caused gales of laughter.
Hefty farm hands next carried in some tubs of water,
And placed them in a ring at the center of the hall.
Bobbing for apples was unique on Halloween
For all the French people assembled there that night.
How many of those present would have known the truth?—

That these apples once expressed those of paradise!—
But Christabelle as Titania had not forgotten.
Thus the evening wore on with games and with diversions,
And everyone seemed to be having a good time.
Unlike our couple, most of the others wore masks;
Though not as fancy, their costumes were just as odd.
But even without masks our couple seemed a little
Unfamiliar that night, more youthful and more handsome;
Still there was something else that could be felt, but not named:
Christabelle herself looked perfectly luminous,
And they both looked just like those figures in the painting.
The masquerade had started right at nine o'clock,
When Christabelle and Perceval had made their entrance.
The three hours until midnight had gone rather fast,
When the huge metal clock—that stood upon its plinth
Of black and white marble against the eastern wall—
Suddenly broke out into sound, striking the hour
From one to twelve, relentlessly, one after the other,
With strange, harsh, chilling, and hollow metallic tones.
One and all stopped in their tracks, and looked at the clock;
Then they looked back to where our couple had been sitting.
Both Christabelle and Perceval had vanished entirely;
There was no sign or trace or track of them at all.
Everyone looked at each other, and in mute wonder.

Where had they gone? A good question. Here is one answer.
Nowhere or Anywhere, Elsewhere or Otherwhere:
They seemed to have lost consciousness while in some limbo,
A place to which they have gone for twenty-four hours.

While they are dead and void to the world, let us pass
An interlude with Titania and with her friend
After their own transition back to Fairyland.
In this instance, but not otherwise at all times,
It looks the same as the Forest of Averonne.
They look the same, but are not the same, as our couple.
Titania speaks to her friend. "Well, Antiphilus,
You have been such a dear, so patient for so long!
This last—what shall I say?—sojourn among the mortals,
This last enchantment, this last dream within a dream,
Took much longer than what we had thought in advance.
I'm sorry, and I apologize most abjectly."
She bows her head, but Antiphilus reaches out,
And takes her hand. "Friend, there is no need to be sorry.
This last experience, this last experiment,
Although much longer than anything else before,
Was quite uncommonly rewarding, don't you think?
Christabelle and Perceval! I shall miss those two,
But it's time for them to take over their own lives
Without our divine guidance, our secret commands."
She rejoins, "The truth is that it was more than time.
Setting up our own transit to come back home here,
Proved more than merely difficult this last occasion,
It proved almost impossible. Setting it up,
All of it, taxed my forces to the maximum.
Oberon flat refused to give me any help
This time, and that was what made it so very hard—
Sometimes it takes two magicks to make a great one—
And you could not help me the way that he might have.

Also, he took offense at the horns on your crown,
When you appeared as he during the masquerade.
It seemed as though we were saying he was a cuckold,
And moreover, we were rubbing it in royally.
I told him that we needed them for our transition,
But he remained upset—after four centuries!
After all that time, how keen he was to see me!
He may be my husband, but *you* are much more fun.
Still we made it back, and I'm not in any rush
To leave again. You are free to go forth once more,
Just as you wish, all on your own. I've held you back
For far too long, against your own actual nature.
After all, my dear, you are a genuine satyr,
And can pretend to be human for just so long;
At last it goes against the grain of your true being.
What is more, pretending to be Oberon himself
Was not easy, never mind running the real peril
Of incurring his wrath. *That* I'd rather avoid.
I suppose that you'll find some suitable companions,
As you generally seem to do. Am I right?"
He responds, "Well, you know my nature and my past:
Yes, as usual, but I'll come back from time to time.
We are after all, you know, much more than mere friends:
We are soul-mates travelling through time and through space.
I suppose that our Christabelle and Perceval
Will get married as soon as they're back home from France:
They were lovers once, and they are lovers again.
Living inside them, sharing their lives, has been fun—
One life after another, for four centuries—

But I'm eager now to get on with my own life."
Here Titania speaks, "I know that I am as well,
And I'm in no rush to set up a new transition
Back into the world of mortals—no, not at all!
Setting up those correlates and co-ordinates.
Those magnitudes and quantities and intersections;
Aligning all those lines, points, planes, angles, and solids,
Those circles, ovals, triangles, rectangles, and squares;
Plus plotting with those four centuries to achieve
Exactly the right position in time and space:
It's a course in pure Euclidean geometry,
And applied mathematics was never my strong point!
I need a rest from all that, from other dimensions.
We may be divine and immortal, but we, too,
Have our limits within which we must work, and remain.
Meanwhile, as I said, you may depart. By the way,
Quite a beautiful nymph is giving you the eye,
Along with her satyr-brother, behind that bush
Over there. We'll visit each other soon enough.
Come, let's kiss and part. Farewell, dear Antiphilus!"
"Farewell, dear Titania!" her satyr-friend rejoins.
From the center of the glade she watches him leave;
Oberon enters the glade, and goes up to her.
He smiles with pleasure, then slips his hand into hers,
And now brings her fingers gently up to his lips.
At least for now they are once again reconciled.

Thus Christabelle and Perceval had disappeared
At the stroke of midnight, but not seen by the people

Gathered in the great hall on Thirty-One October;
And then they reappeared right at the stroke of midnight—
The two of them still in costume—on One November,
But in full view of those regathered in the great hall.
Some persons were sitting near the dais with its thrones,
A vigil headed by Madame Montalambert,
Who had been reading quietly, but who now smiled,
Got up from her seat, and welcomed our couple back.
"Bien, Madame Christabelle et Monsieur Perceval,
Soyez les bienvenus encore chez nous ici!
Welcome back home among us here inside the castle!"
The two themselves had no concept of what had happened,
But they were otherwise all right, and in good health.
This vanishing and then reappearance had happened
Thus exactly four hundred years after the first.
Had it all begun with that dream back in New England?!

That vision of that castle deep in Averonne

Stark-alert, she woke up all at once, her heart thudding:
Once again, that same dream haunting her since her youth!
How many times had she seen the same battlements
Looming up like big teeth out of the darkest night?!
The scene was more or less almost always the same:
The structure stood in ruins, or else it rose intact,
Sometimes by day, or by moonlight, or just by night—
Mostly by night, with cressets flaring, or torches flaming,
Vast walls, turrets, towers, all with massive stonework poised
Solidly far above the river's deepest gorge.

She sat up in her bed, and then lit the large candle
On the stand at her bedside as she paused to think,
"Ancestral memory?"—and smiled. Her heart had calmed.
Within the candle's pallid sphere of light and shade,
Clad in her blue nightgown, her beauty bloomed anew,
A beacon to the pier glass on the wall across,
Whose depths had once thrown back the image of her lovers
Ferociously twining in her secure embrace.
How long ago that was!—even though she remained
As lovely as ever, her blonde hair now pure white;
She did not look that old—well, at least from a distance.

A vision of a castle deep in Averonne.

Some Further Fragments from Atlantis

Dedicated to Don Herron.

Translated from the Atlantean of Prince Atlantarion, through the French of Michel de Labretagne.

Pharanos Descending

Just as Pharanos loved to tell the story about the one single night per year when his master Ullfanon would invite the stars to inspect and study him as he generally inspected and studied them on all the other nights during the year, weather permitting, so did the apprentices of Pharanos love to tell selected others—in confidence, of course—about how Pharanos would stage his own yearly ritual, the accomplishment of which, however, took place over a period of days. As soon as he became astrologer to the Archking—who was at the time my father Atlas CLIII, called Sfamoönophamos—Pharanos instituted this peculiar annual rite following the death of his master Ullfanon, and usually he performed it fairly soon after the vernal, or sometimes autumnal, aequinox. The ritual came about because Pharanos himself had often complained about how those astrologers who studied only the stars, thus those called astronomers—as apart from those who studied the actual or alleged influence of the stars on mice and men and microbes—became so rapt up in their search of the heavens that quite often, unlike the astrologers, they forgot their fellow creatures and their obligations as astronologers to them and to mundane affairs. After all, without society at large and its essential material support, neither astrologers nor astronomers could survive in their high towers, builded upon such elevated places as mountains, high hills or cliff-armored promontories jutting out into the ocean. At least he, Pharanos, would not fall into that regrettable error such as afflicted far too many astronomers. Assisted by his corps of apprentices, no less than his staff of servants—all of whom were essential to the proper functioning of the archroyal observatory rising from the very top itself of Mount Atlantis—he would come down from the central and highest edifice thereupon, would spend one full day while on the ground, that is, on the chief level shared by most of the urban population, and would then ascend back up to the summit of the Acropolis.

This yearly ritual generally required a period of three days: a day to descend, a day to spend on the common level shared by the population at large, and a day to go back up. Descending, he needed little help but in case he might, his apprentices accompanied him. Sometimes he did become rather dizzy from a too precipitous descent in certain places, and he was getting older, not having quite the very same energy of his youth or even early middle age. After visiting the level of the water in the outermost circle of harbor, and then washing his hands therein—thus underneath the Great Place Megalopolitan—Pharanos would pass the first night, as well as the second day and night, at the private palace of some old and highly placed friend. Ascending, he had the services of an entire series of some very strong bearers, who gradually lifted him in an enclosed chair all the way back to the summit itself of Mount Atlantis. The third day always turned out the least interesting even though he did little actual climbing himself during the ascent. However, the often spectacular views no less than the unwonted angles of perspective, thus afforded of the capital city and the surrounding countryside, as Pharanos and his group arose, compensated in large measure for the inevitable tedium of their ascension. Furthermore, without the bearers, all of them fine and lusty fellows in the very flower of their young adulthood, Pharanos could not have made the climb returning to the top. He had already gained middle age when he received the position of astrologer to the Archking after the death of Ullfanon at quite an advanced age.

Descending, however, always proved exhilarating: so many different flights of stairs big and small to go down, so many chambers, so many tunnels, so many halls whether great or medium-sized to pass through, in and out of the massive towered cone, some three thousand feet high, that made up the single mountain standing at the very center of the three concentric harbors, no less than the two circles of land, that occupied one third of the capital city. When Pharanos began his descent, a signal informed the metropolis far below the summit that he was on his way down. In general the signal took the form of a series of three gigantic bright-red flares that blossomed against the early-morning heavens of darkest blue or gray sprinkled here and there with the last few stars yet remaining just before dawn. Those who normally stayed up all night, along with the early risers, would witness the flares, and the word would soon spread throughout the great city. Pharanos was descending! His rare epiphany was at hand.

Once even, when Pharanos had just begun descending, several individuals here and there throughout the metropolis—and all of them trustworthy citizens—claimed unequivocally to have seen at that very moment not merely one iffinnix but an entire flock of iffinnixes. The several individuals averred that they had witnessed a great flash as an enormous mass of gold and flame and rich red-purple suddenly lifted up off the summit of Mount Atlantis, hovered above it briefly, then headed north towards Poseidonis, the mountain-heartland of the Archkingdom. However, others disputed their claim, opining that all that the witnesses had veritably seen was but a kaleidescopic reflection as the light of the early morning sun had first struck the massive objects of metal atop the mountain. These others also maintained that the iffinnix was extinct, or if not extinct, then surely not numerous enough to constitute an entire flock, and that the bird or birds almost never left their preferred habitat, the central and highest range of the mountains that formed Poseidonis. Pharanos with his entourage on their way down witnessed only a gigantic flash that temporarily blinded them. Whatever it might have been, everyone agreed that it was a proper omen with which to signalize that rare descent.

My Mind to Me an Empire Is

> My mynde to me a Kyngdome is.
> —Sir Edward Dyer (1543–1607),
> English courtier and poet.

*Translated from the Atlantean of Athallarion,
but via the recension of Prince Atlantarion.*

Above all else, my mind to me an empire is,
A world of sovereign island kingdoms everywhere:
Above all else, my mind to me an empire is.

How the mind flies!—over the land, into the air,
Into the Ocean Sea where darkling creatures lair,
Inside the mind itself where darker things may lurk.

This Ocean Sea of stars, that endless Otherwhere,
Whether with something strange, or just a little quirk,
Always invites us out inside the sunlight or the murk.

Whether it like an angel or some vampire is,
Above all else, my mind to me an empire is.

Likewise My Mind to Me a Cosmos Is

Likewise my mind to me a cosmos is.
Is it by means of random parallel
That this my mind to me a cosmos is?

The mind may measure, as in yard or ell,
Some dazzling bolt of silk too rich to tell,
Or on that splendor may just opt to muse.

Between some asphodels or hydromel,
The mind like some tense hummingbird may choose
To taste, to drink, to plunge down deep, or else refuse.

Or past unnumbered galaxies the mind may soar,
Freed once again from all constraint, from every ruse,
To make landfall at last upon some star-lost shore.

Through random parallel is it, or it through osmose is?
Wherever, whatever, my mind to me a cosmos is.

Re-ascension

Once the yearly ritual of descending had concluded, and he had regained the buildings at the summit of Mount Atlantis, Pharanos usually confessed that it was less the actual descent that proved exhilarating than the historical revelation that the descent provided. Generally he retired almost at once to his own palatial suite of chambers located in one of the less pretentious edifices that stood not far from the archroyal observatory. All such structures arose inside the sizable compound, wall-engirdled and colonnaded, that spread out over the mountain's pinnacle. Along with the colonnades lining the inside of the all-inclusive wall, several porticos ran outside it, primarily facing north, south, east, and west.

No sooner had Pharanos regained the summit, and then his chambers, than his thoughts immediately descended to the levels through which he with his entourage had just passed while making their way back up. To the dearest and closest acolytes attending him he would confide: he had felt himself literally plunging down through history, down through all the historic levels, floor after floor after floor, as though down through the random geologic or archaeologic layers that made up the various floors or stories. Perceived in rapid succession, the descent became a kind of kaleidescope with all the periods and materials of architecture seemingly jumbled up, one after another.

Pharanos at Sunset

It is a wind-swept evening clear and cool.
The sun, about to sink beneath the west,
Has gathered all its red in one vast pool.

Both heavy-robed, and with an outer vest,
Pharanos pursues his own instant quest,
Pacing that near-the-summit colonnade.

He shields his eyes while glancing towards the west,
And finds his near-impatience well repaid
As he stands still, transfixed, before that sunburst fade.

Out from its vast red pool the sun seems to expand
For one undying hour, an infinite cascade
Of fierce red rays that fill the sea, the sky, the land.

Still unmoving, the old man stands while staring on and on:
Dark grey-blue heavens everywhere, the sun's disk has withdrawn.

Oneiromancy

Yet once more had he dreamed that selfsame dream,
Had Pharanos, as oftentimes before—
That prophetic and cataclysmic dream.

Always that same enormous tidal bore
Viewed from on high, such shook him to his core:
Did the sea rise, did the land sink, or both?

Always he heard that dull, foreboding roar,
And would wake up with some half-scream or oath—
What was it, what could it be, this oneiromantic growth?

At last, poor Pharanos, how much he feared to dream,
So that at times he would become completely loath
To fall asleep lest sleep bring back that selfsame dream.

At long last Mount Atlantis did submerge like all the rest:
And then? He never had that dream again, so he confessed.

AT THE OUTHANOX

How much had happened! That same thought struck Pharanos once again. Each time it hit him almost as hard as a blow to his gut. Yet once again he paused completely in his intermittent pacing. Since arriving at Xonorr, the capital of Poseidonis, he promenaded every day through the endless halls and corridors of the Outhanox, the Great Citadel guarding Xonorr.

How much had happened! The general evacuation of the populace at large into the uplands of the Archkingdom. The terrifying and massive destruction caused first by the widespread earthquakes and then by the submergence of the lowlands, especially around the old capital of Atlantis the City. Not knowing exactly when that Great Cataclysm would occur, the authorities had undertaken the gigantic enterprise of the general evacuation more as a precaution than anything else. In immediate retrospect it had emerged as an inspired move, all survivors agreed.

How much had happened! Despite that precaution Prince Atlantarion as the new king, along with his own immediate family and the imperial court, had planned to return briefly to Atlantis the City, far to the south. Only the need to ensepulchre Pan-Atlantean royalty who not long ago had perished in the catastrophic Battle Before Athens had brought king and court back once again to Xonorr and the Outhanox. Only now no one would ever return to the old capital or Mount Atlantis.

By way of au revoir and envoi

BEAUTY

Translated from the French of Charles Pierre Baudelaire.

Beautiful am I, O mortals, as a dream in stone,
And my breast, where each one, taking turns, has been bruised,
Is made thus, to inspire in the poet a love
Eternal and mute the same as Matter itself.

I throne through the sky like a sphinx misunderstood,
I join a heart of snow to the whiteness of swans,
I loathe all movement that displaces the pure line,
And never do I weep, and never do I laugh.

The poets, before my grandiose attitudes
That I seem to take from the proudest monuments,
Shall consume all their days in unrelenting toil;

For I have—to enrapture my submissive lovers—
Two pure mirrors that make all things more beautiful,
These eyes of mine sublime, with their light from forever.

NOTES

An Enchantress Out of Time.
Dedicated to Indus Arthur, the harpist-singer.

Indus Arthur is an unique performer and entertainment personality on the West Coast of the U.S., and specifically of California, and has often appeared at the Renaissance Pleasure Faire (taking place in the late summer) in the Black Oak Forest near Novato north of San Francisco. Handsome and gracile, a woman of strong presence with a singing voice that haunts the listener, she creates an unforgettable image, whether sitting or standing, dressed in a laced bodice and long skirt flowing virtually down to the ground. She could easily have stepped out of a late mediaeval tapestry, or equally well out of one of the gorgeous tales of Averoigne penned by Clark Ashton Smith. Indus Arthur accompanies her singing by playing on a so-called Troubadour harp, manufactured by Lyon and Healy of Chicago. Its actual shape recalls both the Gothic harp of the High Middle Ages and the Renaissance harp of the 1500s, but in size, range, and number of strings it is, of course, much larger and louder, and is almost comparable to the modern concert harp. In a manner difficult to describe, the Demoiselle Arthur does not so much accompany herself as she literally sings to her instrument positioned before her. Her appearance, performance, and aura constitute the very quintessence and ideal of romance as defined by all the relevant historical connotations of that enduring and amazingly resilient tradition since its inception during the early or middle part of the Middle Ages (from about 400 to 1400 A.D.), and this remains at least one tradition that promises to survive into the immediate future.

In an Atlantean Bath.
Through the French of Michel de Labretagne.

Created by Prince Atlantarion during his wedding voyage with the Princess Aïs amid the divers island kingdoms of the Empire of Atlantis, in the years just before the Great Cataclysm. Specifically it commemorates an experience they had while visiting the island kingdom of Avalonessys, just before going back, at long last, to the great island of Atlantis the Archkingdom.

Copán.
Wednesday afternoon, 14 September 1988.

During the latter half of August, and all of September 1988 (making a total of six weeks), the poet-author visited Central America (primarily Guatemala and Honduras), travelling at first by train but then largely by bus, and passing through Mexico both from and back to California whether going south or then returning north. He sojourned at Copán in the course of 14–15 September, staying overnight at a small hostelry contiguous to the plaza of the little town of Copán Ruinas [sic] which caters to the needs of travellers. He spent a full six hours at the ceremonial center itself on 14 September, from about high noon to about six o'clock in the evening, thus one hour after closing time at five, thanks to the permission and presence of the then Director, who took the author on a special private tour of certain somewhat recondite areas in and around the main part of the ceremonial center, certain areas normally off limits to visitors.

Quo Vadis, California?
New Year's Day, 1991.

It would seem (and we have it on the best authority) that, before the Spanish or any other Europeans first encountered the real, topographical California with its distinguishing and peculiar geography (the peninsula, or almost isle, of Baja California, and then the enormous inland valley of Alta California) they first discovered it, as it were, in their contemporary mythology. When, working from Portuguese into Spanish, he published his translation of *Amadís de Gaula*, the celebrated romance in prose by Vasco da Lobreira, Garcí Ordóñez de Montalvo also published, following it in the same volume, a romance of his own invention, a work also in prose, *Las Sergas de Esplandián*, concerning the adventures of one Esplandián as "the legitimate son of Amadís." Literally invented, imagined, and presented in Montalvo's romance—as part of the elaborate machinery of a book that was essentially a work of science fantasy belonging to the Spanish Renaissance—California made its very first appearance anywhere at all, whether in fact or in fancy, as an island rich in gold and precious gems, inhabited by Amazons and ruled by their Queen Calafía.

When the Spaniards first came across the peninsula, that is, almost island, of what later became known as Baja California, it was assumed that this was indeed *the* island of California as described by Montalvo. The latter evidently based, within the structure of his romance, the episode laid in California on something reported by Columbus after his second voyage to the New World. When the Italian explorer was sailing en route back to the West Indies for the second time—this in 1493—he somehow heard an account of an island inhabited and ruled by women warriors, an island lying, of course, in the further western ocean somewhere. From this mere germ of a story, as it were, Montalvo developed his fabulous demesne of gold, precious gems, and Amazons, doing so by definition with quite a large admixture of imagination and pure fantasy, it should be added and emphasized. This is stated not with an attitude of censure but, rather, of admiration.

Not only was this realm as described by Montalvo a pure invention, or almost so, but the name itself of California, insofar as we can trace it, seems to be likewise a pure invention, but possibly derived, as the name of Calafía herself, from (el) *califa*, the Spanish word for caliph. Montalvo's romance enjoyed a sensational popularity during the 1500s, the last century of the Renaissance that began in the 1300s, and continued through the 1400s. Need we add that the original island kingdom of gold and precious gems, inhabited by Amazons and ruled by Queen Calafía, has not yet been discovered somewhere in the Pacific Ocean?!

(Historical and literary data courtesy of Nancy J. Peters, of San Francisco.)

Our Lady of the Unicorn.
Dedicated to Donna Hall.

A previous unicorn poem, "O Beautiful Dark-Amber Eyes of Old," translated from the French of Michel de Labretagne, has been collected in the First Series of *Songs and Sonnets Atlantean*. The author wishes to acknowledge with special gratitude the assistance given him by Ronald S. Hilger in regard to the final realization of line 6 of stanza II.

Rêverie Gothique.

Line 11: "pagan quoin." *Quoin* here is used in the same sense as *coign* or *coigne*, or as the French *coin*, meaning corner, nook, corner seat, etc.

The daemon satyr-faun that the author had in mind while creating this poem was an entity somewhat along the lines of one of the splendid and charismatic daemons limned by that remarkable artist of the fantastic and macabre, Allen Koszowski. A typical daemon by this artist is that depicted on the cover (dated: '90, i.e., 1990, by the artist) for *Crypt of Cthulhu*, No. 74.

The Monodon monoceros.

Line 9: "The narwhal yet lives on!—a thing of miracle and awe:" The line has an obvious double sense: just as the creature itself is a thing of miracle and awe, so likewise is its mere survival into modern times. Since the narwhal ranks as one kind of unicorn, this poem itself ranks as a kind of unicorn poem.

The small cetacean called the narwhal is unique to the Arctic Ocean, and in Swedish or Danish, *narwhal* means *corpse-whale*, so called in allusion to its pale skin. The mammal ranges in length from twelve to twenty feet, and its horn from six to ten feet, making the horn one-third to circa one-half the length of its body. The horn is basically one tooth, or two teeth fused together, projecting from just above the creature's mouth as a straight, long, spiralling tusk of unascertained use. The single tusk may have given rise to the legends of the presumed purely mythical unicorn. Once pursued and valued for its oil as well as for its ivory, whether in the form of its tusk or its teeth, the narwhal would appear to be no longer generally hunted save sparingly by the Inuit, the native peoples living along the arctic shores and islands of North America and elsewhere.

Although not the smallest whale, it ranks among the smaller species, and compared to the biggest one, the enormous blue whale—the largest creature ever spawned by our planet, larger and heavier by far than any dinosaur, some specimens of the blue whale running one hundred feet and more in length—a typical narwhal would hardly measure, even with its horn, the length of the blue whale's over-all jaw! The narwhal is only a little larger than the bottlenose dolphin but smaller than the bottlenose whale. This little cetacean evidently does not emit any characteristic music or other like sounds in the manner of the humpback whale, which emits sustained, ethereal songs.

Beyond Ultima Thule.
Through the French of Michel de Labretagne.

Labretagne records that the original Atlantean title translates into French as *Au nord du Mhou Thoulanne*, but he gives the poem in his rendering of it into the French of his time the new title *Au delà de l'Ultime Thulé*. The author of the present book has retained the French poet's own title instead of one based on the original. Labretagne further records that Prince Atlantarion, always chafing under the restrictions imposed by his rank, was passing through a severe emotional and mental crisis at the time of the poem's creation, a crisis clearly reflected in the poem itself.

Like "In an Atlantean Bath," this poem was created by the poet-prince during his wedding voyage with the Princess Aïs amid the divers island kingdoms making up the Empire of Atlantis during the years just before the Great Cataclysm. Specifically it commemorates an experience that Atlantarion had in the course of their not quite year-long visit to At-Thulonn and related territories. Their visit lasted from the late summer of one year until the late spring of the next. During their only winter on At-Thulonn, they undertook an expedition with the then reigning king and queen of that island kingdom to the far northeastern end of Mhu Thulan (present-day Greenland). The expedition, representing a huge concourse of people, some on quadrupeds, and some on foot, first went along the relatively ice-free southern and western coasts, beginning more or less at what is now Cape Farewell, and then stopping somewhere north of what is now Disko Island, where the quadrupeds were left to await the return of their human masters from the far north. The entire expedition, climbing up on the great mass of interior (continental) ice, now transferred to an enormous number of sledges drawn by teams of huge polar dogs, and continued on along the western edge of the great sheet of ice covering most of what was once the ancient Mhu Thulan.

The party visited next the series of forts and watchtowers (otherwise previously abandoned) that extended from near what is now Thule Air Base to that section of the northwest coast now known as Peary Land c. 150 miles east of Ellesmere Island. While the main group making up the expedition, including the Princess Aïs, remained here in camp, a very small group including Atlantarion, together with the hardiest and most intrepid of the native guides, continued on with the best dog-drawn sledges to the north pole. This the small group attained, and from this they returned, with no major problem except a terrible polar storm while en route to the pole, a storm that they weathered successfully, but not without experiencing a few days of rather excruciating suspense. It was during their dash to the pole and back that Atlantarion passed through his intense personal crisis, which he survived apparently in better shape than ever.

All in all, the entire expedition and its complete itinerary represented an enormously long trip, c. 2,500 miles from At-Thulonn to their final camp on the northwest coast of Mhu Thulan, and c. 500 miles or more from their final camp (on the ice above land) to the north pole, and then all the way back to At-Thulonn, making a grand total of c. 6,000 miles. The over-all trip lasted approximately from the latter autumn to the latter spring; the dash to the pole and back took place in the depth of winter. As things turned out, the trip would remain as the last such expedition ever undertaken by any Atlantean royalty and nobility, passing into legend among the native peoples of Mhu Thulan, but especially after the Great Cataclysm and the submergence of At-Thulonn along with most of the remaining Empire of Atlantis.

A Miracle in Miniature.
Dedicated to Donna Curry, lutenist-singer nonpareil.

Lines 5–6: "the once rich minimum / Of sound." This is an obvious reference to the curious paradox embodied in the six-course Renaissance lute, such as Elizabeth I herself played (with its relatively limited ambitus, or range, even more limited than that of the modern six-course classical guitar), as perceived *vis-à-vis* its extraordinarily abundant repertoire of extant music, most of which is contrapuntal in character. Beginning c. 1500, or somewhat earlier, and lasting to somewhere between c. 1630 and c. 1650, the lute of all possible instruments of that period offered for the first time to legions of musicians almost the only easy medium for contrapuntal, or multilinear, playing and composition. However, starting c. 1590, the Renaissance lute began to add extra bass courses in such a way that by no later than 1623 some Renaissance lutes had thirteen or fourteen courses in all, the latter representing the maximum development of such with one exception.

As invented by G. G. Kapsberger, one of the greatest of the virtuoso players on the chitarrone or bass lute, there was one type of Renaissance lute—in this case a chitarrone strung with wire that he played c. 1610–1640 at least—that had nineteen courses in all, with a complete set of chromatic bass strings; and such undoubtedly represents the maximum development of the Renaissance, Baroque, or any other lute. Accordingly, if she continued to play the lute during the 1580s on into the 1590s, then Elizabeth would have been using an instrument that had one or more extra bass courses. Since keyboard instruments in their modern form with multiple octaves, etc., had not yet come into existence (apart from the church organ, to which relatively few musicians had access), the lute's facility for contrapuntal playing and composition was alone responsible for its unchallenged predominance in European musical history for some 130 to 150 years until the increasing preference among musicians for the then developing harpsichord ultimately displaced the lute's ascendancy.

Data concerning the portrait, Queen Elizabeth I playing the lute, c. 1580. Nicholas Hilliard, miniature measuring 48 by 39 mm, or about 2 by 1½ inches. Oil pigments with silver and gold on vellum glued onto cardboard. The descent of ownership would indicate that Hilliard painted the miniature as a commission for the Queen's own first cousin and close friend, Henry Carey, first Lord Hunsdon, and that his granddaughter, Elizabeth, brought it with her to Berkeley Castle, Gloucestershire, when she married Sir Thomas Berkeley. The portrait, recorded at Berkeley Castle in 1796 as "Queen Elizabeth Playing on a Mandoline," still finds its home at the same castle.

This tiny painting is the single most outstanding portrait of the Queen done by Hilliard, painted soon after his return from France; he had gone across the English Channel for yet further study in art. The draftsmanship of the hands and the ruffs at neck and wrist, as well as of the geometrically designed rose in the soundhole of the lute, and of the purfling around the edge of the lute body, among other details, epitomizes Hilliard at the height of his graphic powers. Apart from the oxidation of her dress, there has been some slight flaking. The costume would indicate a date around or soon after 1580, and is closely paralleled in a large-scale oil portrait (but without the lute), also probably by Hilliard. There is no precedent for a portrait of a Tudor monarch playing a musical instrument. Although it may be interpreted as an allegory an the harmony of the body politic—such an interpretation in this instance might seem somewhat forced—it probably does honor Elizabeth's own musical virtuosity. Among other instruments it is recorded that she played both lute and virginals, that small harpsichord without legs. Her musical education alone started at an early age, a typical procedure already established in the earlier Renaissance as part of the general education for most of the upper and middle classes, and as part of the then new thinking in education during that period. Her own father Henry VIII had been an accomplished instrumentalist and composer.

The Queen was accounted not only an excellent player on the virginals but also a creditable lutenist. Technically the knowledge of counterpoint alone that she would have gained from playing on the virginals, Elizabeth could then have easily transferred to the lute. In this case she is playing a regular tenor lute, with the four lower courses doubled but with the top two patently single, and thus not just the first string or chanterelle (as was usual), the so-called singing string. Considering its provenance—that is, as a miniature produced as a private commission for Lord Hunsdon—then it was probably done less as an official or imperial icon and more as an intimate portrait of the Queen playing the lute for her own pleasure or for that of a small circle of her close friends in the privacy of her chambers and away from the cynosure of the Court. (This opinion is not an official one.) Edmund Spenser in his epic poem, *The Faerie Queene*, honors Lord Hunsdon in the eleventh of the seventeen dedicatory sonnets, aptly Spenserian in form. This especial sonnet is technically distinguished as one of the exact half-dozen (these being numbers 5, 7, 8, 11, 15, and 17) which conclude with an alexandrine in a manner analogous to that of the regular Spenserian stanza itself.

(The purely historic data concerning the miniature, its provenience, physical make-up, ownership, etc., are courtesy of Eiler Hansen, Custodian, Berkeley Castle, in his letter to Donald Sidney-Fryer, dated 19 February 1992.)

Bialowieza.
Dedicated to George F. Haas, in memoriam.

Bialowieza: pronounced bee-ALL-off-YEZ-huh.

If Bialowieza Preserve, or National Park, comprising not quite twenty square miles, represents the inner core of the over-all primeval forest, then the outer core, of course, immediately surrounds it, being indistinguishable therefrom, at least superficially.

The park is located in the middle of the larger forest of the same name, comprising roughly 500 square miles. The unique value of the forest's core itself lies in the fact that it is all that is left of the primeval forest that once covered most of the European (sub)continent. The forest and the park owe their preservation only to the fact that, from about the ninth or tenth century A.D. on into the early twentieth, a succession of Polish kings, Lithuanian grand dukes, and Russian tsars as well as grand dukes used the forest as their private hunting reserve, thus protecting it against the intrusions of woodcutters, farmers, and poachers by means of royal and other writ.

Located at the edge of the park itself, the neighboring village of Bialowieza grew up originally around the succession of hunting lodges built to house whatever visiting sovereign or other eminent person would be hunting in the forest. Due to the triple partition of Poland that occurred in the last third of the seventeenth century (1772, 1793, 1795) among Prussia, Austria, and Russia; the last-named held the site from that time until the establishment, in 1918, of the independent republic of Poland at the same time and in the same manner as the republics of Lithuania, Latvia, and Estonia. Thus the last rulers to hunt in the forest were Russian, and the Tsar's old hunting lodge in the village remained in ruins for a long time after World War II. The lodge itself has been restored sometime since 1991.

The park itself is "strictly controlled," that is, strictly protected, and the flora and fauna are allowed to develop live, and perish in a completely natural way without interference. The Polish government recognized the forest as the unique treasure that it is in 1921, and prohibits harvesting, planting, and all motor vehicles in the park itself, although horse-drawn conveyances are permitted. This "biosphere preserve" (recognized as such in 1977 by UNESCO) is a classic mixed forest of the northern temperate zone with a particularly wide range of birds and mammals, including not only some spectacular species of eagles, owls, falcons, and other hawks, especially a herd of the ancient European forest bison, or aurochs (otherwise nearly extinct, but basically similar to the American bison, or buffalo, of the great plains).

While the former status of the forest as an enormous hunting reserve helped to bring it basically intact into the twentieth century, and while its comparative isolation has helped to preserve it further, nevertheless the forest and its wildlife suffered because of the depredations of World War I (1914–1918) and World War II (1939–1945). The last free-roaming bison were killed by poachers in 1918, but new ones were introduced in 1929 from the stock luckily preserved in small private herds elsewhere in Europe, and now, thanks to a successful breeding program, a herd of about 300 members or even more wanders at large in the park and environing forest. It is of especial interest to note that this number was about the size of the herd to which the American bison of the great plains were reduced by the early twentieth century before their later repropagation, and thus down from an over-all population during the nineteenth century that has been estimated at its highest at somewhere around 60,000,000 members.

According to those who have studied t, and watch over it, Bialowieza retains the appearance that it had about two thousand years ago, that is, circa the start of the Roman Empire (27 B.C.–A.D. 395). According to Charles T. Powers, "The most striking feature of the forest, on first glimpse, is not the living trees but the dead ones. They lie where they have fallen, grown thickly over with lichen and moss, liverwort and fern, and sink slowly back into the earth. It is an arboreal version of an elephant's graveyard, suggesting the passage of massive living things. It is a place where a respectful hush seems appropriate. But this is not a dying forest or an ecological disaster, so common in much of Poland and the rest of Eastern Europe, where forty years of Communist heavy industry and its noxious fumes have stunted and maimed millions of acres of forested land. Instead, Bialowieza [. . .], with its striking view of fallen trees—among hundreds of thousands of living ones—represents an ecological success story."

Some specimens of the oldest trees have grown to an extraordinary size, whether evergreen or deciduous: pines and spruce trees, about 250 years old or older, that tower up to 160 feet; enormous lindens or basswood trees; no less enormous ash trees; ancient oaks, 500 years old, that tower up to 140 feet; rare and even taller elms that have been spared the ravages of Dutch elm disease because of their isolation. There are very few oaks and elms of such size remaining anywhere else on the entire planet. In the mid-1980s the Scientific Council of the park originated a plan to quadruple the size just of the park itself and then to double the area under strict protection. However, overwhelmed with many other and more pressing ecological problems, the Polish government has not yet adopted the plan. Nevertheless, it remains a wonderful prospect, and one can at least hope that it will be implemented at some future time. All in all, the preservation of the Bialowieza forest is nothing less than a miracle of survival. The United Nations included it as the only such natural site on its World Heritage Register in 1979.

(Much of the information in this note has been taken not only from the standard reference works and encyclopaedias but particularly from the article "A Tree Grows in Bialowieza," by Charles T. Powers, beginning on the front page of the *Los Angeles Times* for Saturday, 16 November 1991. The quotation appearing towards the end of this note is taken from the article in question.)

"Farewell to Zita."

This announcement, in German, appeared as the headline, printed against a background of imperial Hapsburg yellow, on the issue for Saturday, 1 April 1989, of Austria's largest-circulation daily, the *Neue Kronen Zeitung*, on the day of her funeral, which climaxed a week of ceremonies honoring Zita. Born Zita von Bourbon-Parma, she outlived her husband Karl (or Charles) I (1887–1922) by 67 years, and her funeral was the biggest one in Austria since that of Franz Josef I in 1916 during the waning years of the Hapsburg Empire. Although permitted to visit Austria in 1982, she died in exile like her husband; she was 96 when she passed away on 14 March 1989 in Switzerland (in a Roman Catholic home for the elderly). After the reign (1848–1916) of Franz Josef I (1830–1916), one of the longest in recorded history—and thus even longer than those of Elizabeth I of England (1533–1603), reigned 1558–1603, and of Queen Victoria of Great Britain (1819–1901), reigned 1837–1901—Karl and Zita experienced one of the shortest rules of the Hapsburg dynasty. The last Austrian emperor formally signed the Hapsburg abdication on 11 November 1918. Stripped of power and property, he and the empress together with their large family were driven into exile in March 1919, and went to live in Switzerland in relative poverty.

After her husband's death in 1922 on the island of Madeira, Zita always refused formally to abdicate in her own turn. When they went into exile, she was denounced as a spy for her role in a plot to end World War I. Despite Austria's official status as a republic since 1918, the Austrians found a way to contravene their own laws as a republic in order to give her a suitable memorial service. Her funeral, a four-hour ceremony, took place in the towering and magnificent Gothic pile of Stephansdom, or St. Stephen's Cathedral, thus at or near the very center of Vienna's old or inner city, or Innere Stadt Wien. At the end of the two-hour Requiem High Mass, the Austrian citizens assembled therein sang (on what will probably remain the very last occasion) the old imperial Hapsburg hymn, which was replaced with a republican anthem in 1918. Zita thus received a traditional funeral and burial with all the pomp and pageantry of the former Hapsburg monarchy that had reigned for seven centuries. In essence, Zita's own person had become all that was left of the old Hapsburg Empire, and in honoring her the Austrians were also honoring their own history and hence themselves. Vienna's direct imperial associations go back not only to the Holy Roman Empire and Charlemagne as Emperor of the West but also to various illustrious Roman emperors, especially Marcus Aurelius.

(Much of the information concerning Zita von Hapsburg has been taken verbatim from the article *Austria Buries Its Last Empress*, by Roland Prinz, as carried on Sunday, 2 April 1989, by certain newspapers in the U.S. subscribing to the Associated Press Service.)

From the French of José-Maria de Heredia.
Unriming translations from Les Trophées:
Sonnets on Oblivion, Pan, and Priapus.
Dedicated to Stanley D. McNail in gratitude and in memoriam.

    This group of translations is intended as a written memorial in the now chiefly outmoded sense of a "monument" or "tombeau"—but primarily as a tribute to Stanley both as poet and as poetry editor, and more specifically as a male, given the choice of selections concerning Pan and Priapus. It is also an expression of profound affection for Stanley as a close friend for many years, from the late 1960s to the mid-1990s—as well as an expression of no less profound gratitude to him for his work as a poet and on behalf of poetry as an editor of one or more poetry magazines for almost forty years.
    Stanley D. McNail (1918–1995), in addition to being a poet and editor-publisher of divers periodicals, was also a friend and mentor to many poets and other writers for many years in the San Francisco Bay Area. In 1958 he started publishing the Galley Sail Review, his principal magazine (which was devoted to poetry of all schools and styles), and the very last issue that he managed to bring out appeared in the autumn of 1995. Born in Centralia, Illinois, in 1918 (thus the year marking the end of the Great War), he was largely self-educated apart from the usual compulsory attendance in grammar school and then in high school. He worked at the Library of Congress, Washington, D.C., before moving to the Bay Area during the 1950s. During 1968–1983 he worked at a desk job for the Greyhound Bus Lines in San Francisco, from which he retired, moving to Berkeley shortly after that. For a number of years he also served as the poetry editor for the San Francisco Bay Guardian. Among other affiliations he belonged to many fraternal organizations. He had just turned 77 on Wednesday, 14 March 1995, before his death on Tuesday, 4 April, of heart failure. According to the obituary written by Stephen Schwartz and published in the San Francisco Chronicle for Monday, 10 April, "He was described by friends and colleagues as a kind man who stood for intellectual integrity even when his opinions and tastes were unpopular." Even many of Stanley's best friends did not realize the full scope of his activities until after his death. He played a vital role in the poetry renaissance that began in the Bay Area during the 1950s, and was one of the very first persons to sponsor poetry readings in San Francisco and elsewhere, paying the poets himself out of his own pocket. His own specialty as a poet was the macabre and fantastic, which he cultivated very much in his own original fashion, but he was not restricted solely to such themes, and also excelled at so-called regional poetry, in his case descriptive of his own Midwest native area. When Arkham House published his first macabre col-

lection *Something Breathing* in 1965, Stanley came to the attention of both a national and an international audience. Over-all Stanley published some half a dozen books of his own, largely collections of his own poetry. In addition he was quite an effective reader and reciter of poetry. What he accomplished as a poet himself, as well as on behalf of other poets through the *Galley Sail Review* and the series of poetry readings that he sponsored, was chiefly motivated by his deep and abiding love of poetry. As a matter of historical record and personal pride on Stanley's behalf, it should be noted that he published the works of many poets for the first time who later went on to distinguished careers as writers and authors. Within his own particular genres, Stanley ranks as some kind of great figure and poetry editor. Of Scotch-Irish descent he remained faithful all his life, in his own creativity, to his Keltic inheritance of the marvellous and uncanny.

(This overview of Stanley D. McNail and his life and achievements draws upon the obituary appearing in the *Chronicle* soon after his death for much of its biographical data.)

José-Maria de Heredia (1842–1905) is, of course, one of the great French poets of the latter 1800s, the second generation of French Romantic poets. He ranks second only to Leconte de Lisle himself as the chief Parnassian. (It is easy to forget that Baudelaire himself began his career as one of the Parnassian school of poets.) Born at or near Santiago de Cuba, Heredia is often confused with the famous Cuban poet of the exact same name (1803–1839), who was his cousin. The Francophone Heredia began writing poetry in the late 1850s, and having it published in the early 1860s. During much of his life his work appeared for the most part in anthologies, periodicals, etc., but he gathered the best of his poetry during 1892 into his only collection *Les Trophées*, which appeared in book form during 1893. On the strength and success of this remarkable collection, this one volume, he was elected to the French Academy during 1894.

Resembling a little *La Légende des siècles*, that curious epic by Victor Hugo, *Les Trophées* has five sections, revealing an extraordinary scope, variety, imagination, and technical perfection in the 117 sonnets gathered therein: *La Grèce et la Sicile, Rome et les Barbares, Le Moyen Age et la Renaissance, L'Orient et les Tropiques,* and *La Nature et le Rêve. L'Oubli*, or *Oblivion*, is the opening sonnet, and *Sur un Marbre brisé*, or *On a Ruined Bust of Marble*, the closing one. The Pan poems are all included in the first section, the Priapus poems in the second. In the four Pan poems chosen for translation, the Cloven Foot (or Goat-Footed God) whether visible or invisible dominates the given sonnet. In the other three Pan poems not included here, Pan shares the poetic focus with other divinities (as in *Nymphée* and *Le Bain des nymphes*), or is only mentioned, not being actually or potentially present (as in *A Sextius*, included in *Rome et les Barbares*, wherein he is adumbrated as Faunus, his Roman equivalent). Albeit not intended, of course, by the original poet himself to have such an effect, our selection of poems from *Les Trophées* does in fact make a strangely coherent statement.

N.B. In making our translations, especially in our use of the alexandrine as the original meter of the sonnets, we have tried to be as faithful as possible to the original poems, observing the original peculiarities of syntax, grammar, rhetoric, capitalization, and punctuation. However, in a few places we were forced to drop some adjectives, to change the rhetoric in order to preserve the original statement, and to employ a different but similar style of punctuation. To keep the translations as accurate as possible, we decided at the outset to do without rime completely, but therefore, to balance the loss of such a highly musical device, we decided further to make the resultant English as musical and sonorous as the linguistic circumstances would allow, and beyond that need or condition, to naturalize the translations into English-language poems.

However, having stated what is our own translator's credo as a poet, we must also bear witness to *the dichotomy* that may sometimes exist or come about when translating *between accuracy and fidelity*, which are certainly not the same thing in such a context as this. We refer, of course, to the sometimes opposing demands of accuracy on the one hand (according to the *sense* of the original poetic statements) and those of fidelity on the other (according to the *spirit* of the original lines in French). For example, our most salient one, the very last line of "Oblivion" went through more than a hundred versions before we settled on the line as it now stands in English. A completely literal translation, which would not be at all adequate or acceptable, would read: "The Sea who laments to herself [*or*: by herself] while weeping for the Sirens [i.e., unstated, because of their absence]." Although such a statement might be perfect in French, it fails to capture the full nuance of atmosphere and meaning in English.

(Much of the mythological and historical information contained in the following notes is taken, but only in part, from the only and very first critical edition of *Les Trophées* "presented, established, and annotated" by Anny Detalle, professor at the University of Avignon, and published by Gallimard in 1981.)

Oblivion. Whether in Greece, Sicily, or Italy there are any number of eminent promontories crowned by temples. However Heredia may have had in mind certain locales that he had visited when travelling in Italy, especially the coast extending south of Naples to Capo Palinuro, and within that section, from Amalfi to Paestum. This is an area where land and water are locked in relentless combat, and where Homer in *The Odyssey* locates the haunt of the Sirens, those bizarre musical Harpies. Whereas the Earth and the Sea still remember them, Man has forgotten the older divine presences. When renewing the acanthus every spring, the Earth somehow does the same for the old Corinthian column with its acanthus-inspired capital, lying in a ruined state next to the plant itself with its dark-green leaves. Even more maternal, the Sea laments the absence of the Sirens born of her, but most of all she misses their beautiful singing, their wild and fantastic song, which Man can hear no longer, believing no more in the Sirens themselves. Out of the death of the ancient gods, the death of the ancient magic now largely forgotten by the present inhabitants of the Italian coast defined above, Heredia manages to call forth a feeling of tremendous pathos. This poem sets the tone for the entire volume of such "trophies" as these from earlier civilizations, which mementos therefore become symbolic of those preceding cultures.

Pan. This rustic deity, the original Satyr, and variously depicted in ancient sculpture, painting, and literature, is not only the god of fields, forests, wild animals, flocks, and herdsmen but also of fertility, lust, estrus, and rut. Caprine, he appears with the legs, (short) tail, (pointed) ears, and horns of a buck, or male goat. Equine, he appears with the legs, (long) tail, (pointed) ears, and (usually erect) phallus of a stallion (proportionately reduced to suit a being the size of a man). As part goat he usually has a hairy body, especially the lower half. As part horse he usually has a snub nose. Beyond these variable attributes he usually has a full beard and moustache, long hair on his head, and when part caprine, cloven hooves. Extremely alert when required, sinewy, and strong, and (it would seem) capable of assuming a variety of shapes and appearances, he is depicted in ancient Graeco-Roman literature as indulging himself sexually with gods, goddesses, demigods, demigoddesses, and humans and animals of both genders, or by himself.

The son of Hermes by some nymph, he is the inventor of the syrinx, or the musical pipes made out of reeds. Originally from Arcadia, and the special patron of herds and herdsmen, he has an obviously hybrid nature. However, this double nature, such as it is, does not incline him to spleen and violence like the Centaur, or to surpassing himself like both the Centaur and the human male, but rather to abandoning himself to a joyous lechery completely beastlike. The laugh with which Pan usually accompanies his misdeeds—abducting nymphs or youths, appearing suddenly without warning and causing instant and overwhelming fear (the panic named after him), etc.—is the clue to his character as mischief-maker, unsuited to any remorse. However, despite his dark side, and his tendency to lighthearted mockery, he is overall a highly beneficent and utterly necessary god.

The Goatherd. In this poem and in the one following, we find ourselves in Pan's native area. Arcadia, or present-day Arkadhia, is the celebrated pastoral region in southern Greece, located in the central Peloponnesus. Menalos (Greek), or Menalus (Latin), is a mountain situated in the middle of Arcadia. Hecate is, of course, the same as Artemis or Diana, the goddess of the woods and the hunt, but as Hecate she appears in her aspect as a divinity of the moon, the nocturnal earth, and the underworld. Later she becomes the dark goddess of magic as well, no less than Titania (a further development of the name Diana), the queen of the fairies, and the wife of Oberon as the king of the fairies, in mediaeval folklore.

The goatherd and his friend speak low so as not to draw the attention of any malefic presences that might be abroad in the night. Also, by speaking softly, they will not disturb Pan, who may then more likely emerge from his cave, that is, his lair. The familiar spirit of the heights, the most poetic of all the sylvan gods, we see here in his most poetic aspect. If the two men remain quiet, Pan as the inventor of the syrinx will give them a little evening concert. Finally the goat-footed god does come out of his lair, and leads the herd of goats in a whimsical and capering dance.

The Shepherds. Even more than the preceding sonnets, in which he makes an actual appearance, this poem invokes the Cloven Foot in an emotionally powerful way, because he still is present, even though not visible. Kyllenios, or Cyllenius, is one of the highest peaks in the Peloponnesus. According to the commonly received legend, this is the haunt of Hermes, or Mercury, but Heredia also makes it the haunt of Pan as the son of Hermes. With his father (not at all surprisingly) he shares not only the same general area but also a number of characteristics and attributes, including his cunning, as well as his mockery. It is notable that Heredia constantly employs the word *l'antre* in regard to the gods who are half animal such as Pan. Although the word usually means cave, originally it was reserved to indicate a cave that an animal uses as his haunt or home, a place where he sleeps, eats, makes love, is idle, etc. It was the regular policy to make offerings to the gods, but particularly the rustic ones, in products deriving from farming and from domestic animals, that is, in the form of natural products. Heredia lovingly invokes in the last six lines of this poem the carefully cultivated piety of the individual who genuinely believed in the animistic or magical presences existing everywhere in the ancient Mediterranean world.

Hortorum Deus. The series of the five poems under this title, perhaps more than any others in the entire collection, summons forth an emotion of cultivated piety, as well as a true religious feeling, both of which might seem somewhat grotesque under the circumstances, given the nature and peculiar attributes of Priapos, or Priapus. Although Pan in his aspect as an equine Satyr may share certain obvious attributes with Priapus, mainly a large phallus, yet these two gods remain distinct. Specifically in Graeco-Roman mythology Priapus is the god of procreation, the god who personifies the male performance of generation. According to the most commonly accepted legends, as the god of Lampsachus, the city in Asia Minor, he is the son of Dionysus and Aphrodite, or of Aphrodite and Zeus. Priapus was born deformed, because of the jealousy of Hera, or Juno, who—fearing that this child would bring together in himself too many superior qualities, that is, beauty and power—employed sorcery against him while in the womb in order to prevent this. The potential beauty became a generalized cuteness, the power was transmogrified into his phallus and an over-all aura of protectiveness. The shape that the ancient sculptors usually gave him show Priapus as a bearded and grinning man, often with a Phrygian cap, always with an enormous phallus lifting straight up from his groin to the level of his shoulders. The sculptors generally painted the member itself a vermilion, or bright-red. Obviously they did not intend that people should regard such an enormous phallus as practicable so much as emblematic or symbolic! Instead of playing some leading role among the twelve Olympians, as he might have done but for the machinations of Hera, Priapus as the symbol of fruitfulness became not only the generalized god of gardens but specifically the protector of kitchen gardens, as well as orchards, vineyards, etc. However, his very first vocation was a comparatively heroic one, that is, as a battering-ram sculptured out of wood, placed on the prow of a ship, and used to damage or penetrate enemy vessels. As Anny Detalle notes, fully aware of the humorous aspects of such a subject, "The Antiquity celebrated by Heredia is not always [. . .] a tragic, heroic, or delicately erotic. A certain roguishness, a little bit naughty, has motivated him here to dedicate five poems to a god who certainly was very much honored in the Latin pantheon, but who [by modern times], because of his phallic appearance, challenges [conventional] propriety."

I. After a long career as a figurehead and battering-ram all in one on some galley, the Priapus would be "decommissioned" from active duty (as it were) and would be retired to serve henceforth as the guardian of some kitchen garden and orchard, the importance of which in the lives of a given family of farmers or herdsmen cannot be stressed enough. Aegina, a large island located opposite Piraeus, the port of Athens, early distinguished itself by its intense maritime activity, and was the point of departure for the Cyclades. The allusion to the origin, or source, of Priapus designates not the geographic site but the first use of such a figure: as a battering-ram placed on the beak or prow of a galley, and made out of the trunk of some fig-tree, a wood especially hard, but also chosen to include a large branch appropriate for serving as the phallus. In general Phoenician, Greek, and Roman galleys had metallic rams, but the Priapus derived from a fig-tree trunk fulfilled the same role just as well.

The use of a billhook, that ancient implement for cutting and pruning trees and bushes with a hook-shaped blade, in order to shape the figure with its peculiar projection, resulted at best in a rather crude sculpture, the roughness of which did not diminish its efficacy. As a battering-ram it was actually the sculpted phallus itself that did duty as the instrument of aggression and penetration. As a guardian of crops the former figurehead served as a scarecrow. It was only natural that the general aura of protectiveness afforded by such a projection came to include the added association of good luck.

II. In addition to the phallus on the retired figurehead and battering-ram, now serving to frighten birds away, as well as to warn human thieves, the farmer has made yet another large phallus out of another suitable piece of wood. This emblem he has fixed in the ground to do duty as a further warning, not to mention its potential use as a handy club that the farmer can dislodge in a hurry with relative ease, and then wield as quite an effective weapon. However crudely sculptured, whether the Priapus or his emblem, the carvings were fairly specific, and prominently featured the sheath or foreskin clearly delineated (and analogous to the sheath or prepuce on male quadrupeds). The farmer and his family would adorn the Priapus and his emblem with flowers, grains, and so forth, usually woven into garlands, and then placed on the sculptured foreskin as a convenient protuberance.

III. Here in this poem Heredia takes religion, at least in the form of tutelary deities, out of the abstract, and returns it to the everyday realm of concrete reality. He does this by showing that the Priapus as embodied in the heavy club which is his emblem has real clout, real weight, when picked up and used to threaten or to strike a human thief, especially when wielded by a determined and vigorous old man guarding his family's kitchen garden, orchard, and vineyard, their immediate source of food. It is a metaphorical and physical commonplace that tools are extensions of the human beings using them. Perceived in this particular sense, the spectacle of this farmer, who wields with both hands and with full force a giant club carved into the resemblance of an oversized phallus, is not without its broader physiological, philosophical, psychological, and certainly humorous implications.

IV. Whereas in the preceding sonnet the Priapus is eager to get rid of those "damn kids"—in this one he welcomes graciously some other newcomer who seems to be a close friend of the old farmer and his family. The wattle, or screen, mentioned in line seven, that was used in making cheese, was commonly made of the tough pliable twigs from the osier tree or shrub, any of a variety of willows employed for basketry, furniture, and so forth. This poem records the garden god at the height of the family's modest prosperity and, concomitantly, of course, at that of his own success, as he regularly receives from the farmer and his family the offerings of each season in turn.

V. The old peasant has probably died because his family itself has apparently long since moved away, abandoning their former home, kitchen garden, and ancient Priapic guardian, but taking with them, of course, their household gods. Twenty years, or winters, have passed since then, and the poor Priapus has little to do except to observe the passage of time itself whether on a daily or a seasonal basis. The ancient Soracte, today Soratte, that he can still observe, is a mountain of limestone located some 37 kilometers north of Rome and east of the Tiber River. Its northern location predisposes it therefore to be covered with snow, that is, its upper half, from the time of the first real cold. For the inhabitants of Latium it is the sign that winter has arrived. No longer does the garden god receive the offerings that once came his way so steadily and plentifully. Furthermore, he is literally falling to pieces: his paint is chipping off, his wood is splitting, and—ultimate ignominy!—he fears the worms that are weakening and consuming his very substance. What he would not give to be one of the merest and most humble of the household gods who have departed with the family to which they belong. The poet thus adroitly diverts our attention from the sad plight of this Priapus to the ongoing existence of the certain specialized Lar who receives from the sons on their virile day their childhood's amulet. In ancient Rome the virile day was the day when the son turned seventeen, and exchanged his *bulla* (here his amulet of lead that he had worn at his neck since the day of his birth) for the toga of manhood that his father handed over to him personally. The family does indeed live on but somewhere else, and the forsaken Priapus can only look forward to his own dissolution.

On a Ruined Bust of Marble. It is important to note that the very first name of a god stated, among others, is that of Pan, even though his father Hermes in a hierarchical sense is a more significant one. Because Pan and the other divinities are divinizations of nature pastoral and otherwise, then in a sense neither Pan nor any of these other gods can really die so long as the nature giving them birth survives herself. All the rustic gods whether Greek or Latin had the attribution of marking off the boundaries of gardens, fields, etc., but in particular Hermes Criophorus among the Greeks and Terminus among the Romans enjoyed this distinction. All these names—Pan, Faunus, Hermes, and Sylvanus—recapitulate the principal deities in the Greek and Latin pantheons who are associated with the nature typical of the Greek and Roman countrysides, respectively. As Anny Detalle herself aptly summarizes it, "This poem [. . .] admirably closes *Les Trophées* by gathering together again the essential themes: the contrast of epochs, and the death of the gods, but at the same time the illusion of an art rendered eternal by the variableness of the [sun's] light." Whereas "Oblivion" opens *Les Trophées* on a note of tremendous pathos, "On a Ruined Bust of Marble" brings it to a finish on a note of good fortune and good cheer. The illusion alone of the god's face coming to life is indeed a rare and perfect piece of magic.

Postscriptum. As an appendix to the preceding notes concerning Pan and Priapus we should add the following facts and considerations for the reader's contemplation. In the long struggle for dominance between Christianity and the old religion or the old religions long since established in the Roman Empire, the fourth century A.D. played the most strategic role. The old religions embodied the worship of the twelve Olympians and their associated pantheons, together with the other deities and cults not related to them, but enjoying widespread popularity, such as the Persian divinity Mithras, or the Egyptian divinities Isis and Osiris. Not only was it the fourth century A.D. that played the most strategic role in this contest among religions, more specifically it was the period between the triumph of Constantine the Great in 324 as the sole emperor of an undivided empire and the death of Theodosius the Great in 395 after he had just finished uniting once more the western half of the empire to the eastern one for the second and last occasion. By the time of the latter's death the eventual triumph of the Roman Catholic Church was assured in the following centuries. This triumph was first prefigured by Constantine's victory over Maxentius at the battle of the Milvian Bridge in 312, only six years after the army at York had proclaimed Constantine an Augustus following the death of his father Constantius I there in the same year. That religion in general was very much a feature of urban life, with the greatest temples and greatest public festivals, facilitated to the highest degree the spread of Christianity and the Church's eventual triumph. Following his victory at the Milvian Bridge, Constantine secured the "Peace of the Church" through the Edict of Milan in 313, by which the Christian religion became legal throughout the empire. However, the old religions did not give up the ghost that easily and indeed would survive for a long time still to come, and in the countryside above all, of course.

After he had emerged as the sole emperor in 324, and after he had established the foundation of Constantinople as the new capital in the same year, Constantine himself exemplified an admirable tolerance for the most part. He closed or destroyed very few temples of the old religion, even though he favored the Church. Nevertheless, he did strip the old temples almost everywhere of their portable wealth and their property, which he then gave to the Church. By the time that he deprived the temples of their incredible treasures and works of art, the wealth that had accumulated in these fanes after centuries of donations both public and private had become immense. We can imagine the prodigies of art in precious metals and minerals that this dispossession must have destroyed. However, at least a few priests attached still to the old temples would have managed clandestinely to bury or to hide otherwise at least some of the now forbidden treasures.

The major pagan revival that Julian the Apostate instituted in the course of his tragically brief reign (361–363) lasted at least from c. 360 to c. 400 despite the Church's official position and, following him, the largely Christian emperors, on almost all of whom the remarkable Ambrose, Bishop of Milan, exercised an extraordinary influence, and of course, in the Church's favor. Gratian in particular proved extremely hostile to the old religion, and in the course of his reign (375–383) he set about to sweep away what was left of Julian's pagan revival. Among other "impious" acts he commanded the endowments of the Vestal Virgins and other priestly colleges to be confiscated, and the Altar of Victory, that supreme symbol, to be removed from its honored place in the Senate House at Rome. This greatly disturbed and angered at least the many influential non-Christians of the upper classes who still remained. Although Gratian struck at the political heart of the old religion, paganism survived both in humble shrines and in public places.

Notably tolerant himself, Theodosius the Great (379–395) as both a Christian and a Catholic also underwent the almost irresistible influence of Bishop Ambrose. Under his influence this emperor issued two radical orders, one right after the other, that effectively signaled the official change in status of the old state religion from what it had enjoyed only a century before. In 391 the first order closed all the temples, and made all sacrifices illegal, whether public or private. Large fines were imposed on officials who did not enforce the law. In 392 the second order prohibited the ancient worship of the household gods, a form of worship that had existed for centuries in homes everywhere throughout the ancient Mediterranean world. For the Romans these took the form of the Lares, the Penates, and Vesta, a major divinity. No families were allowed to worship them in their own home with the traditional garlands, lamps, and incense. Any property in which the shrines of the household gods were discovered was to be confiscated. Fortunately, despite this extremism, it seems that the actual enforcement of both orders proved ineffective. We should note, however, that these two commands made pagan religious practices illegal, but not the expression of pagan beliefs themselves.

Theodosius intended these extreme orders, that effectively outlawed all pagan worship, to apply to all parts of the empire, of course. However, for the final time the western half rebelled, and under Arbogastes, Eugenius, and Flavianus as a kind of triumvirate the last pagan revival took place. This involved the repair and reconstruction of temples large and small, their re-endowment and reopening, the restoration of the Altar of Victory to the Senate House, as well as the restoration of the great public festivals. This pagan régime (392–394) came to an end when Theodosius returned from Constantinople, invaded Italy, defeated his rivals, and reunited the empire. Eugenius was captured and executed, and Arbogastes and Flavianus committed suicide.

It is curious to note that the gladiatorial games and other entertainments of a like nature that took place in the amphitheatres, and that had come to be such a feature of pre-Christian Rome, continued under the Christian emperors of the fourth century. It was not until the reign of Honorius (395–423) as Emperor of the West that such games were at last officially banned, ceasing to exist in the city of Rome itself above all. Despite Theodosius's official writs and the eventual triumph of Christianity, the last people to be converted to the new state religion were the pagans, literally the people residing in the *pagus*, or village, in the countryside, as the word *pagan* itself indicates. For that reason the intensely personal worship of the rustic gods, such as Pan and certainly Priapus, endured much longer than that of such public and official divinities as the twelve Olympians. However sad the plight of our forsaken Priapus might seem as delineated in the last sonnet of "*Hortorum Deus*," a considerable period would elapse before it became symbolic of universal abandonment.

Return of the Conquistadors.
Unriming translation from the French of Paul Valéry. Dedicated to José-Maria de Heredia, 7 January 1891.

This piece ideally exemplifies the art that, while clear and accessible, conceals much not revealed at once on the surface, or the overt statement, of the poem. Beyond its creation perfectly conceived in the style of Heredia's famous type of Parnassian sonnet, the charm or "conceit" of this poem lies in Valéry's adroit evocation of Heredia, thus in his role as the conqueror of *poetic* gold, as a latter-day and very much a long-delayed successor to the Spanish conquistadors of the last great century marking the Renaissance, the 1500s.

It is a fact that Heredia, born on a sugar plantation not far from Santiago de Cuba, descended (collaterally rather than directly) from one of the most celebrated of the conquistadors of the 1500s, Don Pedro de Heredia, truly an epic or heroic figure, and quite an awesome warrior. Don Pedro had many astonishing adventures, became governor of New Spain, and in 1532 founded Cartagena de las Indias (the treasure-gathering city for the Spanish Empire, from which such cargo went to Spain) on the Caribbean coast of present-day Colombia on the northwest.

"Vers Palas triomphal:" Towards Palas in triumph. Palas, unidentifiable as such. Can Valéry mean Palos, as in Palos de la Frontera or some other place on the southwestern (Atlantic) coast of Spain, such as the conquistadors returning to their homeland aboard ship from the New World would have observed at sea from afar?

Apart from its own intrinsic merit, this particular sonnet provides an excellent example of the continuity characteristic of the older French literature. Before he became one of the great French poets and philosophers of the twentieth century, and certainly somewhat different from his younger self, Paul Valéry (1871–1945) as a young poet came under the marked and surely beneficial influence of Heredia (1842–1905), as did many other poets of the period.

In one aspect, in one particular aspect, Heredia remains quite modern, his general insistence in his own published work (meaning here his poetic output) on brevity or conciseness of statement, but invariably coupled with perfect clarity and grace. In this aspect, he had much to teach his fellow poets, his contemporaries, including Valéry.

The Cuban-born Heredia received general recognition as a great poet in the latter part of his life, second only to Leconte de Lisle (1818–1894), his poetic master or father. Although Valéry created and sent this tribute on 7 January 1891 to Heredia, it did not achieve publication until 1975. Undoubtedly it represents as fine a piece of homage as was ever paid to the elder poet.

Renewal.
(20–21 October 1992.)

This poem reflects not only the first rain to fall after the typically long drouth of summertime, that of 1992, but as it turned out, the first rain of a more abundant wet season after seven years of drought as officially declared by the State of California. The first leaves of that autumn had already fallen (in the middle of October) before the first and very light rain arrived, as recorded here.

Epiphany.
Dedicated to John Law by way of tribute to him for the Burning Man.

The equation of Christ with Pan or Faunus as a shepherd dates back at least to Christian antiquity. However, the equation of Christ with Pan or Faunus in his guise as the *Satyr*, attended by nymphs, is a modern innovation.

A Vision of a Castle Deep in Averonne.
Dedicated to Ronald and Michelle Hilger.

This narrative is founded on a legend of the Auvergne concerning the Citadelle de Merle.

The Citadelle de Merle is a vast and ruined, as well as partly verdure-clad, mediaeval stronghold located in southwestern Auvergne. The name Averonne is a variant of Averoigne (but pronounced AV-er-ONN), the mythicized or mythologized province of Auvergne utilized by the California poet and fictioneer Clark Ashton Smith (1893–1961) as a background for a series of highly imaginative stories mostly depicting the life and folklore of the Middle Ages in France. As a *citadelle* (fortress-town), or a *cité féodale* (feudal city), the Citadelle de Merle was constructed largely during the 1200s and 1300s, and thus in use as a residence from the 1200s on through most of the 1500s by a number of seigneurial families, often all at the same time.

More or less equidistant between Tulle and Aurillac, the citadel, or little city, overhangs the deep gorge of the Maronne river, part of the Garonne river system in the southwest of France. The fortress, no longer inhabited but still notable for its many towers, was as far east as the English (that is, the Anglo-Norman aristocracy with their armies and levies) pushed in this part of the Auvergne. Otherwise considered impregnable, it was captured by them and later by others only or primarily through treason. It thus escaped, unscathed, the depredations of the Albigensian Crusade led by Simon de Montfort l'Amaury, but not those of the religious wars during the late 1500s. Somewhat remote, the place is known locally as *les Tours de Merle*.

(Historical data concerning the fortress are for the most part courtesy of Paul Toffaletti, Grass Valley, California.)

Some Further Fragments from Atlantis.
Dedicated to Don Herron.
Translated from the Atlantean of Prince Atlantarion,
through the French of Michel de Labretagne.

Pharanos Descending. Mount Atlantis, the Acropolis that dominated the very center of Atlantis the City, the capital of the Empire of Atlantis—recorded here at "some three thousand feet high"—is reported elsewhere as at "fifteen hundred imperial feet." Noting the discrepancy, Dr. Ibid M. Andor has insightfully suggested that the use of *imperial feet* in this last instance is intended apparently to double the value, that is, from fifteen hundred to some three thousand.

My Mind to Me an Empire Is. In the surviving works of Athallarion, that is, through the French of Labretagne, as reconstituted by Dr. Andor, this almost completed poem nevertheless remains a fragment, but lacking only a stanza of three lines. Without adding or inventing the missing stanza, Prince Atlantarion as one of Athallarion's former pupils has dutifully and quite successfully pulled this "little song" together, and completed it in a technical or formal sense. The similarity of Athallarion's own opening line, etc., to the title and chief line in the celebrated poem by Sir Edward Dyer (where it recurs a number of times as a highly lyrical repetition) has prompted the quotation therefrom. Athallarion's poem itself has become best known in Atlantarion's recension.

Likewise My Mind to Me a Cosmos Is. Atlantarion created this particular "little song" under the obvious influence of the preceding one by Athallarion, and after he had formally completed the latter. Since there was no true silk until its invention (quite a bit later) by the Chinese, the term *silk* (or *la soie*), as used by Labretagne in line 6, can only mean a (light, strong, and shiny) silk-like fabric. The asphodels mentioned in line 7 may refer either to the daffodil of the early English and French poets, or to the narcissus of the Greek poets, both flowers otherwise belonging to the same genus. The hydromel mentioned in the same line does not so much refer to the pre-fermented liquor of the same name (but called *mead* after fermentation) as it does to any generic honey-water, or sugar-water for that matter, such as that utilized by modern bird-fanciers to attract and feed hummingbirds.

Re-ascension. It needs to be mentioned, as well as emphasized, in this context that Pharanos like many educated Atlanteans had formally studied in his youth both engineering and architecture. In his case he had originally planned on becoming a professional architect, but finally decided to become an astronomer, or astronologer, perceiving the sidereal cosmos itself as the ultimate piece of architecture or architectonics.

Pharanos at Sunset. Atlantarion created this picture or portrait of Pharanos as the result of observing the sunset with him on many occasions. However, what prompted the poem's immediate creation was the very rare instance of a sunset and a sunburst happening at one and the same time

Oneiromancy. Not only Pharanos but also Atlantarion, along with many other Atlanteans, found themselves haunted by the very selfsame dream described in this poem, that is, before the Great Cataclysm, but never again afterwards, oddly enough.

At the Outhanox. The Outhanox (pronounced OO-thuh-nox), the Great Citadel of Poseidonis, was constructed upon, or directly out of, the living rock making up the great stone cliffs, or palisades, that spread out like a great terrace at the southern base of the central and highest of the three ranges that ran along an east-west axis, and that constituted the Archprincedom of Poseidonis, the mountain-heartland or inner core of the Archkingdom itself. Xonorr (pronounced k'zoh-NORR), capital of Poseidonis, lay a little to the north of the Outhanox, and the Great Citadel itself looked out over the verdant upper reaches of the Great Vale of Atlantis to the south. However, following the Great Cataclysm, the fortress then looked out over the roiling expanse of the Ocean Sea, now lapping at the foot of the very palisades themselves.

Beauty.
Translated from the French of Charles Pierre Baudelaire.

Baudelaire (1821–1867) ended his career grouped with the Parnassian school of (French) poets, dominated by Leconte de Lisle, and shared many of the same or similar poetic ideals, a fact easy to forget in the aftermath of his near universal recognition as one of the greatest French poets of all times. During the year, 1866, before that of his death, Baudelaire made his appearance with sixteen poems in the very first anthology, *Le Parnasse-contemporain*, representing the Parnassian group. These poets embodied the second general "wave" of French Romantic authors, taking their cue from the dispassionate manner of Théophile Gautier with his own strategic volume of poems, *Emaux et Camées*. Baudelaire in his renowned sonnet, *La Beauté*, formulates perfectly the austere and uncompromising attitude in regard to Beauty held by these poets: in the strict sense laid out by Plato and Plotinus.

Songs and Sonnets Atlantean

The Third Series

DEDICATED
to my great and good friend
JESSE F. KNIGHT,
brother and colleague in poetics:
Dedicated as well,
through the three series over-all,
to the sustaining presence
of EDMUND SPENSER and *The Faerie Queene*.
the Spenserian stanza, the Spenserian sonnet,
and the posthumous collaboration
involved in the traditionalist innovation
of the Spenserian stanza-sonnet.

CREDITS

For permission to reproduce poems first appearing in their pages, the author would like to thank *The Cimmerian, The Clark Ashton Smith Reader, L'Hebdomadaire cultural de Chalabre, The Klarkash-Tonian, The Klarkash-Tonophile, The Lanthorne of Diogenes, La Revue des Trois Mondes, La Revue du massif central, La Revue littéraire d'Atlantide en exil, La Revue littéraire d'Averonne,* and *Le Zigzag de Carcassonne.*

ACKNOWLEDGMENTS

For their warm interest and encouragement, no less than their practical assistance, during this book's composition, the author wishes to thank the following friends: Lance Alexander, Paul and Susan Dingwell, Cynthia Goldstone, Alan Gullette, Ronald Scott Hilger, Gerda Hoefert-Kennedy, Rah Hoffman, Kathryn Hohlwein, Ted Klein, Jesse F. Knight, Jean-Marc and Randy Lofficier, Terence McVicker, John Miller, Brent Morgan, James Eldon Patterson, Marsha Raleigh, David C. Smith, Brian Stableford, and Gahan Wilson.

Foreword

There was a time when the worth of a poet was measured not only by what he said, but also by how beautifully he said it.

In an age of oral presentation, meter and rhyme enabled an audience to better retain and interpret the poet's message. The poet accentuated his message with a language so rich in sights, scents, and sonorities that the poem took on almost tangible form. In the unfortunate present, the beauties and rhythms of our language have been stripped away, and all that remains to us are a few simple phrases and themes.

The virtuoso wordsmiths of the past are nearly gone—nearly but not entirely. This third and final series of *Songs & Sonnets Atlantean* enables us to relive that oral tradition as it has lasted into the twenty-first century, by means of one such practitioner.

This practitioner has created a unique niche of his own that he defines as "innovative traditionalist"—combining the form and disciplines of his initial inspiration—Edmund Spenser, and fueled by the exotic intoxications of the California Romantics: George Sterling, Nora May French, and Clark Ashton Smith.

Self-described as "the Last of the Courtly Poets," we can ill-afford to lose this lonely Troubadour, as his lute-accompanied recitations return us to a time when the combination of performer, message and word created presentations of rare magic. I hope this volume will aid in negating this self-defined extinction and ignite a following of those who treasure equally the beauties of the written word.

I welcome you now to share with me these Atlantean fragments, by my friend and colleague Donald Sidney-Fryer, hopefully not the Last of the Courtly Poets.

—Terence McVicker

Glendale, California
7 March 2005

Songs and Sonnets Atlantean

The Third Series

TO A DEAD CITY

Cartagena de las Indias.
1532–1583–1697.

Translated from the French of José-Maria de Heredia.

Dedicated to Cynthia Goldstone, friend and artist nonpareil.

Mournful City, Queen of the Oceans long ago!
Today the shark pursues in peace the lesser fish
And only the roving cloud extends the space of shade
Upon your sea road where the giant galleons rolled.

Since Drake and his assault, those English infidels,
Your walls—disabled—crumble down in blackened ruin
And, like some resplendent necklace of sombre pearls,
These gaping holes betray de Pointis's cannon fire.

Between the sky that burns and the sea road that foams,
Where drowsing sunlight sets off high noon's monotone,
You dream, O Warrioress, of the old Conquistadors;

And when the nights hang heavy with their heat and calm,
Soothing your lost renown, O City, how you slumber
Beneath the palms, the long, loud whispering of palm fronds.

Memorial

Dedicated to Keith Allen Daniels, 1956–2001, poet and scientist

(whose ashes his wife Toni Luna Daniels, with her sister, Theresa, cast into the Pacific Ocean at San Francisco on 26 January 2002).

Through cosmic deeps unknown, for numberless light-years,
The spheroid ether-ship with alien crew had sped
Towards that epiphany foretold by alien seers:

Against that vast and galaxy-emblazoned spread,
The planet hung in space: to this their quest had led,
A sea-girt globe enflamed by green and beige and blue:

With island, ocean, continent, and ocean bed,
This panorama, unsurpassed, now held their view,
This destination, Earth, their next new point of rendezvous:

Unheralded, alone, the Earthling women paced aside
Upon that utmost western shore, and with no more ado
They cast the poet's ashes free within that ocean's tide:

Meanwhile, on watch, the spacecraft hovered far above,
    Unseen, unheard, unknown, before it sped away.
    Its crew had eyed in wonderment, that selfsame day,
A great bard being honored, and with all of love.

The Herdsman

Translated from the Atlantean of Aänsess of the Astazhan.

All that night there had massed and swirled and shifted
The strange inchoate shapes, no more than fog,
Before the dense ground-mist with day had lifted:

From where the herdsman sat, perched on a log,
To one side of the reed-infested bog,
The green fields lay revealed with rich ripe grasses:

Saluted on occasion by some frog,
They pastured where they stood, those ill-matched masses
Of munching quadrupeds, the flocks of goats and sheep and asses:

Always alert for wolves and such like beasts, he mused awhile
Upon the great wide world that stretched beyond the mountain passes,
Which led out from that pastureland—he pondered with a smile:

That great wide world, this pastureland—which where?
    Yes, where to fix one's further domicile?
    Yes, which locale might prove the more worthwhile,
Or which mirage might need the greater care?

TROPICALITY

Translated from the Atlantean of an anonymous poet.

In wilderness is the preservation of the world.
—Henry David Thoreau

The huge clump of dark jungle foliage meets
And greets the eye, dazed by heat and by glare,
By parrots and orchids and parrakeets:

Inside this oasis of calm, this lair
Of shade, mute blooms and raucous birds compare
In brilliant plumes, in petal and in leaf:

Bright blue, green flame, vermillion flash and flare
Inside this lushness that defies belief,
Inside this languid gloom like some dream fuelled by kief:

This place that Beauty, *the* perfect sorceress,
Maintains as hers—in fit and righteous fief—
Remains one more stronghold of loveliness:

Here growth commands, untrammelled and supreme,
    In this domain where heat and moisture press.
    Amid this green and lavish wilderness,
On high, the tiny monkeys perch and scream.

Totem

Translated from the Atlantean of an unknown poet.

I

The mouse is our heraldic beast: we shall not fear.
No, our protector animal is not the lion,
Loud, careless, overbearing, but a strong defender—
Quite confident—no wonder: he's all-powerful!
Nor is our totem animal the buffalo,
Unruly, fierce, his horns and hooves not to be scorned,
But to be left alone, unto his own devices!
Nor is our totem animal the elephant—
Never at risk except when old or when a baby—
Calm, lordly, self-assured, the size of some small house!
No, none of these is it that is our special beast—
No, just the mouse, less than the rabbit or the hyrax,
And never summoning attention to himself,
He gets to run away, to run another day.
The poor, grey, furry mouse manages to survive:
That minimum becomes the maximum as well.
The mouse is our heraldic beast: we shall not fear.

II

The mouse is our heraldic beast: we shall not want.
No, our provider animal is not the squirrel,
Nor other animalculum, such as the ant,
The bee, hard-working, patient, and industrious,
Procuring, storing, stashing, squirreling away,

Against need, against want, against a future time.
No, none of these is it that is our special beast—
No, just the mouse, not less than squirrel, ant, or bee,
He too must put away against a future time.
Once the harvest is done, our totem animal
Sneaks out into the fields, zigzagging here and there,
To glean some kernel, to retrieve some seed or grain,
Slowly and patiently building his little pile,
But more painstakingly, perchance, than all the others.
The poor, grey, furry mouse manages to survive:
That minimum becomes the maximum as well.
The mouse is our heraldic beast: we shall not want.

III

The mouse is our own beast: we shall not fear,
So long as we stay quiet, cool, discreet,
We shall survive, and not have much to fear:—
Whether a little hungry, or replete,
Whether with scattered grains, or bits of meat,
The mouse is our own beast: we shall not want:—
Whether to eat light, whether just to eat,
Whether to wax or wane, obese or gaunt,
The mouse is our own beast: we shall not fear or want.

Abandonment

Translated from the Atlantean of Prince Atlantarion.

The silver hippocampus on the stair
Still stands forsaken—tarnished and aloof—
And almost as if with an orphaned air:
Once midmost of the household's warp and woof
That shuttled from the ground floor to the roof,
He still waits in the disavowed abode:
Steedlike he holds aloft a migniard hoof,
As though to beg one further episode,
And have someone sing out his praise in epode or in ode:

The family's life no longer flows around his plinth—
They have moved on, another street, some country road,
And proffer him nor amaranth nor hyacinth:

But soon the family shall return, to claim him as their own,
And have him live again with them, elsewhere, no more alone.

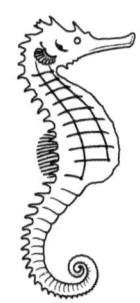

Amaranth

Translated from the Atlantean of King Atlantarion I.

Is it the fabulous blossom that you seek,
The amaranth that never fades or dies,
While here the world remains confused and bleak?
Is it these other blossoms that you prize,
Arraigned in purple, green, and crimson guise,
Whose flowered spikes bear seeds consumed as grains?
Such efflorescence at your footstep lies,
Whereas that rare and fabled blossom reigns
In death-filled wastes of far-off lands that none attains:

For only in the transcendental can you find,
Beyond the hope instilled at birth in human brains,
Those gifts, those treasures, out of sight and out of mind:

That craving towards the transmundane can only turn—
Coiled—back upon itself, to mock that urge to yearn.

Rapa-Nui

A haunted landscape of some seventy square miles,
It looms out from a vast expanse of endless waves,
This one broad high terrain and half a dozen isles:

Where giant statues mix with platforms and with graves,
This compact landmass flaunts its peaks and hills and caves,
When once it climbs out from the ocean's massive depths:

Through alien doors and under alien architraves,
We pass down into what were secret caves or crypts,
Once filled with sacred carvings and hieroglyphic scripts:

Under Make-Make's only eye, the sun's flamboyant rays,
As always, even through the times of death and near eclipse,
Ever from out their great stone heads the giant statues gaze:

The folk of Rapa-Nui have outlived, thus far,
    Their all but Atlantean doom.
    Above the ocean's wrack and spume,
Their home somehow renews its olden avatar.

Pendant

The tall, stone, Titan figures haunt this land,
But most of all along the cliffbound shore,
Like huge chess-pieces tossed by some huge hand:—
And never distant from the great sea's roar,
Now more than ever does it seem the door
To some vast realm, unseen, beyond our ken:—
These huge heads can but hint at all the lore
Lost here, beyond recall by quill or pen,
To shed light on this point of sea, sky, land, and men.

A Game of Chess

(A suggested attraction to those in charge of tourism on Rapa-Nui, as a new tradition or custom, combining indigenous and non-indigenous elements, for the islanders to undertake for the entertainment of the off-island visitors, a novel enterprise that would invoke the island's previous history, the Gospel according to St. Thor Heyerdahl, and that would represent in symbolic form the once lethal struggle between the Long Ears ostensibly of South American origin and the Short Ears of Polynesian ancestry.)

I dreamed a dream, and by means of my mind's eye, during a bright and perfect morning, once again an unseen presence on unseen wings, I flew southwest from the coast of Peru some four or five thousand leagues until I hovered off the northern coast, a little to the west, of Rapa-Nui, or Te Pito o Te Henua, the Navel of the World. Beneath me there spread out the only sandy beach easy of access on the island, south of the bay called Anakena.

A solid and sizeable island of high peaks and hills, a world of pristine and ineffable beauty—an Eden lost of time and space—lay before my gaze, a world wherein entire forests of gigantic palms, interspersed with stands of yellow-flowering toromiro no less than other trees, alternated with lush, fluorescently green savannahs. The deep blue expanses of ocean, mirroring back the deep blue heavens, thundered and foamed against the cliffbound littoral illuminated by the reddish-yellow glare pouring forth from a dazzling but infinitely far-off sun, a small and flamboyant orb hanging all alone in an empty sky.

Presently I saw two large ships approach from the northeast, each with three masts under full sail, and each some ninety feet in length, and some six feet at least in depth, but buoyant upon the water, ships whose decks and hulls and prows were made up of totora-reed bundles tightly compacted and held in that shape by many stout ropes of hemp. The ships now sailed very close to each other, and as though by enchantment they stood still not far from the sandy littoral, despite the winds and the ocean currents impelling them forward.

On both decks a commanding figure stood, in one case a personage who seemed kingly in his bearing, and in the other case another who seemed queenly in her demeanor. A great entourage, made up of courtiers and sailors, numbering some one hundred fifty persons, stood in attendance around each figure, to whom all the others deferred with respect, affection, and obeisance.

Both regal figures and those in attendance upon them wore curious harness and multicolored feathers whether on head or on body. But all, whether king or queen, courtiers or sailors, looked out upon the shore to the south of them with eagerness, wonder, and contentment writ large upon their faces. He was King Hotua-Matua, and she was Queen Avareipua.

Nearing each other on the decks of their respective ships, the regal figures held brief parley, following which they nodded each to the other. Now the ships moved apart, the king's vessel sailing to the east, and that of the queen to the west. Both ships rounded separately the entire island at the same time, and then returned offshore of the same beach bordering Anakena Bay.

At a given signal from both King Hotua-Matua and Queen Avareipua, the mariners now deliberately guided the ships as far as they could venture into the shallows north of the beach. Escorted and assisted by their entourage, the regal figures descended from their ships, debouching into the shoaling waters, and striding boldly onto the shore. They had all now landed at long last after some three or four months at sea.

Some of them noticed more particularly for the first time under the close-woven canopy of the overarching trees a network of stone-paved roads, and here and there lofty stone tombs as of kings or prelates. Some of them now recalled that King Machaa, who with his many followers had preceded them to this island long agone, had colonized it, and had in a sense prepared it for the newcomers.

But, strange to relate, of those earlier people and their habitations the new colonists could see nothing, nor could they surmise what had happened to these predecessors, nor where they might have gone, if indeed anywhere else. Was it possible that at some point they had all departed, seeking those islands further to the west beyond the sunset? The primordial vision then vanished before my mind's eye, and I found myself once again all alone.

An aeon went past in a flash, and I saw the same island but greatly transformed. Alas, most of the pristine and ancient forest cover had vanished as if it had never existed, and in its place there extended great and arid-looking savannahs broken here and there by plantations of eucalyptus trees, and by a few groves of coconut palms.

No longer did I hover off the northern coast of this isolated piece of land, but still an unseen presence I walked inland from the shore over a large stretch of sand until I reached a great platform upon which stood, facing inland, great stone figures with inlaid eyes.

Here, close at hand, between the beach and a grove of coconut palms, in a level space just south of the platform, I saw two men seated at a small table, one with long ears—his lobes curiously elongated, and hanging down to his shoulders—and the other with the usual short ears. They were playing a game of chess.

At the chess-pieces disposed upon the chessboard the two men were staring with marked intensity. Just south of them but north of the grove of coconut palms, placed flat upon the level earth, there extended a gigantic chessboard of wood, with large alternating squares of black and white, eight to a side, and thus making a total of sixty-four in all.

Upon the squares there stood at ease tall people, garbed in curious harness and with multicolored feathers both on head and body. They mimicked the movements of the chess-pieces on the table: as the two men played their game with deliberation, the living chess-pieces enacted their parts in response to the directions of a herald watching the game on the table. In his hand he held a speaking trumpet through which to direct his remarks.

The game had only begun, and the pieces remained more or less as originally set up at the start of any such contest. Near the side of the ahu, or platform, there stood the Long Ears: a king and a queen dressed with harness, with feathers, and with tall headpieces, and in such a manner as to evoke Hotua-Matua and Avareipua, those founding parents of the dynasty that had ruled on Rapa-Nui for almost seventy generations.

On either side of these leading figures, in place of the two bishops, there stood two high priests, and on either side of them, in place of the two knights, two archwarriors, and then on either side of them, in place of the two rooks or castles, two bird-men wearing curious headpieces with exaggerated beaks. Before this line of eight figures there stood the eight pawns, each wearing a helmet that evoked the heads that stuck up out of the ground in the crater of Rano Raraku near the quarry walls, from which the ancestral inhabitants had carved them so painstakingly.

But on the other side of the chessboard, and thus farther away from the ahu, there stood the team of their opponents, the group of the Short Ears, otherwise the same, but with a chieftain and a chieftainess in place of the king and queen of the Long Ears, and with enough of both large and small differences to distinguish them in turn from their own opponents.

The game had only begun, when without warning the dream ended, and I never discovered just how that particular game of chess came out, invoking as it did the quondam struggle of the Long Ears and the Short Ears.

The Chest from Otherwhere

Dedicated to Jesse F. Knight, in gratitude.

The chest was ancient—old beyond belief—
Of quaint, unknown, and curious design,
With strange glyphs deep-engraved in bold relief:

Outside, how keen the pale flame-gold would shine
Like rays reflecting on a moonlit shrine—
Inside, electrum's own pale yellow gleam:

What might have lain within that chest, that scrine?
Within, did some queen's precious gem-stones teem,
Or still within, did some king's treasure-trove daydream?

So now the scrine was empty, void of all but air,
But did not such fit, best of all, the cosmic scheme,
Whether in this dimension, or in Otherwhere?

The empty space, the all-potential nothingness,
Remains the greatest gift, the greatest somethingness.

Another Species of Epiphany

The statue of the general stands on high,
Surrounded by the willows in the square,
A favorite with the pigeons from on high:

With pious mien befitting solemn prayer,
The statue and its tall foundation bear
Long whitish lines upon their stone and bronze:

His head the object of their special care,
The pigeons would not, could not, pass for swans,
Nor all their fluttering crowd for Apollo's paragons:

The general's mottled head—has it been heard to speak?!
"Forgive them their droppings, but let them be bygones—
At least they make me look both ancient and unique!"

The heavenly host with aureole descends
      To leave their blessedness, their special mark,
      Upon the statue's headpiece, bright and stark,
Before that selfsame host once more ascends.

A Ballade of Prospero

An incantation.

Dedicated to David and Janine Smith, with special regards.

No, not the pleasures of the harbor,
    Nor those of haven and of bower,
Nor those of orchard or of arbor,
    Nor those of garden and of flower,
    Nor those of lighthouse or of tower,
Nor those of dock and wharf and quay,
    No, none of these do I empower,
But only the ships that sail out to sea.

Beyond the refuge of the arbor,
    Where vistas open skies that glower,
Beyond the reaches of the harbor,
    Where storm clouds gather, hour by hour,
    Where form the great storms that devour,
Where tempests roar in jubilee,
    Yes, only these do I empower,
And only the ships that sail out to sea.

Yes, only the remoter harbor,
    Unknown and harsh, without a flower,
Only the land without an arbor,
    Austere and stark, without a bower,
    Forbidding, cold, with winds that scour,
With rains that sweep off all debris,
    These do I sing, and these empower,
And only the ships that sail out to sea.

ENVOY

Enchantments born of sweet and sour,
    And philtres made of gloom and glee,
Yes, all of these do I empower,
    And only the ships that sail out to sea.

The Reef of Coral

Translated from the French of José-Maria de Heredia.

Dedicated to Ronald and Frances Fryer, in friendship.

The sun beneath the sea, an enigmatic dawn,
Lights up the forest of the corals Ethiope-red—
Which combines, in the depths of its cool and calm basins,
The sea beast in full bloom and the flower-animal.

And all to which the salt and the iodine give hue,
Moss, long-haired seaweed, anemones, and sea-urchins,
Veils with dark violet, in sumptuous designs,
The bed, vermiculate, of pallid madrepore.

With his irradiant scales annulling those enamels,
A big fish navigates across the coral branches;
In the transparent shade indolently he roams;

And, at once, with one stroke of his tailfin on fire,
He causes, through the crystal, dark and still and blue,
A streak to flash with gold, nacre, and emerald.

Discovery

Beyond the tip of Greenland they had found,
The scientists, upon that southwest coast,
A palace-town of marble, underground:

Such gold and marble, was it not the ghost
Of some refulgent past, a northern post
Of some great southern empire far away?

Such gorgeousness this palace-town could boast
Of pale flame-gold resplendent like the day,
Colonnades on each street, each house, each alleyway:

Agog to tell the world about their great new find,
The scientists emerged, but went at once astray,
Disabled, rendered all but deaf and dumb and blind:

A sudden snow discovered them, engulfing one and all,
And made them vanish underneath, deep and beyond recall.

The Bitch with Tits of Bronze

A ballad.

*Dedicated to Charlotte Barr,
the former Sister Mary Anthony,
poet and teacher.*

So he had come to Mother Rome,
    That Roma Maternalis
Who once maintained a huge domain,
    But based on sword and phallus.

Who was this he? John Quentin Doe,
    Our hero from the States,
Who came across the Ocean Sea,
    And through Gibraltar's Straits.

He went out walking every day,
    Through plazas and through streets!
Museums, churches, palaces—
    He only stopped for eats.

At last he saw the sculptured group,
    There, in the Vaticanus,
The she-wolf suckling those twin boys:
    Yes, Romulus and Remus.

The bitch with tits of bronze, was it,
    Or were they made of brass?
Whatever may have been the stuff,
    The sculpture was first-class.

He stared and stared, quite mesmerized,
    And formed a bond with her,
Across the span of centuries,
    Or did he only err?

Wow, what a bitch, and what a wolf,
    Gee whiz and golly gee!—
As much the Mother of All Wolves,
    As any wolf could be!

At last John Quentin Doe moved on,
    To stare at something else,
Still turning back to look again
    With high and racing pulse.

And so that bitch with tits of bronze
    Still cast her spell abroad,
Across that space of centuries,
    Like goddess or like god.

John still went walking every day,
    Haunting that olden town.
At last he found the great Campagna,
    And walked it up and down:

The countryside that circles Rome,
    The open level plain,
Perfect for walking day or night,
    In sunlight or in rain.

One day at dusk he walked out there,
    And lay him on the grass,
So sleepy, he fell sound asleep,
    Right there, right on that grass.

Midnight it was when he woke up,
    John heard the church bells ring,
And kind of stiff, he yawned and stretched,
    Then stood up with a spring.

Midnight! aye, twelve o'clock at night!
    The church bells echoed on.
Was that a hound he heard far off?
    He felt a little wan.

It sounded odd, more like a wolf,
    But no wolves could be here.
When could have wolves last walked this plain?
    He felt a tinge of fear.

The city's lights seemed far and few,
    No one else was around,
Nothing stirred among the trees,
    He heard no other sound.

Now once again that sound rang out,
    That awesome ululation.
That howling, as of dog or wolf,
    It was no simulation.

What shape was that he saw far off,
    As of a monstrous hound?
Was that the sound of monstrous paws
    That drummed upon the ground?

Perhaps he should go back to town
    With motion that was fleet.
He ran, and he ran fast as hell:
    "Make tracks!" he told his feet.

Again that howl, now not so far;
    He soon would be at bay.
The beast from hell was on his heels:
    John sped upon his way.

He felt hot breath upon his back—
    He surely was a goner!
How to avoid in such short space
    This vile death without honor?

He looked straight back, and was undone:
    The wolf was twice his height!
She loomed above him like a wall:
    When was it she would bite?

Instinctively he dropped him down,
    And rolled up in a ball.
Just like a young one in the womb,
    He could not creep or crawl.

No more pursuit, just utter peace,
    Warm breath, and huge wet nose!
He cringed in fear, he tightened up,
    He dared not breathe, he froze.

But then he felt a huge warm tongue
    That licked, and washed him clean!
The she-wolf lay her down round him,
    To nurse, and not to wean.

One of her tits accessed his mouth,
    Instinctively he sucked,
Then got such instant calm and peace,
    He neither budged nor bucked.

Both wolf and man lay quite content
    Thus nestled with each other,
The picture of pure happiness,
    A nursling and a mother.

His mind went blank from such pure bliss—
    So safe within her keep—
She kind of crooned a wolflike tune,
    And then they fell asleep.

Lost in such sweet unconsciousness,
    He woke up early morn,
And felt outrageously so well,
    In truth as though reborn.

That giant she-wolf, where was she?
    He found nor hair nor hide.
Had she been real, or just a dream?
    Had all his senses lied?

So sad he felt out of her care,
    If only he could bleat!
Of that which he was most bereft,
    He missed her dear warm teat!

Somehow that wolf, or so he mused,
    Had managed to survive:
Then our John Doe walked back to town,
    Content to be alive.

So she still casts her spell abroad
    Close by the Vaticanus,
The she-wolf, yes, of Rome herself,
The mother yet of Mother Rome,
    Through Romulus and Remus.

CODICIL OF CONTRADICTION

Translated from the Atlantean of King Atlantarion I.

Always the end, presumed in sight, appears elusive,
Ambiguous, ambivalent, and self-aware,
Self-conscious, self-righteous, self-mocking, inconclusive:

Finishing anything seems such a big affair,
A big to-do, that breeds disdain, delight, despair—
Forever in all ways has the end appeared the same:

Reaching the close should make the heart so debonair—
Instead it often brings confusion and self-blame,
Nor triumph nor exuberance, but just a sense of shame.

As One Jaguar to Another

Translated from the Atlantean of an unavowed scribe.

*Dedicated to Kathryn Hohlwein,
Patroness of the Arts.*

Or So You Say

Between Greater Antillia and Lesser Antillia the much smaller but rounded island of Atlantillia lies, the so-called Pearl of the Antillias, the capital region and principal port of the Atlantean holdings in that general territory, no less than of the adjacent lands that encircle the Seas of Antillia, which extend between the Antillias proper to the east and the diverse countries of Oöxathan to the west.

Although the capital city of Atzatlan itself lies principally along the western, southern, and eastern shores of Atlantillia—and thus around the island's low-lying central plateau—the Atlantean kings of this particular realm have built their manifold and labyrinthine palace on the northern part of that plateau, and thus facing out over the ocean.

Far from the elongated harbors not quite encircling the over-all island—those harbors that are thronged with ships coming not just from all over the Empire of Atlantis but especially from the lands that border the not quite land-locked Seas of Antillia—and thus removed from all that loud and bustling commerce, it is midnight in the great royal palace, and moreover a semi-tropical middle of the night.

It is quiet in the great inner thronehall of the royal palace where the latter spreads out, where its many structures extend on every side, the over-all architectural masses lifting up tall on their terraces, fixed amid innumerable gardens, whether located in the equally numberless courtyards, or all around the royal palace but beyond its external boundary.

Inside the thronehall no guards are standing on watch, but only in the corridors to and from, as well as around, the vast chamber of black marble, whose columns—carven to resemble the trunks of massive tropical trees—uphold the ceiling everywhere except the open space at the center. There the double throne of black onyx bears nor king nor queen at this late hour.

On either side of the royal seat, celebrated as the Jaguär Throne, a good-sized likeness of that tropical cat, but larger than life, sculpted from a rare dark orange granite, stands atop a low plinth of black marble. The sculptors of these heraldic beasts have inserted bits of black onyx and other minerals to mimic the fur, the eyes, and other aspects of the living animals.

This Jaguär Throne is not to be confused with the other but greater throne of similar name that stands upon the curious and large-scale outdoor platform dominating the great bluff to the north of the royal palace. Such is the Great Jaguär Throne that looks east-northeast out over the sea towards not only the island continent of Atlantis itself but specifically towards Atlantis the City.

But the eyes on the sculpted jaguärs of this lesser throne, placed at the eye level of a human adult, gaze directly into those of the onlooker with a hard and mirrored glare. The light in those alien eyes reflects the fire from the dozen or so ornamental torches here and there that flame and waver against the black marble columns and walls. Conning these carven animals, the observer would never guess that, unlike their fierce demeanor, such creatures have a gentle and whimsical nature, as well as a stern and predatory one.

Whoever the sculptors, they have created a powerful magick in these two forms. By means of a special ritual they have long agone captured the spirits of two dying but long-lived jaguärs, and settled them inside the perdurable shapes. Although suspected by few, these creatures of stone and mineral thus possess a secret and inner life, even though not endowed with mobility—well, at least as observed by official witness.

Even without moving their tongues or jaws the jaguärs can somehow speak, and sounds will issue from their always open mouths. They talk to each other, but quietly, so that only they can hear. They like privacy, and—of course—they speak only the purest Atlantean. Often at night, when alone, they regale each other with stories of their former incarnations, through which individual cycles they have both lived at least nine lives each.

The jaguär on the right-hand side (of the sovereigns themselves) we shall call Dexter, and that on the other, Sinister. Here are half a dozen of their stories as overheard and recorded by some clandestine scribe, or so he thought. Or did the ensorcelled beasts perhaps allow that especial scribe to eavesdrop on their conversation that night, and other nights, because they wanted those especial stories to be recorded?

The Warrior and the Jaguär

(So spake Dexter, sometimes also known with affection as Dextra-Theustra.)

Still more than some little time before the first radiance of dawn, but before he had retired to his lair to sleep through the day, as was his custom, the jaguär was drinking out of a murmuring jungle spring, assuaging his thirst, if not, alas! his hunger. So far that night he had captured only one small rabbit, which served only to pique his appetite. He remained hungry. The thought of any edible flesh at all seemed most enticing.

Suddenly, moving as quietly as the jaguär himself, a handsome young man, a warrior, stood before him. He carried a bow and a quiver of arrows, a hunting knife, and an iron-pointed spear. Despite himself the big cat was a little surprised at the unheralded apparition. The young man's tanned and muscled body looked succulent and very tasty to the hungry cat. The youth, however, had no fear, and appeared a little amused.

He spoke to the cat in the immemorial speech common to the non-humans. "No, my friend, I would not make the best or tastiest meal. Yes, I have divined your serious interest in me as a food supply. But what would you say to a collaboration, instead? Rather than eating me, which would amount to no more than a few hearty meals, why don't we work together? We can get much more fresh meat, working as a team."

Again a little surprised, the cat replied with as much cool as he could muster, "Your proposition interests me. I shall refrain from eating you for the moment." The cat was no fool, and he had, of course, noticed the weaponry carried by the young warrior, who looked quite able to handle any of it quite well at a moment's notice.

The youth smiled, and said, "I know where a small herd of rather substantial deer are eating in a glade. Why don't we stalk them from opposite directions? I'll take us there. No matter which way they may run, one of us will have a better chance of bringing at least one deer down. Agreed?"

The cat decided at once that he liked the suggestion, that the youth had much wisdom, and that he liked the young hunter more than he wanted to eat him. Looking him squarely in the eye, the jaguär smiled, and said, "Agreed!"

The youth reached down, and sensitively scratched the cat's ears, and along his furry jawline. That cinched the deal, and the youth guided the cat to the glade where the deer were browsing on the leaves of some delicious tropical trees. Indeed, the youth could move as softy as the jaguär, and they positioned themselves on opposite sides of the glade. After a silent prayer directed at their quarry, the youth coughed, the deer froze, the jaguär showed himself to the deer, who leapt away into the jungle, right where the warrior stood waiting. He hurled his spear into the buck with great skill and force. Transfixed through the heart, the buck died almost at once.

Amazed at the ease of all this, the jaguär stated, "I am glad, young sir, that I did not attack and eat you. I assume that you will share the kill with me."

By now it was almost dawn. The youth nodded, then skinned and cleaned the carcass, but letting the jaguär feast on the steaming entrails at once. How sweet and savory they tasted! The warrior then split the carcass between them, and even offered to carry the jaguär's portion to the latter's cave. The cat agreed, and guided the warrior to his lair not far away. Meanwhile the youth had quietly said a prayer of thanksgiving once again directed at the quarry.

Arriving at the cave, the youth smiled, and said, "I have kept my word, and here you have enough meat for several days at least," as he put the jaguär's portion inside his lair. "Now I shall take my own portion back to my village. Would you like to repeat this arrangement on another occasion? It has its advantages, and I like having you as my friend."

The cat smiled back, licked the youth's hand in agreement, and without further ado, he proceeded to eat on his haunch of deer meat. The youth nodded his head at the jaguär with respect, and left carrying his own haunch over his shoulder. The adroit warrior thought to himself with satisfaction, "Now that's what I call a civilized jungle!"

Well Met by Midnight

(So spake Dexter, alias Dextra-Theustra. But before he began his next story, his friend and companion—Sinister, or Sinistra-Theustra—from the other side of the large double throne interrupted him to comment on the previous tale involving the young warrior-hunter. "Although I've never enjoyed such an experience myself directly, I have heard of such rare and enlightened examples of co-operative altruism. Your experience ranks as the very best example of such behavior as I have ever encountered, at least as narrated. If we cats were not such a consarned independent bunch, and if we had ever learned to work together, the destiny of our species, the big cats in general, might have turned out markedly different."

("Yes, that is true," Dextra-Theustra responded at once. "But here is another tale, even more uncommon, involving that selfsame young man, who by the way called himself Quoctezu in the language of the humans. With your permission I shall now tell this later and closely related story.")

It had rained with great force for an hour or so during the late afternoon, and the jungle had emerged wet and steaming. By the time that the jaguär woke at twilight in his lair, and went outside, sniffing the slight breeze blowing in his direction, he found, not far away, his small accustomed pool, and avidly lapped the fresh cool water. Although the daylight colors were starting to fade in the increasing dusk, the burnt orange coat on the jaguär with its patterned black pawprints remained somehow more vivid for a little longer. Sniffing again while moving forward, the jaguär suddenly stopped as he savored an odor at once both strange and familiar. But he also sensed anger, bafflement, and frustration, and relatively close by. Intrigued he prowled forward again, and the still wet jungle scarcely betrayed a whisper of sound. The stealthy feline came to a small clearing, and peered into it from behind a lattice of leaves.

There, in the middle of that glade, another jaguär lay, licking his left front paw, then holding it out and growling at it, then whining, then rolling over, then righting himself, only to start the whole sequence all over again. Dextra-Theustra now got a really strong whiff of the other's unique scent. He pondered it for one quick moment. Then he recognized it as a scent similar to his own. This other cat had originated in the same litter as himself, and was none other than one of his own brothers. A rare and altruistic impulse prompted Dextra-Theustra.

Lightly growling to announce his presence, he slipped into the glade, approached the other cat, and spoke to him in the immemorial speech common to felines. "Greetings, brother. I see that you have a problem. May I help?" The other cat's eyes widened even further in the gathering darkness. "Oh, if only that were possible!" he replied, "but you see, it is a thorn, and I can't get it out with my teeth, nor (I doubt) can you."

"Hmm, that is a problem!" Dextra-Theustra said as he nodded in accord, "but I do have an ally, an adopted human brother, the hunter Quoctezu. If we could find him, then I'm sure he'd be happy to remove it for you." "Well, I'll try anything," the suffering jaguär said. "Lead on, by all means!"

Dextra-Theustra did indeed lead the way, first to Quoctezu's village, from the edge of which they surveyed the inhabitants gathered around the big evening fire at the center. But the two jaguärs, careful not to announce their presence either to the villagers or to their domestic animals whether through sound or scent, could not discover the hunter. Dextra-Theustra reconnoitered the main path into the village, however, and was able to pick out Quoctezu's own scent. As was his custom sometimes, he had gone hunting at night. The two jaguärs set out at once on the warrior's trail.

Quoctezu was able to move fast, and cover much territory when he hunted. His trail led the two big cats on a merry chase, as they tracked him through a veritable labyrinth of jungle paths, no less than novel footways that the warrior had blazed through dense copse and near-impenetrable thicket. Dextra-Theustra's brother hobbled along as best he could, sometimes hissing or whining in pain. At long last, when it was almost midnight, they found Quoctezu resting in a small glade after having bathed in a pool fed by a spring close at hand.

The warrior had sensed their presence even before they walked up to him. Marvellously calm and collected, he smiled at them, and in the immemorial speech common to the non-humans he bade them welcome. "Ready for some midnight hunting?" Quoctezu enquired. "I note that you have brought a friend." A pause ensued.

"This is one of my brothers, O noble Quoctezu," Dextra-Theustra replied. "But before we can hunt, and perhaps combine our forces as on a previous occasion, would you be so kind as to remove the grievous thorn afflicting my brother's left front paw?"

Quoctezu had certainly noticed how the other jaguär had hobbled up to him as he favored the paw in question. The warrior had surmised what might be the problem. He went up to the suffering jaguär, and took the wounded paw gently in his hand. After carefully looking at it, he grasped the thorn, and with a quick and skillful gesture he pulled it out. The big cat snarled, but then felt instant relief.

The warrior cleaned the wound, and applied some leaves from a plant nearby, making a kind of poultice with the leaves while tying it in place with some small vines. The big cat could still walk, as the poultice did not impede movement in any way. He licked Quoctezu's hand in gratitude, while the hunter lightly caressed the cat's ears and jaws.

"Well, my brothers," Quoctezu questioned the two jaguärs again, "are we ready now for some midnight hunting? I can lead you to where some deer are grazing. Are you game?"

The two big cats followed Quoctezu as he led them out of that glade onto the trail of some sweet and savory venison. Well met by midnight, in truth!

The Jaguär and the Astrologer

("Now that's what I call a civilized jungle!" A pause. "Did Quoctezu really say that?" questioned Sinistra-Theustra with incredulous bemusement, repeating the sentence after Dextra-Theustra himself had uttered it.

("Yes, he did, the first time just after our third successive midnight hunt, and then, following that occasion, after every nocturnal expedition. Quoctezu said it every time as he was leaving to return to his village at dawn," replied Dextra-Theustra with punctilious courtesy.

(It was midnight again, and the two heraldic jaguärs were once again reminiscing about their former lives. No human being had lingered in the indoor thronehall, and thus could overhear what they said.

("Well," remarked Sinistra-Theustra, "you two certainly had some extraordinary adventures together, and Quoctezu consistently showed himself as unusually fair and trustworthy for a human being." Sinistra paused before continuing.

("And we both know from our long experience of existence, one life after another, just how destructive and vicious, collectively speaking, his especial species can be, thinking themselves as apart somehow from nature, and as absolutely different from, as well as better than, all the other species, their kin and brethren."

(Sinistra-Theustra paused again before continuing. "But I, no less than yourself, have had some extraordinary adventures, and moreover on occasion with human beings, but adventures of quite a contrasting type from yours. The following adventure involved a venerable astrologer who had come from Atlantis the City via Atzatlan, the capital of Atlantillia. Here is one story from my long association with him.")

The jaguär had been prowling for several days now through the jungles covering the eastern highlands of Greater Antillia. This was his usual territory radiating out from his lair, a cave, or a series of small caves, one leading back into another from the entrance. This ample, unobscured opening faced east onto a small glade or natural balcony located up amid a series of high rocky bluffs. Fringed with a narrow belt of trees gapped only at the eastern edge, and at either side where a natural path ran north and south, the small glade looked out over the wide passage of water separating Greater Antillia from the rounded, much smaller island of Atlantillia. At the northern end of this passage lay the waters of the Ocean Sea, and at the southern end those of the Seas of Antillia, beyond the low narrow Isthmus of Quoätzl threaded by its nine canals. Like a dazzling mirror the surface of the water in the passage—on this rare, almost windless day—glittered in the early morning sunlight.

Standing somewhat above the entrance to his lair, but shielded by some foliage, the jaguär had not yet retired from his nocturnal hunting. He found the almost blinding light reflecting off the mirror-like water, if not irritating, at least annoying. Long before now he should have ensconced himself in the innermost cave of his lair, and should have fallen sound asleep. He had hunted successfully, mostly small game, but enough, and had assuaged both hunger and thirst. Although he had other lairs, this cave was his favorite, and his usual one. But he could not enter now for several days, ever since a small party of human beings had beached their large boat far below, had ascended carrying various bales and bundles, and then had pre-empted both the glade and the cave. "Human monkeys," the big cat thought disdainfully to himself.

Not only disgruntled, but more, in an evil mood, the jaguär discovered that the humans had not yet made their departure, the consarned critturs! Would they never leave?! He had no choice but to seek once again his other closest lair, an ample crotch up in a big tree not far away. He snarled, turned round, and left.

Sometime after sunset the following evening, the jaguär had returned to his lookout spot atop his own cave, and found that, to judge by appearances, the humans had at least left the clearing in front of it. The large boat far below had vanished. But had they really departed? The big cat was both angry and hungry. He perceived a feeble illumination spilling out from the cavern's mouth. He also heard one or more voices engaged in conversation. He decided to chance a descent, so he could learn more, but covertly from the shadows.

Peering in, the jaguär noted with amazement the transformation of his cave, or series of caves, into successive chambers luxuriously tapestried and carpeted. Those humans who had effected this major change were the ones who had left. With mounting interest the big cat observed, at some real distance back from the entrance, a white-bearded, and rather frail, old gentleman, dressed in rich dark robes embroidered in curious designs with metallic thread, or filament of gold and silver and orichalch. Dressed only in tunic and sandals, a handsome youth, doubtless the astrologer's assistant and apprentice, was talking to the venerable gentleman. Several candles in candlesticks on a small table nearby gave out a feeble but adequate light.

Growling intermittently, the massive jaguär—an unusually large specimen—advanced into the first chamber. The youth recoiled at once in terror, and snatched up a spear leaning against the wall to one side. But the old gentleman, although somewhat surprised, remained perfectly calm, and put a restraining hand on the youth's arm that held the spear.

Then, speaking in the immemorial speech common to the non-humans, the old man addressed the big cat: "Good evening, O noble and beautiful jaguär!" Startled by such a civilized greeting, the powerful feline was taken aback, but still growling every now and then, he stated, "This is my lair, and arrogantly have you appropriated it. I could kill both of you with ease, and then eat you."

"Know then, O princely jaguär," explained the old man, "that I am a renowned itinerant astrologer who has retired from the imperial court at Atlantis the City. I have come here to the outskirts of Atlantillia to pursue certain esoteric but vital phenomena. I understand that I have usurped your lair; in fact, I deliberately chose it, and because of you, surprising as that might seem. I hope that you will grant me its use, and that all of us three may dwell here in mutual aid and friendship. I have divined that you have already lived your full share at least of the nine lives allotted to cats—and that you have much wisdom, which I would like to record for my own purposes, as well as for the benefit of other notable seekers after both wisdom and knowledge. We have not changed the innermost cave in which you sleep during the day, but we welcome you to continue sleeping there."

Somewhat mollified, but still somewhat angry, the jaguär growled again, and then replied, "I don't know whether I want to share my private space with you. And pray tell, what would you do, what could you do, if I decided to become violent as well as destructive?" Noting the edge of real menace in the jaguär's voice, the astrologer—something of a sorcerer as well, albeit benign—then uttered a sovereign word, a curious vocable, but not from the speech common to the non-humans. The vibrations caused by this vocable seemed to remain suspended in the air, reverberating much longer than ordinary sound or speech. Insensibly they entered the ears and then the heart of the noble jaguär. All at once his anger miraculously ceased, he forgot why he had felt angry, and a great peace came down upon him.

No longer growling, the big cat yielded to the situation. "I find that I can agree now to these altered conditions after all, and I look forward to a prolonged and fruitful collaboration with you, O noble astrologer, and with your assistant. When free from dealing with my own necessities, I shall be happy to co-operate with you in your investigative endeavors. Indeed, I have lived many lives, and have many tales to tell. But I am hungry still, and must now continue hunting. I shall return here at dawn to sleep in the innermost cave." With all due respect astrologer and apprentice presently smiled, and gravely inclined their heads in deference to the wise but also prudent jaguär as he paced majestically out into the night. Such was the beginning of their long friendship and work together.

(Following this tale that he had just finished relating about his first acquaintance with the venerable astrologer, and glancing over at his heraldic friend, Sinistra-Theustra commented, "Now that's what I myself would call a civilized jungle." From the other side of the throne Dextra-Theustra said with singular concision, "Agreed.")

The Apprentice and the Jaguär

(So spake Sinistra-Theustra, telling another story from the time of his long association with the venerable astrologer and his apprentice.)

The jaguär resided now for several years with the frail and ancient astrologer Cyphron and his devoted apprentice Ystros. On occasion the large feline would abandon this easternmost of his various lairs completely to his human colleagues, needing to live alone for awhile as big cats often do, given their solitary nature. At such times he would seek his other most elaborate lair, another cave, or series of caves, but located amid the high rocky bluffs at the western end of the eastern highlands of Greater Antillia, not far from Atlantillia, that rounded Pearl of the Twin Antillias. This other lair faced into the sunset, more northwest than west, looking out over the dense, game-filled jungles that covered much of this part of Greater Antillia.

Meanwhile the first sessions with Cyphron and then Ystros that tapped into the jaguär's past lives had gone exceptionally well. The big cat allowed himself to be hypnotized, and while he remained in such a state, astrologer or apprentice would record what the jaguär could remember on pieces of fresh papyrus. As always, they spoke in the immemorial speech common to the non-humans, thus redacting what the jaguär said in that language as written down phonetically, but later translating it into proper and polished Atlantean. Astrologer and apprentice like many erudite humans never wavered in their allegiance to correct grammar, syntax, and accepted rhetorical usage.

The sessions themselves rarely lasted more than one or two hours. The large feline himself, once aroused from the hypnotic state, could recall almost never what he had just imparted to his human interrogators, or what had otherwise transpired. But he always regained his regular consciousness feeling extraordinarily refreshed and energized, almost as if newly reborn. Like a supernal drug this marvellous condition of superlative well-being evolved into its own incentive for the jaguär to continue the recondite experiments.

More and more Cyphron became unable to study his beloved stars, and to cast his accustomed horoscopes. Less and less could he take an active part in the sessions involving the jaguär, except in an advisory role close by, from whatever chair or couch where he happened to be resting. More and more did he become fatigued and weakened with old age, and albeit as hale as could be considering his general condition, he kept increasingly to his bed. More and more did he perforce come to depend upon his assistant and apprentice, now dearer to him than any son.

Ystros meanwhile had unintentionally developed a passionate fascination for the unique perspective on the world that the sessions with the jaguär had inadvertently opened up for him. Atavistically he soon wished to partake at least a few times in the jaguär's nocturnal prowl and hunt. He wanted to get as close as he could to the actual experience of the hunt and the kill in the wild. That is, as it existed for a predator like the jaguär.

In his own fashion, as much as his nature allowed, the big cat had come to tolerate rather well, and even to like, the two humans with whom he shared his transformed lair. What is more, without precedent or expectation, a real bond soon forged itself between Ystros and the jaguär. What evolved between them had changed into something like love, and sometimes they even frolicked with each other, the jaguär for his part very carefully, knowing as he did the extreme fragility of humans.

One evening as the big cat prepared to leave for the night, the apprentice asked, "Jaguär, might I go with you sometime, overnight, when you hunt?" The feline considered the request, and replied, "Yes, if you can move fast, and make no noise when you run or walk. Do you have such skills?"

"I was born, and grew up, in the margin right between town and forest. I have the skills as woodsman and hunter. All that I need to do is to revive them, and get into practise," Ystros responded, as he slid his hand along the big cat's jaw, and then lightly stroked his ears, before returning to his jaw. The big cat pushed against his hand for added stimulation. "'When you feel that you are prepared, we'll hunt together," decided the jaguär. He licked the apprentice's hand, and left for the night.

Several days later, at sunset, the apprentice announced, "I'm ready." The jaguär was drinking from a small bubbling spring not far from the cave. He looked up, and nodded, "Good." Ystros was wearing a sturdy tunic, but instead of sandals he had put on some snug boots of flexible leather tied somewhat above the ankles. He carried a large hunting knife in a scabbard hanging from his waist, plus a small spear but of metal. The big cat smiled at him with approval.

"Let's go," he urged. "As a special concession to you, I'll roam as much as possible through areas free of heavy underbrush." The jungle lattice work of emerald and sombre green had changed into one of onyx and ebony. The last of sunset had also changed but into a cloud-free night lit only by the vast, unending canopy of stars far overhead.

At first they moved rapidly, going deep into the jungle. Ystros at first could only discern a limited amount in the over-all gloom, but soon he began to distinguish among the varying degrees of darkness. The lucid heavens allowed considerable perception by the pure starlight alone, once a human's eyes became accustomed to it.

The team of cat and human had covered a considerable distance when the big cat stopped, and then began moving forward again but very deliberately and stealthily. He had sensed something. Ystros imitated his every move, and made no more noise than the large feline did. A slight breeze blowing their way brought them the odor of feral swine, which they both instantly recognized.

The jaguär stopped again, his thick tail just barely twitching. Suddenly he sprang forward, hitting in his transit a small branch that broke with a loud crack. Both cat and human heard a confused sound of grunts and squeals, as a small herd of wild boar thundered away deeper into the jungle with the greatest possible speed. The tumult of affrighted forest swine crashing through the jungle gradually died away. So much for the big cat's first attempt for that night!

Once more jaguär and apprentice prowled rapidly forward, but then stopped in a little glade when they heard a sound as of some small animal moving in their direction. The two remained utterly quiet, keeping to one side of the clearing behind some foliage. A baby deer, a little doe, entered the glade. She had become somehow detached from her family or herd, and acted lost, confused, and frightened. Standing next to him, Ystros felt the jaguär's instant reaction, as tension and anticipation took over the large feline. He could also sense the beast's fierce, uncompromising hunger.

The jaguär launched himself through the air, and grasped the deer between his powerful jaws. Before the prey could even so much as bleat or whimper, the jaguär had broken her neck with his big pointed teeth. The little creature lapsed at once into unconsciousness. Not far behind, Ystros could sense the big cat's utter concentration and savage abandon as he bit into the creature's abdomen, and began glutting his hunger immediately by consuming the steaming, delicious entrails.

Ordinarily the apprentice might have become a little nauseated by this instant kill and voracious consumption, but he felt himself so completely at one with the jaguär that the human could only tingle at the fragrance of the blood, of the fresh innards, of the tender sweet flesh. So, this was what it was like to be a predator, to kill and eat in the wild! What a thrill, what a revelation! Man had indeed gained so much in his development on into civilization, but correspondingly how much had he also lost! A primordial shiver coursed through the apprentice's body from head to toe. Ystros even felt a certain atavistic hunger, albeit he had eaten a small but sufficient meal early in the evening before departing with the big cat.

The apprentice withdrew farther back, as the jaguär, his initial hunger assuaged, continued eating, but now more deliberately. The night was waning. The time had gone by faster than what Ystros had foreseen, and he had become a little tired and sleepy. At last the jaguär finished eating, leaving hardly more than a pile of bones. The baby deer had largely disappeared into the jaguär.

The big cat looked at the apprentice, and said, "I trust that you have learned something from this night." Ystros nodded, and replied, "Yes, thank you. Much more than what I had thought. Maybe next time I can take a more active role in the hunting." The jaguär smiled his assent, and urged, "Let's return to the lair." They left the glade, and began retracing their way back towards the easternmost littoral of Greater Antillia.

Quoctezu Bids Farewell

(Once again it was midnight, and once again it was Dextra-Theustra's turn to tell a story. After an initial exchange he remained curiously silent some little while, still pondering Sinistra-Theustra's own last narrative. "Well," Dextra-Theustra broke the silence at last from the other side of the throne, "now surely that last story, the one that you related last night, that was a goodly tale. That young man admitted that he had learned something novel and valuable from that first nocturnal hunt with you, no less than from the others that followed, and about which you have hinted. Ystros just like Quoctezu showed himself as unusually fair and trustworthy for a human being, and quite open to a point of view radically different from that of his own species."

("Precisely," rejoined Sinistra-Theustra. "That young man even went so far, and more than once, as to confess that he would rather have lived the good free life of a jaguär than that of a fragile and vacillating human. How often have you ever heard a human confess anything like that?"

("Not very often, if at all," responded Dextra-Theustra. Then, after a thoughtful pause, he continued, "I still think that it was rather odd—given the fact that we both lived about the same time, and that we both enjoyed some extraordinary adventures with members of their so-called and self-called superior species—that during all those lives and all those unusual experiences that we had with humans, that we, you and I, never came upon each other, that our paths never crossed."

(Another long pause ensued before he continued, "But then I always tend to forget that you passed your succession of lives in Greater Antillia, and I passed mine in the similar but smaller landmass of Lesser Antillia. There I had the benefit of my long and valuable friendship with Quoctezu. But, alas! as we both know rather well, all good things come to an end, and eventually Quoctezu bade farewell to me, no less than our nocturnal hunts and other curious adventures. This is how it happened," and so spake Dextra-Theustra once again.)

It was evening, a little before sunset, when the jaguär awoke with a presentiment that something or someone was close at hand. He roused himself, and paced from the back of his cave to its mouth. There stood Quoctezu, as handsome, tanned, and muscular as ever. He carried not only his accustomed weapons, but a brace of small tropical birds fastened together, and hanging from around his neck. The warrior-hunter had thoughtfully defeathered, gutted, and cleaned the little avians. They were miniature iffinixes, a kind of Atlantean pheasant that the jaguär liked a lot, but seldom had a chance to eat because of their scarcity in the Antillias.

Quoctezu removed them from around his neck, untied them, and placed them on the ground before the jaguär. "Here are a few tasty morsels to take the edge off your hunger," the warrior-hunter said with a broad grin. The big cat grinned back, but wasted no time as he lowered his head, and got to work at once, eating the birds, bones and all. What a delicacy! Like all cats big and small, how he loved the taste and smell of birds!

After he finished, he sighed, "Thank you, noble Quoctezu, for this toothsome treat. You know how much I love these tiny birds. But I'm still hungry. You are proposing a nocturnal hunt? I've not seen you for some little time, and have missed our expeditions."

Quoctezu replied, "Yes, as of late I have indeed sojourned otherwhere than Lesser Antillia, and—yes, let's go hunting!" Off they went with all due speed on into the darkling labyrinth of the nocturnal jungle replete with all its myriad calls and cries of bird and beast. Dear listener, by now you know the familiar litany, and there is no need for an overly detailed narrative.

That more or less familiar litany of the hunt: Their search for some suitable prey, prowling forward always with vigilant care. . . . Then their decision to seek out something exotic, however far and wide the quest might take them. . . . Soon thereafter, quite fortuitously, their discovery of their chosen prey, a wild boar all alone, young but fully tusked. . . . Their deliberate and careful stalking of the quarry as the boar himself searched for his favorite greenery. . . . Their silent and gradual approach towards the beast, as he wandered through the jungle. . . . Given the myriad sounds of the tropical forest at night, the prey never heard the discreet and relentless pursuit by jaguär and warrior, never sensed their presence, until he had paused midway through a spacious glade.

As warrior and jaguär had already done many times before, they positioned themselves fore and aft of their quarry, respectively. Firmly grasping his thick-shafted spear, Quoctezu showed himself to the prey, fixing his attention on him. Startled, the beast snorted a few times, but froze. All at once from behind him the big cat sprang out of the forest, and landed on the creature's back, digging in his claws as deep as he could. In pain and rage, unable to shake his attacker off, the prey charged forward, impaling himself onto Quoctezu's waiting spear.

The warrior-hunter stood solid as a rock as the spearhead pierced the quarry's breast. He drove it in as deep as he could. Almost simultaneously, in an immense display of strength, Quoctezu lifted up off the ground with the spear the front of the wild boar's body, and held it there, with the jaguär still in place on his back. The jaguär had meanwhile sunk his powerful teeth into the animal's neck, exerting such tremendous force at that point that he broke the spine. The quarry soon expired in a violent convulsion of blood, sputum, and trembling. Jaguär and warrior had made their kill for the night.

The warrior-hunter quickly and efficiently skinned and cleaned the carcass, first removing the entrails, and tossing them to the big cat. With practised expertise Quoctezu split the beast down the spine, reducing him to two haunches convenient to carry. The time had passed quickly. Nodding to the jaguär, the human urged, "Let's go back to the cave," as he carried both haunches, one on either shoulder.

Once they had returned to the jaguär's lair, Quoctezu laid one haunch on the ground just in the cave's mouth, and his own haunch he placed up in a tree to one side of the entrance. He found a stream, close at hand, where he proceeded to clean his soiled and blood-smeared body. When he returned to the cave, he found the jaguär inside, assiduously washing himself. The cat had glutted his hunger on the boar's innards, and for the moment was content.

Quoctezu stood before him, and said, "My noble brother, this is our last hunt, and this is how I bid you farewell. The boar is my final gift to you. While away, I visited Atlantillia. There certain officials at court interviewed me for a special position. I am now the Master of the Hunt to the reigning king of Atlantillia. I shall reside at the palace in Atzatlan, but shall direct the principal hunting for His Majesty in both Greater Antillia and Lesser Antillia. But I shall make a point to stay my professional distance from your lair, and I shall never knowingly hunt you."

The jaguär came up to him, and stood on his hind legs while resting his upper body against the hunter's chest. They had done this before, but only on special occasions. Quoctezu held the big cat against him, and embraced him firmly and warmly. Then he lowered him to the ground. Looking up at him, the jaguär spoke in his turn: "My noble brother, I shall miss you, as well as our hunting together, hut I wish you the best in your new life." The warrior-hunter once again slid his hand along the jaguär's jaw, rubbing it sensitively, and then lightly stroked his ears, before returning to the jaw. The big cat pushed against his hand for added stimulation. When the human moved it away, the jaguär licked the hand for the last time as a final gesture of affection.

Quoctezu went over to the tree that stood at one side of the entrance, retrieved his haunch of wild boar, and placed it on his shoulder. He then turned back to the jaguär, and waving his free hand in farewell, he said for the last time, "Now that's what I call a civilized jungle!" His eyes were brimming with tears. He then strode resolutely away, heading back to his village. The warrior and the jaguär never met again.

The Passing of an Astrologer

(So spake Sinistra-Theustra, "Yes, as you so cogently observed before your most recent story, concerning Quoctezu's farewell, all good things come to an end. Eventually both Cyphron and Ystros also bade me farewell. As in your own case it also turned out as a deeply moving episode, if I do say so myself."

(Sinistra-Theustra was holding forth once again from his own side of the double throne inside the great inner thronehall of the royal palace at the northern end of the island kingdom that was Atlantillia.

("Please don't mention it," interjected Dextra-Theustra. "I can still feel the grief and sadness of that farewell!"

(A slight pause ensued before the other jaguär continued, at first somewhat contritely. "I beg your pardon, my noble brother! I mention it only as a point of reference. In my case, at any rate, this is how Cyphron and then Ystros bade me farewell," and so spake Sinistra-Theustra once again.)

For quite some little time now the jaguär had abandoned his easternmost lair completely to his human colleagues, and had taken up ordinary residence at his westernmost abode, the cave, or series of small caves, located amid the high rocky bluffs at the western end of the eastern highlands of Greater Antillia. He did miss his human friends a little, but he did not miss the luxurious tapestries, carpets, and furnishings that had transformed his easternmost lair into a lavish astrological studio.

The jaguär had now resided with the astrologer Cyphron and his apprentice Ystros for several years on an off-and-on-again basis. Like Quoctezu's jaguär, this big cat had picked up by now quite a good working knowledge of the best and purest Atlantean. For the nonce he preferred living alone in the stark and natural cave that was his westernmost lair, and that looked out over the dense tropical forest covering much of that part of Greater Antillia.

Meanwhile Cyphron had become increasingly fragile, as well as weakened by extreme old age, and rarely got out of bed. More and more Ystros had to tend to Cyphron's personal needs. In particular, as a last resort, he helped him cast one final horoscope, his very own. The stars unequivocally foretold Cyphron's impending death in a matter of only a few days.

The astrologer spoke: "Ystros, dearer to me than any son, I shall die soon, and I wish to be buried here. I would also like to say goodbye to our noble and beautiful jaguär. Would you please go to his westernmost lair, and ask him to come back to this cave, so that I may bid him farewell?" Ystros nodded his assent, and held his master's hand so as to reassure him that he would fulfill this last request.

Early the next morning the apprentice got ready for the long journey by foot. Making sure that Cyphron had everything that he needed, and that he could find it close at hand, Ystros kissed his master goodbye, and set out, carrying a backpack with food for a few meals, no less than several weapons—dagger, sword, and spear—using the last as a kind of staff, and thus ready to use for defense at any time. Realistically the apprentice anticipated no problem, either from feral beast, or from any Antillians, for the most part gentle folk who treated the Atlanteans as brothers or cousins.

Ystros made good time. He was a very fast walker. The route to the other lair was a well-marked path that he had often taken to the western edge of these eastern highlands. He reached the jaguär's westernmost lair around noon, and waited outside the cave, moving with utmost quiet. He ate a little food, and rested. Somehow sensing his presence, the jaguär roused himself earlier than usual, and around mid-afternoon came out of his cave.

"Greetings, my noble brother!" The young man stood up, saluted the big cat, and continued talking not only in the immemorial speech common to the non-humans, but just as much in the most polished Atlantean, mixing the twain together in an expert manner. "Pardon me for disturbing your solitude. My master is dying, and wishes to see you one last time so he can say goodbye. Will you not come back with me to your easternmost lair so he may do so?"

"Greetings, my noble brother!" rejoined the jaguär. "Yes, I shall happily accompany you back to the other cave so Cyphron and I can bid each other farewell. But I shall have to make a kill somewhere en route. I have not eaten much for a few days." Ystros answered at once, "I have prepared a good haunch of tender young deer meat against your coming back, if you can wait until we reach the other cave." The jaguär nodded his head in assent, and off they went along the well-marked route back to the easternmost lair.

By mid-evening, or somewhat later, apprentice and jaguär arrived back at the eastern cave that looked out over the wide passage of water separating the eastern end of Greater Antillia from the island proper itself of Atlantillia. From the high rocky bluffs that marked the cave's location they could see the glittering lights tracing the elongated harbors that made up the chief part of Atzatlan the capital city. As apprentice and jaguär came up to their shared abode, Ystros thought with panic, "Cyphron? Is he still alright?!" but then found immediate reassurance. Several candles in candlesticks on the small table stood burning with their small but steady flames. Only Cyphron could have lit the candles.

The twain entered the luxuriously transformed lair, and discovered the old astrologer lightly napping in his bed. This couch occupied a kind of alcove extending laterally from the main space of the cavern. Ystros decided to let him wake up by himself. Meanwhile he fetched the haunch of tender young deer meat that he had prepared, and gave it to the jaguär but out in the small glade beyond the cavern's entrance. Otherwise the noise of the jaguär eating might interrupt the astrologer's needed rest before he might awaken spontaneously.

The young man sat himself in a chair near the bed, keeping a silent vigil. Meanwhile the big cat ate his fill of the preserved haunch, and assuaged his thirst from the small bubbling spring not far from the cave. He then entered Cyphron's bedroom-alcove, and laid himself down close to the apprentice's feet. A great silence descended over all. Only the nocturnal sounds of bird and beast made themselves heard outside the cavern.

Prompted finally by some premonition, but sufficiently rested, Cyphron awoke around midnight, and noted at once his dear apprentice in company with the jaguär. The old astrologer smiled, and greeted them both. Ystros rose at once, and kissed his master. The big cat warmly licked the old man's hand in greeting.

Cyphron sighed with happiness and fulfillment, and now spoke with quiet but palpable conviction, "My dear and noble and beautiful jaguär, thank you so much for coming back here to honor my request. My death is upon me at any time now. I wish to thank you once again for allowing us the use of your favorite lair. It has meant much to me, as it has meant much to get to know your good self in a way normally denied to us human creatures. We cherish the unique wisdom and knowledge that you have shared with us as your friends."

The astrologer paused to catch his breath, and rally his declining strength. "While I still have time and ability to do so, I must now settle one or two questions. First, Ystros, thank you for everything! You have made a perfect apprentice, dearer to me than any son. At my death you become a full-fledged astrologer, and take over all the effects and appurtenances of my profession. Second, dear jaguär, we shall restore to you this your easternmost lair following my death and burial. Ystros will dismantle our astrological studio here, and return to Atlantillia. With your permission, kind jaguär, I shall be buried here outside the cave. There, I am done. I hope that you both agree to my wishes."

Deeply moved, both apprentice and jaguär indicated their acquiescence to Cyphron's last wishes, and continued their vigil, while the venerable astrologer lapsed back into silence and slumber. Sometime a little before dawn, Cyphron suddenly roused up, emitted several sharp coughs, and then gave up the ghost. Ystros rose, embraced his master, closed his eyes, and gave him a final kiss. The big cat himself not only licked Cyphron's hand but even ventured to lick his cheek as a mark of especial respect and affection. Eyes brimming with tears, the apprentice rubbed the back of the jaguär's neck.

With odds and ends of planking that he happened to have at hand, the apprentice made a simple but adequate coffin. He laid his master inside it, arrayed in full astrological robes, together with other personal and professional regalia. Ystros then buried his master at a spot not far from the cave in a kind of outdoor alcove, graced by a small grove of trees, that went back amid the high rocky bluffs. After the burial the young man piously intoned a poem to Cyphron's memory, and poured a libation of his favorite pomegranate wine over the fresh earth tamped down over the grave. It had used up most of the day for Ystros to accomplish all of this. In the late afternoon the jaguär had roused himself out of sleep, and had stood in attendance while Ystros had read the poem, and poured the libation.

After the little ritual Ystros retired to a well-deserved rest, while the jaguär departed to go hunting for the night. The big cat now resumed his accustomed life at his easternmost lair. Meanwhile the apprentice-become-full-fledged-astrologer began packing up all the paraphernalia and personal effects, taking down the tapestries, rolling up the carpets, and readying the furnishings for shipment to Atzatlan. When the large boat arrived that came with supplies every thirty days or so, Ystros informed the captain and sailors of Cyphron's death and burial, no less than the decision made by astrologer and apprentice that Ystros would now return to Atlantillia with all their effects, furnishings, and paraphernalia to set up a new life there for himself.

The jaguär prudently made himself conspicuous by his absence until he could find himself alone once again with Ystros. Everyone soon began carrying the various bales, bundles, and furnishings down from the cave's location amid the high bluffs, and then storing them aboard the boat that captain and crew had left floating, but secured, off the small dock that they had built sometime after Cyphron and Ystros had first settled in at the cave. The former apprentice climbed back up to the cave one last time to say goodbye to the jaguär, now dearer to him than any brother. But even after he had established a prosperous astrological business for himself in Atzatlan, Ystros would still return every now and then to visit the jaguär and the site of his former master's grave, sometimes even staying overnight to go hunting with the big cat, just as in the days when they had lived together.

When Ystros climbed back up to the cave one last time, to bid farewell to the jaguär, something happened that neither jaguär nor human could ever forget. As he had often done before, the former apprentice bent down to rub the big cat's jaw, no less than to stroke his ears, before bringing his hand back to the jaw. The jaguär as usual pushed against his human brother's hand for added stimulation. When the hand moved away, the jaguär licked it as a gesture of affection.

But then Ystros did something that he had never done before. He dropped down on one knee, very gently picked up the big cat's right front paw, and licked it in his very own turn! Who could say which one, the human or the jaguär, found himself the more astonished by such a spontaneous gesture of reciprocal tenderness?!

Epilogue

(So spake Dexter, or Dextra-Theustra, and so spake Sinister, or Sinistra-Theustra, sharing their tales, anecdotes, and reminiscences, presumably through all eternity, or a fair imitation of it. And when Atlantillia sank beneath the salt seas all on that single day and night of rain, earthquakes, and supercolossal waves—along with the rest of the Empire of Atlantis—so the royal palace with its great inner thronehall, together with its double throne flanked by the two heraldic jaguärs, went beneath the ocean as well, down to the bottom of the wide passage that still exists between Greater Antillia and Lesser Antillia. There presumably the granite images holding captive the souls or spirits of the two once-alive jaguärs now rear up from the ocean floor, and there presumably the statues continue their unending conversation. But as powerful as the magick of the sculptors who made them may have proven in Atlantean times, it did not, it could not, transcend the Great Cataclysm. The spirits held captive in those images for centuries found freedom and expansion at last, whether to fade into blissful oblivion, or to develop on into further lives or incarnations.)

Cephalopod in Residence

Translated from the Atlantean of Prince Atlantarion.

Dedicated to Gahan Wilson, in mysterium.

The chambered nautilus, so closely furled
Inside his carapace of spiral shell,
In splendor sits alone, enthroned, empearled:
Eddying throughout, in every nook and ell,
The mothering ocean swirls around the shell
Where coral gardens breathe, unknown and cool:
Encased within the armor of that cell,
The little squid inside is no one's fool,
But glides about, from place to place, a rare but vibrant jewel:

Howevermuch poeticized he might appear,
This chambered nautilus—he, too, must seek renewal—
Through need of sex and food, that knot of love and fear:

Whether by sun, by moon, by underwater gloom,
    The chambered nautilus shall thus live out his term,
    Unless devoured by squid, or fish, or wee small worm,
Until that spiral shell becomes at length his tomb.

Colossal Chambered Nautilus

Translated from the Atlantean of Prince Atlantarion.

Dedicated to Marsha Raleigh, in recognizance.

This *Architeuthis princeps*, what a squid!—
Whose looks alone might give most people angst—
In what dark ocean-deeps has he not hid?
His sixty feet and sometimes more in length
Endow his tentacles with tactile strength
That more than one sperm whale has cause to rue:
But what exists to cause this *princeps* angst?—
Except those whales, those mollusks, that pursue
The squid himself, and more, with all their famished retinue:

Sometimes the squid ejects, behind his nest of arms,
A pitch-black ink that stains the seas with witches' brew,
Insuring by that mix his own protective charms:

Some half a billion years agone, another giant squid,
    But clothed in armor, here deployed his tentacles,
    More potent talismans than any pentacles—
That one colossal chambered nautilus with giant id.

Hippokampoi

Translated from the Atlantean of an anonymous poet.

Two small seahorses drifting through the ocean
Had lodged themselves amid some offshore kelp
To rest a spell from all that endless motion:
Incapable of whimper or of yelp,
Each one but little more than sea-born whelp,
They idly swayed and shifted with the tide:
Instinct apart, they had no need of help,
But managed on their own to feed, to glide,
To live in that vast world of seaweed . . . to one side:

At the pouch of the one of greater girth
The tiniest horses came out from inside—
It was the male, himself, who gave them birth!

So forth they came, one little horse after another,
Out of their father who was also thus their mother!

As One Seahorse to Another

Translated from the Atlantean of Prince Atlantarion.

*Dedicated to Robin Rowe Reynolds III,
Patron of the Arts.*

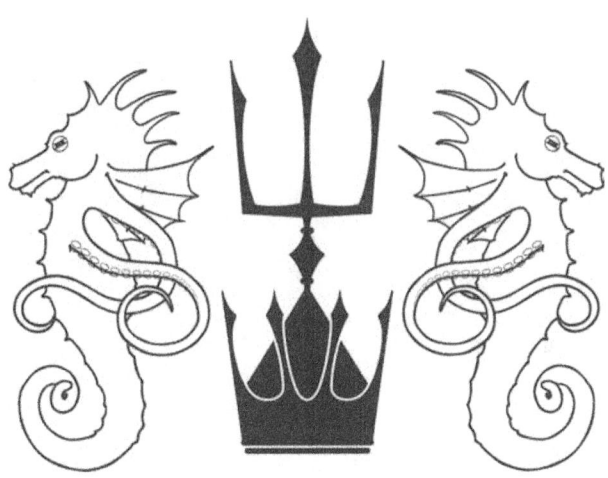

The Little Horses of the Ocean Sea

The little horses of the Ocean Sea? You find them where they find their habitat in grass-filled inlets and in shallow bays, and sometimes even in those undisturbed lagoons near mangrove swamps.

You find them there where warm or lukewarm waters, green or yellow-green, transform from blue green depths to gleaming shoals, and where those very shallows radiate and sparkle in the sunlight.

You find these little horses of the sea where oftentimes they twine their tails around sea whips, or blades of ocean-grass, or strands of dark-brown kelp, or other species of sea wrack, those larger classes of seaweed.

They drift and glide and float below the chartreuse waves, themselves like insects with their hard-cased shells, but more like half-transparent or half-solid ocean-steeds, perchance for ghostly riders that return from the seas of Otherwhere.

The little horses of the Ocean Sea? You find them where they find their habitat in grass-filled inlets and in shallow bays, and sometimes even in those undisturbed lagoons near mangrove swamps.

An Oldster Gives Advice

In the grass-filled inlet of a shallow bay, where the wide blades of tall sea-green sea-grass reflect the sunlight much less than the sea-green seawater itself, an oldster, a much older male seahorse, was holding forth to a large school of much smaller seahorses with great big eyes, born but a few days before.

"Welcome once again into our midst, you newcomers! You have been among us now long enough, at least a few days, to have gotten your bearings. By now you should feel quite at home in our safe and pleasant inlet. And more than that, speaking protectively, I note with approval that your pigment cells—or chromatophores, to speak more properly—are functioning perfectly well. Just as much as us oldsters you have now become a nice bright green just like the nice bright green of the sea-grass that sways and shifts with the tide here in our home."

The oldster paused to gather his thoughts, and then began again. "Let me reassure you. I think that all of you will do just fine here on the edge of the great ocean. But as for you male youngsters, a special bit of advice and encouragement. Yours is the responsibility to bring forth the next generation of seahorses, and out of your very own bodies. That's a real struggle, but you'll manage alright. Yes, you'll find out soon enough what it's like, what it's all about. Any questions before leaving?"

A Mating Dance by Sunlight

It is a sparkling expanse of grass-filled, sea-green shoals lying somewhere off the western coast of Lesser Antillia. It is the mating season, the spawning time. It is the mating dance by day, by daylight, by sunlight—and all of it underwater.

En masse it seems, the generally mute seahorses have all at once found their voice, and send forth an intense, insistent, relentlessly monotonous drumming sound. This drumming makes a kind of fanfare, a multifarious roll of drums that call all the dancers to the dance!

Line up with all the other dancers, dos-à-dos, and face your partner, still do-se-do! So now they start, and away they go! They nod, they glide, they bow, they scrape, they twirl, they pirouette! They glide past, they glide close by, they glide together, and the dance is over. They clinch.

Without further ado the lady seahorse produces the eggs, depositing them inside the male seahorse's empty brood-pouch, but empty now no longer. As the eggs enter the pouch, the male seahorse fertilizes them. This is without a doubt a moment of rapture for both partners. Male and female unclinch. Gestation belongs now for some ten days exclusively to the male. Her task done, the female gets out of there but fast!

Labor and Deliverance

Our poor pregnant male seahorse has been drifting and feeding now for days, gradually shifting down from the sparkling expanse of grass-filled, sea-green shallows on into a slightly deeper space of somewhat bluegreen water.

Here there flourish in this locale not just the usual sea-grasses and sea-ferns but vivid and many-colored anemones, brilliant clusters of red and orange and golden-yellow sponges, along with little forests of corals displaying the very same colors.

Here the seahorses that habitually live in this locale exhibit well-near the same opulent shades of orange and red and yellow gold as the sponges and the corals.

Our pregnant male has at last come to rest, his tail wrapped around a piece of sea-fan. His time of deliverance is at hand, and in an ambiance of unearthly loveliness. Every few moments our grave and gravid ocean-steed pushes his bulging pouch forward. The pouch's little aperture, like an eye closely shut, begins to open and widen.

Twitching and trembling, the seahorse undergoes the keenest labor pains, tensing his entire physique at such times. He squeezes hard, and the tiny first foal comes out. During a series of spasmodic or convulsive jerks more sea-foals emerge, one after another. After several hours the adult male is done, surrounded by several dozens of his own brood. Exhausted, he drifts off to find another perch, on the stem of some sea-fern.

At first these littlest ocean-horses drift around, quite helpless, wrong end up, but not for long. Almost at once they position themselves upright, gliding away to roost on underwater twig or tendril. How tiny they appear, but how big seem their eyes! Is it with wonder that their sage and bulging eyes look out, and then turn around? Each big insectoid eye swivels free from the other, and one eye looks behind while one eye looks ahead. Exhausted, the father—or is it the mother?—pays the brood no heed, he needs his well-earned rest. Parent or no parent, it matters not at all, their instinct shall suffice.

A Proper Mode of Life

> Eaters of death are all: Life shall not live,
> Save that its food be death: No atomy
> In any star, or heaven's remotest moon,
> But hath a billion billion times been made
> The food of insatiable life, and food
> Of death insatiate: For all is change—
> —Clark Ashton Smith, "The Ghoul and the Seraph."

In the grass-filled inlet of the shallow bay that we have overseen before, where the wide blades of tall sea-green sea-grass reflect the sunlight much less than the sea-green seawater itself, our oldster, the much older male seahorse, is holding forth again more or less to the same large school of seahorses first observed soon after their birth. Only now, some sixty days or so later, the young seahorses have almost matured, and are just about ready to mate. "Well, here you are again, all or most of you! Here you are, almost grown up! By now you have learned our mode of life, our proper mode of life, and are now comfortable with it. We feed, we mate, we give birth, we hang out, we hang around. We sway, we shift, we glide, we drift, we float, and in particular we stay out of strong ocean currents. But possibly most of all, we feed, we snack, we hang out. And few are the predators that chase after us. Such is our life!"

The oldster clears his throat before continuing. "As protected as we may seem, we still must obey Mother Nature's laws, just as any other form of life must. Our mode of existence, our proper mode of existence, is direct and simple. We have few natural enemies, and we survive by living right at the margin of things, whether the lagoon, whether the shore, or whether the sea. There is a moral somewhere in all that, but I leave it for you to figure out. Whatever, it's not a bad life at all!"

A Ghostly Dance by Starlight

It is a vast expanse of coastal shallows during a calm and a clear night. All the brilliant colors that rule here during the day—within the shoals below the surface—have transmuted into blacks and greys and ghostly whites.

This is the setting for an otherworldly dance, the mating dance by night, by nightlight, by starlight. This illumination permits only the least perceptible colors. If any such whatsoever survive, they have all changed to ghostlike hues.

The living seahorses are all asleep, or immobile. But at midnight the everlasting sound of the waves on the shore, that music that has played since the sea herself has existed, summons forth from the depths of aeons past the legions of the multifarious ancestors of the present ocean-steeds.

And forth they come, fantastic little creatures, made only of gleaming witchlight, or fading amaranth, or evanescent silver, or spectral mother-of-pearl. All at once the ghostly seahorses appear, to dance atop the quiescent waters. They nod, they glide, they bow, they scrape, they twirl, they pirouette!

All through the nocturnal hours the little phosphorescent entities dance and counterdance, until at last at the first flush of dawn they glide back deep into the nothingness that gave them their ghostly renaissance.

Dominium atque Apotheosis

Yes, we find our little seahorses, and some not quite so little, inhabiting all or most of the seven seas, but for the most part the warm or warmish waters that encircle our planet.

But lately, more and more, we have found them in cool, if not outright chilly, as well as in deeper, waters. And they range in size or length all the way from the width of one or two human fingers through the width or even the length of a human hand to the very length of a big human foot.

And they say that the fishermen who live on the remnant islands of Mu and Lemuria have discovered off their own shores these last and largest specimens. What then can we make of these ocean-steeds that have appeared in colder waters, or even at considerable depths? What can all of this portend?

If it were not for the fact that seahorses cannot sustain themselves in the very coldest waters, or where the most powerful currents operate, then we could almost state, according to the rate at which this charming and apparently harmless creature reproduces, that they might soon take over the world by sheer force of numbers!

Such a possibility might then lead to their inevitable domination of our entire planet, and thus even to their consequent and ineluctable apotheosis!

Hadrian and Antinous

He, Hadrian, and he, Antinous—
Whose lives, linked at one time, no one could sever,
Whose names, thus linked, have now come down to us:
What fate or circumstance brought them together,
So that their love would join their names forever,
The Emperor of Rome, *the* youth divine?
What wisdom did that emperor not gather
Out of his lover's lips, which would combine
What beauty from his mouth like honey mixed with wine?

That lover's death—amid the Nile—had made of him
A god, like those of field and flock, of grove and vine,
One last new god, one more than fair of face and limb:

His death—was it an accident, a suicide?
    Impelled by dire prediction and from inner strife,
       Himself he sacrificed?—to save his lover's life?
Who knows? The Nile reveals—what? An enigmatic tide.

Pan and Priapus

How many generations have gone by
Since Pan and since Priapus, unashamed,
Last reared their manhood in the public's eye?!
Be-plinthed, be-flowered, and all but picture-framed,
They nonchalantly stood where we have named,
In kitchen garden or at city gate:
The Satyr still remains at large, untamed,
And like Priapus he is free to mate
With whom or what he will—beast, human, curved or straight:

Why have men made these laws against themselves,
Against their phallus, thus to militate
Against the frank depiction of themselves?

At least the Greeks and Romans proved upright
    While dealing with themselves in life and art—
    At least they showed more ballocks and more heart.
In this one way were they not more upright?!

A Ship Sails Out to Sea

Translated from the Atlantean of an unknown poet.

The ship was breezing out to sea by sunset,
Leaving behind the seaport's little town,
About the same time as the moon's own onset:
The moon came up just as the sun went down,
Leaving behind a blaze, a fiery crown,
A coronal of purple, gold, and flame:
Inside this blaze the ship appeared to drown
As it sailed straight into that very same,
As from the bow the shaft shoots out dead right on aim:

The moon's pale disk now rode above Earth's eastern rim
When whim of happenstance enforced its elder claim—
Both crown and ship had vanished in that interim:

The sunset had turned grey, but where had that ship gone?
    The trireme with her crew had vanished through some gate,
    Into another realm, dimension, or estate?
Or had that sunset changed to just another dawn?

Barcarolle

Translated from the French of Michel de Labretagne.

While smaller fish swim everywhere around,
The monsters of the deep, from squid to shark,
From whale to octopus, no less abound:
Noah, how many creatures in your ark
Could find no place, nor yet in any barque!—
By circumstance—what's a flood to a fish?
The Ocean Sea, so deep as it is dark,
Holds many secrets, gem or skull or dish—
Statue, jar, ship, well-near whatever one might wish:

Not only can the sea bring back the lost and old,
But she first nurtures all of life, and not just fish,
A primal cause unemphasized and unextolled:

Considering the miracles of Time and Space
    There is no greater one than this, of life and sea:
    How life, implanted in her depths, developes free,
To leave that element, and find another base.

On Reading Edmund Spenser Once Again

> Upon a great adventure he was bond,
> That greatest *Gloriana* to him gave,
> That greatest Glorious Queene of *Faerie* lond,
> —Spenser, *The Faerie Queene*, I: I: III.

Discovering anew *The Faerie Queene*
After so many years, is not unlike
Finding a source of water deep and clean:
Chaucer, that "well of English undefiled,"
As he by Spenser has been quite well styled,
Is not more deep, full, pure, and eloquent:
But better, and more apt, what it is like,
Is finding some entire new continent
With fields, hills, rivers, mountains, all of broad extent:

But only woods and woodlands link this whole terrain
Below the vast and all-enclosing firmament,
This realm ruled by Panthèa's distant châtelaine:

For she who sovereigns this Faerie-land's demesne,
    Who rules from her grand capital Cleopolis,
    And from Panthèa, palace and acropolis,
Is that same châtelaine who is the Faerie Queene.

Nine Happy Goldfish

Translated from the Atlantean of Prince Atlantarion.

*Dedicated to Gary H. W. Wong, in gratitude
for his dynamic watercolor
coincidentally of the same name.*

Nine happy goldfish swimming in a pond
Descend through dark-green depths, each in a swirl,
As though from seas of space that lie beyond:
While bright or sombre hues flit, flash, unfurl,
Their nimble bodies curl and then uncurl,
Three red, three gold, three black, these little carp:
They dance and counterdance, whirl and unwhirl,
As if in time to lute or lyre or harp,
How small, how precious, and how frail, these little carp!

An Archaeologist Uncovers the Past

> Where dolent griffins weep for some forgotten dream,
> And crowns and thrones and tridents lost from old Atlantis gleam:
> —Sidney-Fryer, "A Summoning of Shadows."

A thousand miles to the west of Portugal, the ancient Lusitania, there lies the far-flung archipelago of the Azores, extending four hundred miles farther to the west, somewhat south of latitude forty degrees north, almost on the same degree of latitude as Lisbon, or Lisboa. At the east-southeastern end of the archipelago, there lies the largest of all the islands, São Miguel, and at that island's western end there opens out the enormous chalice of a very wide crater, or caldera, the remnant that a colossal volcanic explosion created long ago.

This is the valley of Sete Cidades, thus named after the legendary King of the Seven Cities, reportedly of Atlantean provenance. The environing caldera walls, rising hundreds of feet on all sides, resolutely protect the verdantly lush and incredibly fertile interior from the powerful oceanic winds that sweep across São Miguel. This interior contains an entire unique world of its own: productive farms, evergreen and other forests, the one single town of Sete Cidades, the two great lakes of contrasting colors—emerald or turquoise or sapphire—separated by the narrow land-bridge that connects the terrain on the north and south shores of the twin lakes.

Rising up from the tremendous depths of the Atlantic Ocean, São Miguel and all the other islands making up the Azores are actually the mountain peaks of the former island continent of Atlantis, the home terrain of a vast maritime empire: that is, according to ancient legends that ultimately derive most likely from Plato's Atlantis Mythos, or it might be, possibly, from some other sources as well. Who knows?!

Peh Ng Wen had awakened a little earlier than what he would have liked, and could not return to sleep. Still he felt sufficiently rested, and this day's events, as planned, made him so excited and energized that he decided to get up, and go outside his own solo tent that he rated as the little expedition's leader. The shelter was comfortable enough, what with its window flaps and built-in floor.

Because he was a small man, but muscular and well-knit, he had no trouble clearing his head below the tent's roof. He doffed his thin summer pajamas, and then donned in a jiffy his daytime gear: levis, low laced-up boots, sturdy long-sleeved shirt, and a ranger's hat to cover his black, straight hair that lay flat, and that harmonized nicely with his yellow-tan skin.

Was that a small earthquake tremor that he just managed to sense? He shrugged, no big deal. Such tremors happened often.

Since he generally woke up earlier than the other expedition members—the six other archaeologists and the small support staff also in place—it was Peh, more often than anyone else, who woke everybody up. It was five o'clock, and much too early to arouse the entire camp yet, reveille generally taking place around six thirty. Besides, as he often did, he liked to enjoy the early morning by himself, to collect his thoughts and emotions, and to review things past, present, and future. This was his meditation or contemplation time.

Although of mixed Vietnamese and Cambodian origin—his wealthy parents had fled to South America when the French abandoned French Indo-China way back in the middle 1950s—Peh, as their last child born in 1975, had grown up exclusively in Uruguay, and spoke not only Vietnamese and Cambodian but also Spanish, Portuguese, French, and English.

His family still resided at their seaside villa surrounded by lush gardens in that Atlántida that lies some twenty-five miles east of Montevideo, the capital of Uruguay, sited on the northern littoral of the Rio de la Plata, and some hundred and twenty miles east of Buenos Aires, the capital of Argentina, located in turn on the southern littoral of that same great estuary.

Perhaps because he had grown up in Atlántida, the Spanish form of the name Atlantis, Peh had nurtured a special fascination since his early childhood for that semimythical place. Of course, as a budding archaeologist he soon realized that Atlantis as described by Plato was in all likelihood no more than a glittering dream. However, that had not lessened his fascination with the subject, even as he had risen with phenomenal rapidity in his chosen profession. Now at the age of only thirty-two he had arrived at the pinnacle of his precocious career. To date he had successfully headed three far-separated expeditions, one in Outer Mongolia, one in southwestern U.S., and one in eastern Poland. The present and completely secret expedition, done under the aegis of the Portuguese government in Lisbon during the spring of 2007, and based at the western end of São Miguel, represented his fourth and quite unprecedented one. It bid fair to turn the world of orthodox archaeology right plumb on its head. This thought brought a fleeting but wide grin to the young man's face as it flashed through his mind.

After setting his sleeping bag in order, and noting again the heavy condensation on parts of the tent's interior, Peh went through the largest flap that served as his front door, and stepped outside. Was that another small earthquake tremor that he felt? He shrugged as he walked into the heaviest fog that he had ever encountered in his entire life, an absolute cloud lying all over the caldera and hugging the ground, a mist so dense that he could hardly see six or seven feet before his face. Because of the near absolute stillness, he had suspected some kind of fog even before leaving his tent but nothing like this.

The density of the fog imposed a preternatural quiet, an almost absolute silence, over everything. The near eternal oceanic winds had ceased, and in that stillness the fog had formed over the ocean, and had covered the land evidently during the night and earliest morning. From where he stood, Peh could not hear the first awakening sounds from the nearest farms. The cessation of the winds, the utter stillness, the opaque fog had already marked this day of all days as extraordinary beyond all precedent.

Presumably just another group of carefree campers, or so it might well have seemed to a casual observer, the seven young archaeologists and their small support staff had set up their encampment just a few days beforehand. They had sited it in a little glade inside the woods at the extreme western, or actually northwestern, end of the caldera. There the southern shore ceased at the limit of the western and much larger of the two volcanic lakes, where it abutted against the caldera's tall environing walls, preventing any further movement around the lake on dry land. Despite the fog Peh knew his route easily from the camp to the almost hidden entrance of the outer cave that he had found. He had been camping by himself on vacation just a month or so beforehand.

The cave descended into a very long tunnel, apparently natural, that descended in turn into what seemed a man-made tunnel, and equally long. Following this, one descended yet again into a vast man-made chamber, Peh's crowning discovery. Urging secrecy, he had communicated his extraordinary find at once in person to the authorities at Lisbon. His report in turn had led to the present archaeological expedition. Moreover, the report had set it up under top-secret conditions out of necessity. The Portuguese government had permitted him to choose his collaborators and support staff as he had wished.

Lost in thought about the sequence of events leading up to the present moment, Peh suddenly regained full consciousness of his surroundings, and found himself standing in front of the almost invisible entrance to the cave. The penetrating chill of the dense oceanic fog made him shiver all at once. He turned around to go back to his tent, and put on a jacket until the fog lifted. He decided to remain inside until it became time for him to rouse the camp.

Today was the big day when at nine o'clock he would guide the other young archaeologists and most of the support staff on into the cave for the very first time, and show them his mindboggling discovery. The other six specialists included a Portuguese, an Azorean, a Spaniard, an American, a Frenchman, and an Egyptian. He had gotten to know them all on previous digs. Peh had now gotten them all worked up to a rare pitch of excitement. He could hardly wait to have everyone get up, fix and eat breakfast, clean up the camp and set it in order, and then put everything in motion.

Was that yet another little earthquake tremor that he felt? He shrugged again, no big deal. One often felt such quick, small tremors. The Azores, after all, were volcanic in origin. One expected these tiny, often almost-imperceptible tremblings to happen at just about any odd moment.

By nine o'clock the expedition had everything ready to roll, the near impenetrable fog had completely lifted, the sun was dazzling in its brightness, and the air was radiantly fresh and buoyant. Two members of the support staff manned the gasoline-fuelled generator inside the camp. They had it functioning perfectly.

Two other members stood as guards by the almost hidden mouth of the outer cave. Strange, how nobody could find it until they stood right there, virtually within its mouth. A black rubberized safety wire went from the generator to the very large wooden spool from which still two more members of the support staff were slowly unwinding the wire as they rolled the spool forward inside the cave descending into the first long, seemingly natural tunnel.

The seven archaeologists, the four men and the three women, with Peh in the lead, followed by the rest of the support staff, had all gone ahead, carrying floodlights, tripods, cameras, and other equipment. Everyone going underground wore miners' helmets with little electric lights. It would require the better part of the morning to set everything up inside the vast man-made chamber. Probably by early afternoon, after lunch and a little rest, the expedition members could begin measuring, photographing, and recording the find in other ways under the brilliant floodlights.

As everyone going to the great chamber was descending from the natural tunnel to the man-made one, another mild tremor took place, but so mild that hardly anyone noticed or commented. The two guards at the almost hidden mouth of the outer cave felt it much more strongly. "Let 'er rip," said one. "Maybe next time it'll be the really big shake, rattle, and roll," joked the other.

Setting up all the technological paraphernalia took much longer than anticipated. Lunch was late, and almost everyone who had gone underground experienced a curious lassitude, falling asleep, and then staying asleep, for something more than just a little nap. The air inside the vast man-made chamber, despite its obvious depth under the earth and then the ocean above it, proved strangely fresh and buoyant. It seemed anomalous, and the scientifically knowledgeable could not explain it. Where did the air come from? By the time that the expedition members returned to their tasks underground, and had everything ready, it was the middle of the afternoon.

Under the rather dazzling floodlights Peh smiled, and complimented his crew for their work. He gestured around him, like an artist surrounded by the diorama that he has designed and painted, and engineered with the help of assistant painters. "Look," he said, and they looked. It seemed as if they had not really looked before, so busy had they kept themselves handling equipment and setting it in place. Assimilating the scene consciously for the first time, they let out a collective breath of wonder and awe. The high-ceilinged chamber was immense, unique, superb, and not like anything else that they had ever seen, at least in the over-all sense.

The floor plan was not quite a perfect square, but with major rectangular recesses marking the four cardinal points of the compass—north, south, east, and west—each recess marked in turn by a huge metal door with double valves and ponderous ornate frame. The expedition had made their entrance into the chamber from the long man-made tunnel through what was the eastern portal. The double doors had opened readily, the hinges evidently in perfect working order. Although designed to seem functional, the double doors on the three other portals would not open, and evidently could not open. When struck with the fist, they gave off a sepulchral and hollow sonority. On all sides massive columns of an unusual design, some fluted, some not, supported the overhanging surface above except at the large open center, where the ceiling, curiously cantilevered right there, rose to its highest point. How precisely the ceiling supported itself with nothing beneath it thereat was not at all clear. The engineering appeared anomalous.

A typical column, designed so as to seem to taper downwards, impressed more than one archaeologist present as rather resembling the Minoan columns of the great labyrinthine palace at Knossos, but mounted on a triple base like those of the Ionian columns on the Temple of Artemis at Ephesus in its final version. An enormous volute, resembling a scroll, or the unequivocal coil of a spiral shell, adorned either side of the simple but elegant capital on each pillar, which thus resembled again an Ionian column, except that the volutes proportionately had a much greater size. Despite these inadvertent resemblances the chamber created an over-all effect of alien, unknown, and quite exotic architecture and culture.

The double doors on all the portals appeared to be cast from some unknown metal. The few metallurgists among the expedition members hazarded the guess that the metal, patently an alloy, consisted of copper and gold immingled with some silver. Whatever the metal, it suggested a kind of pale flame-gold, and gave off a brilliant redlike sheen. Also, despite what seemed the obvious antiquity of the metal, it showed no, or little, sign of age, but appeared to have undergone some kind of unknown galvanizing process.

The over-all stone of the vast chamber like that of the long man-made tunnel seemed to be carved from some kind of especially hard marble, generally off-white but also slightly mottled. With a shock changing to something akin to stupefaction, the archaeologists and their staff suddenly realized that the builders of the entire chamber had sculpted it from the living stone itself, from what was in essence an enormous marble quarry. And there was one other thing, in spite of its blatant obviousness, that they had not consciously noticed before: *Nor was there any dust on marble or metal*. Everyone looked at each other in pure amazement, if not in utter dumbfounderment! It was anomalous.

But the principal thing that rivetted everyone's attention, utterly and inevitably, stood within the wide open space at the center of the vast chamber, and moreover completely filled the sunken floor hemmed in by three descending steps on all sides. Piled everywhere, great heaps of treasure towered over the tallest of the expedition members: objects of art and state and religion, from what seemed a patent variety of historical periods, but of a history still awaiting decipherment, if not indeed its actual discovery.

Gleaming in a half dozen metals or even more, both known and unknown—apparently at least gold, silver, brass, copper, bronze, electrum, and the pale flame-gold already perceived—there arose on all sides in mind-boggling profusion what appeared to be crowns, chests, vases, thrones, tridents, tables, chairs, crown and tridents with the tridents emerging from the pointed caps of the crowns, and so much more, all of it lying heaped up in those great massy piles.

Like the metal of the four great double doors marking the four cardinal points of the compass, all this bewildering kaleidoscope of treasure appeared to have undergone the same unknown galvanizing process. Also like the great doors of metal as well as the columns and carvings of mottled marble, none of the treasures in this colossal thesaurus, or treasure-house, showed any appreciable sign of age, or of dust or detritus of any kind. This was anomalous.

The task alone of disentangling, sorting out, and cataloguing all these objects represented an enormous challenge that would require a great amount of time, patience, and expertise. All the expedition members realized this fact at once, and continued to look at each other in unalloyed amazement. And they were supposed to do all this merely preliminary work under conditions of relative secrecy! Ha!—some fat chance of that! Peh had indeed made an unprecedented and all-astonishing discovery.

The Azorean archaeologist grinned at Peh where he stood with the others, and said, "Well, we better get to work. Lights, camera, action!" This broke the tension that everyone had been feeling more and more, and they all gave a great big cheer that echoed thunderously inside the chamber. Everyone's ears rang resoundingly.

They worked late that night, until nineteen hours, per Euro-time, or seven o'clock in the evening, per Britanno-American reckoning. But starting on the second day they would work strictly nine to six, taking an hour for lunch, from one to two, plus the time spent walking to and from the vast inner chamber. When they returned from the subterranean fastnesses that first day, the staff above ground reported that they had felt several sharp seismic jolts. The news amazed those working underground, because they had felt nothing at all. Somehow, or so they reasoned, the man-made tunnel and treasure-chamber were constructed so as to reduce almost completely, or otherwise to negate, the force of mild or even severe tremors. On the second day the expedition members used their video cameras as much as possible to record the specific location of each treasure-pile, as well as the precise location of the items within each pile. They soon found that it was possible to thread their way among and between the piles in what had seemed at first glance no more than a bewildering labyrinth. The variety and richness of the objects at first appeared to defy merely simple describing as well as cataloguing.

What Peh had stumbled upon, they collectively decided, was nothing less than some kind of treasury, but the seemingly helter-skelter piling-up of objects appeared to challenge any kind of immediately intuited logic. It was almost as if whoever had carved this place out of the living rock had intended it to exist somehow, somewhere beyond ordinary time and space. What would the third day reveal?

That night after supper the expedition members, continuing to pose as patent-applied-for happy campers, gathered around a rare but hearty campfire to discuss their amazing find. As a safety measure Peh mentioned that he had sent for a small contingent of military guards from Ponta Delgada. The newcomers would join their encampment, and provide some much needed security for the inestimable treasures underground. Ponta Delgada, the capital and economic hub of the Azores, was located only ten or twelve miles to the southeast of Sete Cidades.

At a gesture from Peh the Azorean archaeologist Fernando Noronha, who hailed from the capital itself as his native city, took over the discussion. "Peh has asked me to talk about the theory that we've come up with to try and explain that chamber that we've been exploring. And the only way that we can make any sense out of it is in light of certain little known Theosophical insights or concepts purveyed by Madame Yelena Blavatskaya." Some of the happy campers began to laugh, but Fernando smiled, and raised his right hand with the palm facing outward and the fingers extending upward. "Please hear me out. Okay?" The group fell silent, and listened.

"As far as we can figure it out, ahem, according to conjectural prehistory, Atlantis as described by Plato, or the major part of it, submerged about 13,000 B.C., about the time the last ice age was ending. The cataclysm left a substantial island behind, a former mountain heartland, that the Theosophists have identified as Poseidonis. This major fragment lasted another 3,000 years. Then it also submerged, about 10,000 B.C., leaving the present Azores. Sometime before that final submergence some Atlanteans knew somehow what was going to happen, and that the highest peaks would somehow survive. With rather amazing prescience, or pre-science, if you like, they selected the particular site that we've stumbled upon, filled it with as many precious objects as they could—probably racing against time—sealed it, and then left it as a kind of gigantic time-capsule."

Fernando had paused, and looked at the faces gathered around the campfire. Then he finished, "There, that's our theory. If anybody has a better one, let's hear it." Suddenly plunged into introspective reverie, the group remained without a word.

It was on the third day, however, that the expedition made another major discovery that had unexpected consequences. Some little time after lunch, about mid-afternoon, while reconnoitering the frescoes and the crisply sculpted bas-reliefs that rose above the dados with their richly geometrical ornamentations, Peh noticed a curious detail in the wide rectangular bas-relief to the right of the great western portal, presumably a false double door like those on the southern and northern portals. Measuring and photographing, the other expedition members were focussing totally on the treasures heaped up in the large open space at the center of the vast chamber itself. No one appeared to notice just what their leader was doing.

The very large tableau depicted some nocturnal scene. Although some lateral illumination came from the floodlights arranged around the middle of the chamber, Peh was using an old-fashioned, but powerful, electric torch to pick out the details in the bas-relief. As he conned the picture, he realized all at once that it portrayed the Pan-Atlantean royalty when they would meet in Atlantis the capital city every five and six years, respectively, on an alternating basis. The Atlantean kings and princes would convene at midnight in a sacred grove, among other meetings at other times, to hold strategic parley concerning serious issues confronting their Empire of Atlantis. Here was the depiction of such a meeting exactly as described by Plato.

An awe and wonder settled on Peh as he studied the picture. A group of kings was assembled in a grove of what appeared to be tall, stately, and very dark cedars or cypresses. In the upper background the black sky was dotted with innumerable silver pinpricks representing stars, and at the center what might have been the moon possessed only half the size of that death-pale disc.

Dressed in very full, all-encompassing purple robes, the monarchs—some ten or eleven of them—were seated on great carved thrones of stone arranged in a semicircle opening out toward the viewer. They all wore massive crowns upon their heads with tall, pointed spikes on the periphery of each crown. From the cone shape that tapered upward in the middle of each crown there arose a kind of diamond shape that supported a large trident. The right hand of each king held a heavy metal staff with a crown and trident at the top exactly like the one worn on his head. However, the king, or archking, at the center wore a crown with a triple trident, and held a staff whose crown supported another triple trident. Each crown and trident, as well as each staff with crown and trident, was made of the same pale flame-gold that constituted the four great double doors.

Of course, Peh thought, this metal was that orichalch, or orichalcum—*oreichalkos* in Greek—mentioned emphatically by Plato in his Atlantis Mythos. He studied now more particularly the staff with the crown of the triple trident, firmly held in the hand of the archking. This projected out from the bas-relief noticeably more than any other of its type. Instinctively Peh reached out to touch it. He grasped it securely toward himself. To his great surprise it moved outward about an inch or so farther. Suddenly and silently the huge double doors of the western portal opened inward, and on into a dark descending tunnel with wide sculpted steps. Mute with amazement, and almost hypnotized, his electric torch illuminating the way before him, Peh descended the steps on down into the utter darkness, and then vanished. The doors remained open.

It just happened that nobody noticed what Peh had managed to do, nor yet his disappearance. A massive tremor struck right at that moment, a tremor so strong that it registered even in that vast chamber presumably somewhat proof against earthquakes. Peh staggered back through the double door. He had to close this portal at once. "Get out," he screamed as loud as he could. Almost instantly a cloud of what appeared to be some kind of darkish vapor came pouring up and out through the open doors on the west in a great and ever-thickening mass, filling the chamber. Everyone began coughing violently. This volcanic gas not only asphyxiated all the expedition members and staff assembled in that vast chamber, but killed them at once. It had all taken place so fast that not one of them had much of a chance even to cough, never mind to escape, before they died.

On that same day, 25 April 2007, only a little while after this, a temblor of unparalleled, if not unprecedented, strength struck the eastern Azores with the greatest force, and shook the entire archipelago. The temblor was recorded as 9.5 on the Richter scale. The destruction proved enormous, not only in property but also in human and other life. The tsunamis generated by this temblor raced around the world, but they ravaged the shores of the North Atlantic Ocean with ferocious power, it seemed almost beyond repair.

At the western end of São Miguel the outer cave and the outer tunnel, thus leading into the man-made tunnel and the vast inner chamber, suddenly collapsed, and were buried under tons of earth and rock. No feasible way existed to extricate the dead expedition members out from their inadvertent mausoleum. By chance the few members above ground also perished in the earthquake. But given the circumstances a long time would pass before the Portuguese government was able to give any specific attention to what had happened to the expedition.

Macabre Arabesque

Dedicated to Paul and Susan Dingwell, in thanks.

Cadaver, and mummy, and skeleton,
Inserted in a tomb, or in the ground—
The masquerade of life has had its run:
Inside a cairn, a pyramid, a mound,
The old remains of men and beasts are found,
Hinting that life might just be some burlesque:
Our funerary practises astound,
With liturgies and customs picturesque,
With sepulchre, sarcophagus, and adjunct statuesque:

Let us therefore apparel Death in all due pomp,
Elaborate it with macabre arabesque,
Transform our obsequies to one resplendent romp:

The masquerade of life has had its run,
    And ends up where, perforce, it shall have found
    Its remnants in the tomb, or in the ground—
Cadaver, and mummy, and skeleton.

The Scallop Shell

Translated from the Atlantean of an unknown poet.

Emblem of pilgrimage, emblem of quest,
Emblem of trade, emblem of merchandise,
Emblem of argosies advancing west:
Their ocean-route of fearless enterprise
A long way past the twin Antillias flies
On through the Isthmus-Gates that lead beyond:
The remnant isles of Mu, their goal, their prize,
Their course to them runs never vagabond,
Their course runs fixed, unswerving, and expressly conned:

Just what perfumes and spices come from there,
Those remnant isles of Mu that lie beyond,
Plus other items more than passing fair?

Is merchantry *the* alkahest of true renown?
So serves the scallop shell as crest as well as crown.

Triolets du Jour

(In memory of the day trip by boat on Sunday,
28 December 2003, taken by three good and joyful
friends from San Pedro, the port of Los Angeles, to Avalon,
Santa Catalina Island, and then at last back to the mainland.)

From the mainland to the island let us go
Where the greening hills and valleys rise
Above the sea's opaque and sombre glow.
From the mainland to the island let us go
Where the tall palms and the date palms grow,
Where the crowds walk with delighted cries.
From the mainland to the island let us go
Where the greening hills and valleys rise.

(There it was that three friends found,
    and tramped through, paradise.)

So from the island let us now return
Through the darkness without sun or moon,
With only stars to light our backward turn.
So from the island let us now return,
And on the mainland let us then adjourn—
We have had our sweet, warm afternoon.
So from the island let us now return
Through the darkness without sun or moon.

(Let the day's dregs drain back in,
    on into Time's unstoppered urn.)

A Villanelle Not à la Mode

(A villanelle-cum-virelay.)

*Dedicated to Dr. Ibid M. Andor, in memoriam,
who cherished the forms of villanelle and virelay.*

I do not sing of kitchen sink, or of commode,
Or if you will, of chamber pot, or toilet bowl,
But this I sing, a villanelle not à la mode.

To sing of things beyond our ken still is my goal,
Of towering castles that loom on the horizon's line.
I do not sing of kitchen sink, or of commode.

Can villanelle for once with virelay combine?
Should such things be? If some say not, then I insist:
But this I sing, a villanelle not à la mode.

I ask: Can barnyard fowl with eagle co-exist?
I say they can, but that the eagle needs more care.
I do not sing of kitchen sink, or of commode.

We dream of castles built in Spain, yet would we dare
To build skyscrapers on the moon? And at what cost?
But this I sing, a villanelle not à la mode.

What challenges and perils might we not accost?
Whatever! Such the goal, the slogan on our scroll!
I do not sing of kitchen sink, or of commode,
But this I sing, a villanelle not à la mode.

Item: Ariel Sings

*Dedicated to T. E. D. Klein, in gratitude,
and in ceremonious appreciation of his own dark gods.*

ARIEL'S SONG

Full fathom five thy father lies;
    Of his bones are coral made;
Those are pearls that were his eyes;
    Nothing of him that doth fade
But doth suffer a sea change
Into something rich and strange.
Sea nymphs hourly ring his knell:
    Burden. Ding-dong.
Hark! Now I hear them, ding-dong bell."
    Shakespeare, *The Tempest*, Act I, Scene II.

Others more Ingeniously doubt
whether there hath not been a vast tract
    of Land in the *Atlantick* Ocean, which
Earthquakes and violent causes
    have long ago devoured.
    Sir Thomas Browne, *Christian Morals*,
        Part the First, Section XVII, the fourth period.

Is this Atlantis just a mix of lies,
A tissue of extravagance, but made
By someone who saw things with alien eyes?
A few distorted facts that would not fade,
A myth that quite a few could not evade,
Became the tocsin for a stronger knell:
But more, a charm that beast and man obeyed,
Nor could ignore—nor scallop in his shell,
Nor wise man in his cave, nor magus in his cell:

Thus Plato's terse and moralistic tale, herewith,
Has changed now to a stranger charm, a deeper spell,
A piece of necromantic lore to conjure with:

To quote not quite, this myth hath suffered some sea change
    On into something splendid and phantastical,
    And so much more than merely mythological,
A piece of magic so supremely rich and strange.

Ancestral Memory Revived

(Mynydd Prescelly, on one of whose higher spurs
there once ascended Apenderragon,
the Great Watchtower of the Atlanteans in Great Britain.)

The traveller had come from far away
To southwest Wales, to Mynydd Prescelly,
To con the view southwest of there by day:
Out on the slate-grey, calm expanse of sea
He looked, and thought, "Nobody could foresee
Just how that sea-green isle might disappear."
Avalonessys! Who would wish to flee
From there? The distant notes of trumpeteer—
Was that what he had heard, faint in his inner ear?

He saw behind him, on the spur below the peak,
Above the massive flanks, Titanic stones uprear—
The tower's base—built way back in time beyond antique:

How high, those waves, they must have washed, to touch this high—
    The sea, one foam-filled mass, as far as eye could veer—
    The rolling surf of thunder constant in one's ear,
The blast of mighty fanfares blowing on for aye!

The Scroll

Translated from the Atlantean of an unknown poet.

A scroll it was of time-defiant stuff—
Vellum, perhaps, or parchment, both of hide—
And that alone proved mystery enough:
Off-white and lustrous gleamed the scroll's outside,
With only heraldry to serve as guide—
The blank end claimed a crown and trident plain:
But how distinct the volumen's inside—
Line after line of glyphs one scanned in vain,
The sound and sense of which no one could ascertain:

It was unknown, an older Atlantean script,
The key thereto who was there who could now regain?—
The key that evermore into the dark had slipped?

That olden scroll alone proved mystery enough—
      Vellum, perhaps—who knows?—or parchment, both of hide,
          But evermore unknown its glyphs would still abide—
That ancient volumen of time-defiant stuff.

To a Conch

Translated from the French of José-Maria de Heredia.

By what cold Ocean Seas, and since how many winters,—
But who will ever know, Conch frail and rainbow-hued!—
Have both the tidal bore, the surge below the sea,
Impelled you through the basin of their green abysses?

Today, below the sky, far from the bitter ebb,
You have made a soft bed out of the sands of gold.
But your hope is in vain. Prolonged, full of despair,
The great voice of the seas laments in you forever.

My soul, it has become an ever-sounding prison:
And just as in your coils the wail of that refrain,
That ocean's ancient cry, sorrows and sighs anew;

So from the depth of this my heart, too full of Her—
Slow, deaf, insensible, but somehow still eternal—
In me there groans that ocean's restless, distant roar.

Of Some Eternal Realm

*Dedicated to Lauric Guillaud, with gratitude,
the foremost Atlantologist following Dr. Ibid M. Andor.*

Poet or prince, I may not know
My perished name, nor bring to mind
Years that are one with dust and wind,
Nor songless love, nor tongueless woe—
          Clark Ashton Smith, "A Fragment."

A un prince atlantéen d'un royaume eternel,
à l'abri du bruit and de la fureur
du monde contemporain.
     Lauric Guillaud, from an inscription in a book.

(To an Atlantean prince of some eternal realm, a refuge from the tumult and the violence of our contemporary world.)

Although our ship has no one at the helm,
We seek beyond the further shores of space
The citadel of some eternal realm:
With varying degrees of luck or grace,
We seek a refuge, more, a great good place,
Assured somewhere beyond the cosmic storm:
Unyieldingly secured upon some base,
Could this locale endure in such a form
That it would stay the same, no further to transform?

But is not such a hope itself pure blasphemy,
To seek this place beyond the stars' unceasing swarm?
Is this not counter to the cosmic alchemy?

Yet thus it is, in this way are we made—
    Poor creatures, but unique, if commonplace—
    We live in inner space and outer space,
No less than interspace, before we fade.

Past, Present, Future

> Man
> In whom illusion doth itself behold.
> —*The Black Book of Clark Ashton Smith.*

Poet or prince, captain or sailors' mate,
Whatever!—nothing could be better than
To choose the fine details of one's own fate:
Klarkash-Ton has it right—to let each man
Pursue his phantom-dream, as best he can,
On into death—his future unforetold:
Under the constant threat—or goad—of Pan,
Man always is that phantom, as of old,
Himself the dream "in whom illusion doth itself behold."

The present, gripped and nourished by the past,
Forever makes the future tense unfold,
The bud that makes the future perfect past:

No facile optimism can assuage
    Or minimize this fate or this emprize,
        Can yet reduce this quest, this enterprise,
Can yet negate this dream, this fire, this rage.

Demeure Exotique

Hommage à Philippe Gindre, en reconnaissance.

> Where the brazen griffins guard
> From the satin-footed pard,
> And the lion of the sands,
> All the wealth of elder lands—
> Rich and unremembered things,
> Tombs and crowns of crumbled kings,
> Ebon lutes with silver strings,
> Pearls, and ivory, and nard.
> —Clark Ashton Smith, a fragment, c. 1918.

Amid the desert sands in sejant style
Two griffins all of bronze still stood on guard
Outside the gateway to that old stone pile:
The structure, dark, perdurable, and hard—
By war, simoon, or earthquake never jarred—
Permitted no intruders through its door:
With massive iron valves the door was barred,
Denying facile access, as before,
To all the treasures heaped inside around that floor.

A treasury where kings had made their tombs,
It even served as palace for some queen
Who danced amid its mortuary glooms:
She mimed with gestures broad and unforeseen
As lutenists, their fingers quick and keen,
Would play their ebon lutes with silver strings:
Her nakedness deployed but not obscene,
Her arms and legs agleam with gems and rings,
How many trysts she brought to pass, and midnight flings!

Entombed within, she too had changed to dust,
With all her lovers, but where then had flown
The passion, where the rage, and where the lust?
Within, all now lay mute—no lover's moan,
Nor sob of disbelief, nor gripe nor groan,
Nor sigh of discontent, nor yet of dread:
Her strongbox had remained, and had not flown,
The gem-stones flaunted in or out of bed,
Displayed on foot and leg, on hand and arm and head.

With massive iron valves the door was barred—
Were the same valves then welded shut, besides?—
No griffins really had to stand on guard?
Somehow this place resisted history's tides,
Eternal flux of calends, nones, and ides,
Bequeathed perchance from Atlantean times:
Was this not magick so to thwart those tides?—
But is it only in those other climes
That such takes place, and only in those other times?

Safeguarding all that wealth of elder lands,
Way past those outland peaks, it still stands there,
This treasure-house amid the sun-drenched sands:
With fierce, with stern and, yes, with brazen stare,
Those owl-eyed griffins all of bronze still glare
Outside that doorway, just outside that gate:
Out through that door sometimes a ghostlike air,
A phantom tune, would seem to infiltrate,
But all the lutes lie silent where, within, they rest in wait.

The Fugitives

*Translated from the Atlantean of Aänsess,
through the French of Michel de Labretagne*

Dedicated to Louis and Susan Irmo.

I

All in a springtime dawn of amaranth and gold
Whose flags and banners flared up above the horizon—
With daybreak-gonfalons fraught of empurpled rose,
With sunrise-oriflammes of gleaming orpiment—
The boy, the girl, they met within the village square
Close by the fountain set amidst of All-Neph-Rom,
Far west of the capital Atlantis the City,
But not too far west of the Amphus river delta,
The town secured upon its own flood-safe plateau.

All in that springtime dawn of amaranth and gold
The girl, the boy, they met, or met yet once again—
Since childhood, great good friends, but now gone from each other
For more than several years as they were growing up.
The youth was Cartha, and the maiden Aviol—
She was twelve, he fourteen—near, but not quite, adult.
No longer children, but not quite adult, they eyed
Each other long and hard, then they grinned all at once:
Goddess and god they seemed, or more than merely human.

Each felt deep in the gut a warmth, a flame that passed
Through the heart, through the throat, and then into the head,
Where it lodged to expand like a flower in one moment,
Or like a lightning bolt that starts a blaze right then.
Stabbed to the quick, but caught off guard, they well-near swooned,
And fell, but grabbed each other, in the nick of time.
Then they embraced, and kissed, and almost fell again,
But caught themselves at once. He whispered in her ear:

She shivered as his lips, warm and moist, touched the lobe.
"Why not meet around noon in that high grassy meadow
To the west of the village," and she breathed back, "Yes!"

Due west of All-Neph-Rom, in that high grassy meadow,
Close by a rural shrine, old-fashioned and roofed over,
Where the stream formed a pool, near-choked with giant lilies,
The sun stood at high noon more or less overhead.
A shrine it was devoted to Atalantossa,
The greatest of all deities throughout Atlantis,
That earth-and-nature mother-goddess of them all—
One with the Cosmic Mother-Deity herself.
Flanked by two giant ballocks at the base, there stood
Her curious emblem or device: an ithyphallus
That held aloft a perfect delta, upside-down,
On top of which, to either side, two large round teats.

Through a break in the trees to the east one could see,
Way far off in the east, the top of Mount Atlantis
That marked the mid-point of the great metropolis.
Cartha the black-haired youth, and Aviol the golden,
He from the west, she from the east, approached the pool,
But by way of the shrine, where they both stood and prayed,
Making a sign from throat to groin, from right to left.
Then afterwards they met there at the water's edge,
Each looking at the other, but in utter silence.

Now they embraced, and kissed, feeling a great excitement,
A great relief, and a great heat, their pulses pounding,
Devoured mutually by their hunger for each other.
Oblivious of everything except their passion,

They sank down deep into the high, protective grass,
Amid the lush-green grass, in the shade by the pool,
Seeking a nourishment that neither could have named,
A benediction granted only by their senses
Concentered to this magic warmth shared equally,
During that breathless hour that never seemed to end.

Such was their midday meal, but food they did not miss;
Such was their secret now, the secret pact between them:
A day, a date, an hour they never would forget.
Leaving by different paths, they returned to their village,
Their absence noted, but not that of them together,
A consummation dearly to be sought again,
And yet again, as one would search for an oasis,
A taste of paradise that only two may share,
A great good place that otherwise is lost forever.

The days and nights elapsed, the spring deferred to summer,
In All-Neph-Rom, an honored home of farming life,
An honored home as well of ancient arts and crafts.
The farmers and the artists and the artisans
Somehow resided with each other all in peace,
Not only side by side, one house next to another,
But sometimes even in the selfsame families.
A farmer and a poet, just like his farmer father,
Cartha lived still at home, as one of many sons.
The only daughter of two frail and ageing parents,
And now their one and only source of real support,
Aviol earned their keep, an artist just like them:
Sign-painter, wood-carver, house-painter, all in one.

The days and nights elapsed, the spring deferred to summer,
As girl and boy pursued their passion, one on one,
As often as they could as circumstance allowed,
As unobtrusively as it was possible.
That she did not conceive was just an accident!
Yet inescapably the other villagers
In All-Neph-Rom could not but note their love affair,
As girl and boy matured, and grew more beautiful:
He waxed more masculine, and she, more feminine,
As in that old refrain from dim antiquity:
Goddess and god they seemed, or more than merely human.

It was only a matter of time, place, and age
Before Cartha would have asked for Aviol's hand.
Whatever plans that they had made, or had not made,
An unforeseen event would set them all askew.
The Archking of the Empire of Atlantis had
His deputies and secret agents everywhere,
To guard against—and to report—injustices,
Inequities, corruptions, and unfairnesses,
So that all things of this type could be put to rights.

But these same proxies also served another purpose,
To notice anything at all supremely fine,
And bring the matter to the Archking's cognizance,
Whether for recompense, or for encouragement,
For payment or award, for prize or yet reward,
Whether it might involve objects or living creatures.
The reigning Archking was both young and passionate,
Who had not only wives, but also concubines,

And some of these he valued higher than his wives:
He could choose anyone to be his Archqueen Consort.

One fine day, well-near noon, into the village square
Of All-Neph-Rom there strolled a seeming traveller—
One of the Archking's deputies, incognito,
Who sought wood-sculpted beasts both colorful and quaint.
Idly he came upon our Aviol's display,
But noticed even more the artisan herself.
The agent bought some specimens, and then he left,
At once returning to the great metropolis,
To tell the Archking of the find that he had made.

Regaining access to the Archking but in private—
Where he sat in a room, set amid Mount Atlantis,
A balconied room overlooking the sacred grove
That flourished to the north at the base of that mountain—
The agent spoke about the beautiful young maiden.
The Archking pondered, smiled, then commanded at once,
"Bring her here. Let her grace our court and capital.
Settle it with her parents. Offer the standard fee.
Perchance a something more. We can be generous.
Agreed?" The agent nodded, then he bowed, and left.
The Archking turned back to the papers on his table.

Now back in All-Neph-Rom, a few days later on,
The Archking's agent sat with Aviol and parents,
The golden maiden with her frail and ageing parents:
The family sat there, pensive, pallid-faced, and quiet.
It was high noon in the main room of their small house—

Small, neat, and unpretentious, but comfortable:
Carvings of every type fantastic thronged the walls.
The agent held a scroll, examining it close,
Rolling it up at last, placing it in its tube,
A special tube of pale flame-gold, and then he spoke:

"You have all signed this paper voluntarily;
You shall receive the fee the day of her departure.
I need not stress the honor that this represents."
(He looked at Aviol away from both her parents.)
"You may not be his wife, but you shall have respect,
A place of honor in the household over-all.
The Archking treats his people well, and with great kindness,
Not always a common courtesy with every ruler."
The father smiled, and asked the daughter to bring wine,
A special pomegranate wine, and silver cups,
So that they could all drink a toast to celebrate:
Aviol kissed her parents as she left the room.

Due west of All-Neph-Rom, in that high grassy meadow,
Cartha had rendezvoused with Aviol that night,
But they did not make love, and only said farewell.
She had explained to him what she had had to do:
"I have sold myself to the Archking for a fee
In order to provide an income for my parents,
As they live through their final and their failing years.
It was the only certain thing that I could do.
I may be able at some point to have them come,
And live at court with me, but all that will take time."
He said, "I understand." She added, "Pray forgive me."

He countered, "There is nothing to forgive. I love you,
And I shall always love you. I shall not forget."
They both wept, and embraced—they wished each other well,
Embraced, and wept again—and then they said goodbye.

The Archking's agent had arranged this whole affair
So that both Aviol and parents could enjoy
One final time of family happiness together
Before the agent, Nanotep, returned for her
To take her back to court with proper entourage,
For which the Archking had commanded something special:
A trireme, a litter, a great concourse of people,
Banners and bannerettes, a cavalcade of knights,
With heralds and with drummers and with trumpeteers,
With flashing oriflammes and gonfalons afloat.

At last the day dawned: what an honor for the village!
At dawn a ship of state, a trireme, left the City,
A crown and trident spread across its one great sail,
Heading west past the Amphus delta's many mouths,
Then rowing up the Alphis, the last big stream to-west,
Finally docking at the little port of Ymtron,
Where everybody but the ship's crew disembarked,
Joined by the horses for the cavalcade of knights,
The marshals bringing order on into the groups,
Before the company went west on foot or horse.

The company had reached the eastern end of town,
Of All-Neph-Rom, where they had stopped before high noon
To organize their entrance in the village square.

First came the heralds, drummers, trumpeteers, and then
The standard-bearers with their sculptured heraldries
Of crown and tridents, made from wood or lustrous metals,
Going before the Archking's emissary-agent
Surrounded by officials, richly gowned like him,
And followed by the cavalcade of knights at last.

The villagers had gathered in the central plaza,
Leaving the center open for the group from court
As they marched in, as drummers and as trumpeteers
At once proclaimed—with all the thrice-resplendent clang
Of hard metallic tones—the Fanfare of Atlantis,
The Archimperium Salute, exploding forth
In sombre counterpoint quite of resounding brass
That energized the heart, and speeded up the pulse,
Instilling silence, and a wonderment of awe:
And in that very midst the litter-bearers came,
And lowered to the ground a flame-gold palanquin
That bore upon its roof a giant crown and trident.

The knights dismounted, and assembled round their chief,
The agent Nanotep, in his high-crested helmet.
Speaking in unison, loud with solemnity,
Gowned in their vivid robes, the heralds next announced,
"Our emissary bears a message from the Archking."
Nanotep cleared his throat, and spoke with tones of brass,
"The Archking calls to court the maiden Aviol
To take up her new post of Singular Companion."
The crowd gasped from awe: what an honor for the village!

Two courtiers took a chest into the maiden's house
That stood off to one side around that open space.
Anon the father, mother, daughter came outdoors,
And slowly walked to where the palanquin stood tall.
They bowed to Nanotep, and he to them, and then
The family all embraced, the daughter went inside,
And took her seat within the flame-gold palanquin.
The litter-bearers picked it up, and headed east,
The courtly company soon following behind,
As once again the Fanfare of Atlantis played.

The villagers, amort at such magnificence,
Came back to life at once, and gathered all around
In order to congratulate the daughter's parents
In that spot where they stood, their arms around each other,
Weeping and mourning for the daughter who had gone:
No chest of coins could mitigate that maiden's loss,
Although there was the chance that later they could join
Their offspring, and reside with her at court themselves;
But now they turned their steps back to their house bereft.

Cartha had been there, too, had witnessed all of it,
Had briefly crossed his glance with that of Aviol
Before she stepped inside that flame-gold palanquin.
That night he interviewed his father quite alone,
And said, "My years of wandering have come at last—
I desire to go forth, with my lute and my sack,
To seek my fame and fortune, in the world at large.
Dear father, may I have your blessing and your help?"

The father said, "I think I understand." He paused,
And smiled. "Of course, you have my blessing and my help."
Father and son embraced. Next morning Cartha left.

He took the high road out of town, but going north
On into the Great Vale, far from the capital.
The island continent had other towns and cities
Dispersed throughout its plains, its mountains, and its valleys,
Where he could try his luck like any other youth.
In this way he began his years of wandering,
His years as poet singing almost everywhere
Throughout the island continent, its breadth and length,
Until at last he came to Atlantis the City,
That great metropolis and capital no less,
Where it sits tall amid the Amphus river delta.

Preceded by his reputation as a poet,
The handsome Cartha fit right in his new milieu,
A maker of sad songs, lamenting evermore
A goddess peradventure evermore departed.
Such sweet but melancholy songs, now sung in person,
Such songs in which for other folk he had transformed
His private pain on into such uncommon pleasure,
Now gained for him another vital audience
More avid than his former ones for his new songs:
Thus Cartha found at last a measure of contentment.

Thus Cartha found as well a source of ready coin:
He could replace at last the simple bardic lute

That he had used since latter childhood for his songs,
And what he had in mind was pure extravagance:
A giant wire-strung lute with nineteen single strings,
Not just the six or seven single strings of gut
That some lutes have, but this would have a full bass choir
Of twelve half tones, chromatic, all of brass or bronze,
The deepest bass strings carried on a harp-shaped prop.

When Cartha made his first appearance with that lute,
As soon as it was ready to be played, he caused
A great sensation in that humble ambiance,
Some hostelry or tavern in the Outer City,
The popular report of which soon spread its fame,
And people came from everywhere to hear his songs
Moving in time to that relentless novel clang
Resounding full above the drinkers' cries and shouts,
His mournful songs renewed somehow by that archlute.

A state official came, inviting him to court:
The Archking had expressed a certain interest
In hearing Cartha sing his songs accompanied
By that new archlute almost without precedent.
The concert would take place a few days hence, at night,
That hour about mid-evening, favored by the king
When he sat in a hall of his own private suite,
Surrounded by his intimates of either gender—
In the same private suite set amid Mount Atlantis,
In the same hall that overlooked the sacred grove
That flourished to the north at the base of that mountain.

To sing and play for no one other than himself,
That is, the Archking of the Empire of Atlantis—
There was no higher patronage in all that world—
What an honor to have befallen the young Cartha!
Or thus his artist friends all hastened to assure
The poet-lutenist, but he stayed calm and cool,
Or merely smiled, or grimaced, back at all of them.
He said, "Let's hope that I don't get hoarse before then.
Croaking the words—well, *that* does not improve my songs."

II

Attended by a friend who carried in a case
His archlute, Cartha went, a few nights later on,
To Mount Atlantis, where it stood right at the heart
Of Atlan-town, across the rings of land and water:
First off, the Great Place Metropolitan led on
Above the canyon of the merchant harbor's curve
Whose terraces and colonnades descended to
The water's edge with all its docks and quays and ships,
That breadth of water thronged with ships from everywhere,
From half the planet's many seas, and still beyond.

Leaving the Outer City, plaza, harbor all behind,
They passed, the twain, across the first great curve of land,
And crossed in turn, though but in part, the Hippodrome,
Which could contain near half the people of the city.
The twain crossed next the Great Place Hippodromical
Above the canyon of the second harbor's curve
Whose waters served as the archroyal navy's home.

The twain then passed across the second curve of land,
And walked with haste right past the public gardens there,
Open to king or commoner or anyone,
And came out in the Great Place Acropolitan
Above the canyon of the third great harbor's curve
Whose breadth of water lodged the Archking's private fleet.

That plaza was the center of the Inner City:
The last great gate awaited Cartha and his friend
Where, just beyond, the mountain's peak loomed far above:
This Mount Atlantis was the Empire's heart itself.
Little time had gone by while they walked, but their talk
Had made it seem to go by faster than it had:
Yet in another way—how strange!—it also seemed
As if an aeon had gone by while they had walked,
Had talked, had passed above those rings of land and water:
How much work did those rings over time represent!

They arrived at the gate that rose up overhead,
Almost blocking out the bulk of the mountain itself,
Whose temples, towers, and palaces now stood in shadow
Save where highlighted by lanterns and by flambeaux.
The guards there on duty inspected the two men,
Then signalled to a courtier standing to one side,
Who nodded at our twain, and signed for them to follow.
He explained, "The Archking has changed his plans a little.
Instead of receiving you in his private chambers,
He shall hear you sing in his Great Thronehall Archroyal,
A mark of rare respect, and seldom shown to poets."

The sacred way beyond the gate went straight on through
The sacred grove with all its height of darkling trees,
And led up to the massive portal, double-valved,
Left ajar at the base on the south of the mountain.
Ushered beyond the vestibule, they found themselves
In a huge cavern-space lit by a few flambeaux.
They saw a giant statue, crowned—man, king, or god—
Standing tall in a chariot drawn by six horses:
Faintly the stone and metal gleamed in that dim light.
The suave, old, and sophisticated courtier paused,
And spoke with practised awe: "This is none other than
Our Poseidon the First, the Father, the Earth-Shaker."

The young man carrying the lute had placed it down,
Had joined his hands, had closed his eyes, had bowed his head—
He prayed—towards that colossal eidolon, and Cartha
Did the same, the old man noting this with approval.
The three resumed their way, the courtier turning right,
On towards a smaller door set in a larger one:
With that small door ajar, the brilliance lured them on.
The Great Thronehall Archroyal stood, lit up beyond,
Waiting in readiness for Cartha, friend, and lute.

Ushered inside, the twain observed, such as they would:
How much of it seemed carven from the solid rock!
A long hall running north and south, a long high hall,
And rectilangular: thus triply tiered on either side,
A broad expanse between three floors of colonnades,
Which featured that distinctive type of pillar-post
That seemed to taper downward, crowned by thick volutes,

That Atlantean column type above all others.
The brilliant light came forth from candles and flambeaux,
From candelabras, and from flambeaux-chandeliers.

Across from our two youths a massive fountain played,
Set in a massive niche, sporting a hundred jets,
The largest jets projecting high, then thundering down,
Splashing upon a hundred shapes, fantastical
And multi-hued, upon a hundred sculptured forms:
Nymphs, naiads, nereids, and oceanides,
With dolphins, and cephalopods, and porpoises;
Mermen, mermaidens, underwater cavaliers
Mounted upon seahorses every here and there.
This was the Fount of Atkastalia, world-renowned,
Metals and gems commingling on its terraced cone,
The light reflecting off it in a burst of rays.

At either end of this long hall a wide long flight
Of shallow steps led to the second floor or tier
Of colonnades, to where a spacious landing spread.
A line of smaller fountains bordered either side
Of each staircase, the light reflecting on their jets.
Divers musicians occupied the southern end,
Drummers and trumpeteers attired resplendently,
Who proudly stood before a *soleil rayonnant*,
Positioned flat against the wall in pale flame-gold.

But at the chief, the northern, end of this long hall
A massive scallop shell, quarried of porphyry,
With curls and curlicues like waves on either side
Quite rivetted the sight upon that other landing.

Positioned flat against the off-white wall above,
Three crowns and tridents in a complex heraldry
Gave off the flame-gold blaze of purest orichalch.
Centered against the scallop shell the Archking sat
Upon his massive throne, set high upon its dais,
Both quarried of, no less, the selfsame porphyry.

Surrounded by his intimates of either gender,
Who sat on either side in casual array,
The king, likewise relaxed, was dressed informally:
Apart from those eternal guards, they were alone.
Their usher paused, with Cartha and his friend in tow,
Both youths astonished by such unaccustomed splendor.
All such as we describe, they saw but in a flash,
For as the old man guided them on towards the throne,
After turning left from that thronehall's midmost point,
All the musicians there, quite unexpectedly,
Began to play right then: what a tremendous crash!
The Fanfare of Atlantis, with all its pomp and brass,
The Archimperium Salute, burst forth at once.

The three came near the foot of the stairs to the throne,
The music stopped as suddenly as it began,
Their usher signalled to the youths to stop, to bow.
All three bowed low, and held the bow, then stood erect.
Their usher spoke. "Here you perform. The king will speak
To you erelong. Here are some chairs if you need them.
After the concert I shall guide you back outside."
The courtier smiled, while vanishing amid the columns,
While one last phrase came back to these two youths: "Good luck!"

Cartha's friend had meanwhile placed the case on the floor,
Had taken out the lute, and handed it to Cartha,
Who—seated on a chair—was tuning it forthwith.
He then secured the lute against his middle torso
With a strap round his back, to his waist at the right,
From his left shoulder, baldric-wise. Cartha stood up,
He briefly bowed his head, then faced up towards the king.
The Archking smiled. "We bid you welcome to our court,
Both yourself and your friend—and your lute! Pray begin."

(Both Cartha and his friend, like the king and his group,
Wore summer tunics with the customary sandals,
An apt attire.) First Cartha played a little piece
As a taste of the sound and the scope of that lute,
Which struck the group with its relentless novel clang,
And soon enchanted them. Then he sang his first song
To the sound of this unique accompaniment,
One of a series that lamented evermore
Some goddess peradventure gone forevermore.

He sang with such expression and such longing that
He touched the hearts of all to thrills as well as tears:
The hour flew by while he sang his most poignant songs.
He finished as he had begun. He played the piece
That introduced the sound and the scope of that lute.
He removed it, and handed it back to his friend;
Then he bowed long and low while he took a deep breath.
The group around the king exploded in applause,
And the king proved himself the most vociferous.

Inviting Cartha with his friend up to the throne,
The Archking spoke. "Come, drink a cup of wine with us,
And Cartha, we have here a small reward for you."
The twain went up the stairs, where one and all were struck
By how much Cartha and the king looked like each other,
The former like, in truth, the latter's younger brother!
Cartha began to bow, but the king stopped him short,
And smiled, "We're not in state. Here, have a cup of wine,"
Addressing both young men as courtiers plied their cups.

The king then handed him, and from his very hand,
A heavy massive coin of purest orichalch,
The highest coin-piece of the realm, a crown and trident.
"You sing divinely well. Your archlute is unique.
We would like you to sing for us on other nights,
But in our private suite. Meanwhile please meet our friends,
Chief of whom is our foremost Singular Companion."
He pointed out a maiden hitherto obscured,
And Cartha well-near swooned. *There* was Aviol the golden,
A little older now, *but* more beautiful than ever!

She was more gracile than the swan that swims the lake:
Her lustrous flame-gold hair hung down on either side
Of her fair face—with all its vivid coloring
On lips, on cheeks, around her blue-green eyes that glowed—
Her hair in giant curls, which hung down to her waist,
Gave off a sudden splendor all around her chair,
Dazzling the eyes and hearts of everybody present.
Her summer tunic ended in a long full skirt—
Some shiny teal-green stuff—that almost swept the floor.

For support Cartha grasped the arm of his young friend,
As he bowed low towards her, while she smiled back at him:
He stood up, and they crossed their glances with each other.
The Archking spoke again. "Aviol tells me that
You both have come from All-Neph-Rom, and have grown up
As childhood friends. Well, surely, on some other night
You will revive your friendship, talking of old times."
Cartha inclined his head at king and concubine,
Closing his eyes in deference and in respect,
Hiding the tumult of emotions that he felt.

Cartha and friend met other people there that night,
Some of them being peers of the realm, of the highest,
With whom as with the king the youths conversed as equals,
At least for that one night, as they had been instructed:
Just as the king repeated plain, "We're not in state,
We're all here among friends, no need of ceremony."
Aviol even got to speak a bit with Cartha,
While they exchanged, unseen, a sweet and subtle glance,
While whispering to each other, "Another time, perhaps."

The social hour continued thus, with pleasantries,
Both Cartha and his mate, best known as Enzalor,
Making a good impression on the king and friends.
The king arose, and spoke. "Thank you all! We retire."
While walking over to the poet-bard, he said,
"And thank you, Cartha, for your songs. Another night!
And we shall tell you in advance." Cartha bowed low.
The Archking left with all his entourage of friends.
The suave, old man appeared at once from out the columns,
And guided our two youths back towards the Outer City.

The time was getting close to midnight when, at last,
Our Enzalor and Cartha found themselves, once more,
Outside the Inner City with all of its rings,
With its concentric circles both of land and water—
Out in the Outer City, past the merchant harbor,
And thus beyond the Great Place Metropolitan—
Together all at once they heaved a great big sigh!
Then Cartha said, "Look, Enzalor, I'll give you half
The value of this coin of purest orichalch
For all your help to me tonight, but otherwise
I want to keep the coin itself a souvenir.
Alright?" And Enzalor spoke back, "Alright, and thanks."

III

That was the first of many times that Cartha played
For king or court or inner circle of his friends,
And even several times for grand affairs of state,
No less than for diversions planned and held at court,
Performing instrumentally for dance events.
Cartha and Aviol revived somehow their friendship,
As best they could, and even somewhat more, in time.
The Archking's concubines were free to come and go
More or less as they wished, and sometimes to have lovers,
Above all when he ceased to favor certain ones,
But such was not the case with Aviol the golden.

She ventured several times out from the Acropolis,
Into the outer town, where she met Enzalor,

Who guided her to the place that he shared with Cartha,
Where she and he were free to talk alone at last,
To talk as they could not amid the courtly crowd.
Whether at first, or afterwards, once more it happened:
Each felt deep in the gut a warmth, a flame that passed
Through the heart, through the throat, and on into the head,
Where it lodged to expand like a flower in one moment,
Or like a lightning bolt that starts a blaze at once.

Now they embraced, and kissed, feeling a great excitement,
A great relief, and a great heat, their pulses pounding,
Devoured mutually by their hunger for each other.
Oblivious of everything except their passion,
They sank down deep on Cartha's bed, amid the covers,
Seeking a nourishment that neither could have named,
A benediction granted only by their senses
Concentered to that magic warmth shared equally,
During that breathless hour that never seemed to end.

Each time that she came, they made love, and then they wept,
Holding each other in their warm and moist embrace,
Mourning the might-have-been, the nevermore-to-be.
They exchanged news and notes about each other's lives;
Thus they learned quite a bit the one about the other.
She told him of the king, how passionate he was,
And more than generous to her and to her parents.
With health improved, they had decided not to move
From All-Neph-Rom; instead, they visited her quite often,
And she was free to visit them in turn whenever.

But Aviol confided in him somewhat further.
The Archking had considered altering her status
Of Singular Companion to the rank of wife,
Moreover of Chief Wife, and would have changed it further,
On into the exalted rank of Archqueen Consort.
However, it turned out that she could not conceive,
And this remained an insurmountable impasse,
Because Chief Wife or Consort had to bear him heirs.
That she had not conceived with Cartha was no fluke!

Now, prudently, she kept her times with Cartha brief.
Guided by Enzalor, ostensibly she shopped
Amid the Outer City's markets and bazaars,
And then returned to Mount Atlantis after shopping.
Cartha meanwhile had learned from Aviol two facts—
Two central facts—about the king, Memtellidon:
That he was kind, though strong, and was not prone to vengeance.
Meanwhile a plan was taking shape in Cartha's mind
Whereby the lovers might escape their own impasse.

Cartha one day confided, "Aviol, I must
Return to All-Neph-Rom, to visit with my folks.
I haven't seen them now some six or seven years.
My father and my mother won't be any younger,
And I'll be gone from court and capital awhile."
He paused, and smiled. "Why don't you come, and join me there?
While you stay with your folks, we could wander around,
Away from idle eyes. Who knows where we might go?
What refuge west of All-Neph-Rom . . . or even overseas?"

She smiled, and kissed him on the lips. "I understand.
You go ahead of me. I'll follow somewhat later."
They made yet further plans, but told no one of them,
Not even Enzalor, their best friend and ally.
(Why burden anyone with needless information?
If questioned later on, they would in truth not know.)
Saying farewell to friends at court or in the City,
Cartha would only add, "I'm going home to visit!"
With sack, with lute in case, a few days later on,
He took a small ship to the little port of Ymtron,
Where he debarked, and walked the road to his own village.

The little town turned out en masse for his return,
And Cartha's name was heard on everybody's lips—
Cartha!—he of the dancing eyes and flashing smile,
The night-black hair and olive skin: he had such charm!
He greeted one and all, but closeted himself
Soon with his family and his friends, his closest friends,
Announcing first that he would give a gratis concert
Within the village square at some point later on,
A concert of his poems, with archlute nonpareil,
Of which the villagers had heard the best reports.

Some thirty nights had passed when Aviol arrived
At high noon, one cool day, coming in from the City,
She and her group on horseback, with no fuss or fanfare,
Her beauty cloaked in cape and hood, with few attendants,
Whom she sent back at once, after they ate and rested—
Her parents had one servant girl—that was enough.
Thus Aviol herself came back to All-Neph-Rom,

And settled quietly back into village life,
Enjoying once again those other ways and rhythms.

Cartha and Aviol visited back and forth
Just a bit, not too much, and aroused no suspicion,
While they conceived and made the plans for their escape,
Their flight, to other towns or lands across the seas.
Again the lovers told no one of these new plans,
But shortly after Cartha's concert that was free,
And that achieved a great success with one and all,
He packed the lute and case inside a larger case,
Ostensibly to have it shipped back to the City.

But what he really did, he had it shipped himself,
Yes, from the little port of Ymtron, on the Alphis,
But not back to the City, as he might have done,
And rather to a port in far Oöxathan,
Far to the west, so very far, thousands of leagues,
Past Atlantillia, past the Seas of the Antillias,
Thus all that long, long way to far Oöxathan.
Meanwhile he had his other lute, his bardic lute,
Which would suffice, and would not serve to point him out.

He withdrew now and then, a few days at a time,
While he did all those tasks that had first to be done,
For their flight, their escape, but before they could leave:
First, near the swamp that lay due west of All-Neph-Rom,
A league past that high grassy meadow dear to them,
Where Cartha and where Aviol had first made love.
Then he left a small chest at the inn "for a friend"—

So he said—at Ur-Orm, the tiny fishing village
That sat high by the coast that lay south of the swamp.

Both he and Aviol by chance had saved much coin,
Small chests of which he sent ahead to certain towns,
But from Ur-Orm, where people knew him not at all.
Once he had everything in readiness at last,
Then he came back to rest awhile in All-Neph-Rom,
Before they each set out alone, to meet ahead.
Cartha now told his folks, he wanted to explore
Those isolated villages west of the swamp
That he would need to go around far to the south.

In secrecy he had arranged with Aviol
To follow him but only after several days,
And on whatever pretext that she cared to give.
Soon Cartha said goodbye to family and to friends—
With bardic lute, with sack, he headed west afoot
Along the ancient route that went south of the swamp.
Once those few days went by, then Aviol announced
To parents and to friends: "Long have I wished to make
A pilgrimage to all the little rustic shrines
That lie round All-Neph-Rom, but starting towards the south."

Travel she would afoot, at least part of the way
With long-term friends, in relays as it were, for aid
And for companionship, staying most of the time
At nearby inns and other hostelries at night:
She would not be gone long, or not for very long.
Meanwhile she sent a note to reassure the king

Of her eventual return, but only after
The pilgrimage that she was undertaking now,
And travelling as light as ever she could manage.

In her own turn she said goodbye to folks and friends,
And gave her parents such a sweet and warm embrace.
She whispered something in the ear of each in turn
That puzzled them a bit, but also gave them comfort:
"Whatever otherwise that you may chance to hear,
Know then that I am well, wherever I might be.
Remember only that, have faith, and be serene,
Even if we should never see each other again."
Then off she went, attended by an old boy friend,
With but her two small sacks depending at her back.

They left at noon, and headed south of All-Neph-Rom,
Stopping at several shrines along the shaded road,
And at the end of day they fetched up at an inn
Where they would eat, would rest, would then stay through the night.
At this inn the next day she would meet her next friend,
After her old boy friend would bid her a farewell.
No sooner had he left the next day than she left,
Aviol by herself, heading west, always west,
Along the ancient route that went south of the swamp.

Now scarcely had she gone a thousand paces west,
When some young man forthwith approached from that direction:
Blond, smiling, simply dressed like her in summer tunic.
Only when he came close, did she see who it was:
None other than her very Cartha in disguise!

No longer raven-haired, but pale blond, hair cut shorter,
No longer clean-shaven, but with a small moustache!
Astonished, Aviol began to laugh and laugh,
And so did Cartha, too, himself no less than she!

He held her in his arms, and laughing they fell down
Upon a patch of grass by the side of the road,
Until that storm of merriment had quite subsided.
He smiled at her, and said, "Well now, dear Aviol,
Let's see what you look like when we get done with you!"
She hastened to remark, "Dear Cartha, you look great,
So different, though, that I . . . I could not help but laugh!
My turn is next, I know. Let's see how I turn out."
They lingered there awhile, secure in their embrace.

They next stood up, brushed off each other's clothes,
And so continued on their way on through those woods.
They met few people on that shaded, quiet road,
And soon had walked the league that led up to the swamp,
Then to a hidden bower by the edge of a pond
That Cartha had already chosen with great care
As the place to effect Aviol's transformation.
He cut off all her hair to a boy's handsome cut,
Then dyed it raven-black: how different then she looked!

She still was beautiful, but seemed another person!
He held a little mirror up, so she could see.
She smiled, and looked at him. "Well, we make quite a pair,
And I doubt that our friends would recognize us now."
He agreed, and cleaned up, bundling up the cut hair,

Tying it to a rock, hurling it in the pond
At some length from the shore. They sat, and ate the lunch
Of bread and cheese and beer that he had brought with him;
They rested in each other's arms a little while.

Soon they stood up, gathered their sacks, and walked elsewhere
As Cartha guided them to a spot near at hand.
He pointed out, "The deepest quicksand around here,"
Retrieved some clothes, a bundle from a bush nearby,
And laid them on the knoll at the edge of the quicksand,
Two mantles, one of hers, one of his, on that grass.
Tenderly then he placed near his cape his old lute,
As if it were a child that he were laying down.
"Let people make of this whatever they might wish."

"Well, Aviol, we still have time to change our minds.
Do you still want to go through with this as we planned?"
He smiled, and looked at her. She nodded back at him,
And said, "I have not changed my mind, unless you have."
He shook his head, and smiled again. "Then let's do it.
We'll reach Ur-Orm this afternoon before it's dark."
They kissed while they embraced, picked up their sacks, and left.
Mid-afternoon they reached Ur-Orm, and got a room
At the inn, where—disguised as "the friend"—Cartha claimed
The small chest that he had left there sometime agone.

Descending to the cove that sheltered ships and boats,
He booked, and paid for, in advance a double passage
For Aviol and for himself, not on a boat,
But just on some small merchant ship that plied the coast,

That would sail after dawn straight for Aliddium,
The last port of its type on that part of the coast.
That evening, while in bed in their room, Cartha said,
"You know, there's no going back, we start a new life."
She replied, "Yes, I know." Cuddling, they fell asleep.

Getting up before dawn, the two boarded the ship,
With small chest, with their sacks, and settled in their cabin,
Where they would take their meals. Unless delayed by storm,
The ship would reach Aliddium in a few days.
The unireme cast off, at first propelled by oar,
And westward held her course, once she had cleared the cove,
Sailing close to the coast. The two came up on deck,
Once the sail had been spread: they marvelled at the views,
The greenery of woods and farms, the bluffs and beaches;
The few days on the waves went pleasantly and fast,
Without mishap they reached their port mid-afternoon.

Aliddium itself sat high on rocky bluffs,
Secure against the storms that rarely struck this coast
Except in wintertime with frequent winds and rains.
Bolstered by merchant wealth, it was a pretty town,
Located at the angle where the great west prong,
The great western peninsula, projects southwest
Into the depth and vastness of the Ocean Sea:
Stark mountains with steep slopes and sharper peaks and summits,
Near-barren tablelands and shelving terraces,
Blind shores and hidden coves and beachless littorals,
High rockbound cliffs that plunge to sounding waves below.

Lightly burdened, our two ascended to the town,
And going to the inn, to which Cartha had shipped
One of the little chests that he had sent ahead,
He claimed the chest, and booked a room for several days,
Where they would take their meals. They settled in at once,
A pleasant room in quite a first-class hostelry.
They visited the town a little every day,
But otherwise they would rehearse their music act.
They did not have to fret about sufficient coin;
Cartha had bought another lute that he could play.

Aviol, so he found, had quite a lovely voice,
Quickly she learned, and soon they had a repertoire,
A music act, that they could sell to earn their keep
At inns or taverns or—more to the point—on board
Of ships or argosies that sailed to western seas.
Soon they auditioned, thus, and won their passage on
An argosy of trade, an ocean-going trireme,
As that ship's minstrels, on the way to Atlantillia,
And past the inland seas to far Oöxathan,
Where Cartha's archlute would await our lovers there.

Cartha, of course, no longer sang of one unnamed,
His goddess peradventure evermore departed,
Nor any song identified with his past life.
The repertoire he shared with Aviol was new,
Hornpipes and sailor's tunes, but mostly comic songs,
Or mock laments, such as made people burst out laughing.
At last the great ship sailed, clearing the great west prong,
The great southwestern prong, extending out to sea,

On a trip that would last much more than several days,
Taking our twain thousands of leagues to their new life.

Their further plans involved, beyond Oöxathan,
Beyond the Isthmus-Gates that open south of there,
The remnant isles of Mu in those great seas beyond.
Meanwhile in All-Neph-Rom much time would need to pass
Before the folks of Aviol became concerned
About her absence, and about no word from her.
Getting no note from her himself for quite some time,
It was the king, impatient for her due return,
Who stirred things up: he sent enquiries to her folks.

Since *he* became alarmed, then *they* did so in turn,
And sent him back a note, that she had not come back,
But that they would send news as soon as they found out.
Where then was Aviol, and where could she have gone?
Some close friends volunteered to trace and find her trail,
Assisted by her former boy friend at the start,
So that they tracked her down with ease through her first day,
An easy half-day's walk away from All-Neph-Rom,
Arriving at that inn to the south at day's end.

They asked the workers there anent her whereabouts,
And learned that Aviol, once she had said goodbye
To him, her old boy friend, had not waited around,
Expecting the next friend who would walk on with her,
But she had left almost at once, that early morning,
Had headed west alone, two small sacks at her back,
Along the ancient route that went south of the swamp,

And vanished from their sight, ere little time elapsed.
So now this group of those close friends in their own turn
Veered right, and then went west, along that ancient route.

The searching party met few people on that road,
But these few were not those who had seen Aviol,
And when addressed, these few could not remember her,
Nor was the road inhabited on either side.
Walking about a league or so along that route,
The seekers reached the swamp, coming abreast of it,
Just to the south, and here they amplified their search
Along that marshland's edge, between that and the road,
Past quagmires and quicksands and reed-infested waters,
Checking out the terrain for any sign of her.

The searchers found, though somewhat hidden from the road,
The grassy knoll on which the two capes had been spread
By Cartha, with his lute laid next to his own mantle.
A tiny crown and trident sewn upon the collar
Served to identify one cape as Aviol's—
All three things looked the worse for their outdoor exposure.
Saddened, the searchers reached the obvious conclusion:
Rather than be apart, the lovers—still in love—
Had chosen death by drowning in the quicksand there.

Some of the searchers wept. They picked up lute and capes,
Retraced their route, first east, then north, to All-Neph-Rom,
Telling their tale along the way to one and all,
Restoring lute and cape to Cartha's dad and mom,
And giving Aviol's cape back to her old parents,

As they with all of All-Neph-Rom were plunged in grief.
Her parents in their turn gave her cape to a friend
To take it to the king, Memtellidon himself,
To tell the tale to him of how the lovers died.

In spite of all his other wives and concubines,
Memtellidon was greatly shattered by this loss,
And with no fanfare and with no large entourage
He visited the site, and ordered there a tomb
To be raised up of marble and of orichalch,
To honor those two lovers, both so dear to him,
With this inscription in the oldest Atlantean:
"Here lie two lovers who thought it was best to die
Together, rather than to live without each other."

Meanwhile that argosy of trade continued sailing west
Without mishap or tempest ruffling up the route.
Cartha and Aviol, featured as that ship's minstrels,
Nightly were holding forth with song and lute and quip,
With sailor's tunes, with comic songs, with mock laments,
With hornpipes and with other jolly dancing riffs.
The two musicians proved a great hit with the crew,
With captain and with crew, as minstrels and as persons,
En route to Atlantillia, then Coöxathan.

How far away seemed All-Neph-Rom and their old life—
And that sham death of theirs, with burial, in the swamp!
Was all that not a cruel hoax, as well as heartless?
Or was it really that? Or only *their* decision?
The old saw says that all is fair in war and love—

Survival by all means is Nature's foremost law.
But our two lovers paid a price for their escape:
They had to die, to folks, to friends, to their old life,
Eternal exiles from the world they loved and knew.

Once they had gone beyond the reach of legal force,
They would send back a message to their families,
Enjoining utter secrecy for one and all:
It would not do to have the Archking learn of this,
For fear that vengeance or retaliation fall
With full blind force on blameless individuals:
Choosing the course that they had seen fit to fulfill,
Despite whatever qualms that they might well have had,
They would explain in brief what they had done, and why.

Their further plans involved, beyond Oöxathan,
Beyond the Isthmus-Gates that open south of there,
The remnant isles of Mu in those great seas beyond:
The ancient remnants of a greater continent,
A greater empire, than Atlantis ever knew,
Or could have ever known, allured our lovers on:
The scent of alien spices and perfumes began
To haunt their dreams and waking visions all the more,
The blaze of alien stars would soon beguile their nights.

The Music of the Spheres

(Upon reading *The Theory of Everything*, by Stephen Hawking, late in 2002.)

Dedicated to John and Lola Morgan, in gratitude and esteem.

The music of the spheres that vibrates out in space,
Do black holes quench this music that lured Plato's ear,
As they draw matter to their mass, to leave no trace?
And when these particles resume in some new sphere,
A planet or a star, is it those that we hear
Ghostlike in our tympanum, tintinnabulous?
And is it in this way, this roundabout career,
In this and other ways much more than fabulous,
That particles go forth from us, and then come back to us?

Expansion and contraction, dissonance and consonance—
Begun at once, the cosmos needs no further impetus—
Its particles need but recharge, as on and on they dance!

This music of the spheres that vibrates out in space
    Is the cosmos in sound, unceasing, huge beyond huge,
        One labyrinthine fugue and cunning subterfuge,
Polyphonies that sing at every kind of pace. . . .

TO RINALDO
FOR CLARK ASHTON SMITH

(On behalf of Saturday, 11 January 2003,
in honor of Smith's birthday, 13 January 1893,
the one hundred tenth anniversary of the same.)

Dedicated to Ronald Scott Hilger, in gratitude.

With vision undeterred by sound and hue,
He sought the means to state at once his praise
For one who never had received his due:
Shaping with art his eulogies and lays,
His odes and sonnets, *he* had passed his days,
A prophet honorless in his own land:
Instead of proffering some crown, some bays,
He chose to honor *him* with his own brand
Of honest monument, which somehow should withstand:

Big boulder with footing, and plaque with words engraved,
Uncluttered and straightforward but still somehow grand,
A legend of great art superbly lived and braved:

The lichens, with the moss, upon the rock remain,
  The wine and earth and ashes all have now been poured,
   As at some feast of gods, or at some king's own board,
As from an antique urn, inside an antique fane.

Forevermore the Rose

> To sing again that oft-sung tale:
> The May-Rose and the Nightingale!
>   —Eulalie, "Approach of May."

Dedicated to Violet Nelson Heyer, in memoriam,
and in honor of her own poem "Forever the Rose."

Whether extolled by one Pierre de Ronsard,
Or by gold-mining Auburn's Eulalie,
The rose in May abides the springtime star!
Despite the modern ban—is it decree?—
Against the rose of any pedigree
As topic for a poem, the rose endures:
In ways antiquity could not foresee,
In brand-new colors, in still new contours,
In limitless varieties the rose today matures:

As if the blossom thrived in Eden's garden-close—
Such glamours it revives, such glamours it procures!—
This is the rose today, forevermore the rose:

As for the nightingale, that night-bird troubadour,
     He, too, has relevance, still of the very best.
         His song inspires young lovers, on their lovelorn quest,
To find, and then to follow up, their own amour.

Tableau Sous-Marin

Translated from the Atlantean of an unknown poet.

Dedicated to Deirdre McVicker and Timothy Ray.

Down in the deep black darkness of the sea,
Where light is little more than phosphor-gloom,
The strange and lamp-armed fish manoeuvre free:

Where undersea volcanos fret and fume
In rumbling incantations without plume,
Dead silence otherwise unfurls its pall:

Where all things undergo some outré doom,
The deep-sea hills and mountains rear their wall,
Vast ridges and sheer peaks that thrust up over all:

Here all things come to rest in this dark ocean's womb,
As in some shadow-filled, enormous temple-hall,
Where everyone foregathers, just in one huge room:

Assured and patient as the fates,
    Far from her surface toil and spume,
    As both the matrix and the tomb,
The mothering ocean waits and waits.

Predicament

The nymph may fear, may flee, the rampant faun,
The satyr-faun, perhaps insatiable.
And Nature? Unconcerned. She just moves on.

The ins and outs of individual
Affairs to her are less than trivial.
Nature has one concern: this! *Thou shalt mate*.

The who, when, where are immaterial.
But, *Thou shalt couple, thou shalt fornicate:*
Above all, *Thou shalt procreate, and procreate, and procreate.*

Six billion human beings are the end result,
And more, upon this Earth that we still formicate.
The question? Should we weep, or should we not exult?

Is this whole biosphere but one big pod
     From which the human race will catapult,
        In ways overt, or yet in ways occult,
To other planets? Huh?! "We trust in God."

Huh?!

Remonstration

Translated from the Atlantean of a modern poet.

Dedicated to William Kostura, in expostulation.

My songs and sonnets from this latter day
Do not seem Atlantean quite enough
To certain connoisseurs, or thus they say:
But just as metaphor all this rare stuff,
Ephemeral perhaps as foam or fluff,
Is of Atlantis, hence not ordinary:
Her seas alone make treasure-house enough,
Where iridescent creatures, lapidary,
Glide through the coral-gleaming depths extraordinary:

For, all things beautiful but lost, forevermore,
Are Atlantean-like, and intermediary
Between Atlantis and that bright but final shore:

Even without some tangible remains,
    With splendors only metaphorical,
    It all transmutes to one dim oracle:
The mythoglyphical, as always, reigns.

Enlightenment

To C. A. S.

Embattled and beleaguered individual—
    A solitary beacon on the coasts of night,
    Dispensing fitful gleams of half-enshadowed light
Amid the general gloom of everything and all—

You have endured, you and your works, against the odds,
    The prejudice against imagination's fire
    That fountains forth, transfigured, through your antique lyre,
Whose tones remind us yet of goddesses and gods!—

Our lost inheritance from that long vanished world
    That flowered upon the shores round our great inland sea,
    Before there came upon the scene the Christian Three,
Where that Imperium Romanum once unfurled.

But yet your antique lyre sings in another key,
    Of sky-tall city towers whose peaks far off astound,
    Of interstellar flight, of Space-Time without bound,
One poet's dream, one vision towards futurity!

False prophets, poetasters, and such other frauds—
    Some grown rich from their wares—all of these notwithstanding,
    You have bequeathed a greater gift, beyond outstanding:
You have endured, you and your works, against the odds.

For me your works remain one cosmic treasure-chest,
    Piled with the spoils and lore and wealth of centuries,
    Concealed behind which lurk yet further treasuries,
Which always lead to one more world and one more quest.

A Rendezvous with Pierrefonds

> Les fourriers de l'Eté sont venus
> Pour appareiller son logis,
> Et ont fait tendre ses tapis,
> De fleurs et verdure tissus.
> —Charles d'Orléans, "Rondeau de l'Eté."

Remembering the towers of Pierrefonds
That rise like pepper-pots above her walls,
I must go back again to Pierrefonds!
I must return to where nostalgia calls,
To roam again her corridors and halls,
To climb yet once again her stairs and towers!
Still Viollet-le-Duc's design enthralls,
And I must haunt again those hidden bowers
Where Louis and Charles d'Orléans long since beguiled their hours!

And if the Middle Ages mark the outside of this fort—
Where pearl-grey clouds pledge once again their half-eternal showers—
The Renaissance comes back to life inside her inner court:

There still her towers lift up below that lowering sky,
Where but one cat looks on, to greet the passersby.

Rondeau of Winter

*Unriming translation from the French
of Charles d'Orléans, poet and prince.*

The season has laid forth his cloak
Of wind, of coldness, and of rain,
Has dressed up in embroidery
Of sunlight, sparkling, clear, and fine.

There is not any beast or bird
That in his tongue nor sings nor cries:
The season has laid forth his cloak
Of wind, of coldness, and of rain.

River, fountain, and little stream
Bear on their handsome livery
Drops made of silvered jewelry;
And everything is dressed anew:
The season has laid forth his cloak.

Rondeau of Summer

*Unriming translation from the French
of Charles d'Orléans, prince of poets.*

Lord Summer's harbingers have come
To dress his lodging in advance,
Have made his carpets delicate,
With flowers and verdure intertwined.

Spreading his carpets, velvet-piled,
With green grass, through the countryside,
Lord Summer's harbingers have come
To dress his lodging in advance.

Our hearts, long numbed by dreary cold,
Are happily still hale, still good:
Out from this place go somewhere else,
Lord Winter, lodge no longer here:
Lord Summer's harbingers have come.

Pierrefonds, Poème en Pierre

This castle of Pierrefonds, poem in stone . . . Gigantic poem in quarried rock, in limestone, made thus of that same calcium carbonate still retaining the remnants of desiccated seas incalculably remote in time. . . . How high the site itself alone lifts up, about a hundred feet, above the ambient ground!

Imperial silhouette of projecting walls and of lofty towers fashioned like giant pepper-pots. . . . Massive late-mediaeval skyscraper built at the command and expense of Louis d'Orléans, during that long-agone fin-de-siècle of 1393–1407, by a succession of master constructors and stoneworkers. . . . What an epic of effort and aspiration to build, rebuild, and maintain this fabric through the centuries!

A long interval of disaster and recovery would follow from 1406, the inauguration of the castle, until 1440. Late in 1407 a small company of armed men in the hire of Jean Sans Peur, the rival Duke of Burgundy, brutally waylaid and murdered Louis, the Duke of Orléans, during the dark of night on a street in Paris. After losing his father, the adolescent Charles became the new duke, and then after losing his mother to grief in turn the following year, Charles continued pursuing justice in his father's death. This led to civil war between the partisans of Orléans and Burgundy, civil war that laid waste much of France, before Burgundy triumphed at Paris sometime before 1411.

After the disastrous battle of Agincourt, late in 1415, Charles d'Orléans was taken prisoner by his cousin Henry V of England, and began his captivity of twenty-five years in Great Britain, not to find ransom and release until 1440. During this long exile Charles developed into the great poet whose works we read and love today. Meanwhile, what of Pierrefonds?

Besieged and damaged several times, repaired by Charles d'Orléans and his own son Louis XII . . . Besieged and damaged with cannon a final time decisively, during the spring of 1617, by the Count of Auvergne at the command of Cardinal Richelieu, and then dismantled a few months later at the command of Louis XIII. . . . The vast structure would now stand abandoned, spectacularly ruined, for almost two and a half centuries. . . .

Alas! used but as an occasional residence or a hunting lodge, the castle has existed either as an immense but often underinhabited stronghold, or as a grandiose and picturesque ruin, inspiring poets and painters as well as the general public of succeeding centuries. . . .

Thanks to the combined attention of the Count of Auvergne, Cardinal Richelieu, and Louis XIII, truly that spring of 1617 had proven fatal to the ambitious original poem in stone of Louis d'Orléans. . . . How many castles and estates did that magnificent prince not possess or build or rebuild in the course of his fourteen years of rule, begun in 1392, before his assassination late in 1407?!

Reconstructed—and on the inside into a Renaissance château—at the command and expense of Napoléon III, during 1858–70 (thus at the height of the Second Empire, begun in 1852), by master builder Viollet-le-Duc (1814–1879) with his principal assistant Wyganowski, and finally continued at the command and expense of the Third Republic, during 1878–85, by Viollet-le-Duc again, and after his death by his own son-in-law, the architect Ouradou. . . . The château survives. . . .

Nevertheless, despite its neglect, abandon, or partial ruination, yes, despite the terrible damage or destruction that it has endured, it has on occasion served as the focus or setting for several outstanding occurrences. . . . To inaugurate the almost completed palace encased within the mighty fortress, Louis d'Orléans during 1406 opted to celebrate at Pierrefonds the marriage of his then ten-year-old son, the future prince and poet Charles d'Orléans, and invited his brother Charles VI and his court to attend the celebrations, to which they travelled through the great forest from the little city of Compiègne situated at the confluence of the rivers Aisne and Oise to the northwest. . . . What a pageant and kaleidoscope of color and ceremonial that must have called forth in such a setting!

More than four centuries later, in the summer of 1832, the first King of Belgium, Léopold I, arrived in Compiègne. In the chapel of the Versailles-like palace built there by Louis XV, Léopold married the much younger daughter of Louis-Philippe, Louise d'Orléans. To celebrate this union, the same Citizen King hosted at Pierrefonds a great banquet that lasted long into the night, but inside the picturesque ruins of the great inner courtyard. . . . How brightly the candles and flambeaux must have flamed and flared against the nocturnal darkness of the high surrounding walls!

After the fall of the Second Empire, signalized by the defeat of the French by the Prussians at the disastrous battle of Sedan, the imperial family went into exile in England. Napoléon III thus died in exile while in Great Britain during the winter of 1872–73. His only son, the prince imperial

Louis, died in South Africa during 1879, killed by the Zulus, whom he fought while voluntarily wearing the Britannic uniform. Each spring from 1891 onward, thus in the course of her exile from France, the French government allowed the former Empress Eugénie to pass her winters in the warmer climate of the Riviera. During her exile she bore the self-given title of the Countess of Pierrefonds, a descriptive name at once precise and nebulous. . . .

Indeed, she still bore this title when in 1912, given leave by the authorities, Eugénie visited the village and especially the reconstructed castle of Pierrefonds, which she had last seen sometime during 1870. Now seeing the reconstruction as completed by Viollet-le-Duc and then finally by Ouradou, she wept there among the other visitors at the castle. Something of the pomp and circumstance and initiative of the Second Empire had survived after all! Born in 1826, Eugénie died in 1920. One who had once danced to the waltzes of her own court pianist Emile Waldteufel, waltzes composed expressly for use in the imperial ballrooms of her husband's own régime, she passed on thus at the very threshold of the Jazz Age!

One final and prolonged look back at that elegant Empress of the French, while the strains of some suave and slow-paced waltz by Waldteufel, perhaps *Mon Rêve*, soothes and beguiles our inner ear. . . . Let us not recall her as the grande dame in exile—always dressed in black, and always in mourning for husband and son, emperor and prince imperial. Let us invoke, instead, the young and exquisitely beautiful sovereign, yes, as portrayed by the brothers Winterhalter, when during 1855 they painted her and eight ladies of her court, somewhat in the mode of the nine Muses, only two years after her marriage to Napoléon III in a ceremony of great splendor amid the Gothic magnificence of Notre-Dame de Paris during January of 1853.

L'Imperatrice Eugénie et sa cour . . . *The Empress Eugénie and her court.* . . . How variously and widely has that painting appeared in reproduction!—but how many people who have seen it thus, have never beheld the original, and so have no concept of its actual size! With its lifesized figures this enormous picture towers over the observer, and has an elaborate and gigantic frame that must rest on the floor for support. As posed in some lovely glade of park or garden, perhaps at Fontainebleau, the mannered grace and studied refinement of these women, as arranged in a circle with their very full skirts and their tasteful décolletage, recall directly some artful grouping of ballet dancers—in some big action ballet of the period 1853–59—as choreographed by the then chief ballet-master Mazilier at the then Paris Opéra in the Rue Lepelletier! Was this the Eugénie who confided the reconstruction of Pierrefonds to Viollet-le-Duc?

But now during the spring of the year 2000, I think that I like the reconstructed castle best. It has extraordinary and even haunting qualities that a mere academic restoration could never possess. All my studies prior to coming here in person could not have prepared me for the actual experience. One is completely taken with surprise not only by the castle's very site high above the charming village but above all by the enormous castle rising even and ever higher than the site itself. On arriving from Compiègne, suddenly emerging from the surrounding forest, one seems to discover the castle ascending out of the trees almost at once as if by magic. Truly the towers and walls of such a fortress literally loom overhead, and make a genuine epiphany.

Yes, I like the reconstructed castle best when, in the absence of other visitors during a late overcast morning, the resident cat, a certain Mistress Graymalkin sitting in the great inner courtyard, follows me through the official kitchen entrance that now leads into one of several exhibit chambers. Coming up close, she meows at me with such a clear and poignant cry that I cannot resist. I stoop not to conquer but to caress. Moreover, I hunker down, and after I stroke her affectionately for a minute or so, she seems content, and walks back out into the courtyard. A cat may look at a king, and a poet may fondle a cat. Ainsi soit-il, so be it, amen!

A Ballade of Duality

A dialogue.

Dedicated to Louis and Susan Irmo, with affection.

CALIBAN:

Greetings to you up there from me the mole,
    I, who am not the apple of your eye!
To be like you one bit is not my goal,
    Angelic harpy, prancing butterfly,
    Mincing and insubstantial flutterby,
You mote aswim in some cask of vermouth!
    You can but threaten me, not edify,
Here, on this island of still-vexed Bermooth.

ARIEL:

You muckworm, such a foul and filthy troll,
    Yes, you are not the apple of this eye!
If you are the flesh, then I am the soul—
    If you are the earth, then I am the sky—
    If you are the lid, then I am the eye—
If you are the mouth, then I am the tooth!
    For you I play nor lute nor lullaby,
Here, on this island of still-vexed Bermooth.

CALIBAN:

As one we make one undivided whole,
    Nor you nor I as such can truly die!
Without the flesh, say, where would be the soul?
      Without the earth, speak, where would be the sky?
      Without the lid, pray, where would be the eye?
Without the mouth, tell, where would be the tooth?
    Thus always you yourself I here defy,
Here, on this island of still-vexed Bermooth.

ARIEL'S ENVOY:

There is no happy ending for us two,
    Nor hope of peace between ourselves in truth.
We cannot mesh aright, but just askew,
    Here, on this island of still-vexed Bermooth.

Conundrum

He had awoke inside the cryptic dungeon,
Or worse, inside some darker oubliette,
Down deep below the castle's massive donjon:

Why was he there? What had he done? He let
His mind float free. But how could he forget?
He thought and thought, but came up with no clue.

He felt a sense of panic, then of threat.
Again he thought and thought, but still no cue.
His head ached bad. His mouth was dry. What should he do?

Had he come to this place to state a grievance?
And had he quarreled, caused a big to-do?
A hard blow to his head? A disappearance?

Yes, had he disappeared for challenging his lord?—
He might have got instead the sharp end of a sword.

Rondel of Time

Time is, time was, and time will be
While tick-tock scans the metric line,
Just like the clock's pulse, by design:
Each verse means work, and none comes free.

If tick is tock, and both can plea,
Then their two voices must combine:
Time is, time was, and time will be
While tick-tock scans the metric line.

If tock is tick, but truth is key,
Epistemology is fine,
An inference more than benign,
This axiom-fact that none can flee:
Time is, time was, and time will be
While tick-tock scans the metric line.

Rondel of Space

They say, there is no end to space,
And that the cosmos has no limit:
Whether for elephant or emmet,
The cosmos has no end of space.

The cosmos with no end in space,
What image can we use to limn it?
They say, there is no end to space,
And that the cosmos has no limit.

So many folk live in Earth-space
That we all soon shall over-brim it,
And in that process over-grim it,
At this our procreative pace!
They say, there is no end to space,
And that the cosmos has no limit.

The Ghost of a Dream

(In collaboration with Jesse F. Knight.)

Did not some Atlantean ship once glide,
Bordered with trees and fields, up this broad stream,
As all her flashing oars dripped from the tide?

Her wide right-angled sail, as in a dream,
With woven crown and trident quite agleam,
Pavaned up to this dock by sunset's glow:

With ship secured, framed in the sun's last beam,
The crew soon swarmed ashore, all at one go,
Followed by merchants and their goods, the same as long ago:

The natives brought much stuff, to trade by flambeau-light;
Some goods the merchants took on board, and stored below;
Then drank, and feasted, everyone—all through that night:

How fast the night unfurled, as in a dream!
    Well pleased at adding to their vessel's hoard,
  At dawn the foreigners went back on board;
The ship slipped quietly back down the stream.

A Fanfare from Atlantis

Richard Rodgers and Robert Russell Bennett,
The Song of the High Seas.

Dedicated to Michael and Renée Halverson, with much gratitude.

It sounded faint at first, and then a little loud,
A disembodied noise—that clangored from the past—
Like trumpet notes and drum beats echoed through a shroud:

A series of huge waves, each louder than the last,
Was heard to surge, transcendent, on the wind's great blast,
Pausing with clarion calls like those intoned by fate:

And then, above all this, an anthem proud and vast
Was heard there—at the pause itself—to sound, to state,
To sing full force, its hymn divine—majestic, broad, elate:

A song it was that sang of open seas, and high—
Of kings and fabled courts, of awesome things of state—
Of boundless waves profound, whose waters touch the sky:

Returning to the source out of which it had come,
    That final hymn of empire from an elder day,
    The fanfare from Atlantis fiercely died away,
One final trumpet blare, one final roll of drum.

Notes

To a Dead City.

Cartagena de las Indias, founded in 1532, functioned as the treasure-gathering-and-exporting city for the Spanish Empire in the New World from the early 1530s until about 1800. Here the treasure fleet left every year to bring its lavish cargos to the Court of the King of Spain headquartered at Madrid and El Escorial to the north of the capital. Cartagena de las Indias inevitably fostered a whole culture of avaricious and ferocious parasites (read *Pirates of the Caribbean*), most of whose depredations in the long term had little real effect on the vast bulk of precious materials destined for the Court of Spain.

The two greatest pirate attacks occurred, sic: in 1583 under Sir Francis Drake, and in 1697 under Baron Jean-Bernard Desjeans de Pointis, but other attacks only a little less notable took place under French corsair Robert Baal in 1543–1544, followed by Martin Cote between Baal and Sir Francis. Baal sacked the town just as the treasure fleet had assembled to set sail for Spain. Drake began burning the port, block by block, until the local authorities agreed to pay the ransom that he demanded.

Despite the formidable walls erected in the latter 1500s, Jean de Pointis managed to besiege and ultimately to take the city. He came with a huge fleet and 9,000 buccaneers, not to mention quite a few then state-of-the-art cannon that played the decisive role in conquering the city. In the last two decades of the 1500s, the local authorities by order of Philip II erected the still extant walls out of coral, 60 feet high and 40 feet wide, and studded the walls with some 30 stone forts. All of this availed for the most part, except in the case of Jean de Pointis.

Memorial.

Born in Rantoul, Illinois (4 June 1956), but raised and educated in Rhode Island, Keith Allen Daniels attended the University of Rochester, New York, earning his B.S. in chemistry. After four years in the U.S. Navy, he attended the University of Florida in Gainesville, and earned his M.S. in materials science. As a scientist he pursued the humanities and literary arts on his own, having never attended a college-level English class. He worked as a materials engineer first in Florida and then in California, where he died while working at China Lake and residing in adjacent Ridgecrest, all in the Mojave Desert, faithfully attended at home to the last by his loving wife, the artist Toni Luna Daniels.

Keith began writing poetry in 1967, and having it published in 1970. In latter 1993, while attending a science-fiction convention in San Francisco, he met and fell in love with Toni Luna, a native of the Philippines who had relocated to California. Later that same year Keith himself relocated from Tallahassee, Florida, to San Francisco, where Toni and he lived together (while he worked in Palo Alto), and where they eventually married.

Despite his early death at 45 (18 December 2001) from metastatic colon cancer (which he valiantly battled from spring through autumn of 2001), the poet left a considerable output of his own work, including especially the two major collections *What Rough Book* and *Satan Is a Mathematician*. Through his own Anamnesis Press, which he founded and managed from 1990 onward, he specialized in publishing science-fiction poetry, just as he did in writing it. Keith brought out many significant books in the genre, whether single collections or wide-ranging anthologies.

A fact deserving special mention, Keith through his own press sponsored an annual poetry contest during 1996–2001 for the best short collection of new poems (that is, of an imaginative nature), the prize involving $1,000, plus publication of the winning MS. as a distinctive chapbook. Beside furnishing the prize money himself, he had to read and judge hundreds of MSS. for the contest, not only thus demonstrating his great love of poetry but also his generosity towards other poets, a rare altruism, indeed.

Keith combined the practical knowledge of the physical scientist with the keen imagination and sensibility of the instinctive poet, the latter deriving perhaps from his Keltic inheritance. He based the speculative flights of his poetic output on a solid bedrock of hard science, as preached by the late great science-fictioneer James Blish. Keith was that rare phenomenon, the fantasy and science-fiction poet who combined profound scientific thought with the forms and standards of traditional English and other prosody, including meter and rime, all of which he deployed with unusual skill, naturalness, and musicality.

His work was widely published in genre magazines of all types (whether prozines or fanzines), and was nominated for, and indeed won, several distinguished prizes. From some point following 1970 until his death in late 2001, Keith Allen Daniels became perhaps the foremost science-fiction poet of his time, and compares as an imaginative writer in verse, no less than poetic propagandist, with the late, great Stanley McNail (1918–1995).

The present poet-author enjoyed an especially warm friendship with Keith from April 2000 until the latter's death, as well as with Keith's wife Toni Luna Daniels, who provided much of the art for the books that her husband published from the mid-1990s onward. Anamnesis Press continues in operation.

The Herdsman.
Through the French of Michel de Labretagne.

Most of the surviving poems by Aänsess deal with the pastoral culture and life typical of the Astazhan, the vast pastoral plateau that occupied the southeastern extension of the largest island in the Empire of Atlantis, that is, Atlantis the Archkingdom. The Astazhan was the native region of Aänsess, Archknight, and the last Archroyal Governor of the Atlantean Forts and Watchtowers in what is now Cornwall, Wales, and southern Ireland. These last-cited installations Aänsess eventually abandoned to return to what was left of the Archkingdom after the Great Cataclysm. Because there was more than one well-known poet with the name of Aänsess in the period just before the Great Cataclysm, the poet under immediate discussion became generally recognized as "Aänsess of the Astazhan."

Tropicality.
Through the French of Michel de Labretagne.

Like the preceding selection, "Tropicality" is an expanded sonnet, or song archroyal, and is taken from the Late Atlantean but Pre-Cataclysmic *Anthology of Anonymous Poets*, compiled by the last great Atlantean poet Athallarion during his young adulthood. The collection became an universal favorite before the Great Cataclysm (and remained that even long afterwards). The "tropicality" of the title may refer to one of two tropical island kingdoms belonging to the Empire of Atlantis: either Atlantillia, the site between the Greater Antilles and the Lesser Antilles (in the present West Indies) or Iffrikonn-Yssthia, the site marked today by the Cape Verde Islands.

Totem.
Through the French of Michel de Labretagne.

This whimsical poem, half prayer and half exhortation, its author may have intended as a paean to modesty, patience, and frugality, and as a lesson to Atlantean children specifically. Whoever the poet, he may also have authored some of the other poems for children included in this third series of songs and sonnets translated from the Atlantean.

Abandonment.
Through the French of Michel de Labretagne.

Although the context of this rueful poem does not make the situation overly clear, the fairly large hippocampus that is the subject (the conventionalized image of a horse fused with a sea monster) has apparently functioned as a kind of mascot or as an addition to the household gods that the family who formerly lived in the house has already removed. Also, the abandonment is only temporary, now that the dwelling has already emptied itself of most of the departing family's possessions. Prince Atlantarion in his notes observes that a night watchman in charge of a small group of (armed) workers is residing in the house until all the family's effects have gone. A venerable work of art, the (hollow) hippocampus is made of cast silver, suitably enchased and planished.

Amaranth.
Through the French of Michel de Labretagne.

This opus typifies the poetic output of the exceptionally long-lived King Atlantarion I, as written down following the death of his beloved wife, the preternaturally beautiful Queen Aïs. Its vague disillusionment exhibits perfectly the rueful and questioning tone that came to characterize almost all the poetry scrivened by Atlantarion not just after the Great Cataclysm but above all after the death of Aïs, who had always functioned as his best friend.

Rapa-Nui.

Rapa-Nui: the name Easter Island is here discarded in honor of the somewhat earlier Polynesian term, even if not the original native title. Thanks to the efforts of many scientist-mysteriarchs, we now know that the island's older human life or culture is primarily South American (mostly Peruvian, Bolivian, and Chilean), two successive periods, with a later admixture that brought the locale into the far-flung Polynesian world of the Pacific Ocean, and thus long before the arrival of Columbus into the Americas during the 1490s. By the mid-1870s, due to various adverse events and circumstances, the island's population had sunk to a mere 111 persons, but the annexation of Rapa-Nui by Chile during 1888 has permitted their gradual recovery and renaissance (that began in the mid-1870s) to continue without a break up to the present time, 2002. The population grew from c. 900 in 1955 to c. 2,000 in 1988. Around 1,000 Chileans had immigrated to Rapa-Nui by the last-cited year. The resident people have now reached a total of c. 6,000 or 7,000, more or less the maximum that the island supported at the height of its pre-European technology.

One non–Rapa-Nui scientist-author-adventurer of the highest caliber and humanity stands out in the continuing rehabilitation of the island and its culture, human and otherwise, the Norwegian explorer and anthropologist Thor Heyerdahl (1914–2002). Thanks to the extraordinary success attendant on his Kon-Tiki expedition of 1947 and on his book that followed, *Kon-Tiki*, and thanks to the two archaeological investigations that he sponsored or headed on Rapa-Nui during 1955–1956 and, thirty years later, during 1986–1988, Heyerdahl finally managed to resolve or solve the basic mystery or mysteries about the island. His three books on Easter Island alone take pre-eminent place among the dozen or so major works that he wrote: *Aku-Aku: The Secret of Easter Island* (1958); *The Art of Easter Island* (1975); and *Easter Island: The Mystery Solved* (1989).

Pendant.

There are somewhere between 600 and 1000 giant statues on Rapa-Nui (possibly more, but as yet unexcavated and hence undiscovered), but because the bottom half of any given example has arms and hands that do not project out from the torso, the same bottom half gives the appearance of being more sculptured bust or conventionalized support than anything else, and thus emphasizes the gigantic size of the head in and of itself. Therefore the over-all resemblance of any given Titan figure to an exotic but generic chess-piece (perceived as one of the absolutely needed group of pawns, let us imagine) is really not that far-fetched.

At a certain point, a very low point, in the island's (human) history, what was left of the diminished population had toppled all the giant statues erected on the platforms all over the island. Thus the only statues that still stood until the re-erection of a small number of them in modern times were only those left upright at the quarry in the crater of Rano Raraku, statues deeply embedded in the talus that had accumulated at the site, leaving only the giant heads exposed, and in some cases looking out towards the sea on the south. Given that estimates of Rapa-Nui's over-all area have changed since first recorded by European explorers, and vary between 64 and 69 square miles, it follows that no part of the triangular-shaped landmass finds itself remote from the eternal sound of the great ocean surrounding it. The island may have thus totalled even more than 70 square miles much earlier in geological history, but the ceaseless work of the ocean's waves has gradually eroded significant parts of the coast all over the island, especially along the western half of the northern littoral.

A Game of Chess.

Our account of the history as presented in this poem in prose (preserved only in the oral record among the older indigenous Rapa-Nui population) follows the synthesis effected by the author of *Kon-Tiki* (English-language edition, 1950), i. e., the Gospel according to St. Thor Heyerdahl as outlined in *Aku-Aku* and *Easter Island: The Mystery Solved*—rather than the painstaking synthesis put together by a scientist first working under Heyerdahl's direction, i. e., the revised Gospel according to William Molloy, now deceased, but formerly an archaeologist at the University of Wyoming. This latter figure launched the systematic archaeological survey of Easter Island, the restoration of selected stone houses, and the selective re-erection of toppled moai (i. e., the giant statues commemorating the many dead kings and possibly other eminent people), beginning in 1968.

The period of cultural competition and internecine conflict between clans or tribes, or between the Long Ears and the Short Ears, seems to fall after 1500. This tragical competition and conflict led inexorably to environmental destruction or degradation on the one hand, and chronic warfare and cannibalism on the other, and finally ecological and societal collapse.

It is possible that Heyerdahl overemphasized the influence coming directly from South America (although his evidence appears to be reasonably convincing), and thus to the disparagement of the Polynesian presence on the island. Moving in a general southwestern direction from off the northwestern coast of South America on into the Tuamotus (French Polynesia) as well as past Rapa-Nui, the Humboldt Current certainly facilitates any travelling by sailboat, large raft, or large canoe from, say, selected areas of South America's western coast. This is indisputable.

However, contrary to Heyerdahl's assertions, the Polynesians were for a fact quite capable of creating any and all megalithic monuments and other architecture. It is odd that in this connection almost no one seems to have remarked the existence of the megalithic urban remains far to the west in Micronesia, some 6,500 miles west-northwest of Rapa-Nui. The island cities of Nan-Madol at Pohnpei and Leluh at Kosrae, each complete with its own canal system, respectively—each one a veritable Venice of the Pacific—embody some of the most original, as well as most spectacular, archaeological sites on the entire planet of Earth.

The Chest from Otherwhere.

Many years ago his great and good friend Jesse F. Knight sent the poet-author a color picture postcard showing a large chest of extraordinary beauty and elaborateness, a chest made of precious or semi-precious metals and adorned with various gemstones, whose provenience like the postcard itself is now lost. As a fellow scrivener Jesse had playfully suggested in the small message part of the card that the chest had probably originated in Atlantis. Certainly the scrine suggested some unknown realm, if not Atlantis herself, then some geography hitherto undiscovered in Otherwhere. Hence, the dedication to Jesse, in gratitude.

A Ballade of Prospero.

In that supreme dramatic poem called *The Tempest* by one William Shakespeare, Prospero as the former Duke of Milan, shipwrecked on an uninhabited island, raises a storm by magic, the tempest of the title, during which Prospero's brother Antonio, who has deposed him, is in his own turn shipwrecked upon the same island. It is possible that some direct influence on this unique play by Shakespeare (first produced in 1611), the product of his final years as a dramatist, may have emanated from Spenser's own *Mutabilitie Cantos* (first published in 1609), the only surviving fragment from Book VII of *The Faerie Queene*, as well as the product of its own poet-author's final years as an epic poet and supreme romanceer.

The Bitch with Tits of Bronze.

The Vatican, or Vaticanus, the independent city-state located within the commune of Rome (Italy), is the seat and home of the (Roman Catholic) Pope, the headquarters of the Papacy. Formerly the capital of the Vatican States, a virtual empire that sprawled over much of Italy (the northern and central parts of the Italian peninsula)—during the Middle Ages, the Renaissance, and on up into early modern times—until its dissolution in 1870 by Victor Emmanuel II; the Vatican, or Vaticanus, takes its name from the Mons Vaticanus, or the Vatican Hill, situated on the western bank of the Tiber River.

Made of bronze, today the statue of the she-wolf suckling Rome's two legendary founders stands in the City Hall of Rome on the Capitoline Hill, but a copy is on display in one of the museums of the Vatican. An unknown Etruscan sculptor originally made and cast it in the 400s B.C., and Antonio Pollaiuolo added the twins themselves in the 1400s A.D.

Codacil of Contradiction.
Through the French of Michel de Labretagne.

This opus, like *Amaranth*, is another typical piece produced by King Atlantarion I in the final decades of his life, following the death of his profoundly cherished wife, the Queen Aïs. In fact it is one of his very last poems. By the time that he wrote this, the king had virtually abdicated in favor of his eldest son, and was devoting most of his time to his art, his music, and his poetry. He had just completed his final sequence of connected poems, but instead of experiencing a sense of release and elation, he felt only a sense of defeat, as adumbrated in this one of his final pieces of verse.

As One Jaguär to Another.
Through the French of Michel de Labretagne.

The scribe who recorded these half-dozen fables (as well as others) did not sign his name to them perhaps from fear of some negative karma deriving from the very fact of having overheard and recorded them. The other fables concerning the two jaguärs (as featured in the present series of short stories and intertextual conversations) reportedly exist somewhere among the extant papers of Michel de Labretagne in the Bibliothèque Nationale in Paris, but no scholar to date has found them. Labretagne complains in a letter to a friend about the difficulty that he has encountered in translating these fables into (Renaissance) French, not so much the literal meaning of the words but how to establish the precise and rather whimsical tone. This latter has also proven to be a major concern for the present translator.

Quoctezu Bids Farewell.

The miniature iffinixes that appear at the start of this fable, while distantly related to the huge birds that resided in Poseidonis (the mountain-heartland of the island continent of Atlantis), were much smaller birds, and lived primarily in foothill areas. However, like their much bigger cousins, or like modern parrots, they characteristically had brilliant plumage that usually featured several vivid and often contrasting colors: blues, greens, reds, yellows, etc.

Cephalopod in Residence.
Through the French of Michel de Labretagne.

This lyrical poem, like *Nine Happy Goldfish* among other pieces, also stems from the period just preceding the Great Cataclysm. Some Atlantologists perceive a certain linkage with *Tableau Sous-marin*, and unlike Michel de Labretagne himself, have speculated that Prince Atlantarion might very well have authored the latter poem, and moreover before the Great Cataclysm, rather than after it. If Dr. Ibid M. Andor has left any notes for *Cephalopod in Residence*, they have not yet surfaced.

Colossal Chambered Nautilus.
Through the French of Michel de Labretagne.

This less poetical companion-piece to *Cephalopod in Residence* stems likewise from the period just preceding the Great Cataclysm, but not in advance of the Battle Before Athens, which destroyed most of the Pan-Atlantean royalty together with the highest nobility.

The giant squid and its occasional combat with sperm whales at great depths in the ocean were common knowledge to the ancient Atlanteans. The squids invariably lost, and the whales consumed them, the whales and any of their own hangers-on. The titanic grappling with the whale invariably left the imprint from the suckers of the squid's tentacles unremovingly marked upon the whale's own skin. In spite of this, the squids in general seemed to have formed a preferred item in the cetacean diet, but the squids themselves often cannibalized other squids, whatever the precise species.

Furthermore, the Atlantean marine scientists and marine archaeologists also certainly knew of the archaic armored squids, protected by a spiral shell (similar to that of the chambered nautilus). At least as large as the giant squids of Atlantean or modern times, the giant armored squids evidently had existed in the Cambrian period, although some experts date them somewhat later.

Hippokampoi.
Through the French of Michel de Labretagne.

It is obvious that seahorses, related to the pipefishes, do not neigh, but they do give forth, during the season when they spawn, a monotonous but intense drumming sound, that is, under the water. It is a fact that the female seahorse deposits her eggs directly into the male's brood-pouch, after the couple has performed their simple mating dance. (The female calls it quits right after depositing her eggs.) Inside the male's pouch the eggs are fertilized and "gestated" until the baby seahorses are ready to be born, this development taking over-all around ten days. Depending on the species of hippocampus, or hippokampos, the male seahorse can give birth up to 12 or 36 "foals." The usual habitat of the seahorse is the grassy inlets and shallow bays of warm seas.

As One Seahorse to Another.
Through the French of Michel de Labretagne.

According to Labretagne, it was none other than Prince Atlantarion himself who wrote this sequence of vignettes in prose, and moreover for his own children, such as were born during the very long wedding voyage of Atlantarion and Aïs during the five or six years (or even more) before the

Great Cataclysm struck. From the fact of their being written for his children derives the gentle and often whimsical tone, similar to but yet different from that distinguishing the sequence of the fables in As One Jaguär to Another.

A Ship Sails Out to Sea.
Through the French of Michel de Labretagne.

It is obvious from the reference to the moon that this poem is by an unknown poet of the post-Cataclysmic period, and hence before the eventual foundering of Poseidonis, the last major fragment of the original island continent of Atlantis. It was the capture by Earth of the moon, or of Sfamoön (as the Atlanteans called it), that triggered the Great Cataclysm that led in turn to the submergence of (most of) the Empire of Atlantis. Before this capture Sfamoön had existed as an independent planet of its own that vacillated between Earth and Mars, but that yielded eventually to Earth's greater gravitational pull during the moon's last perihelion to Earth. Every five and six years, respectively, the moon had come into perihelion to Earth in regular alternation, which dictated the convening of the Pan-Atlantean royalty to Atlantis the capital city, in order to deal with issues confronting the over-all Empire of Atlantis, as well as their individual kingdoms.

Barcarolle.
Translated from the French of Michel de Labretagne.

This is one of the few rare poems by Labretagne uniquely of his own authorship, and not directly Atlantean, except by inference, given the story of Noah and the flood. However, the thinking in this particular poem (lines 7–9, 10–12, and 13–16) seems more Atlantean, rather than Renaissance French, especially originating from someone who was perforce a nominal Christian, or Catholic, the Biblical reference to Noah notwithstanding.

Nine Happy Goldfish.
Through the French of Michel de Labretagne.

This little poem stems from the period just preceding the Great Cataclysm. "As though from seas of space that lie beyond:"—It is thought that this line refers to the well-known (Atlantean) theory of how life began hereat within the earliest oceans of Earth, that is, as fertilized by "the seeds of life" borne on the ether-winds that move between the galaxies and the stars making up the said galaxies.

An Archaeologist Uncovers the Past.

The terrible disaster that ended what would have turned out as one of the greatest archaeological feats of all time—how close it came to fruition!—the Portuguese government as the chief sponsor of the expedition established west of the town of Sete Cidades (under the immediate supervision of Peh Ng Wen, the Uruguayan of mixed Cambodian and Vietnamese parentage) deliberately under-reported (if not distorted and misrepresented), and for a variety of complicated reasons, as one might expect.

The Scallop Shell.
Through the French of Michel de Labretagne.

This curious lyric derives from the general period sometime before the Great Cataclysm. Although many Atlantean ships continued to use the crown and trident in differing styles upon their enormous main (or only) sail, the conventionalized symbol of the scallop shell had come to supplant that piece of heraldry in a great many instances, and had become as universally recognizable as the crown and trident itself, that is, as identifying something as Atlantean, whether ship or anything else.

A Villanelle Not à la Mode.

Although not emphasized in previous accounts of the late great, and once pre-eminent, Atlantologist; the fact remains that, in addition to being quite a capable poet himself, Dr. Ibid M. Andor was a great connoisseur of poetry in quite a range of modern and ancient languages. The considerable Atlantological tradition that he left behind, Dr. Lauric Guillaud, formerly *maître de conférences* in the English Department at the Université de Nantes, has entirely appropriated, and continues in the most enlightened manner today.

The Scroll.
Through the French of Michel de Labretagne.

Another curious lyric, this also derives from the general period sometime before the Great Cataclysm. The location of this renowned scroll is unknown at present ever since its disappearance from the Louvre. It has been rumored most recently to be in the possession of an extremely wealthy collector.

To a Conch.

In the collection *Les Trophées* by José-Maria Heredia, the title is *La Conque*, or *The Conch*. Interestingly enough, at least in American English, probably as an influence in the South (of the U.S.) from the West Indies, conch is pronounced either *conch* (from the Spanish *concha*) or *kongk* (from the French *conque*).

Of Some Eternal Realm.

It is a debt of honor on the part of Donald Sidney-Fryer as the translator and poet largely responsible for the three series of *Songs and Sonnets Atlantean* to acknowledge the inspiration for these last two poems given him by Dr. Lauric Guillaud as the greatest Atlantologist of today following in the noble footsteps of Dr. Ibid M. Andor—a direct inspiration for *Of Some Eternal Realm* and an indirect one for *Past, Present, Future*. See the separate note on the latter poem below.

Past, Present, Future.

In Clark Ashton Smith's commonplace book, there are three or four fragments of poetry that seem to be the first sketch of a poem that Smith apparently did not finish, or did not actually create as such, but that runs parallel to his finished but much longer poem *Soliloquy in an Ebon Tower*. Although widely separated from each other by other materials, these items 128, 153, and 218–219, seem to be manifestly linked. They appear below, presented as if in the form of a rough draft.

Item 128:

> Taught by me, [the poets yet to be] they will
> Reject the fading phantoms called the Real,
> And choose in place of them those other phantoms
> That fade not, being immaterial.

Item 152:

> Say, wouldst thou have
> Wisdom, or love, or empire? Let each man
> Follow some chosen phantom into death.

Item 218:

>   Man
> In whom illusion doth itself behold.

Item 219:

> Through ultimate cycles, as in cycles old,
> Phantoms, and apparitions manifold,
> Shall pass before the spectral eyes of man
> In whom illusion doth itself behold.

These four items are taken from *The Black Book of Clark Ashton Smith*, edited by Rah Hoffman and Donald Sidney-Fryer, Arkham House, Sauk City, Wisconsin, 1979. It should be remarked that *illusion* is an obsolete meaning for phantom, and that Klarkash-Ton is the playful term employed by H. P. Lovecraft to designate Smith in his correspondence and elsewhere, a term picked up and used by others then and since. Klarkash-Ton is pronounced KLAR-kash-TONN.

Demeure Exotique.

> Somehow this place resisted history's tides,
> Eternal flux of calends, nones, and ides,
> Bequeathed perchance from Atlantean times.

It was the firm belief of Michel Labretagne, as the foremost Atlantologist of all time (after Plato himself, of course, and thus long before Dr. Ibid M. Andor and other modern Atlantologists), that the Roman system of calends, nones, and ides of each calendar month represented a specific inheritance from the ancient Atlanteans, bequeathed somehow to the (later) Romans, but long after the foundering of Poseidonis, the last major fragment of the original island continent, or archkingdom, of the Empire of Atlantis. However, lacking any direct evidence for this belief (at least as it has managed to survive into modern times), it is difficult to see in what manner it conforms to the known historical or archaeological record.

The Fugitives.
Through the French of Michel de Labretagne.

During much of the twentieth century, following Dr. Andor's lead, it was assumed that this curious love story was the work of Athallarion, but now the evidence, carefully re-examined by the current generation of revisionist Atlantologists, would seem to favor the conviction, promulgated by Labretagne as the original translator (at least into French), that the original author was Aänsess (that is, Aänsess of the Astazhan), because the tale features the kind of morally equivocal subject that fascinated him, but generally did not intrigue the morally straightforward Athallarion.

Memtellidon, about whom little appears to be known, apparently reigned as Archking of the Empire of Atlantis at some period around the middle of the Empire's third and last millennium. His reign was evidently a fortunate one, happily not marred by war or catastrophe of any type. The little recorded about him would seem to suggest that he was a great patron of the arts and sciences, and was himself a poet of no mean ability.

Although Aviol and Cartha did not commit suicide, or actually decease, while in the relative wilderness bordering the great marshland located west of All-Neph-Rom (as described close to the end of the story), this tragic ending, as believed by everyone but their own two families, is the one that passed into both popular legend and official history.

Working evidently from different sources than those of Michel de Labretagne, Clark Ashton Smith created a version of the story that enshrines the tragic ending, making his version the subject of a romantic drama that he did not complete apart from four songs and a few pages of blank verse. Smith describes the stage piece, as follows, in a letter to R. H. Barlow dated 23 November 1936.

> "The Fugitives" ran only to two and one-half pages of blank verse and several songs that I planned to intercalate in the dialogue.... The plot was a simple and quite romantic one: it began with the mutual dawning of love in an Atlantean boy [Cartha] and girl [Aviol], soon to be separated. Later, they were to meet again: the boy a wandering poet of recognized genius, the girl a king's concubine. Their old love reawakens, they flee the Atlantean court and capital, to perish in the wilderness after several days and nights of mad happiness. On this framework, much lyric beauty and romantic imagery could have been strung. But somehow the impetus failed me and I never went on with it.

All that survives of this drama is a fragment dated 17 September 1922, and the four extant songs: "The Song of Aviol," "The Love-Potion," "The Song of Cartha," and "Song." Smith first published the songs in the *Auburn Journal* during April and May 1923, and subsequently gathered them in *Sandalwood* (1925), his third major poetry collection. The few pages of blank verse have not yet been discovered.

The Music of the Spheres.

Although the fact concerning the existence of the black holes appears to have become established in scientific and other circles only during the latter half of the 1900s, yet it is only today—during the 1990s and earliest years of the twenty-first century—that the brilliant theoretical physicist Stephen Hawking and other theoretical scientists have identified the special role of black holes as galactic (and possibly other cosmic) generators and regenerators, particularly in regard to the particles making up all matter.

Even if he could not possibly have known or intuited, or otherwise foreseen or foretold, the existence and function of black holes, the poet and fictioneer Clark Ashton Smith (1893–1961) did in fact anticipate, in his early poetry (1910–30) and his later fiction (1928–38), the concept (in literary terms) of the repeated usage by the cosmos of the particles making up the matter that constitutes that unlimited universe.

Smith features this concept in many poems and stories, usually to brilliant effect and often with great poignance. For just a few typical examples chosen at random, we need cite only the playlet "The Ghoul and the Seraph" (first published in 1922)—see particularly the final speech of the ghoul Necromalor in biting response to the taunting remarks and questions of the seraph—the sonnet "The Last Oblivion" (first published in 1924), and the much later poem "Dominium in Excelsis" (first published in 1951).

Forevermore the Rose.

Eulalie is, of course, Mary Eulalie Fee (1824–1854), Mrs. John Shannon, celebrated as the Auburn Poetess, and California's first (known) woman poet in English. She resided in Auburn, during the time of the great Gold Rush, from late March or early April 1854 until her death in late December 1854, while giving birth to a child. Her one and only collection of poems—*Buds, Blossoms and Leaves*—appeared in book form during November 1854 at Cincinnati, Ohio, and thus only a poignantly brief time before her death.

Violet Nelson Heyer, a great friend to both Clark Ashton Smith and Donald Sidney-Fryer, resided most of her life in Auburn, apart from the short and unhappy period of one year or so passed in San Francisco during the 1920s. Her family lived not far from the Smith's for some ten years or so (c. 1909–1918). Violet apparently was in her early nineties when she died sometime in the 1990s. Among other accomplishments she became a notable admirer of Clark Ashton Smith as great poet and great thinker, as well as a notable collector of his published books.

Late in life, to hone her appreciation of poetry modern and otherwise, Violet took a poetry class at Sierra College in Rocklin south of Auburn. In urging the students to write their own poetry as part of appreciating poetry in general, the professor of the class forbade them the usage of well-known subjects and themes long cultivated by the traditional prosody, such poetic properties as flowers, especially the rose. Instead, the teacher encouraged the students to employ more modern and less hackneyed subjects, e.g., the urban or metropolitan nitty-gritty with such characteristic elements as conflict, struggle, and protest, an area of experience in which Violet had obviously little experience.

Violet rightly refused to heed this professorial proscription, and instead wrote quite a competent poem in free verse entitled "Forever the Rose," taking as her theme this very prohibition itself vis-à-vis the sempiternal aesthetic worth and beauty of the rose. Despite her genteel defiance the professor actually relented, and gave her and her poem quite a good grade. She subsequently told this anecdote concerning her poem's creation to Donald Sidney-Fryer, and read the poem aloud to him, during one of his occasional visits from Sacramento to her home in Auburn. In turn Sidney-Fryer found the poem itself to be lovely, the theme of it to be worthwhile, and the specific point that it made to be completely valid.

Tableau Sous-marin.
Through the French of Michel de Labretagne.

Labretagne in his notes for *Submarine Tableau* confesses that he cannot figure out if the unknown poet in question created this poem before or after the Great Cataclysm, but then goes on to note that, apropos of the final stanza of this expanded sonnet, or song archroyal, the concept of destiny or fate as one or more female entities, as in Graeco-Roman mythology, was evidently not unknown to the ancient Atlanteans, and indeed appears distinctly to have anticipated that much later and better known concept, the three goddesses representing fate: Clotho, Lachesis, and Atropos.

Remonstration.
Through the French of Michel de Labretagne.

This particular expanded sonnet, or song archroyal, Labretagne apparently intended to include in his renowned novel, *Le roman de la princesse Aïs et du prince Atlantaryon*, but it evidently never evolved beyond the condition of a rough sketch (disregarding whatever original Labretagne may have been translating from the Atlantean), and it never left the poet-translator's own study (maintained as a museum today) at the top of "la Tour d'yvoire," the family library kept up in his ancestral castle-stronghold, the Château Bretagnesque indeed situated in Brittany, not far from Mont-Saint-Michel.

The authorities who run the library-museum have graciously allowed the present poet-translator to copy the rough sketch in French, and to use it as the basis for the sonnet under discussion. The original Atlantean poet is unknown, and all that Labretagne has recorded on the sheet of high-quality rag paper is "Translated from the Atlantean of a modern poet"—unless the original is really by Labretagne, and the detail of the "modern poet" is a playful allusion to himself. As we know, the French poet never scorned a good scholarly joke.

A Rendezvous with Pierrefonds.

The present poet-annotator sojourned in France during mid-May to mid-June 2000, and first visited the city of Compiègne, and then the village and castle of Pierrefonds, only a few days after his arrival in the country. So diverted was he by both Compiègne and Pierrefonds that he revisited Pierrefonds for about a week in early June shortly before his return to Los Angeles.

Deserving special emphasis is the fact that it rains often and much in northern France, or for that matter in much of the country over-all. The village of Pierrefonds itself, with its little lake (lying to the southwest of the village just off the main street), is utterly charming, and boasts all the modern amenities, including several noteworthy hostelries and restaurants. One may also secure worthwhile accommodations in Compiègne.

Pierrefonds, Poème en Pierre.

Charles d'Orléans (1394–1465). Often personal but rarely dealing with major issues, his clear and accessible poetry is unusually graceful, as well as impeccably but simply crafted. Like the duke himself, it is sensitive and charming, and with him the courtly poetry of the Middle Ages came to a final but beautiful conclusion. The lightly allegorical elements in his poetry pose no real problem for the modern reader, and can be simply understood in general psychological terms. In his own time, although it was well known that he was an extraordinary poet, his poems themselves were known only to a select group of intimate friends and relatives (not to mention scriveners, illuminators, and makers of books, that is, before printing existed) whether in Britain or in France. After the copies of his poetry were duly and carefully placed in the archives of what later became the Bibliothèque Nationale, they were forgotten. His poetry did not become generally known until its rediscovery and general publication sometime during the 1700s.

His own personal library, including the books that he had inherited from his father Louis d'Orléans, and from his grandfather Charles V, became the nucleus of the later Bibliothèque Nationale. Both Louis d'Orléans and his wife, Valentina Visconti, were notable readers, or scholars (if you will) in their own way, and presided as patrons of learning and of those who literally made books. The library of Charles d'Orléans probably numbered some 200, or perhaps even 300, volumes. This total would not strike the attention of the modern reader or scholar as being exceptional unless he realizes that these were of necessity all hand-made volumes requiring intensive labor whether for text or for art, being largely produced before the invention or innovation of printing with movable type by Johann Gutenberg (1400?–1468?) during the fifteenth century. It should be mentioned that Louis d'Orléans himself was a skillful and charming poet.

Franz Xaver Winterhalter, born 1806 in Menzenschwand (the Black Forest), died 1873 in Frankfurt am Main. Leading German portrait painter (very fashionable and very successful), who nevertheless made his international reputation in France. He arrived in Paris in 1834, and was patronized by Queen Marie-Amélie, wife of Louis-Philippe. Winterhalter's portrait of the French queen helped establish his fame and subsequent vogue in the French capital as well as elsewhere. However, his previous appointment in Karlsruhe helped establish his fame in Germany, and it was from that city that he went to Paris. His brother Hermann Winterhalter (1808–1891), another portrait painter, moved to Paris in 1840, and the brothers worked together henceforth, presumably until Franz's death in 1873, but it was the elder brother who had established the artistic beach-head at Paris, and his paintings became *the* fashion in portraiture not only in France but throughout Europe.

The fame of the elder Winterhalter brother rests on his reputation as "the painter of the Second Empire" (i.e., of Napoléon III), and he either alone or in collaboration with his brother painted the portraits of most of the European royalty, no less than the leading aristocracy, of his time. Technically impeccable, his work gives us an excellent visual account of many of the leading figures of his over-all period. Some of his paintings have been widely and variously reproduced, especially his enormous and most famous work, *L'Impératrice Eugénie et sa cour,* now no longer in the Louvre but in the Museum of the Second Empire, located within the palace built by Louis XV at Compiègne, or the Château de Compiègne. The correct title in full is *L'Impératrice Eugénie et les dames de sa cour;* i.e., *The Empress Eugénie and the ladies of her court.* The brothers Winterhalter created the painting, probably their single biggest one, during 1855. It was exhibited in a special room at the Exposition Universelle in Paris during 1855; and Winterhalter was awarded a first-class medal for his contribution to that show. A peculiarity of this work is that none of the persons depicted therein seems to be looking directly at anyone else.

Emile Waldteufel (1837–1915). French-Alsatian musician, he was appointed court pianist to the Empress Eugénie in 1865, then orchestra conductor for the court balls in 1866. He began composing elegant and individual waltzes as early as 1859, and continued to do so all during the 1860s as his other musical activities allowed. He volunteered to take part in the Franco-Prussian War, 1870–71, continuing as conductor for the court balls until he enlisted in the French military. However, it was not until the cessation of war, and the hugely successful publication of his waltzes (beginning with *Manolo*) in Britain during 1875 (first published in France during 1873) that he became internationally celebrated, and that he decided to devote himself completely to the creation of dance music. By the end of his life and career he had composed c. 270 individual dances, most of them waltzes, but also polkas, galops, etc. After Johann Strauss II he is the best-known waltz composer, and the only pre-eminent French one. (*Mon Rêve*, composed, published, 1877.)

The Empress Eugénie, born in 1826 at Granada, died in 1920 at Madrid. A spirited woman of great beauty, considerable intelligence, and extraordinary charm, she possessed notable charisma, and was an excellent conversationalist, able to discuss intelligently a wide range of topics. Both Napoléon III and Eugénie were also notable patrons of the arts, sciences, industries, etc., and put much energy, intelligence, and even their own money on a continuing basis behind the "Gothic Revival" directed by Prosper Mérimée and Viollet-le-Duc all over France. Even in consideration of that, Pierrefonds represents an exceptional case in point. By the phrase "Gothic Revival" we mean the repair and restoration, or reconstruction, of Gothic structures all over France, mostly churches and cathedrals, but also non-ecclesiastical places like Pierrefonds and Carcassonne.

Both emperor and empress were also notable patrons of the ballet at the then Paris Opéra (the opera house located on the Rue Lepelletier), 1853–70. The fall of the Second Empire did not materially affect Eugénie, given that she had her own wealth. She was closely related to the Spanish royal family, as well as a close friend of theirs. Eugénie and Queen Victoria were notable and faithful friends, and Victoria in particular greatly admired Eugénie. Following her departure from France, their friendship deepened and even developed further. Eugénie played the role of the grande dame in exile to the hilt, something which her wealth permitted her to do with ease. She moved from Chislehurst, England (where her husband had passed on), to Farnborough, during 1881, where she lived in a large mansion, and where she built a tomb for her husband, her son, and herself.

A Ballade of Duality.

This ballade is intended as a companion-piece to the ballade included in the first section of this third series, "A Ballade of Prospero." Given that "A Ballade of Duality" features the two opposing characters Caliban and Ariel highlighted in *The Tempest*, it is perhaps more closely tied than the first ballade to this most Spenserian of Shakespeare's plays. Prospero himself as enchanter is a fairly close relative to Spenser's own archetypal great magician, Archimago, who makes his appearance for the most part in the first two books of *The Faerie Queene*.

A Fanfare from Atlantis

It was the well-known musician and musicologist, Dr. Ragù von Hoffmann, who first pointed out, sometime after the television season of 1952–53, the rather startling resemblance of *The Song of the High Seas* (from *Victory at Sea*) to the traditional Fanfare of Atlantis, or the Archimperium Salute, as that just happened to survive, along with some other pieces of music, and of course in the original Atlantean musical notation, deep under Apenderragon, the Great Watchtower in southern Wales.

Like all the other Atlantean governors who preceded him in what are now the British Isles, Aänsess of the Astazhan, as the very last governor, deposited and sealed his records, correspondence, and manuscripts (later known as the *Codex Atlanteanus*) in the lowermost vaults of the central tower of Apenderragon, the over-all complex of heavily fortified buildings making up the Great Watchtower (that is, of the Atlanteans in Great Britain), which crowned an only somewhat lower spur of the highest peak in southwestern Wales, that is, Mynydd Prescelly. Today this peak rises about 1,760 feet above sea level, but evidently rose about 2,000 feet at the time of the Great Cataclysm.

Apparently it was also none other than Aänsess who deposited the pieces of music in question, together with selected musical instruments, presumably just on a whim, in the same lowermost vaults of Apenderragon, before he and his garrisons (as the last remaining Atlanteans) departed from the British Isles forever, and immediately before they went back to what had survived of Atlantis the Archkingdom, that is, the very core of the Empire of Atlantis, the great mountain-heartland known as Poseidonis. As far as we can estimate now from the available evidence, this took place about 13,000 B.C.

It is indeed an amazing coincidence that the Archimperium Salute, otherwise the Fanfare of Atlantis (this famous melody appears prominently mentioned in Parts I and II of the narrative in verse *The Fugitives*), just happens to resemble so closely *The Song of the High Seas*, by Richard Rodgers (1902–1979) and Robert Russell Bennett (1894–1981), who collaborated on many musical shows first presented on Broadway. Perhaps their most celebrated collaboration (if that in fact is what it is) emerged as their music for *Victory at Sea*, for which *The Song of the High Seas* functioned as the musical signature at the start of every half-hour program, and often within it as well, as a kind of unifying leitmotif.

Working with the U.S. Navy during the early 1950s, NBC television produced 26 half-hour episodes, each dealing with a different facet of the Navy's ubiquitous role around the world in securing the eventual American triumph during World War II. (Whether lasting an hour or half an hour each, 26 episodes have often constituted a complete series for a typical television season extending from the second half of one year on into the first half of the next.) The network first aired the series during 1952–53. The music played a decisive part in the overwhelming success of this unique documentary series whether artistically or popularly, the documentary series itself representing a first achievement of its kind for a major television network. Although Richard Rodgers, usually considered *the* composer involved, received a Congressional Medal of Honor for his contribution, Robert Russell Bennett functioned as the individual who really composed and orchestrated this music, possibly the single biggest commission that he ever undertook.

Rodgers initially supplied Bennett with a dozen tunes, over-all about a half-hour's worth of music only, but admittedly all melodies of superior quality. Employing these 12 themes freely, Bennett fleshed out, orchestrated, and then timed the music for each episode. Starting in April 1952, he also conducted the recording sessions, for which he had the express use of Arturo Toscanini's excellent NBC (also known as the RCA Victor) Symphony Orchestra, an experience that he found most enjoyable.

After the series first aired, RCA Victor produced and released a long-playing record with a suite of music (also under the title *Victory at Sea*) derived from the 26 episodes. Bennett himself, of course, prepared the suite, as well as a separate version for orchestral concerts, necessitating much rescoring or rerecording as required. (Later RCA Victor produced and released a second suite, also arranged and conducted by Bennett.) During this enormous task, spread out over a year or more at least, Bennett's own composing almost ceased, no less than that done for other commissions, that is, for the duration of his then chief assignment.

For each of the 26 episodes, he prepared about 26 minutes of all new music (although re-employing the same 12 themes, or variations of these, but of his own invention), making more than *eleven* hours of continuous music over-all. This means that almost nonstop music accompanies the full duration of each episode. All this music Bennett had to redact at great speed, easily filling more than 5000 pages of orchestral manuscript. How many music lovers realize the huge amount of hard labor involved in a technical sense that such redaction requires?!

However important his contribution may have turned out, a half-hour's worth of melodic material does not entitle Richard Rodgers to be considered *the* composer of this music, whereas more than *eleven* hours of continuous music does thus entitle Robert Russell Bennett! Nevertheless, Richard Rodgers received the commission, and the ensuing credit, because he had become probably the single most popular American composer during the 1940s and 1950s, that is, the composer whose music American orchestras most often performed almost invariably by means of orchestral arrangements created by Robert Russell Bennett!

An enormously prolific and gifted composer, orchestrator, and conductor, Robert Russell Bennett (not to be confused with the British composer Richard Rodney Bennett), born in Kansas City, Missouri, undertook his earliest music lessons with his music-loving parents, and then with the Danish composer and conductor Carl Busch. He went to New York City in 1916, and his work as copyist and arranger for G. Schirmer and T. B. Harms led to his first theatre orchestrations for Broadway during 1920, this musical work being interrupted briefly by his required military service in the U.S. Army during World War I.

Upon the death of Frank Saddler (1864–1921), Bennett became the U.S.'s foremost theatre orchestrator, an eminence that he held unchallenged for four decades, thus filling the role formerly held by Saddler himself. This activity he interrupted only during a significant part of 1926–29 on behalf of the private studies that he understood with Nadia Boulanger in Paris, funded in part by a Guggenheim Fellowship. His recordings in the 1930s and 1940s led to frequent live performances of his orchestral compositions during the same decades, he himself often presiding at these concerts as a highly effective and completely professional conductor. He spent the major part of

1936–40 in Hollywood, mostly at RKO, working on orchestrations and original scoring for a variety of movies.

After the tremendous labor involved in writing the music for *Victory at Sea*, Bennett went on to score some 35 television documentaries for NBC television, employing the NBC, or RCA Victor, Symphony Orchestra yet again. Among his most performed works, he created more than 30 wind-band scores for first and repeated playing by the Goldman Band of New York City. Bennett's own major compositions include seven symphonies, an opera *Maria Malibran* (lavishly premiered at the Julliard School of Music in 1934), a ballet-symphony, concertos, chamber music, studies for solo or accompanied instruments, etc. However, despite all his own compositions of all types, he remains best known for having furnished the orchestrations (in whole or in part) for more than 300 Broadway musical shows.

As is obvious from this account, Bennett was a magisterial orchestrator like the film composer Bernard Herrmann, albeit in a different genre. In his prolificness as composer and orchestral arranger, Bennett ranks with such other fecund (primarily theatre) musicians as the Italian composer Cesare Pugni (1802–1870), who claims the credit for furnishing the music for 312 ballets, 10 operas, and 40 masses, among other compositions. Although he functioned and prospered as the consummate and very busy professional that he was in fact—from roughly 1920 to 1960—Bennett had the misfortune in a critical or artistic sense to live at a time when atonal and abstract music, along with the controversies attendant on it, was dominating the attention of the serious music world whether in the U.S. or abroad. As primarily a composer for the Broadway theatre, his music, although distinguished in its own way, is tonal and programmatic, qualities not then cherished by the musical avant-garde. Nevertheless, his career and compositional output deserve every respect.

(Much of the information for the preceding account of Robert Russell Bennett's life and career derives from the entry on this composer by George J. Ferencz, Volume 3, pp. 280–281, the *New Grove Dictionary of Music and Musicians*, the second major edition by Stanley Sadie, Oxford University Press, 2001. For his help in clarifying divers aspects of both Atlantean and post-Atlantean music and musicology, the present writer wishes to express his gratitude to Dr. Ragù von Hoffmann.)

As readers will recall, it was at some point in the 400s A.D. that a Cambrian, or Welsh, lord (not Saxon, as previously stated) incorporated what remained of the Great Watchtower (primarily the massive foundations of Apenderragon) into the donjon of his castle, actually a refurbished hill-fort of the Iron Age. During the reign of Uther Pendragon as High King of Britain (evidently in the latter half of the same 400s A.D.) the same resident family of nobles discovered in the lowermost vaults from Atlantean times the records, correspondence, and manuscripts that became known as the Codex Atlanteanus. In addition, of course, the family discovered the selected pieces of music in the original Atlantean musical notation, along with the selected Atlantean musical instruments (miraculously intact still), as placed there by Aänsess of the Astazhan. Later the same family brought both the *Codex* and the assemblage of musical instruments to King Arthur's court at Camelot, evidently the immense and refurbished hill-fort of the Iron Age later known as Cadbury Castle.

Although the musical instruments did not long outlast the end of Arthur's reign as High King of Britain, as well as the subsequent abandonment and ruin of Camelot, or Cadbury Castle, someone at his court had prepared an inventory of these instruments that had survived from Atlantean times, along with the *Codex Atlanteanus*. Later still, after many vicissitudes, the whole mass of ancient writings, together with the Latin and Cambrian translations done by the clerk-scholars at Camelot under Merlin's guidance, came into the possession of the Labretagne family, whose chief estate lay not far from the Abbey of Mont-Saint-Michel. It was from this famous monastery that they by express permission took the *Codex* into their ownership, and made it part of their own private library lodged in the olden tower called "la Tour d'yvoire," which some scholars claim also had an Atlantean foundation.

Michel de Labretagne himself discovered the *Codex* in the selfsame Château Bretagnesque during 1503. Among other materials he translated the Arthurian inventory of Atlantean musical instruments, and this register survives along with other papers of his in the Bibliothèque Nationale at Paris. We reproduce the list as abstracted from Michel's translation (into Renaissance French), as follows:

one harp
one lyre
one large lyre
one small, or tenor, lute
one large, or bass, lute
one long-necked lute
one flute

one double flute
several panpipes (various ranges and sizes)
one pair of small drums
various large drums

one zaör (a lyre and a harp combined, both with wire strings; i.e., a large lyre with a very large sound chamber, combined with a harp carrying extra bass strings, and using the lyre's own sound chamber, or an extension of it).

Although these instruments managed to survive under the special sealed conditions obtaining in the lowermost vaults of the Great Watchtower, apparently no one learned how to play them in King Arthur's court at Camelot, and they did not long survive the abandonment and ruin of that site over-all, especially of the Royal Library there. Whereas the *Codex Atlanteanus* did manage to survive, placed as it was in a subterranean vault, and moreover with the scrolls themselves protected inside their original pieces of metal tubing. Preserved in the Bibliothèque Nationale at Paris, the pieces of music in the original Atlantean musical notation remained in their undecoded state until Dr. Hoffmann succeeded in deciphering them during the mid-twentieth century, and rendered them into modern musical notation. He published the results of his arduous labors in 1951, shortly before NBC television aired *Victory at Sea* during 1952–53. The musical signature provided by *The Song of the High Seas* immediately caught the attention of Dr. Hoffman, who correlated and identified it with the Fanfare of Atlantis, otherwise the Archimperium Salute, almost at once.

N.B. (The poet-author's final note, Winter Solstice, 22 December 2007.) Donald Sidney-Fryer began the first poem in the First Series, "Avalonessys," in March of 1961, and he completed the last poem remaining to be finished in the Third Series, "The Fugitives," in March of 2005. He completed the notes for the Third Series in early summer. The composition of the First Series over-all took place over the ten years from early 1961 until early 1971; that of the Second Series over-all took place over the ten years from sometime 1988 until early summer 1998; and that of the Third Series over-all took place over the three years from early 2002 until mid-2005. He supplemented the Second Series with a handful of new poems (preceding "A Vision of a Castle Deep in Averoigne") in the spring and summer of 2007. Over-all the composition of the entire three series extended not quite over twenty-five years dispersed not quite over half a century.

It was the mythopoeic poetry of Clark Ashton Smith (first experienced in early 1958) and then of Edmund Spenser (first experienced in early 1961) that inspired Sidney-Fryer as an adult poet to continue poeticizing in the same general direction. The same poetry likewise inspired him to demonstrate—by writing new poetry of the same general type—the truth of Smith's apothegm, "The forms and themes of poetry do not become outworn or exhausted. The exhaustion is in the individual poets." (However true this might seem in certain specific aspects, the just or evenhanded critic must grant any poet or other artist the inalienable right or necessity to experiment.) The concept of the three series as a more or less interconnected sequence in form or theme, our poet-author borrowed from Swinburne and his three series of *Poems and Ballads* (1865, 1878, 1889). The poetic forms employed in the three series for Sidney-Fryer's own mythopetization derive overwhelmingly from Spenser and his epic-romance-allegory *The Faerie Queene* (1590, 1596, 1609).

In addition to the attention given to a broad spectrum of poetry in half a dozen languages (including four years of Latin, eight years of French, and two years of Spanish whether in high school or college) a lifelong devotion to French literature, especially poetry, has exercised a residual, even if mostly general, influence on Sidney-Fryer's writing in poetry or prose. Despite its division into three parts or series, *The Atlantis Fragments* essentially remains a more or less unified collection, or gallimaufry, of prose and verse.

APPENDIX

August Derleth, owner-editor of Arkham House, permitted Donald Sidney-Fryer to write the front and back blurbs for the dust jacket of the First Series. The self-authored blurbs therefore became part of the over-all book presentation, and are reproduced here as historical items.

[Front blurb.]
SONGS AND SONNETS ATLANTEAN
by Donald Sidney-Fryer

Donald Sidney-Fryer's first book embodies the first extensive selection of Atlantean poems translated into English—even if only through the French of the Renaissance Atlantologist, Michel de Labretagne. Dr. Ibid Massachusetts Andor, the premier Atlantologist in today's world, rightly hails this collection as a major contribution to Plato's Atlantis Myth.

To do justice to the original poetic forms in Atlantean, the translator has not only revived the Spenserian stanza but has also innovated a special form, the Spenserian stanza-sonnet, based upon both the Spenserian stanza and the Spenserian sonnet.

Now retired and resident in the Azores for many years, Dr. Andor has provided an erudite and informative introduction, together with a concluding section of notes. These notes and Sidney-Fryer's translations evoke the strange, opulent, and unforgettable pageant of the last days of the Empire of Atlantis, a world overwhelmed by the Great Cataclysm, circa 13,000 B.C.

Upon these translations, the result of about a decade of sustained labor, Donald Sidney-Fryer as poet and scholar has brought to bear the fruits of a varied career in life and literature. The present volume also includes translations just from the French, as well as a selection of original poems expressly written for it.

* * * * *

The jacket, fashioned after an original design invented by the author, is the work of the young Denver artist, Gordon R. Barnett.

[Back blurb.]

DONALD SIDNEY-FRYER

A young California poet and scholar, Donald Sidney-Fryer spent his first 18 years in New Bedford, Massachusetts. Of English descent on his father's side, and of French on his mother's, he served for three years in the U.S. Marine Corps. At U.C.L.A. he majored in theatre arts and French language and literature. He also studied classical ballet for one year.

Though he has lived in both New England and Florida, he bas been a Californian by adoption since late 1955, and has made his home in San Francisco since 1965. He has held various positions over the years, but as Master Donald Sidney-Fryer—the Last of the Courtly Poets, and San Francisco's only Neo-Elizabethan poet-entertainer—he has found his true métier, practicing the ancient and honorable art of incantation. In late 1969 he married Gloria Kathleen Braly.

Donald Sidney-Fryer has compiled A *Checklist of the Ballet Scores of Cesare Pugni* (*Enciclopedia dello Spettacolo,* Volume VIII, Rome, 1961) as well as A *Bibliography of the Writings of Clark Ashton Smith* (Grant). He has contributed scholarly essays on Clark Ashton Smith, H. P. Lovecraft, and Lord Dunsany to amateur periodicals, and has edited the text of three books for Arkham House—*Poems in Prose* (1965) and *Other Dimensions* (1970), both by Clark Ashton Smith, and the forthcoming *A Vision of Doom,* poems by Ambrose Bierce, to two of which he has also contributed introductory essays.

* * * * *

Donald Sidney-Fryer, clad in his troubadour-poet costume, in San Francisco's Buena Vista Park. The photograph is by John Frazer.

Index of Titles

Abandonment	361
Alpha Huge, The	80
Amaranth	362
Amphus Delta, The	84
Ancestral Memory Revived	445
Another Species of Epiphany	370
Apprentice and the Jaguär, The	396
Archaeologist Uncovers the Past, An	428
Argosy of Trade, An	132
As Buds and Blossoms in the Month of May the Rose	50
As One Jaguär to Another	383
As One Seahorse to Another	413
Ashes in the Rose Garden, The	61
At the Outhanox	317
Atalantessys	125
Atatemthessys	127
Atkantharia	123
Atlantean Obelisk, The	88
Atlantigades	122
Atlantillia	126
Atlantis	45
Atlantis	120
At-Thulonn	128
Aubade	102
Avalonessys	43
Avalonessys	129
Ave Atque Vale	64
Ballade of Duality, A	504
Ballade of Prospero, A	371
Barcarolle	425
Beauty	318
Beyond Ultima Thule	211
Bialowieza	215
Bitch with Tits of Bronze, The	375
Black Poppy and Black Lotus	104
Cephalopod in Residence	410
Chest from Otherwhere, The	369
Codicil of Contradiction	381

Colossal Chambered Nautilus	411
Connaissance Fatale	111
Conundrum	506
Copán	201
Crown and Trident, The	54
Crown and Trident Imperial, The	44
Cydnus, The	68
Demeure Exotique	451
Discovery	374
Dominium atque Apotheosis	421
Enchantress Out of Time, An	195
Enigma	230
Enlightenment	495
Epilogue	409
Epiphany	235
Fanfare from Atlantis, A	510
Fantaisie Médiévale	232
Farewell to Zita	216
For Master Edmund Spenser: His Great Song	143
For the *Black Beetles in Amber* of Ambrose Bierce	112
For the *Shapes of Clay* of Ambrose Bierce	110
Forevermore the Rose	491
Forsaken Palace, The	109
Fragment, A	66
Fugitives, The	453
Gades	121
Game of Chess, A	365
Garden of Jealous Roses, The	89
Ghost of a Dream, The	509
Ghostly Dance by Starlight, A	420
Goatherd, The	221
Golden Mycenae	69
Green Sleeves	107
Hadrian and Antinous	422
Herdsman, The	357
Here, where the fountains of the deep-sea flow	119
Hippokamp, The	74
Hippokampoi	412
Hortorum Deus	223
House of Roses, The	105
Iffinnix, The	98
Iffrikonn-Yssthia	124
Illumination	233
Imperial Crown Jewels of Atlantis, The	85

Title	Page
In an Atlantean Bath	198
Inspiration [Ian M. M. Law]	140
Invocation, An	213
Item: Ariel Sings	443
Jaguär and the Astrologer, The	392
Kilcolman Castle: 20 August 1965	101
Labor and Deliverance	418
Legend	117
Letter from Valoth, A	134
Likewise My Mind to Me a Cosmos Is	313
Lilac Hedge at Cassell Prairie: 27 May 1967, The	103
Little Horses of the Ocean Sea, The	415
Lo Primordial	199
Lullaby	70
Macabre Arabesque	439
Mating Dance by Sunlight, A	417
Memorial	356
Memories of the Astazhan	133
Merchant-Princes, The	131
Midnight Visitant	212
Minor Chronicles of Atlantis	71
Miracle in Miniature, A	214
Monodon monoceros, The	210
Music of the Spheres, The	487
Musical Note of Swans . . . Before Their Death, The	106
My Mind to Me an Empire Is	312
Nine Happy Goldfish	427
No, not until the final age of Earth,	135
Notes	317
O Beautiful Dark-Amber Eyes of Old	108
"O Ebon-Colored Rose"	48
O Fair Dark Eyes, O Glances Turned Aside	67
Oblivion	219
Of Some Eternal Realm	448
Offrande Exotique	113
Oldster Gives Advice, An	416
On a Ruined Bust of Marble	228
On Reading Edmund Spenser Once Again	426
Oneiromancy	316
Or So You Say	385
Our Lady of the Unicorn	203
Pale Fragile Unicorns	231
Pan	220
Pan and Priapus	423

Passing of an Astrologer, The	404
Past, Present, Future	450
Pavane	52
Pendant	364
Pharanos at Sunset	315
Pharanos Descending	309
Pierrefonds, Poème en Pierre	500
Poseidonis	130
Predicament	493
Proem [Michel de Labretagne]	73
Proper Mode of Life, A	419
Quo Vadis, California?	202
Quoctezu Bids Farewell	400
Rapa-Nui	363
Re-ascension	314
Reciprocity	97
Recompense	57
Reef of Coral, The	373
Remonstration	494
Rendezvous with Pierrefonds, A	497
Renewal	234
Return of the Conquistadors	229
Rêverie Gothique	209
River Called Amphus, The	81
Rondeau of Summer	499
Rondeau of Winter	498
Rondel of Space	508
Rondel of Time	507
Rose and the Thorn, The	46
Rose Escarlate	47
Rose Verdastre	63
Scallop Shell, The	440
Scroll, The	446
Secretest [Fritz Leiber]	141
Shepherds, The	222
Shepherd and the Shepherdess, The	94
Ship Sails Out to Sea, A	424
Some Further Fragments from Atlantis	307
Song	55
Sonnets on an Empire of Many Waters	115
Spenserian Stanza-Sonnet Empourpré	59
Strength of Dreams	200
Summoning of Shadows, A	196
Symbol for All Splendor Lost, A	60

Tableau Sous-Marin	492
Tale of an Olden Love, The	91
Thaïs and Alexander in Persepolis	65
"Thy Spirit Walks the Sea"	56
To a Conch	447
To a Dead City	355
To a Youth	58
To an Atlantean Poet [Margo Skinner]	139
To Clark Ashton Smith	51
To Edmund Spenser (1552?–1599)	62
To Gloria Kathleen	142
To Rinaldo for Clark Ashton Smith	490
Totem	359
Triolets du Jour	441
Tropicality	358
Valediction	197
Villanelle Not à la Mode, A	442
Vision of a Castle Deep in Averonne, A	237
Vision of Strange Splendor, A	99
Warrior and the Jaguär, The	387
Well Met by Midnight	389
When We Were Prince and Princess	53
Your Mouth of Pomegranate	49

Title	Page
Tableau Sous-Marin	492
Tale of an Olden Love, The	91
Thaïs and Alexander in Persepolis	65
"Thy Spirit Walks the Sea"	56
To a Conch	447
To a Dead City	355
To a Youth	58
To an Atlantean Poet [Margo Skinner]	139
To Clark Ashton Smith	51
To Edmund Spenser (1552?–1599)	62
To Gloria Kathleen	142
To Rinaldo for Clark Ashton Smith	490
Totem	359
Triolets du Jour	441
Tropicality	358
Valediction	197
Villanelle Not à la Mode, A	442
Vision of a Castle Deep in Averonne, A	237
Vision of Strange Splendor, A	99
Warrior and the Jaguär, The	387
Well Met by Midnight	389
When We Were Prince and Princess	53
Your Mouth of Pomegranate	49

Special Acknowledgments

Special acknowledgments are made here to the following individuals for their support of the original edition:

Mikey Clagett, Rio Grande, New Mexico
John D. Haefele, Sussex, Wisconsin
Gerda Hoefert-Kennedy, Sacramento, California
Dennis Rickard, Fresno, California
Gavin E. Smith, Irving, Texas
Jay T. Yamamoto, Aiea, Hawaii

ABOUT THE POET

Poet, performing artist, critic, and literary historian, Donald Sidney-Fryer is the last in the great line of California Romantics that reaches from Ambrose Bierce to George Sterling and Nora May French, from Sterling to his protégé Clark Ashton Smith, and from Smith to his disciple Sidney-Fryer.

Carrying on the tradition of "pure poetry" begun in early modern English by Edmund Spenser and revivified by the English and American Romantic poets (Samuel Coleridge, John Keats, Percy Bysshe Shelley, Alfred Lord Tennyson, and Edgar Allan Poe), long after the mainstream poetic establishment had abandoned it, the California Romantics created two monuments in verse, Sterling with A Wine of Wizardry and Smith with The Hashish-Eater.

During his long career Sidney-Fryer has given dramatic readings from these poets and from Edmund Spenser's epic The Faerie Queene, across the U.S. and Great Britain. He has written and edited some two dozen books and booklets. He has edited four books by Smith for Arkham House, and three paperbacks, also by Smith, for Pocket Books, in addition to A Vision of Doom, 50 best poems by Ambrose Bierce, published by Donald M. Grant, who has also brought out Sidney-Fryer's monograph Emperor of Dreams—A Clark Ashton Smith Bibliography.

From 1980 through 1999 Sidney-Fryer assembled The Case of the Light Fantastic Toe (still awaiting publication), his historical monograph on the Romantic Ballet. As a poet Sidney-Fryer has crafted Songs and Sonnets Atlantean (the first series), the final book to appear from Arkham House under the personal supervision of its founder August Derleth; as well as the Second Series, published by Wildside Press; no less than the Third Series brought out by Phosphor Lantern Press. In 2004 Black Coat Press issued his translation and presentation of Gaspard de le Nuit by Aloysius Bertrand.

Moreover, Sidney-Fryer has accomplished his chief prosodic innovation, the creation of the Spenserian stanza-sonnet, long before the recent and welcome emergence of the group of poets known as the New Formalists, who have restored a much needed and long overdue balance to the ongoing evolution of American poetry and poetics.

Although he resided in Northern California during 1965–98, the self-styled Last of the Courtly Poets presently lives in Westchester, Los Angeles.

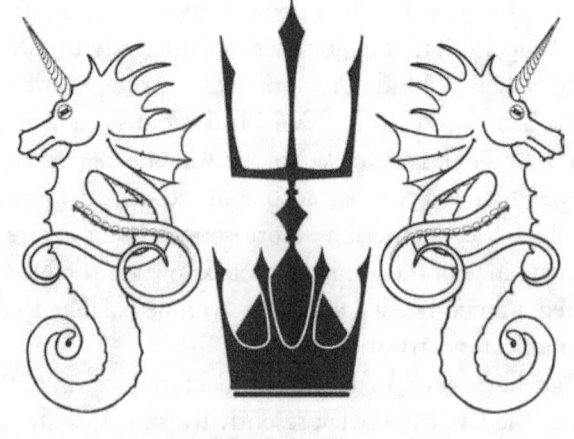